INTRODUCTORY READINGS IN

Archaeology

Photograph courtesy of Sir Mortimer Wheeler and the Society of Antiquaries of London

Maiden Castle, England. An air photograph showing earthworks and excavations in progress.

INTRODUCTORY READINGS IN

Archaeology

Edited by **BRIAN M. FAGAN**
University of California, Santa Barbara

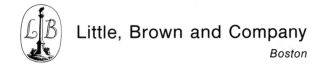

Little, Brown and Company
Boston

FOURTH PRINTING

*Published simultaneously in Canada
by Little, Brown & Company (Canada) Limited*

PRINTED IN THE UNITED STATES OF AMERICA

To

KATHY, KATHY, JOAN, and SUE

with gratitude for their hospitality

PREFACE

The teaching of introductory archaeology[1] involves exposing the student both to the basic methodology of the subject and to the results of archaeological research. A number of textbooks are available that describe the techniques of archaeological research, and survey the broad outlines of world prehistory. These volumes are usually insufficient in themselves because they are, at best, a summary of original literature and give little insight into the basic approaches to archaeology found in the scientific literature.

This volume is designed to give the introductory student the opportunity to read a series of excerpts both from scientific reports and from general essays to complement and amplify the other textbook assignments. The offerings in this volume make no pretensions to being either comprehensive or the final word on the subject. They have been chosen to represent a wide cross-section of points of view and types of archaeological problems. Some are excerpts from basic textbooks or theoretical papers. Others are selected from original site reports to convey an impression of how the excavator or analyst arrived at his conclusions using archaeological data. We begin with a chapter which presents a series of pieces reflecting differing approaches to archaeology. The sections on field survey, chronology, excavation, and economic reconstruction are designed both to illustrate the principles of such research and to show how archaeological evidence can be used to make convincing reconstructions of the past. We end with chapters on artifacts, the field of settlement archaeology, and a series of papers on the interpretation of archaeology.

One of the problems of archaeology is that it is a young discipline and

[1] For the purposes of this volume, the word *archaeology* is taken to cover the field of prehistoric archaeology unless specifically stated to the contrary.

has as yet generated little "great literature." Some of the extracts appearing in this volume have been published in other readers. We make no apologies for using them again for they represent the best and most articulate approach to the subject concerned so far published. It is worth guiding the reader toward two other volumes of selected readings in archaeology which will amplify this book: Dr. Glyn Daniel's *Origin and Growth of Archaeology* gives a more comprehensive treatment of the history of archaeology, while Professor R. F. Heizer's *The Archaeologist at Work* goes into many aspects of field archaeology in much more detail than is possible in this reader. These authors' pioneering efforts have been valuable in the preparation of this volume, the content of which is based on experience obtained by teaching introductory courses in archaeology at the University of California at Santa Barbara.

I am grateful to the authors and publishers whose works are reprinted below for permission to reproduce their published writings. Individual acknowledgements are made at appropriate places in the text.[2] Much of the burden of producing this work was undertaken by Michael Bisson and Mrs. Phyllis Frezin, and I am very grateful to them. Lastly, a word of thanks to Milton Johnson for encouraging me to undertake this work. Nothing would have been achieved without his interest and encouragement.

[2] Where a paper has been reproduced in its entirety, the references have been left intact. With extracts, however, we decided to omit all references and most footnotes, in the interests of clarity, and have so noted. The reader is referred to the original publication cited at the beginning of each extract for substantiation of statements in the extract. Much of the material reproduced in this book is obtainable from university, college, or city libraries.

CONTENTS

CHAPTER ONE   What Is Archaeology?   1

Grahame Clark   The Discipline of Prehistory   3

James Deetz   A New World Viewpoint   10

Gordon R. Willey
and Philip Phillips   American Archaeology and
Anthropology   14

Joseph R. Caldwell   New World Archaeology   19

CHAPTER TWO   Field Survey in Archaeology   31

R. J. C. Atkinson   The Principles of Archaeological
Air Photography   33

Gordon R. Willey   Air Photography in Peru   39

CHAPTER THREE   Time in Archaeology   45

Sir Mortimer Wheeler   Stratigraphy and Relative Chronology   47

John Howland Rowe   Stratigraphy and Seriation   58

John Howland Rowe   The Law of Association   69

x ▣ Contents

Jane Gray
and Watson Smith   Pollen Analysis   83

Willard F. Libby   Radiocarbon Dating   99

CHAPTER FOUR   Archaeological Excavation   117

Sir Mortimer Wheeler   The Strategy of Excavation   119

Sir Mortimer Wheeler   A Prehistoric Battle   124

CHAPTER FIVE   Prehistoric Economies   133

Joe Ben Wheat   A Paleo-Indian Bison Kill   135

Charles F. W. Higham   Domestic Animals and Agriculture   149

Wilfred Shawcross   Prehistoric Diet in New Zealand   154

Johannes Iversen   Pollen Analysis and Prehistoric
Agriculture   161

Brian M. Fagan   Hunter-Gatherers at Gwisho   168

Grahame Clark   Prehistoric Trade   175

CHAPTER SIX   Artifacts   183

Irving Rouse   Classification of Artifacts   185

Albert C. Spaulding   The Dimensions of Archaeology   201

Albert C. Spaulding   Statistical Analysis   218

CHAPTER SEVEN   Settlement Archaeology   235

Bruce G. Trigger   Settlement Patterns in Archaeology   237

CHAPTER EIGHT Culture Change, Social
              Change, and Analogy   263

V. Gordon Childe   What Happened in Prehistory?   265

Irving Rouse   People in Prehistory   278

Bruce G. Trigger   Culture Change   297

Lewis R. Binford   Archaeology as Anthropology   325

James Deetz   Prehistoric Social Systems   339

Robert Ascher   Analogy in Archaeology   347

Raymond H. Thompson The Subjective Element in
                    Archaeological Inference   356

                    Index   363

INTRODUCTORY READINGS IN

Archaeology

𝄢𝄢𝄢𝄢𝄢𝄢𝄢𝄢𝄢𝄢𝄢𝄢𝄢𝄢𝄢

CHAPTER ONE

What Is Archaeology?

The four extracts in this chapter
are included to show the differences
between New and Old World archaeology,
and to highlight differing approaches
to American archaeology.

THE DISCIPLINE OF PREHISTORY

The first selection presents an Englishman's view of prehistoric archaeology, taken from GRAHAME CLARK's Archaeology and Society. Old World prehistorians tend to consider archaeology as a branch of historical study, and as a discipline for studying antiquities in order to reconstruct the past. The role of anthropology is recognized as being important, but less so than that of history. Clark's words clearly state the European position.

Archaeology may be simply defined as the systematic study of antiquities as a means of reconstructing the past. For his contributions to be fruitful the archaeologist has to possess a real feeling for history, even though he may not have to face what is perhaps the keenest challenge of historical scholarship, the subtle interplay of human personality, and circumstance. Yet he is likely to be involved even more deeply in the flow of time. The prehistoric archaeologist, in particular, is confronted by historical changes of altogether greater dimensions than those with which the historian of literate civilizations is concerned, and has to face demands on his historical imagination of a commensurate order; further, at a purely technical level he is likely to be met with much greater difficulties of decipherment, difficulties which can as a rule only be surmounted by

From *Archaeology and Society* by Grahame Clark, pp. 17–26, copyright © 1939 by Grahame Clark, and published by Methuen and Co. Ltd., London. Reprinted by permission of the author and publisher. Footnotes are omitted.

calling on scientists and scholars practised in highly specialized branches of knowledge.

Much of the fascination of archaeology indeed resides in its many-sidedness. One can safely say that there are few faculties, experiences, or fields of special knowledge that cannot contribute to or are not stimulated by its pursuit. The complete archaeologist, if such a being existed, would need to have a genius for travel, exploration, and reconnaissance; to be adept at business and administration, skilled at raising funds and obtaining all manner of permits from authorities and owners, few of whom can hope to gain from his activities, and capable of administering and directing excavations which may well turn out to be large-scale enterprises; to be a competent surveyor, draughtsman, and photographer, so that what he finds can be adequately recorded; to combine a gift for exact description and analysis with a power of synthesis and a flair for journalism; and to have the gift of tongues, or at very least an ability to digest the reports of his foreign colleagues without which his own will lack the authority that only wide reading and comparison can provide.

In addition to all these talents of the market-place, without which even the finest scholarship is likely to prove ineffective in this field, our para-gon must be endowed with other qualities of a higher and a rarer order. The fruitful practice of archaeology involves to a unique degree an ability and a willingness to comprehend the aims, methods, and potentialities of fellow-workers in the most diverse branches of both humanistic and scientific study. To express the matter differently, the quality of the contributions an archaeologist is likely to be able to make depends on the degree to which he recognizes the limitations as well as the possibili-ties of his discipline in the elucidation of the past. The first step is to recognize that archaeology is in fact a discipline, but only one of the many disciplines needed to throw light on the more or less remote past, and the second that success is likely to depend not only on the rigor of its own proper methods, but also on the skill and sympathy with which its practitioners combine with those of cognate disciplines to solve com-mon problems.

The discipline of archaeology imposes special requirements of its own. All archaeologists, whatever their precise field, have to depend primarily on the study of artifacts, and the classification and understanding of these call for a highly developed sense of style: the archaeologist has to rely in the first instance very largely on his appreciation of form, texture, and artistic convention if he is to distinguish correctly the products of separate cultures, discern stages of historical development, or detect the interaction of different traditions. Further, so soon as he concerns himself with at-tempting to reconstruct the lives of the societies responsible for the artifacts he studies, he is brought up against a new set of requirements. Even to appreciate ancient works of art it is necessary to combine with a capacity for aesthetic appreciation a wide knowledge of the techniques and history of architecture, sculpture, and painting. But the range of artifacts with the production and use of which the archaeologist has to be familiar is coextensive with the life of society. Indeed, technical processes and the artifacts shaped by them can only yield their full historical meaning in relation to the economic and social systems of which they formed an integral part. This means that archaeologists need to be aware of the work, not merely of economic and social historians, but still more, in the case of those working on preliterate societies, of the findings of social anthropology.

Again, since artifacts are made by and for people and since societies are constituted by individuals, it is vital to study the mentality and actual physical characteristics of the bearers of his cultures, and this the archaeologist can only do indirectly, since in the case of the former he is often studying people without a literature and whose language is unknown to him, and in the case of physical type and condition he is as a rule confined to skeletal traces which may often be very incomplete: for his knowledge of mentality he will have to rely mainly on what he can infer from the way in which the people he is studying have utilized their environment, behaved to each other and come to terms with nonmaterial, unseen forces, though where skulls are available he may get some help from the size and convolutions of their brains; and for physique, racial type, age, sex, medical history, nutrition, and deformation he will have to rely on anatomy and forensic medicine and, where ancient, fossil material is concerned, on human paleontology, branches of knowledge which, if he is lucky, he will find combined in the person of a physical anthropologist.

Further, the archaeologist, and more particularly the prehistoric archaeologist, must study his cultures in their geographical setting, if he is to bring them to life in all their dimensions or even understand their economic basis. It is not sufficient to study the relationship between traces of former stages of settlement and the present geographical situation: such studies may and indeed must be misleading, and the more so the older the cultures studied, since the geographical environment can no more be taken as a constant factor than can human settlement itself. What the prehistoric archaeologist has to study is the history of human settlement in relation to the history of the climate, topography, vegetation, and fauna of the territory in question. One of the greatest difficulties in such a study is to distinguish between changes in the environment brought about by purely natural processes and those produced, whether intentionally or incidentally, by the activities of human society, and this can only be resolved by intimate cooperation in the field with climatologists, geologists, pedologists, botanists, zoologists, and paleontologists in the comradeship of Quaternary research. The archaeologist wants to know precisely what geographical conditions obtained at each stage of human settlement; the extent to which the economic activities of any particular community were limited by the external environment; and above all how far the economic activities of the people he is studying are reflected in and can be reconstructed from changes in the geographical surroundings. It is only by observing the human cultures of antiquity as elements in a changing ecological situation that it is possible to form a clear idea of even the economic basis of early settlement, see precisely how early man utilized his environment and so arrive at a fuller understanding of his intellectual, economic, and social progress.

Archaeological methods can profitably be applied to any phase or aspect of history insufficiently documented by written records, however recent in time; indeed, archaeology can not only be used to fill gaps in the documents, but also to check or corroborate them. In this respect archaeological evidence bears some analogies to the circumstantial evidence of the law courts. Human testimony, whether written or oral, has a directness of appeal that may at first sight seem to be lacking from the fragments and traces on which the detective relies for his circumstantial evidence, but the very humanity which appeals to us in literature or speech involves grave limitations. Human memories are fallible and the motives of witnesses, writers of state papers, and even historians are more mixed than they know themselves. Cross-examination in the courts and critical analysis in the study may do something to rectify or at least check the unveracities of human testimony, but they can hardly do more than reduce the area of uncertainty. Although the interpretation of scientific data by hired experts is notoriously liable to point to opposing conclusions, the value of circumstantial evidence can hardly be doubted as a check on personal testimony. In dealing with the past it is the gaps even more in many cases than the imperfections in the surviving written record that enhances the value of archaeological evidence. For instance, it has been found that more precise information about the proficiency of the men of medieval times can be obtained from a study of their scientific instruments than from their treatises alone. Similarly, excavation has recently been throwing more light on the history of medieval settlement in Denmark than could be obtained from the documents, and even in England, where the documentary record is relatively complete, there are large spheres of economic activity never or only incidentally recorded in writing.

As a general proposition it must be accepted that the value of archaeological evidence as a source of information about human history varies inversely with the extent and nature of documentary sources in the broad sense of the term. The more incomplete the historical record the heavier the reliance that must be placed on alternative kinds of evidence. Thus the value of archaeology is likely to be higher in relation at any rate to the earlier stages of the older oriental civilizations than to the classical or later European ones. Yet even in the study of the earliest literate communities archaeology is bound to play an ancillary, if not a subservient, role where any considerable bulk of inscriptions has survived, since these give an insight into the mentality and values of early societies more direct than material things can ever do. Conversely, it is in the reconstruction of prehistory, the unwritten history of all but a comparatively brief span of all humanity, that archaeology can render its greatest contribution to human understanding. . . .

No precise delimitation of the range of prehistory is likely to find wide acceptance, though it would probably be agreed by most English-speaking archaeologists that it is concerned with preliterate societies. At the lower end of the range no hard and fast line can be drawn between animal and human societies, but for practical purposes one may take the appearance of tools shaped in conformity with a recognizable tradition as a useful datum. As regards an upper limit one might accept the appearance of a more or less continuous written record as marking the end of prehistory and the beginning of what is conventionally regarded as history. Quite clearly, though, some difference of opinion is likely to exist as to precisely at what stage preliteracy gives way to literacy: attainment of literacy must in the first instance have been a slow process; and the spread of literacy was so uneven that it has taken about five thousand years for it to extend from the earliest centers over the world as a whole.

One of the results of this slow diffusion of literacy is that the prehistoric period lasted much longer in some regions than in others. Thus even in Europe marked differences can be noted as between different areas: over much of the Mediterranean coasts the prehistoric period was brought to an end by Greek and Punic colonization already by the middle of the first millennium B.C.; the extension of the Roman Empire during later centuries incorporated the rest of the Mediterranean and parts of the temperate zones within the sphere of history and, even if outlying provinces suffered a relapse into barbarism, the experience of Imperial rule was sufficiently profound to mark the end of an age; but extensive territories in the northern, central, and eastern regions of the continent remained prehistoric until gathered into the fold of Christendom in the course of the Middle Ages. Most of western and parts of southern Asia had already been drawn within the sphere of ancient oriental civilization long before Alexander's famous march, and the rise of an independent, if in part derivative, civilization in North China and its attainment of literacy soon after the middle of the second millennium B.C. had already brought prehistory to an end over extensive tracts of the Far East before direct contact was established with the West. Much of Africa on the other hand remained prehistoric until quite modern times; influences from ancient Egypt had early penetrated extensive areas of North Africa, but it was not until the establishment of Phoenician trading-stations on the coast that any part of the continent outside the Nile Valley and its immediate area passed into history; trade and commerce from the Indian Ocean must have opened up parts of the east coast comparatively early, and on the west the Portuguese extended their influence as far down as the Gold Coast before the end of the fifteenth century; but it was not until 1652 that the Dutch disturbed the prehistory of South Africa, and much of the tropical interior remained prehistoric until the middle of the nineteenth century. Australia remained for all effective purposes prehistoric until the founding of Sydney in 1788 initiated a process that was not to affect the greater part of the continent until well into the nineteenth century. When the New World was first effectively discovered by Europeans it is true that indigenous civilizations existed and that in certain of these historical records were maintained, but by far the great part of both the Americas remained prehistoric until opened up by exploration and settlement during the post-Columbian era.

It follows from this not merely that there was a broad overlap in time between the later prehistoric communities and those recording their own histories, but that simpler cultures in proximate and even in quite distant regions would even in quite early times have been liable to more or less profound influence from civilized centers. This means that the later prehistoric cultures must needs be studied in the same context as their literate contemporaries. With characteristic clarity our French colleagues have long recognized that this necessity in turn serves to differentiate the phases of prehistory anterior to the rise of the early civilizations (or at least to their impact on the prehistory of whatever area is in question) and those which betray in metallurgy or other traits the impact of ideas deriving ultimately from literate communities: it is the former alone, running from the beginning of the Old Stone Age to the Neolithic, that for them comprise *la préhistoire*; the latter they consign to *la protohistoire*. British archaeologists have generally preferred to hold to the concept of prehistory as a unitary field. Yet it is important to recognize the existence of a polarity of interest as between those concerned with the primary evolution of culture up to the discovery and spread of an elementary farming economy and those whose main interest is with the secondary devolution of culture and the transformation of primitive farming communities under impulses from civilization up to the stage at which they were capable of beginning to record their own history: for some purposes it may even be useful to speak of primary and secondary prehistory.

The general aim of prehistory is to recover as much as possible about the history of preliterate societies which by their very nature were incapable of recording it. This makes it hardly necessary to emphasize that the kind of information to be won from the prehistoric past differs profoundly from that to be gained from the history of even partially literate societies. In a sense there is justice on the side of those who have claimed that, since prehistoric peoples have and can have no history, prehistorians are attempting the impossible in trying to recover it. The distinction we have to preserve is that between history in its rigorous, academic sense, which began only when it was written down, and history in its broader evolutionary connotation, the product of the last two centuries of scientific thought, which comprehends the whole story of mankind in society. The fact that we now recognize a continuity of development, and one that can only conventionally be restricted to human societies, should not prevent us from recognizing Natural History, Prehistory, and History as separate disciplines, disciplines which differ not merely in their procedures, but still more in what they can tell us about the past.

It is the glory of history that by means of it one is enabled not merely to check general trends by reference to a multitude of particularities—one can often do this for prehistory—but actually to study the relations of individual men to one another and to the circumstances in which they found themselves, and even to discover the motives that determined or at least influenced specific choices. The prehistorian, on the other hand, lacking documentary sources, is precluded from identifying individuals; so soon as the names even of the most prominent are known we sense ourselves on the threshold of history proper and begin even in the English-speaking world to qualify our studies as protohistoric. Prehistory, as I have written elsewhere, is a social study: it deals "not with individuals or with the relations of individuals to one another and to society in general, but with societies, including their internal stratification and their local organization, and their relations to one another and to the world of nature of which in the final resort they form an integral part." Yet, though the units with which it deals are larger and though it has to work at a higher level of abstraction than history proper, prehistory is nevertheless fundamentally historical in the sense that it deals with time as a main dimension.

A NEW WORLD VIEWPOINT

JAMES DEETZ's brief introductory essay on archaeology is rapidly becoming a classic, and the short extract reprinted here comes from the first chapter. He considers archaeology as a part of the discipline of anthropology, and the archaeologist as an anthropologist who studies extinct peoples. Deetz's approach is typical of New World archaeologists, whose research is intimately connected with the anthropology of modern Indian groups. Their ancestry lies directly in the prehistoric past, and in ancient societies which flourished in the same areas in which these groups live.

Archaeology is the special concern of a certain type of anthropologist. We cannot define archaeology except in reference to anthropology, the discipline of which it is a part. Anthropology is the study of man in the broadest sense, including his physical, cultural, and psychological aspects, and their interrelationships. Archaeology concerns itself with man in the past; it has been called the anthropology of extinct peoples.

Archaeologists are anthropologists who usually excavate the material remains of past cultures, and through the study of such evidence, attempt to re-create the history of man from his earliest past and to determine the nature of cultural systems at different times and places around the world. Archaeology is similar to history in part of its purpose, that of delineating sequences of events in the past and their importance to mankind today. This kind of reconstruction is called prehistory, a term which stresses a basic difference between archaeology and history. Prehistory treats the time before man learned to write and therefore record his own career on earth. It begins with man's first appearance on this planet, almost two million years ago, and usually ends with the beginnings of written history in all parts of the world. This later date can be as early as *circa* 3500 B.C. in the Near East, or as late as A.D. 1850 in parts of the state of California. While such time limits can be imposed on archaeological studies, they are somewhat flexible and blurred at the later end of the scale. In recent years, archaeologists and historians have become aware of the value of working together in certain situations. The archaeological and historical records combined often yield a richer picture than either would separately. We know from history that Plymouth Colony was founded in 1620, that the ship bringing the first colonists was the *Mayflower*, that separate land grants were given the settlers in the cattle division of 1627, and that the first houses were probably made from sawn clapboards. Yet no known historical documentation tells us exactly what animals were used for food by the Plymouth colonists, what types of dishes were used in the homes, when the first bricks were produced locally, or what types of nails, window cames or door hardware were used in constructing the houses. Archaeological investigation of seventeenth-century house sites in Plymouth has given the answers to all these questions, fleshing out much of the bare bones of the historical accounts.

In the missions of southern California, we know from the historical record that quarters were constructed for the Indian neophytes, and that they were occupied by family groups. Such a structure was built at La Purisima Mission in 1814, but the resident Padre was satisfied with simply noting in his diary that the building had been erected. Archaeological excavation showed it to be 540 feet long, of adobe brick with heavy tile roof. Study of the contents of the apartment units within this barracks structure provided valuable insights regarding Indian life in the missions not forthcoming from the historical record.

If historical documentation is of value at the later end of the archaeologist's time scale, the earliest end leans heavily on the natural sciences. The older the material, the less perfectly preserved it usually is, and the greater the need for supporting interpretations with data drawn from other disciplines. The excavation of a 40,000-year-old site in France requires the assistance of paleontologists, botanists, soil specialists, and geologists, to name but a few of the non-anthropological scholars who work with the archaeologist in the analysis of the materials recovered. Through the application of results from these supplementary fields, the archaeologist is given a good idea of the environment in which man lived at the time, and the types of problems which life presented.

The "where" of archaeological work is as important as the "when." Modern archaeologists are pursuing their investigations in all those places where man lives or has lived at any time in the past. Sites are excavated in the frigid Arctic, in the jungles of tropical America, Africa and Asia, on the open plains of the United States, beneath the streets of London, and even under the waters along the coastlines of many parts of the world.

With the entire world from which to draw his materials, and a two million year span of time represented by them, it is the task of the archaeologist today to integrate this immense yet imperfect corpus of data into a meaningful picture, and in so doing provide an understanding of cultural process in time and space.

CULTURE

Archaeology seeks to learn about culture from the fragmentary remains of the products of human activity. What, then, is culture? Culture can mean many things: a growth of bacteria in a petri dish, the correct way to behave in various situations, or what we get when we read "good" books, listen to "good" music, or learn to appreciate "good" works of art. To the anthropologist, culture means none of these things. On the other hand, to say just what it does mean to an anthropologist is by no means simple. In fact one entire book has been devoted to the definitions of culture used in anthropology.[1] Assuming that you could find them, ten anthropologists selected at random on the street would probably give ten somewhat different definitions.

Since we are concerned with culture in our discussion of archaeology, we must attempt a definition in the face of so many others; there is some comfort in numbers, however, and our treatment of culture in this case will not be too different from the consensus. Culture can be defined by making several statements about it.

CULTURE IS LEARNED BEHAVIOR. We inherit many things from our ancestors through genes; the color of our hair, our blood type, the shape of our face. Other things are given to us by our ancestors, but not biologically. There is no gene for speaking English, wearing a necktie, calling our mother's sister's children "cousin" or using Arabic numerals. Yet, generation after generation does these things, having learned them by a process separate from the genetic and biological, a process termed *extrasomatic*, apart from the body. We might even say that culture is everything a person would not do were he to grow up completely isolated on a desert island.

CULTURE IS UNIQUELY HUMAN. This statement might cause some disagreement. Many species of animals learn certain patterns of behavior in a way not too different from that by which man learns cultural patterns. But man is the only animal who uses culture as his primary means of coping with his environment. Culture is man's adaptive system. While bears and rabbits in the Arctic have developed heavy pelts through biological evolution that protect them against the cold, the Eskimo makes a snug fur suit and lives in an igloo. Over the ages, man has elaborated culture into an ever more complex buffer between him and his world. Remove this cultural

---

[1] A. L. Kroeber and C. Kluckhohn, *Culture: A Critical Review of Concepts and Definitions,* Papers of the Peabody Museum of American Archeology and Ethnology, Vol. 47, No. 1 (Cambridge, 1952).

screen from the picture, and we would find man so ill adapted to his environment that he would probably become extinct. Even a brief loss of electrical power places urban man in an unfamiliar and uncomfortable relationship to the environment, and an apartment dweller who cannot use his electric can opener is in much the same predicament as an Australian aborigine who has lost all his spears while hunting far from home.

CULTURE IS PATTERNED. The array of habits and customs which make up culture for any group of people is integrated: each part relates to every other part in a systematic manner. Anthropologists categorize culture in certain conventional ways. Language, religion, economics, technology, social organization, art and political structure are typical categories. In any culture, the form of the political structure is in some way contingent on the social structure; art reflects religion, social organization shapes a part of technology, and so on. In studying the nature of cultural patterning, anthropologists have come to understand how culture is structured in hundreds of cases.

SOCIETY IS THE VEHICLE FOR CULTURE. The distinction between culture and society is clear. Societies are groups of interacting organisms, and man is but one species of social animal along with other primates, many insects, and even certain lower forms of life. In the human case, society is the repository of culture; it carries it; its members participate in it; and culture is the dominant determinant of social behavior.

Culture can thus be defined as a uniquely human system of habits and customs acquired by man through an extrasomatic process, carried by his society, and used as his primary means of adapting to his environment.[2]

To this definition we might add one qualification as archaeologists. Culture is highly perishable, and therefore cannot be excavated. No one has ever dug up a political system, a language, a set of religious beliefs, or a people's attitude toward their ancestors. Yet such things as political and religious behavior, language, and social interaction affect what the archaeologist does recover. The patterning which the archaeologist perceives in his material is a reflection of the patterning of the culture which produced it. Pots, arrowheads, house floors and axes are the products of culture, not culture in themselves, but they are linked to culture in a systematic manner. It is the archaeologist's task to discover how cultural behavior is shown in its products.

---

[2] Anthropologists also distinguish between culture on the one hand, and individual cultures on the other. This latter, somewhat different use of the term signifies individual groups of people the members of which share in a particular culture system. Thus we can speak of American culture, Chinese culture, Navaho culture, etc. Another definition of culture in these terms would be the shared habits and customs of a single society.

AMERICAN ARCHAEOLOGY AND ANTHROPOLOGY

*In 1958 GORDON R. WILLEY and PHILIP PHILLIPS published a
short monograph on method and theory in American archaeology
that has become a classic exposition of the theoretical rationale
behind the subject. The volume explores the relationship between
archaeology and anthropology, and the introduction to this work,
quoted below, expands the position set out by James Deetz in the
preceding selection. The interested reader is recommended to study
Willey and Phillips' book in detail, for it sets out frankly and critically
the relationship between cultural anthropology and archaeology in a
lucid and penetrating manner.*

It has been said that archaeology, while providing data and generalizations in such fields as history and general anthropology, lacks a systematic
body of concepts and premises constituting *archaeological theory*. According
to this view, the archaeologist must borrow his theoretical underpinning
from the field of study his work happens to serve, or do without.
Whether the latter alternative be an admissible one does not seem to be an
arguable point. Acceptable field work can perhaps be done in a theoretical
vacuum, but integration and interpretation without theory are inconceivable.

The above remarks apply to archaeology in general, but the sole concern
of this study is American archaeology. It seems to us that American
archaeology stands in a particularly close and, so far as theory is concerned, dependent relationship to anthropology. Its service to history in
the narrower sense, i.e., as the record of events in the past with the interest centered on those events, is extremely limited, because for pre-
Columbian America there is in effect no such history. The use of traditions
derived from native informants and other documentary sources of the
contact period as starting points for pushing back into the unrecorded
past—the "direct historical approach"—is not archaeology serving history,
but the reverse. As a technique of investigation, American archaeology,
like archaeology generally, provides useful data for geology, paleontology,
climatology, etc., and it recovers valuable materal for art museums and

From *Method and Theory in American Archaeology* by Gordon R. Willey and Philip Phillips,
University of Chicago Press, 1948, pp. 1–7. By permission of the authors and the University
of Chicago Press, copyright holders.

the study of aesthetics, but it is not involved theoretically with any of these subjects. To paraphrase Maitland's famous dictum: American archaeology is anthropology or it is nothing. The American archaeologist, unless he thinks he can dispense with theory altogether, is therefore obliged to take a stand on some of the basic questions of general anthropological theory. This we shall do briefly in the following pages.

The methods outlined in this study, and our arguments in their behalf, are predicated on two general theoretical assumptions: (1) that anthropology is more science than history, and (2) that the subject matter of anthropology is both society and culture. The first part of this statement appears to settle out of hand the position of anthropology in respect to the dichotomy science-history, a question that has vexed philosophers ever since the emergence of anthropology as a field of study. It seems to us that the force of this antithesis is largely spent. There is now considerable agreement among theorists that the world of anthropology is a mixture of recurrent and unique events acting and reacting upon each other in a tremendously complex fashion. The only serious disagreements are in respect to the role and importance of the two components of the mixture. Our view is that the part played by recurrent events, though it may be the smaller, is the more significant; and that this is just as true for an archaeology devoted to the service of anthropology as it is for anthropology itself. Archaeology, in the service of anthropology, concerns itself necessarily with the nature and position of unique events in space and time but has for its ultimate purpose the discovery of regularities that are in a sense spaceless and timeless.[1] And, since it appears that a comparative method will be most likely to disclose such regularities, it follows that the archaeologist is faced with the responsibility of finding, in the seemingly endless flow of cultural and social events, forms and systems of forms that are not only comparable to each other but also comparable to, or at least compatible with, the forms and systems of forms of cultural or social anthropology.[2] We shall return to this point later.

The second article of belief referred to above is that the subject matter of anthropology is both society and culture, another polarity that is not standing up under analysis. The interpenetration of social and cultural facts now seems to be taken as axiomatic. Following Kroeber and others,

---

[1] This we hope will not be taken to mean that the events referred to take place outside space and time. In this and all subsequent references to space and time in this study, it is of course geographical space and chronological time that are denoted.

[2] "Social anthropology" in England, "cultural anthropology" in the United States—these are not precise equivalents but are closer, it seems to us, than practitioners in the two countries appear to believe. From the detached point of view of the archaeologist, at any rate, they are practically synonymous terms. In this study we follow the American usage but without any convictions regarding the predominance of the cultural over the social aspect of our subject matter.

we have chosen to regard them here as *aspects* of the same basic reality. Definition of this basic reality is fortunately outside the scope of the present inquiry. It is sufficient for our purposes to characterize it loosely as patterned human behavior. Archaeology, of necessity, deals very largely with patterned human behavior in its cultural aspect. In American archaeology especially, we have tended to suppress the social aspect altogether. Some Americanists have been drawn into the extreme position that sees in culture an independent order of phenomena, intelligible in terms of itself alone—the "cultural superorganic." Most of us, without subscribing to the superorganic view of culture, have nevertheless operated "as if" it were a fact. In our opinion even this moderate position, though operationally expedient and to a certain extent inevitable, is ultimately detrimental to the main task of archaeology, which is to organize its data in terms of a real world, a world in which cultural and social phenomena (to name only these) are inextricably mingled.

The reader will have noted by this time that we are driving toward an accommodation between the seemingly opposed methods and outlook of archaeology and cultural anthropology. Comparison may be facilitated by considering the operations of the two disciplines on three levels of organization that are generally applicable to all scientific analysis: *observation, description,* and *explanation.* The accompanying diagram is a crude attempt to show how the operations of archaeology and cultural anthropology can be considered as converging toward a synthesis from one level to the next.

Explanation	Processual interpretation	Ethnology
Description	Culture-historical integration	Ethnography
Observation	Field work	Field work
	ARCHAEOLOGY	CULTURAL ANTHROPOLOGY

On the observational level, archaeological and cultural anthropological field work are placed far apart on the diagram because of wide differences in the phenomena observed. These differences, however, can be too easily overemphasized. Cultural anthropology observes group behavior and the products of group behavior in their twofold aspects, social and cultural. Its primary concern is with the social aspect, but certain categories of behavior, notably those which are symbolized in language, art, myth, etc., may be studied very largely in their cultural aspect. Archaeology observes primarily the materialized products of group behavior but has considerable opportunity to observe symbolized behavior in the forms of art, iconography, and (rarely) written language, and occasionally touches social behavior through inferences, as in the interpretation of burial practices, house plans, settlement patterns, roads, irrigation systems, and the like. Thus it appears that the raw materials of the two disciplines are not so different after all; what is different is that archaeology is obliged to view its material almost entirely in the cultural aspect. It has sometimes attempted to turn this limitation into an asset by embracing the cultural superorganic, as already noted.

The term "culture-historical integration," as used here, covers almost everything the archaeologist does in the way of organizing his primary data: typology, taxonomy, formulation of archaeological "units," investigation of their relationships in the contexts of function and natural environment, and determination of their internal dimensions and external relationships in space and time. However high-sounding these terms, it appears that the activities represented by them remain essentially on the descriptive level. Explanatory concepts, such as acculturation, diffusion, and stimulus diffusion, are utilized, but the aim is primarily to describe what happened to specific cultural units at specific times and places; no attempt is made (on this level) to draw generalizations from these observations and descriptions. Culture-historical integration is thus comparable to ethnography with the time dimension added, but we dare not push this analogy too far, because the archaeologist's descriptive formulations, like his observations, lie mainly in the cultural aspect of his subject matter. Later . . . we make a plea for unit concepts that are intelligible in the social aspect as well, but we are under no illusion that any except the very smallest of them can be precisely equated with correspondent units of social structure. Nevertheless, we have placed culture-historical integration and ethnography closer together on the diagram than their respective field operations, in the belief that archaeological unit concepts can and should make more sense in terms of the social aspect than is generally supposed.

So little work has been done in American archaeology on the explanatory level that it is difficult to find a name for it. It might have been left blank on the diagram to emphasize this lack. The term "functional interpretation," which has gained a certain amount of currency in American studies, was used in the original version of this diagram but is not entirely satisfactory, since it implies that the functional is the only explanatory principle involved. We have substituted here the broader "processual interpretation," which might conceivably cover any explanatory principle that might be invoked. In the context of archaeology, processual interpretation is the study of the nature of what is vaguely referred to as the culture-historical process. Practically speaking, it implies an attempt to discover regularities in the relationships given by the methods of culture-historical integration. Whatever we choose to call it, the important consideration is that, on this explanatory level of organization where we are no longer asking merely what but also how and even why, our formulations must be viewed in both their cultural and their social aspects.[3] It is not possible to go about investigating culture-historical processes and causality without reference to the efficient causes of cultural change, which are people or groups of people, and therefore lie in the social aspect of reality. Perhaps it is fair to say that there has been a lack of progress in processual interpretation in American archaeology to date precisely because unit formulations have been put together with so little reference to their social aspect. In the same vein of optimism already displayed, we have put processual interpretation and ethnology (which includes among its many meanings the operations of cultural anthropology on the explanatory level) side by side on the diagram to suggest a further convergence of aims, if not of practice. At this point, the archaeologist is in effect a cultural anthropologist,[4] but it is well to remember that his activities on this level are conditioned by his formulations on the descriptive level and that these in turn have special characteristics which it is our purpose to describe.

Diagrams and models have the happy faculty of proving whatever they are designed to prove, and ours is no exception. Nevertheless, we think that this model, in spite of the crude simplification inherent in any system of "levels," represents a pattern that is not wholly fictitious. As archaeology, in the service of anthropology, moves from one operational level to the next, it is compelled to pay more attention to the social aspect of its subject matter, until there takes place on the explanatory level an actual convergence with cultural anthropology and the possibility of an eventual synthesis in a common search for sociocultural causality and law.

---

[3] To name only two of the important factors in a complex equation. Geographical and ecological factors, already present on the descriptive level, carry over with increased importance onto the explanatory level. These have been deliberately ignored in our diagram, which is focused on the special relationships between the cultural and social aspects of anthropology. The same neglect of physiological and psychological factors should be noted.

[4] This point has been very well put by Walter Taylor, who also rationalizes the operations of archaeology on a series of levels that differ in detail from ours but can be reconciled with them, as in the following passage: "When the archaeologist collects his data [observational level], constructs his cultural contexts [descriptive level] and on the basis of these contexts proceeds to make a comparative study of the nature and workings of culture in its formal, functional, and/or developmental aspects [explanatory level], then he is 'doing' cultural anthropology and can be considered an anthropologist who works in archaeological materials" [A Study of Archaeology, 1948, p. 43].

NEW WORLD ARCHAEOLOGY

American archaeology has undergone some basic changes in the last twenty years which are the subject of JOSEPH R. CALDWELL's article, "The New American Archaeology." The old emphasis upon the description and definition of prehistoric cultures, the principal concern of Willey and Phillips' study, is seen to have given way to a concern for historical problems and generalizations concerning culture as a whole. Thus the new archaeology is not only of importance to anthropology but can also prove useful in answering some of the age-old problems of philosophy and history. The reader is advised to read both extracts one after another to emphasize the contrast between the two points of view.

▣ It is well known that the fortunes of archaeology have been greatly improved by new technical aids such as radiocarbon dating. A more important but far less celebrated advance is represented, I think, by a shift of interest in recent years toward problems of far greater generality than pertain to any single excavated prehistoric site. Part of this shift of interest to more general problems must be ascribed to the outstanding work of V. Gordon Childe and others in the Old World, but the greater reason perhaps is to be found in the close ties which most American archaeologists have maintained with general anthropology and through this, more tenuously, with the wider domain of social studies.

This juxtaposition of anthropology and archaeology in North American universities came about for the good historical reason that this continent contained living primitive cultures as well as prehistoric ones. The work of Americanists has with reason been called social-science archaeology. Not only do many Americanists have a cultural anthropological background but they find fruitful applications in archaeological thought of the studies, for example, of social anthropologists such as Julian Steward and Robert Redfield. A series of papers in a . . . volume entitled *Seminars in Archaeology: 1955* (*1*) comprised the following titles: "An archaeological classification of culture contact situations"; "An archaeological approach to the study of cultural stability"; "The American Southwest: A problem in cul-

Joseph R. Caldwell, "The New American Archaeology," *Science* 129, No. 3345 (6 February 1959) 303–307. Reprinted by permission of the author and the Editors of *Science*. A revised version of this paper was published in *New Roads to Yesterday*, Joseph R. Caldwell, Editor, Basic Books, 1966.

tural isolation"; and finally, "Functional and evolutionary implications of community patterning." Had a sociologist found himself at these meetings, he would have had no trouble recognizing the problems, even if the factual data seemed a little strange. An anthropologist writes of these four seminars that they domonstrate "a growing together rather than a falling apart of archaeology and the other special disciplines of anthropology" (2).

FIRST APPROACH

The understanding that is emerging as a result of shifting interests and new problems can be shown by comparing recent archaeology with the older variety. Since American archaeology is regionally specialized—Andean, Eastern, Middle American, Southwestern, and so on—and because some of these regions were ahead of others in development, I find it easier to use the older archaeology of eastern North America as a base line for the kind of contrasts that I propose to make.

Up until World War II the chief concerns of eastern archaeology—with some exceptions—seem to have been the description of archaeological sites and the description—often simply the definition—of prehistoric cultures. The latter might be presented individually or in terms of culture provinces (3). Sometimes particular categories of material culture—for example, all the known prehistoric pottery from the eastern United States—were presented in terms of provinces (4). Some fine work was done on the identification and methods of manufacture of prehistoric stone tools (5).

A considerable advance was represented in the Midwest by a Linnaean-like taxonomic system (6) which appeared just at the time it was beginning to be realized that cultural stratigraphy was present in the Eastern areas. The Midwestern taxonomic system was regarded as a necessary first step. It organized archaeological materials into categories based on degrees of likeness of the assemblages being unearthed. Unfortunately, there was a tendency to regard classification as the end of research, and some archaeologists who were obtaining long stratigraphic sequences, which in some cases showed gradual culture change, were hard put to classify these in Midwestern terms, although they continued for years to do so. In being able, now, to observe material culture changes in time and space, they already have part of the means for establishing *kinds* of historical connection, whereas the taxonomy they tried so hard to employ could only specify something about degree and could not deal with continuities.

I think it is fair to say that before World War II American archaeological studies were in a condition similar to that which Northrop (7) has characterized as the natural-history stage of inquiry. The emphasis was on archaeological data as things in themselves rather than on the values offered by different ways of looking at them. Moreover, it was considered, in practice, as important to excavate a site meticulously and to record every scrap of evidence which might conceivably bear on any future problem as it was to have a reason for excavating the site in the first place. One result of all this was the development of a specific kind of problem which treated classificatory entities as independent realities; one might inquire into the content of cultures known from preserved material objects, examine their temporal or spatial boundaries, or try to establish the degree of relationship among them.

A second result was the development of a specific kind of analysis to set up the comparisons required to solve problems of this nature. Types were routinely established as an economical means of describing small objects, pottery, constructions of one sort or another, and burial customs. These types were considered adequate for all comparisons which might later be made but were not designed to solve particular problems. Problems might certainly occur to one after the types had been established. Types of this kind, since they were immediately apprehensible regardless of problem, were in some quarters considered to be real entities, and rightly so.

The third result was the development of a specific kind of history—a history of material culture—which, at best, described the succession of the preserved archaeological assemblages in each culture province. At worst, such a history was confined to the area of a modern state and made unnecessarily complex by the assignment of different names in different states to cultural manifestations which, on the basis of the criteria in use, should have been assigned the same name.

The essentially dull and uninteresting character of this "culture history" was a matter of concern to some archaeologists. Walter W. Taylor (8) called for the construction of fuller cultural contexts—for attention to "the interrelationships which existed *within*" each cultural entity. Others attempted to inject a lifelike note by substituting the word *people* for *culture* whenever possible. Thus, in a semipopular book (9), the "Savannah River Culture" became the "Savannah River People," with corresponding shifts in referential pronouns.

TRANSITION

A trend away from local specialization was initiated in the 1940s in monographs by Ford and Willey in 1941 (10) and by Griffin in 1946 (11). These men made themselves familiar with a vast amount of uncollated and unpublished data which had emerged from the hundreds of excavations undertaken under various federal relief agencies. The prehistory of the eastern United States was found to be most readily susceptible to presentation in terms of a succession of pan-Eastern periods or eras, reflecting the importance of time and continuity in contemporary archaeological thought. The picture obtained from these formulations was of a steady development of material culture and of the essential unity of the East: The various prehistoric cultures assigned to each period in this vast region were usually more alike than were the temporally separated entities within any particular subarea. Hence, each of these major periods could also be regarded as a developmental stage.

In 1958, Willey and Phillips (12) applied what is essentially the same kind of formulation to the whole of the New World, as a series of pan-continental stages. The theoretical foundations of their work were stated at length, some hundreds of areally based prehistoric cultures were characterized, and many special hypotheses regarding the interrelationships of these were proposed, weighed, or discarded. The result of this method was again to show the cultural interconnectedness of the area treated—in this case the entire Western Hemisphere—and to suggest that the civilizations of Mexico and Peru emerged from the same background as the other American cultures but proceeded through additional stages leading to civilization.

American archaeology still leans heavily on the idea of areally based cultures and probably always will. We have even improved the utility of this view by the concept of tradition—a culture area having depth in that it is allowed to shift its boundaries through time. If we now suggest some new ways of thinking about areal traditions, this does not mean that we are ready to dispense with them. They do represent more or less closely one kind of natural or common-sense division among the primary materials we have to work with. Where we have improved on the older archaeology is by asking different kinds of questions of the materials, and this is directly bound up with the new interests we have noted.

THE NEW ARCHAEOLOGY

The new archaeology in America is tending to be. more concerned with culture process and less concerned with the descriptive content of prehistoric cultures. There are now two kinds of problems, historical and general, which can be suggested either by distinctions seen in the data themselves or by results of archaeological research in other parts of the world, or which can emerge out of other disciplines such as ethnology or philosophy, and then be brought to the data as propositions to be tested.

We may characterize our new interests in the following way. Where formerly we were concerned with the identification of things and of cultures—whether, for example, a particular artifact should be regarded as a knife or as a scraper, or whether a given archaeological assemblage should be classed with this culture or that—we have added an interest in the identification of culture processes and situations. Thus, W. R. Wedel's "Environment and Native Subsistence Economics in the Central Great Plains" (13) examines culture-environment connections in that area, and since that time other archaeologists, stimulated no less by A. L. Kroeber's

"Cultural and Natural Areas of Native North America" (*14*) than by the fine Virú Valley Project in Peru (*15*), have turned their attention to the interrelations between natural ecology and human populations and settlement patterns, with respect to cultural level.

Another approach to cultural and historical processes is seen in the wealth of inferences which can be derived from changes in cultural forms seen through time—that is, through stratigraphic and constructed sequences. Whether or not changes were diffused from another region can be inferred from knowledge of whether or not they occurred earlier elsewhere. That changes are of local development can be inferred when their prototypes occur locally at an earlier time. Something about the historical situation can be inferred from rates and magnitudes of changes in cultural forms. A sudden change in a whole series of artifact forms may herald a prehistoric invasion; gradual changes in forms occurring at different times suggests a period of comparative tranquility during which cultural development was not greatly influenced by outside areas. Whereas the older Midwestern taxonomic system could establish degrees of connections among cultural assemblages, we are now finding various methods of inference which will enable us to see the kinds of connections.

Present archaeology still reflects an indiscriminate use of the notion of a prehistoric "culture," by which is sometimes meant a few artifacts of some former society and, at other times, a number of societies historically related, but perhaps in different ways and in different degrees. We are increasingly sensitive to the value of making distinctions between cultures as opposed to societies (*16*). Observations which can be made about behavior are for the archaeologist mediated through cultural forms, but his inferences need not always refer back to culture. Sometimes it is better to use the concept of interaction area instead of culture area; not only is thought thus referred directly to the behavior of people instead of to a "culture," but in some cases this idea is better suited to the archaeological facts of continuous intra-areal diffusions of cultural forms. In other instances we can make inferences concerning social organization itself (*17*).

Still another basis for our changing interest stems from the idea of pattern or configuration, which has had a considerable vogue in anthropology although it is not new with that science. The archaeologist is inclined to see cultural patterns in developmental terms. A pattern represents some kind of regularity or organization. If a pattern can be recognized, the features we use to account for its presence may perhaps be stated in terms of the processes which brought it into being or perhaps in terms of the factors which operate to maintain it.

With the idea of cultural patterns and developmental patterns, modern archaeology has reached a point where many possible patterns and hypotheses can be suggested, each of which seems to propose cultural "facts" that are not necessarily mutually exclusive and that do not necessarily contradict each other but which *in the same body of materials* reflect various aspects of a many-sided reality. To take a very simple example of the way in which a given body of archaeological materials may mirror different historical facts, suppose that a stratigraphic sequence of flint projectile points is used to suggest the answer to the question of whether these points were javelin tips or arrowheads. If both types are present, it may be that the bow and arrow was replacing the javelin during this range of time. We could perhaps arrive at an answer to this problem by using a type system with criteria based upon the size and weight of the specimens. On the other hand, the question might be whether the flint was being obtained from a distance through trade, and for this we should have to examine the projectile points in the light of another type system based on kinds of flint correlated with different localities—not on sizes and weights as in the other case.

In the foregoing example it is relatively easy to see how a given body of archaeological materials represents different historical or cultural facts. In the case of cultural pattern or configuration, however, the "reality" of proposed fact is less apparent because the particular interests of the investigator, and perhaps the historical development of the science, intrude more strongly into the result. Thus, Willey and Phillips' stadial conception of New World prehistory is also concerned with a particular reality; they might have devised other conceptions of equal validity had their interests been other than what they were.

New Understandings

The views held by Julian Steward, a social anthropologist (*18*), show how additional understanding has been reached by a different approach. Steward rejects "unilinear" cultural evolution, maintained at the end of the last century by ethnologists like Tylor and Morgan and now in part by Willey and Phillips (*19*), which says that with certain allowances for diffusion, all human cultures pass historically through similar developmental stages. According to Steward's theory of "multilinear" evolution, all cultures do not pass through similar stages but we can discern a finite number of parallel evolutions in which societies adapted to particular environments and natural resources pass through successive and distinctive levels of "sociocultural" integration. Steward's comparisons deal with societies from various parts of the world. Features of these societies are treated by Steward as types, and certain recurrent associations of important features represent "cross-cultural types."

Conclusions concerning processes involved in particular evolutionary sequences are regarded not as natural laws but as regularities or generalizations of limited range, upon which, one supposes, we may in time build further. Steward says: "Ecological adaptations can be considered as causative in the sense that a degree of inevitability in cultural adjustments is directly observable. Patrilineal bands of Bushmen, Australians, Tasmanians, Fuegeans, and others represent a type in that the ecological adaptation and level of integration are the same in all these cultures. In these and other cases, factors producing similar types such as environment, food resources, means of obtaining food, the social cooperation required, population density, the nature of population aggregates, sociopolitical controls, the functional role of religion, warfare, and other features, will have an understandable relationship to one another."

Steward's work is concerned with processes of culture change manifested in a number of distinct developmental sequences and arrives at generalizations of limited range stated in terms of cultural process, whereas, the Willey-Phillips formulation stresses the interconnectedness of the prehistoric societies of the Western Hemisphere and arrives at a series of cultural levels applying to the area.

Some of Steward's proposed cross-cultural types, such as Formative, Regional Florescent, Empire, and Conquest, are designed to show the processes leading to civilization. They are nearly parallel to the later stages of the Willey-Phillips formulation. Steward's types are now being examined and somewhat modified by archaeologists familiar with the various regions (20). The developmental similarities of Steward's types may be stated in causal terms, because between the Old World and the New World there is not much chance that the similarities are due to historical connection.

A new approach sometimes brings a wealth of understanding. Archaeology seldom affords direct evidence of social institutions, although Childe has suggested some means by which these can be inferred, and recently Sears has been able to propose a correlation between prehistoric burial mounds on the Gulf Coastal Plain with the presence or absence of strong social classes in the societies involved (21). Now Steward provides another method for arriving at such inferences, as Eggan has pointed out (22). Archaeology usually does offer data (for example, the bones of food animals and the size and locations of sites) concerning ecological adaptation. Some social institutions can be satisfactorily inferred from this if, as Steward maintains, they are causally connected with ecological adaptations.

I recently proposed (23) a conception of the development and spread of early civilizations which, like the Steward and Willey-Phillips formulations, rests on a hypothesis. The body of available data is here divided differently, and in thus shifting the focus of our interest, new cultural "facts" are created. According to this scheme, there has been, in the areas which developed civilizations as well as in those which did not, an "Archaic" culture type with certain definable developmental features.

These developmental features can be used to account for the emergence of civilizations in some areas as well as for the absence of civilization in other areas. Once a civilization has developed, however, some of the processes involved in its spread are best seen in terms of a contrast between two additional culture types: "nuclear civilization" and, in the areas outside of civilization, "nonnuclear culture."

The most important developmental feature of the Archaic culture type in eastern North America was the achievement of primary forest efficiency. This was a cumulative process manifested in the development of ambush hunting, in seasonal economic cycles (transhumance), and in the discovery of new sources of natural foods. It is supposed that something like this may have occurred wherever Archaic cultures are found in forested lands. An extension of this idea leads to a definition of a "plains efficiency" for the hunters of large migratory game and a "maritime efficiency" in coastal areas. These various "efficiencies" are meant to be the logical counterparts of "primary farming efficiency"—a term originally used by Braidwood (24) to describe the economic platform upon which civilization may arise.

Plant raising was known in areas where nuclear civilization did not arise. However, it was *only* in areas of nuclear civilization that food production was the economic basis for society. Perhaps the plants used had greater potentialities; perhaps growing populations or the progressive depletion of other resources, or both factors, brought about a Toynbeean challenge which was successfully met.

In the nuclear civilization culture type, it is the achievement of primary farming efficiency which permits the changes leading to civilization. In the nonnuclear culture area of eastern North America, where primary forest efficiency was well established, it was this very efficiency which tended to direct subsequent economic innovation along lines previously established. Changes only represented further development of hunting-gathering systems.

While a degree of residential stability and comparative freedom from want can be achieved by peoples who live by hunting, fishing, or gathering (witness the American Indians of central California and the northwest Pacific coast), it appears that urbanization and civilization cannot appear without the development of food production on an extensive scale.

The growth potential of different economic patterns is clearly delimited in comparing the nuclear and nonnuclear culture types. The mechanics of the limiting factors can be seen in comparing each of these two with their common antecedents in the Archaic culture type.

What new understanding can be reached by viewing culture developments in the Western Hemisphere in terms of two contrasting types, nuclear civilization and nonnuclear culture? Such a view suggests one way to find connections which became established between the areas of civilization and the areas beyond, and the outward spread of civilizations can be formally examined both in time and in space. It becomes possible to ask certain questions about the spread of civilizations, and although the particular historical events may seem to be of infinite variability, it may be possible to account for these in terms of a finite number of general processes. Within the framework of the contrast between nuclear civilization and nonnuclear culture, it is relatively easy to describe certain intermediate cultural balances as of mixed descent. To do so emphasizes the role of such hybrid cultures as active agents in the spread of civilizations. Finally, it calls attention to the different developmental patterns between the spreading civilizations and the cultures which confront them. An acculturation situation consists of far more than the simple adoption of features of the greater culture by the weaker. Both are affected, and both reinterpret culture transfers in terms of their own views and interests, which we *can* see as patterned in terms of a particular historical development.

CONCLUSIONS

It is supposed that behind the infinite variability of cultural facts and behind the infinite and largely unknown detail of historical situations we shall discover the workings of a finite number of general cultural processes. This hypothesis underlies much of recent archaeological thought despite the view, often propounded, that because of level, cultural facts are much more complex than those of the physical sciences. This latter assertion does not make our task impossible. Not all cultural facts are of equal importance in determining a given pattern or trend. Certain developmental patterns must surely be overriding in their effects upon other patterns. A major historical pattern may serve to unite or in some cases to subordinate other patterns of more limited range.

Although, as I have tried to show in this article, cultural facts vary with the hypothesis, and although the hypothesis varies with the special interests of the investigator, this does not mean that archaeological formulations at the pattern level cannot be tested and that some kind of validation cannot be secured. The pathways of archaeology are strewn with the wreckage of former theories which could no longer be supported in the light of new data. Some hypotheses are concerned with different aspects of a reality reflected in a single body of materials. There are also hypotheses which can be shown to be logically inconsistent with each other and among which a choice must be made. As time goes on, tests of compendency will become increasingly specific. Finally, here in the realm of postulated cultural facts there are some from which test cases can be constructed, and in this way the truth of the postulates can be tested. One way to disprove the Willey-Phillips postulate that all the cultures of the New World went through similar developmental stages would be to show that an important area of New World cultures did not go through these stages but did go through others.

I said in the beginning, and have tried to show with reference to the convergence of archaeology with anthropology and social studies, that archaeology is now turning to questions of greater generality than pertain to any single excavated prehistoric site or culture. I think that our interests will become still wider. The similarities between Steward's views concerning the importance of the food quest in determining the institutions of the simpler societies and Marx' production relationships, which formed the basis for his labor theory of economics, may already have occurred to the reader. V. Gordon Childe apparently found much in Marx' historical formulations to stimulate his own conceptions of prehistory.

Since archaeology expects to deal with a range of problems pertaining to former societies and often seeks the aid of other sciences to do this, it tends to make connections among various kinds of studies. Moreover, the appropriateness of archaeological data for questions which have arisen in general studies of history or art has long been recognized. Archaeological findings from the earth, viewed in terms of time, space, and cultural behavior, offer a vast body of material for inference. And as for philosophy, I think that the usefulness of archaeological data will be recognized and that closer connections with that discipline will be established. What does a stratigraphic sequence of changes in cultural forms have to say about the nature of historical causality? What does the regularity which such changes often show imply concerning historical determinism as opposed to human liberty?

If it is the wise archaeologist who now restricts his formulations to the development and persistence of civilizations, cultures, technologies, arts, and lesser matters, it must also be the very dull archaeologist who could be unconcerned with the implications of these for some of the perennial problems of Western man.

References and Notes

1. "Seminars in Archaeology: 1955," *Soc. Am. Archaeol. Mem. No. 11* (1956).
2. E. H. Spicer, *Am. Antiquity* 23: 186 (1957).
3. H. C. Shetrone, *The Mound Builders* (Appleton, New York, 1930).
4. W. H. Holmes, *Bur. Ethnol. 20th Ann. Rept. 1898–1899* (Washington, D.C., 1903).
5. ——, *Bur. Ethnol. Bull. 60* (Washington, D.C., 1919).
6. W. C. McKern, *Am. Antiquity* 4: 301 (1939).
7. F. S. C. Northrop, *The Logic of the Sciences and the Humanities* (Macmillan, New York, 1948).
8. W. W. Taylor, *Am. Anthropologist Mem. No. 69* (1948).
9. P. S. Martin, G. I. Quimby, D. Collier, *Indians Before Columbus* (Univ. of Chicago Press, Chicago, Ill., 1947).

10. J. A. Ford and G. R. Willey, *Am. Anthropologist* 43: 325 (1941).
11. J. B. Griffin, *R. S. Peabody Foundation for Archaeology Publ. No. 3* (1946), p. 37.
12. G. R. Willey and P. Phillips, *Method and Theory in American Archaeology* (Univ. of Chicago Press, Chicago, Ill., 1958).
13. W. R. Wedel, *Smithsonian Inst. Publ. Misc. Collections* 101, No. 3 (1941).
14. A. L. Kroeber, *Univ. Calif. (Berkeley) Publ. Am. Archaeol. and Ethnol.* 38 (1939).
15. G. R. Willey, *Bur. Ethnol. Bull. 155* (Washington, D.C., 1953).
16. ——, and P. Phillips, *Method and Theory in American Archaeology* (Univ. of Chicago Press, Chicago, 1958).
17. V. G. Childe, *Social Evolution* (Shuman, New York, 1951).
18. J. H. Steward, *Theory of Culture Change* (Univ. of Illinois Press, Urbana, 1955).
19. G. R. Willey and P. Phillips, *Method and Theory in American Archaeology* (Univ. of Chicago Press, Chicago, 1958), pp. 70–71, assure the reader that theirs is not an evolutionary scheme. I found their arguments unconvincing, and the reader may wish to judge this matter for himself.
20. *Irrigation Civilizations: A Comparative Study,* "Social Science Monographs" (Pan American Union, Washington, D.C., 1955).
21. V. G. Childe, *Social Evolution* (Shuman, New York, 1951); W. H. Sears, *Am. Antiquity* 23: 274 (1958).
22. F. R. Eggan, in *Archaeology of Eastern United States,* J. B. Griffin, Ed. (Univ. of Chicago Press, Chicago, Ill., 1952).
23. J. R. Caldwell, "Trend and Tradition in the Prehistory of the Eastern United States," *Am. Anthropologist Mem. No. 88* (1958).
24. R. J. Braidwood, *The Near East and the Foundations for Civilization* (Univ. of Oregon Press, Eugene, 1952).

CHAPTER TWO

🔲🔲🔲🔲🔲🔲🔲🔲🔲🔲🔲🔲🔲🔲

Field Survey in Archaeology

How do you find an archaeological site?
This is one of the perennial questions
encountered by the teacher of archaeology.
The most effective way to answer this question
is visually, with single-concept films.
Therefore, the discussion here is confined
to air photography.

THE PRINCIPLES OF ARCHAEOLOGICAL
AIR PHOTOGRAPHY

*Air photography is a well established technique of archaeological
survey, and has been since the 1920s. R. J. C. ATKINSON's
exposition of the basic principles involved is included to demonstrate
the potential of the method, especially on sites where no surface
traces remain on the ground. The frontispiece to this volume is an
example of an air view of a conspicuous archaeological site.*

▣ During the last twenty years the work of Mr. O. G. S. Crawford, the
late Major G. W. G. Allen, and others, together with the cooperation of
the Royal Air Force, has given archaeologists a new weapon of research,
the air photograph. Indeed, the use of air photography marks the greatest
advance made in the technique of field archaeology since the introduction
of scientific methods by General Pitt-Rivers, and the archaeological aspect
of many areas has been completely changed by the discovery of hundreds
of hitherto unrecognized sites. . . .

Fundamentally, all archaeological sites (and, of course, all non-archaeological disturbances of the ground) are revealed as differences of tone
on a photograph. These tone differences are due to two causes, namely,
differences in the reflecting power of surfaces on the ground, and actual
differences in the color of growing crops and grass, or of the bare soil.

From *Field Archaeology* by R. J. C. Atkinson, pp. 18–29, published by Methuen and Co. Ltd.,
London, 1953. Reprinted by permission of the author and the publisher. References are
omitted.

Sites made visible in the first way are known as *shadow-sites*; those revealed in the second way are called *crop-marks* and *soil-marks*.

SHADOW-SITES

These sites include the ramparts and ditches of hill-forts, boundary-ditches, barrows, and any other earthwork whose surfaces in relief are capable of casting a shadow. On sites where the relief is slight shadows are usually cast only in the early morning or late evening, when the sun is low; at these times details are often visible from the air which cannot be picked out at all by an observer on the ground.

Shadow-sites of another class may sometimes be seen in growing crops in July or August. A crop growing over a silted-up ditch or pit may, owing to the greater depth of soil, grow high enough above the surrounding plants to cast a slight shadow, although, because of the ripening at that time of year, no difference of color will be discernible, as might have been earlier in the season (*v. infra*, Crop-Marks).

A third type of site may be included under this heading, although its appearance is due not to the casting of a shadow but to the unequal intensity of reflection from inclined surfaces. For instance, when lynchets (cultivation terraces) are photographed facing a setting sun, the sloping faces of the terraces, being steeper than the general slope of the hillside, and therefore more steeply inclined at right angles to the sun's rays, will reflect more light than the surrounding ground and will appear on the photograph as light lines on a darker background.

On rare occasions snow may show the position of earthworks in a striking manner. In a heavy storm with a driving wind, mounds and hollows will cause differential drifting of the snow. When the main blanket of snow has melted, the remains of the drifts will mark even very slight changes of relief, which can be recorded with great clarity by air photography.

CROP-MARKS

Whereas the shadow-marks just described are all due to differences in the relief of the ground, which can always be detected by an observer at ground-level either by eye alone or by careful use of levelling instruments, crop-marks often betray the position of sites of which there is no indication in the surface relief at all. Photographs revealing crop-marks are therefore of particular value to the archaeologist.

Marks in crops (which term here includes pasture) are due to two causes, namely, differences in the color and differences in the growth of the crop. Both these differences arise from disturbance of the ground in which the crop is growing. The growth and color of a crop depends largely upon the amount of moisture and other nourishment which the plants can derive from the soil and subsoil. Where, therefore, the depth of soil has been increased by the digging and subsequent filling up of a pit or ditch, or by the heaping up of additional soil in the form of a bank, more nourishment will be available, which will be reflected in the rate of growth and color of the overlying crop. Conversely, where the available depth of soil is decreased by the presence of impenetrable surfaces, such as walls, floors, and roads, the overlying crop will tend to be thin and stunted and lighter in color. This weak growth may be shown either by patches of corn flattened by the wind, or by darker or lighter areas where the soil shows more clearly through the thin crop.

Generally speaking, therefore, a well-defined dark mark in a crop may be taken to indicate a pit or ditch beneath the surface, and a vaguer, more smudged mark a weathered bank; while a light mark, or patches of flattened grain, will probably overlie foundations or some other hard surface.

We may here include for convenience what may be called *soil-marks*, that is, differences in color appearing in bare soil prepared for sowing. These differences are due to the spreading and exposure by the plough of material from banks, mounds, and even walls and floors, which shows up as a lighter patch contrasting with the darker plough-soil around it. The effect is particularly marked in chalk country.

All the contrasts described above are intensified by parching of the ground in a hot dry summer. The effect is particularly marked on grassland, where crop-marks normally only appear under such conditions (it may be noted, however, that the position of pits and ditches beneath grass is sometimes indicated not by differences in the grass itself but by the flourishing growth there of thistles and other weeds). Parching too will show the position of walls, roads, etc., as light patches on bare plough-soil, though usually only when the rough surface of the field has been smoothed out by rain some time beforehand.

Changes of tone analogous to crop-marks and, like them, indicating the position of buried ditches and pits, have occasionally been seen when the ground is completely covered with snow. The effect is evidently due to the relatively greater thermal conductivity of the ditch-filling, which causes the overlying snow to melt faster than on undisturbed ground.

The degree in which soils and crops are capable of producing visible marks is variable. Generally speaking, crop-marks do not appear where the soil and underlying "rock" are of similar consistency, as is the case with clay and sand. Disturbances in harder "rocks" such as chalk, gravel, and limestone will produce marks, but only if the topsoil is comparatively shallow. Crops, too, vary in sensitivity; grass rarely shows any marks, except under parched conditions, while among grain crops oats, and among leguminous plants lucerne (alfalfa), is probably the most sensitive.

It will be clear, therefore, that the absence of crop-marks does not necessarily indicate an area archaeologically barren; it may be due simply to the lack of suitable conditions. Conversely, by no means all crop-marks should be assumed to be of archaeological interest. Ditches may be relics of comparatively modern drainage systems; banks may mark the site of destroyed hedges or old plough headlands; and many a promising set of circular marks has turned out upon inspection on the ground to be nothing more than fungus rings. Even Mr. Crawford, the pioneer of archaeological air photography, records how he spent a day discovering that some interesting "barrow ditches" were in fact the result of circular browsing by tethered goats.

The moral of these examples is obvious. Observation from the air is a very valuable method of research, but it is not enough. Every site seen or photographed from the air should be visited on the ground as soon as possible, so that the observations may be checked. Until this has been done it is very unwise to speculate or to indulge in hopes which may easily be proved vain. . . .

THE STEREOSCOPIC EXAMINATION AND INTERPRETATION OF AIR PHOTOGRAPHS

It is well known that the ability to see objects as three-dimensional solids depends upon the fact that the two eyes register images which differ slightly owing to their separation. A single photograph cannot give a three-dimensional view since it incorporates only one image taken from a single viewpoint. If, however, two photographs of the same scene are taken from slightly different viewpoints, and if the prints are arranged so that the right eye sees only the right-hand image and the left eye the left-hand one, stereoscopic vision results and the two images will combine to give an impression of three-dimensional relief.

Any pair of vertical air photographs which overlap one another will thus contain an area common to both which, if viewed so that each print is seen by one eye only, will be seen in stereoscopic relief. It is for this reason that prints of the 1/10,000 survey overlap each other, each adjacent pair showing a common area of ground approximately ¾ by 1¼ miles which can be examined stereoscopically.

Stereoscopic examination, since it adds a third dimension to the photographs, enables details to be seen which cannot be appreciated in a single print. Moreover, owing to the great separation in space between the viewpoints from which adjacent photographs are taken, the effect of three-dimensional relief in these photographs is enormously exaggerated, so that even very slight eminences and depressions on the ground are seen clearly in relief. For this reason it is essential that these photographs should be examined in pairs under a stereoscope; it is always undesirable, and often quite useless, to order single prints of individual sites.

It is possible with practice to view a pair of prints stereoscopically with the naked eyes alone, but it is liable to lead to eyestrain, especially for those with defects of vision. It is preferable to use a simple stereoscope . . . which enables a magnified image to be viewed in comfort. The instrument consists of two positive (bi-convex) lenses whose separation is adjustable, fixed in a metal frame with folding supports. The lenses are adjusted so that the eyes look through their inner halves; the photographs are then placed so that corresponding points on their respective images lie beneath the centers of the lenses, and are orientated with respect to each other and to the stereoscope in such a way that a three-dimensional image results. Once proper orientation has been obtained the instrument may be moved about over the prints to examine different features in the area of overlap.

For proper interpretation of relief two conditions must be fulfilled. First, the photographs must be correctly positioned and orientated; if the positions of the prints are reversed right for left the relief will be inverted, heights being seen as depths and vice versa; advantage may occasionally be taken of this fact deliberately, in order to determine with greater certainty whether a feature in very slight relief is in fact a depression or an elevation.

The second condition is that the apparent direction of lighting *in the prints* should correspond with the *actual* direction of lighting at the place where they are viewed. In the majority of these photographs the light comes from the bottom edge (i.e., the South), and they must therefore be viewed with this edge furthest from the observer and nearest to the source of light, which will be in front of him. Failure to do this may result in the apparent inversion of the relief seen. . . .

Correct interpretation of archaeological features from stereoscopic pairs of prints can be learned only with practice. Generally speaking, if the orientation and the lighting is correct, structures of marked relief will stand out with great clarity; but where the relief is only slight some difficulty may be found in deciding whether elevations or depressions are seen. In such cases the position of the shadows is the determining factor; in a pit or ditch, the shadowed side is nearest the source of light, and on a mound or bank, furthest from it.

Not only does stereoscopic examination of photographs enable structures to be identified that would be invisible to the naked eye of an observer in the air, and sometimes even to one on the ground also; it presents, in addition, a picture of the topographical setting of an ancient site that cannot be obtained in any other way. Moreover, even on quite flat ground, where sites show only as crop- or soil-marks, it will be found that the stereoscopic view will usually reveal more than can be seen on a single print. This applies also to the examination under a stereoscope of duplicate prints of the *same* photograph (e.g., an oblique aerial view); even though no real stereoscopic image is seen, a more satisfactory image of the photograph is obtained, especially if the observer is practiced in the examination of stereoscopic pairs.

PLOTTING FROM AIR PHOTOGRAPHS

Air photographs may often serve usefully as a basis for archaeological plans and sketch-maps. For many purposes a simple tracing of the main features from a vertical photograph will suffice, but it is desirable to know the limitations of accuracy of this method. A vertical photograph has the characteristics of a map only if the ground it portrays is flat and level, and if the photograph is taken in a strictly vertical direction; undulating ground and tilting of the camera introduce distortions of scale.

In the 1/10,000 survey the degree of camera-tilt is regulated within narrow limits, and distortions due to this cause may be neglected. Distortions due to surface relief are more serious; they arise because the tops of hills, being nearer to the camera, are necessarily reproduced in the photograph at a larger scale than the more distant bottoms of the valleys. Thus two structures of identical diameters but at different heights will appear to be of different size on an air photograph; the maximum apparent change of size from this cause on any one photograph is unlikely to exceed 4 parts in 100. For accuracy of plotting it may thus be necessary to determine the scale of a photograph at more than one point on each print.

The scale of a vertical photograph may be found in three ways. In the first, the focal length of the lens used is divided by the height of the aircraft (in the same units) to give the required representative fraction. Thus a photograph taken at 16,400 ft. with a 20-inch lens has a scale of 20 ÷ 16400 × 12, or 1/9840; but this is only a rough method of finding the approximate average scale of a print, owing to the continual variations in the actual height of the aircraft and of the ground.

The second method requires a map on which points visible in the photograph can be identified with accuracy. If the distance between two points on the map is A, the corresponding distance on the photograph B, and the representative fraction of the map 1/C, then the scale of the photograph is given by B ÷ A × C.

In the absence of a map the scale of the photograph may be found if the length of an object appearing in it is known. Thus if the length of the image on the photograph is B, and that of the object, in the same units, is A, the scale of the photograph at that point is B ÷ A.

If a piece of semi-transparent tracing material, such as *Kodatrace* or

Ethulon is placed over one print of a pair viewed under a stereoscope, rough contours or form-lines can be sketched in to indicate the basic features of the relief.

AIR PHOTOGRAPHY IN PERU

This classic passage from GORDON R. WILLEY's monograph on the prehistoric settlement patterns of the Virú Valley, Peru, demonstrates the use of air photographs in locating sites where the terrain is arduous, or maps nonexistent. Virú vegetation is scanty, and the survey party was able to locate a large number of sites by using air photographs.

🔁 The procedures in field and laboratory for the Virú Valley program have been described previously. The present section will paraphrase these earlier accounts but will also consider certain problems, methods, and techniques that have a specific bearing upon the settlement-pattern study.

The basic data for analysis and synthesis of prehistoric Virú settlements are the descriptive observations on archaeological sites or other prehistoric works in the Valley. These data were compiled as notes, maps, and photographs during the course of a 4-month survey of the Valley. In this period 300 sites were recorded. They were visited by Ford, who was conducting the ceramic survey, myself and two workmen. At each site notes and photographs were made, and at many of them a detailed map was prepared.

The mapping techniques were based upon aerial photography, and to describe the processes it is necessary to refer back to initial preparations which were made before entering the field. In embarking upon an investigation of settlements or site layouts it was obvious that maps would be crucial and would represent the greatest expenditure of time and effort in the field. If a large number of sites were surveyed, adequate

From "Prehistoric Settlement Patterns in the Virú Valley, Peru" by Gordon R. Willey, *Smithsonian Institution, Bureau of American Ethnology,* Bulletin 155, 1953, pp. 3–6. Reprinted by permission of the author and the Smithsonian Institution. References are omitted.

instrument maps could not be prepared in the field time allowed. The problem, then, was to find a way of making a relatively accurate site map in a short time. I am indebted to Ford for a solution to this problem through the use of aerial photos and for his help in setting up the mapping laboratory at our Trujillo headquarters.

Before leaving Lima we had purchased air photographs of the Virú Valley. These had been prepared three to four years previously by the Peruvian Air Force and were assembled at the National Air Force Laboratories at Las Palmas near Lima. The prints were coordinated quadrangle mosaics, each of which encompassed 2 minutes of latitude and 3 minutes of longitude at a scale of 1:10,000. Twenty-two of these quadrangles, each measuring 23 by 16 inches, were needed to give adequate coverage of the cultivated valley bottoms and margins of Virú.

Study of the air photos showed numerous archaeological sites in the Virú Valley, most of which were unreported; and this preliminary review proved to be most helpful in the field survey. Walls of dwelling sites, mounds, ancient roads, and canals were sharply defined; and, in many cases, features could be appreciated in the air photographs that would have been missed if we had passed over them without previous knowledge in a ground survey. It was this clarity of definition in the photos that suggested the particular mapping technique employed. Such a technique is feasible in country like the Peruvian coast where there are large areas without vegetation cover and where there are abundant structural remains visible on the surface.

Preparatory to going into the field, a site map was made from an air photograph with the aid of an epidiascopic projector. This was done by placing one of the 1:10,000-scale air photographs in the epidiascope and projecting the image, in a dark room, onto a screen equipped with drawing paper. The section of the air photo so projected was a small rectangle about 3 by 2 inches. This was arranged to include the site, or sites, in question and the surrounding country. The enlarged projection was then traced in pencil, and this tracing formed the outline map which was then carried into the field to the site under consideration for detailed checking. The projection enlargement was a little over 15 diameters of the original on the air photograph. This particular ratio was accidental, being arrived at by adjusting for a convenient distance between epidiascope and screen. As the air photos were on the 1:10,000 scale, the projected tracings were at a scale of approximately 1:700. This scale was standardized and used throughout our Virú mapping work. All of the site maps illustrated in this report were made in accordance with it.

Field checking included chain measurements made on the ground. In many cases, there would be features which did not show to advantage on the air photos. These were then measured and plotted. Wall thickness, wall heights, doorways, subfloor cists, room banquettes, masonry and adobe types, and a multitude of other details not revealed in the air photographs were measured or recorded during our visits to the site. In addition, the relationship of one site to another, of sites to canals or cultivation plots, of sites and refuse heaps, and similar observations were noted during the ground survey, sometimes with reference to the air photos.

The sites, as surveyed, were numbered in a consecutive system with the prefix "V" (for Virú), hence the designations V-1, V-2, etc. As the survey progressed these sites were marked on a duplicate set of the large aerial photo quads which were carried with us in the "jeep." Later, they were copied onto the second, and cleaner, set of quads which were kept in the laboratory and from which the projections were made. The sites were also entered on a master site map of the Valley. This map was prepared by the geographer, F. W. McBryde, who worked from an aerial photograph taken at a 1:25,000 scale.

There are a number of comments to be set down concerning the site maps made with the help of the epidiascopic projections. It should be emphasized that they are not as accurate as a plane table or instrument map, but are more accurate than sketch maps or maps made only with compass and chain. There are a number of reasons for their lack of accuracy. We have mentioned the indistinctiveness of site features in the air photos. Besides this, there is the element of distortion in the photograph. I am not technically competent in aerial photography and cannot discuss the error factor with precision, but, in comparing ground and air-photo projection measurements, I found this margin of error to be small for practical purposes. For example, if a wall measured 50 meters, by scale, on the projection map, there would be an error of less than 1 meter in the measurement of this same wall on the ground. Thus the projection maps seemed effective and accurate enough for the settlement-pattern study.

There were, of course, sites which did not show to advantage on the photographs and for which any but the most gross projections were impossible. Steep terrace dwelling sites, because of the slope, could not be satisfactorily projected. The maps which I made of many of these are little more than sketches supplemented with chain measurements and occasional compass readings. At other times, heavy *monte* growth covered a site so that it was impossible to use the air photographs for anything more than general location data. These sites, which were usually on flat ground, were more successfully mapped than the hillside sites, as the chain measurements were more simply and accurately taken. For most site maps the direction arrow indicated the true north, as this was obtained from the aerial quads. There are some exceptions to this, however, where, because of a lack of a projection, a direction reading was taken by compass. In these instances, the map has been reproduced with a magnetic north designation.

Throughout, heights of mounds, buildings, and walls have either been estimated by eye or checked with a hand level. Contour elevation, as it is used on some maps, was taken in another way. The Servicio Aerofotografico provided us, in addition to the air-photo quads, a partial series of contour maps at the same scale. These contour maps, with intervals of 10 meters (and 2-meter subdivisions in some cases), had been made from the air photos, not from ground surveys. They did not offer a complete valley coverage; but, where available, we used them for epidiascopic projections in the same manner as the air photographs. After completing a site tracing from an air-photo projection, the matching contour map was inserted into the epidiascope at the same place and orientation as the air photo. This was done by means of north-south coordinate lines drawn through both. When the contour map was properly adjusted in the machine, the contours were traced onto the map projection, over the site outline, and the meter elevation figures recorded. These superimposed contour projections were only moderately successful. Many of them are inaccurate. For example, the reader will note that canals will occasionally cross from a lower to a higher contour when actually the canal is running down grade. In these cases it is certain that the air-photo projection is the correct one; the contour projection wrong. In spite of this, I decided to use the contour lines, when available, to indicate general slope and elevation of terrain. A 10-meter interval is a large one, and is useful only for steep slopes; but there are many of these in Virú, and the fact of a site being on a precipitous hillside or relatively flat ground was worthy of indication. Within the contour lines there were often lesser elevations that were significant, and these have been indicated by a hatched symbol.

Site mapping was carried out on those locations or features where, in effect, there was something worthy of mapping. Of our 315 Virú sites, at least half showed no noteworthy surface features. These were "mapped" in the sense that they were located on the air quads and, eventually, the master-site map, but individual drawings were not made. Such sites were midden piles without rock or adobe walls, earth and refuse mounds of the Lower Valley which appeared only as low hillocks, and many of the smaller dwelling-construction of pyramidal mounds about which no surface data seemed particularly significant except gross size and general location. Because of the differential in the construction of sites in the Valley, those in the middle and upper portions having rock foundations while those in the lower sections being of adobe, more middle and upper region sites were mapped in detail. There are numerous exceptions to this, however, as there are many adobe-walled Lower Valley buildings whose surface outlines are reasonably clear.

A series of symbols have been used in the site maps. These indicate stone masonry walls, adobe walls, superimposed terraces, and all the other necessary features of the map. In some cases these are supplemented with names, such as "road," or "canal," "massive wall," etc. Proportion and scale have been sacrificed slightly to the symbols. For example, in the scale we used it was impossible to indicate a stone wall in proper symbol that would be rendered less than 1-meter wide on the map. Actually, most rock-walled dwellings had thinner walls than this; however, features of this sort are described in the text where dimensions are given.

Theoretically, the survey sites were selected at random. Actually, a number of factors tended to skew our sample, and these should be pointed out. As indicated in the previous paragraph, sites of the upper drainage offered better possibilities for mapping; hence, we included in our sample more upper- than lower-region sites. Also, as any archaeologist knows, the big impressive sites command one's attention before the minor midden heap; and it is only fair to say that we have, proportionately, given a better coverage to big sites than to small ones. In retrospect, we see the Virú-settlement job as a much larger one than we had anticipated. Our total of 315 is no more than one-quarter of the total prehistoric sites in the Valley. This estimate is made from observations in the Valley and from inspection of the air photographs. . . .

CHAPTER THREE

🏛🏛🏛🏛🏛🏛🏛🏛🏛🏛🏛🏛🏛🏛

Time in Archaeology

The distinction between absolute and
relative chronology is one of the first
archaeological concepts important to the
student. This chapter concentrates on
relative chronology; with the exception of
the article by Libby, the subjects cover
stratigraphy, association, and seriation,
as well as pollen analysis.

STRATIGRAPHY AND RELATIVE CHRONOLOGY

SIR MORTIMER WHEELER's classic exposition of the principles of stratigraphy is one of the most frequently quoted passages of archaeological scholarship. His unrivalled experience of complex stratigraphic sequences in European and Asian sites is evident in the following discussion of the problems involved in stratigraphic interpretation, which is taken from his handbook of field archaeology.

▣ In this context [stratigraphy's] principles are—in theory, at any rate—simple enough. The human occupation of a site normally results in the accumulation of material of one kind or another on and about the area occupied. Objects are lost or discarded and become embedded in the earth. Floors are renewed and old ones buried. Buildings crumble and new ones are built upon the ruins. A flood may destroy a building or a town and deposit a layer of alluvium upon its debris; and later, when the flood has subsided, the levelled site may be reoccupied. Sometimes, the process is in the reverse direction: evidences of occupation may be removed, as in the deepening of an unsurfaced street by traffic, or the digging of a pit for the disposal of rubbish or for burial. At Sabratha in Tripolitania, a Roman temple was found in 1948 to have been rebuilt at a *lower* level than its predecessor on the same site, through an intentional lowering of the

From *Archaeology from the Earth* by Sir Mortimer Wheeler, Clarendon Press, Oxford, 1954, pp. 41–46, 48–55. Reprinted by permission of the author and the publisher. Footnotes are omitted and figures renumbered.

whole *temenos* at the time of rebuilding. In one way or another, the surface of an ancient town or village is constantly altering in response to human effort or neglect; and it is by interpreting rightly these evidences of alteration that we may hope to reconstruct something of the vicissitudes of the site and its occupants. . . .

. . . The successive layers in the soil, in other words stratification, [are] compared to the successive pages of a book. The analogy is essentially a true one, and includes the corollary: a prime condition of intelligibility is that the layers, like the pages, shall be brought to our eyes reasonably intact and in proper sequence. Of course, mass-excavation has not always been devoid of all merit. In a rudimentary stage of research, it may help to point the way and stimulate advance along it. We may be grateful to Schliemann for plunging his spade into Troy, Tiryns, and Mycenae in the seventies of the last century, because he showed us what a splendid book had in fact been buried there; but he tore it to pieces in snatching it from the earth, and it took us upwards of three-quarters of a century to stick it more or less together again and to read it aright, with the help of cribs from other places. On a smaller plane, I remember my gratitude in 1944 to certain ardent but highly unskilled French antiquaries at Pondicherry in south India for scraping up a heterogeneous mass of material from an ancient site because, although they knew it not, their spoliation showed that the site contained imported (and dated) Arretine pottery which subsequently, by more orthodox methods, enabled us to determine the first archaeological datum-line in pre-medieval south India. But the accidental benefits conferred on us by our Pondicherry friends, or even by Schliemann himself, are no longer a valid excuse for archaeological illiteracy. Today, the digger must learn to read his sections, or he should be constrained from digging.

In practice, the identification and correlation of the strata or layers which represent the successive phases in the archaeological "history" of a site is one of the principal tasks of the excavator and will occupy the major portion of his time. So important is his task that, at the risk of wearying the reader either with the excessively unfamiliar or, more likely, with the excessively familar, it would be wrong to forbear from certain rather arid technical details. The task is one which involves clear and logical thinking reinforced by experience and infinite patience. Normally, the strata are differentiated by variations in color or material or content. Not infrequently, however, these variations, particularly under the bleaching influences of an African or Asian sun, present difficulty even to the experienced eye: so much so that more than one archaeologist who ought to know better has denied the presence of stratigraphy (in the Western sense of the term) on Eastern sites. "There was no clear stratification," writes a well-known American archaeologist with reference to a Palestinian site, "during a good part of the period covered because there was no complete destruction and rebuilding at any one time." This, of course, is nonsense; by "stratification" the writer quoted means merely "continuous building-levels," oblivious of the no less important layers which on any site may be expected to supplement and interrelate phases of actual construction. The fact is that the observer had simply failed to observe. There are in practice various ways and means of dealing with the reluctant, sun-baked section of the Orient, or indeed with many sections in the West. Damping, and careful scraping with a knife or turf-cutter, will often provide the remedy by bringing out the more subtle variations of color or material. Observation in different lights at different times of the day may help. In a difficult and important section, observation may be continued over a period of days before certainty is reached. And finally an attempt must be made to "read" the section—to discriminate, without prejudice, between the more significant and the less significant differentiations of strata: for example, between a mere "tip-line" in a continuous accumulation on the one hand and a substantive and emphatic occupation-level on the other. It is not enough to identify layers, although that is, of course, the essential first step; it is the task of the archaeologist to *interpret* them, to understand the sentence as well as to transliterate it.

On this all-important question of interpretation something more must be said, always with the proviso that the written word is no sort of substitute for field-experience. The most that the professor can do is to offer such hints or warnings as shall create in the mind of the student a healthy wariness and a proper regard for trifles. Let us take once more as our theme the first and universal question . . . . : What is the time-value of archaeological strata? How long did it take, say, 4 feet of stratified deposit to accumulate? A very searching and important question, well worthy of the most careful consideration: if we could always answer it, half our battle would be won.

Reference has already been made to a famous lead which geology has given us by the recognition of the varved clays of Sweden (and elsewhere) as the annual deposits of the retreating ice, and as the time-table, therefore, of a related human phase. But it is rarely, in all conscience, that geology deals with us so straightforwardly; while man-made strata are capable of every sort of perversity. Some of them, indeed, are of no chronological import whatsoever, and, as instructive disturbers of all faith, these nonentities shall be considered first.

It has been my practice, from time to time, to persuade my students towards the end of the day's work to cut a section through the dump which is the outcome of their digging. They normally discover, as is to be expected, that the section thus cut is replete with stratification—tip-lines, streaks of variant soil, a miscellany of the materials through which they have been working in the course of the day. Nothing is more calculated to disturb their faith in the time-significance of stratification. Here, in front of them, is the variegated accumulation of a few hours; how is that to be reconciled with the interpretation of the adjacent strata below ground in terms of centuries?

In theory the answer is difficult, in practice it is usually easy. It will often be found that certain of the strata cease towards one end or both, in such a fashion that the underlying and overlying layers unite to clasp them and hold them within a uniform mass, as it were in suspension—a sufficient proof of contemporaneity. A succession of layers may join up laterally, like fingers extended from the palm of the hand, essentially integral therefore with one another in substance and date. Very rarely do deposits of this sort consistently ape a prolonged and systematic accumulation. On the other hand, they present a warning: a selected portion of them may be found to simulate a consistent and logical sequence, and so serve to point the danger of argument from small sections. Figure 1 shows a problem of this kind, solved on the right by an extension of the section. It should in any event be axiomatic that no chronological sequence can be regarded as established securely on the basis of a single section. . . .

Figure 1. Section Illustrating (A–B) an Apparent Succession of Strata (3–7), Shown by an Extension of the Cutting (B–C) to Have Been Deposited Simultaneously.

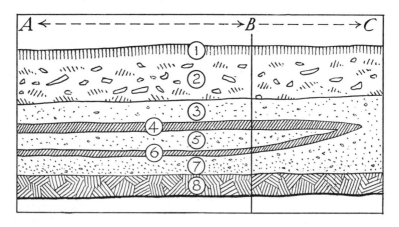

[Wheeler continues with an example of the use of stratigraphy and associated finds to provide a relative chronology.—Ed.]

In 1947 I was digging a town-site on the Mysore plateau in south India, in the vicinity of an undated Iron Age megalithic cemetery, with a view to the correlation of the culture of the cemetery with one or other of the phases of the town. In fact, the sections through the town-site revealed three successive and quite different cultures, of which the middle one was that of the cemetery. For the understanding of the sequel I must burden you with names. The topmost culture was known as "Āndhra," from the name of a local kingdom, the middle culture as "Megalithic," since it was also that of the local megalithic tombs, and the lowest as "Stone Axe," from its characteristic product. Of the three, the only datable culture was the Āndhra, which could be ascribed mainly to the first century A.D. The problem was to relate the other two cultures to this and so, for the first time, to obtain some sort of chronology for them.

For this purpose it was obviously of cardinal importance to ascertain whether the three cultures formed a continuous succession or whether they were divided from one another by time-gaps. Examination of the sections failed to reveal any intervening weathered or exposed surfaces; and indeed, had there been such surfaces, laboratory facilities for their analysis were not available in India. Accordingly, recourse was had to other types of data. In one instance, chance played happily into our hands: a pot-burial of the distinctive Stone Axe type was found inserted into the lowest over-lying stratum of the Megalithic culture, implying a co-occupation by the two cultures at this point. But even without so incontrovertible a demon-stration of continuity, the matter was set at rest by what I may call the actuarial analysis of our sections. Such actuarial analyses should, in my view, be made more frequently than they are, and the Mysore example may therefore be described in some detail. Briefly, the method was this.

In an extensive cutting, chosen as free from complication in the form of intrusive pits or structures, a careful register was kept, layer by layer, of every potsherd found, and the results were tabulated [Figs. 2 and 3]. Fortunately the fabric and technique used by the three cultures were so distinctive from one another that their classification was beyond doubt; the pottery of the Stone Axe people being coarse, hand-made stuff, that of the Megalithic folk being a polished and beautiful black and brown and turned slowly if at all, that of the Āndhra at the top being turned more mechanically on a fast wheel and otherwise elaborated with glaze and patterning. Now the table shows a substantial overlap, running through three successive layers, between the Stone Axe and the Megalithic series, followed by a similar overlap between the Megalithic and the Āndhra series. In estimating the significance of these very substantial overlaps, due allowance must be made for the fact that, from a variety of causes, the subsoil is always in a state of less or greater movement. Animal and vegetable life, and climate, are constantly at work in it. Relics of one stratum are always liable to find their way sporadically into another and to confuse our exact minds. But the thrusting-upwards respectively of 239 and 219 sherds from one culture into the next above it in this single section is not to be thus lightly dismissed. The only acceptable explanation

Figure 2. Section from Brahmagiri, Mysore State, India, Showing Three Cultural Phases with Overlaps.

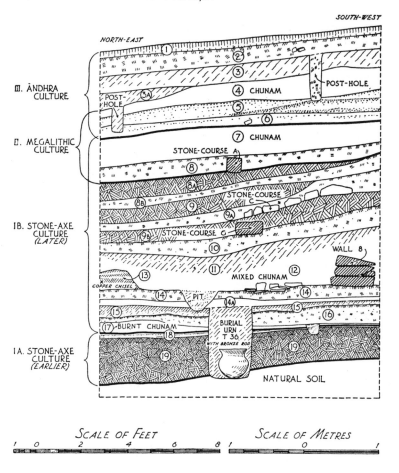

is that on neither occasion did the arrival of the newer culture on the site involve the immediate extinction of the older: in other words, that the cultural sequence was *continuous* and, in our estimate of its chronology in relation to the fixed point at the top, we can ignore the possibility of unknown factors arising from interruptions in the occupation. . . . Details of this specific Mysore example do not concern us; it will suffice to observe that the overlap thus demonstrated between the Megalithic culture and the overlying first-century culture proved that the megalithic tombs were there in use until the first century, and so provided the first firm date for this very abundant category of south Indian structures.

Well, there are examples of various kinds of stratigraphical evidence:

of layers that are contemporary with one another, layers that are separated by greater or lesser time-intervals, layers that have accumulated in unbroken succession. The reading of a section is the reading of a language that can only be learned by demonstration and experience. A word of advice to the student. However practiced, do not read too hastily. Be your own devil's advocate before passing judgement. And, wherever possible, discuss your diagnosis with others—with colleagues, with pupils, with your foreman. ("The testimony of one person is no testimony," declares Hywel Dda, the wise Welsh law-giver.) Be humble. Do not ignore the opinion of the uninstructed. "Everyone knows as much as the savant. The walls of rude minds are scrawled all over with facts, with thoughts." Emerson said

Figure 3.   Tabulation of Sherds Representing the Three Cultures at Brahmagiri. (See Fig. 2.)

LAYER	I STONE AXE	II MEGALITHIC	III ĀNDHRA
1	. .	. .	52, including 1 yellow-painted sherd
2	. .	. .	384, including 10 yellow-painted sherds
3	. .	. .	480, including 68 yellow-painted and 1 rouletted sherd
3a	. .	. .	67
4	. .	36	269, including 51 yellow-painted sherds
5	. .	68	219, including 10 yellow-painted sherds[1]
6	26	115	405, including 7 yellow-painted sherds
7	63	407	. .
8	150	199[2]	. .
8a	36	. .	. .
8b	89	. .	. .
9	76	. .	. .
9a	196	. .	. .
10	46	. .	. .
11	33	. .	. .
12	23	. .	. .
13	26	. .	. .
14	48	. .	. .
14a	15	. .	. .
15	198	. .	. .
16	7	. .	. .
17	45	. .	. .
18	25	. .	. .
19	321[3]	. .	. .

[1] In adjacent cuttings, layers equating with 5 and 6 of Br. 21, i.e., the lowest "Āndhra" levels, produced 7 sherds of rouletted ware.

[2] In an adjacent cutting, the layer equating with this contained an urn-burial of the "Stone Axe" culture.

[3] Including 18 "Early Painted" and 6 incised sherds of the IA culture, which this layer represents.

so, and he was right. Even if you do not accept the views of those you question, the mere act of questioning is at the same time a restraint and a stimulus.

We turn now from interpretation to record. But first reference must be made to a method of recording that not long ago was widespread in the East and may in fact still survive there. If so, it is the survival of a fantastic and monstrous device evolved in the alluvial plains of the great river valleys of Egypt and Mesopotamia as a substitute for exact observation in ill-controlled "mass excavations." Its origin is probably to be found in Petrie's belief that on an Egyptian town-site it was possible to equate the accumulation of material with a specific time-scale. The validity of this "principle" was doubtful and dangerous enough in its original specialized context; it has no place whatsoever in the general technique of modern field archaeology. Yet in India, for example, as recently as 1944 it was still the only method known.

Briefly, it consisted of the mechanical recording of every object and structure in relation to a fixed bench-level. Thus in the excavations at the great prehistoric city of Mohenjo-daro in the Indus valley, in 1927–31, the records were prepared from bench-levels, in one area "178.7 ft. above mean sea-level" and in another "180.9 ft. above sea-level," the assumption being that all objects and structures at the same level below (or above) datum line were in the same "stratum," i.e., contemporary with one another! I have described this system as "incredible" and I repeat the description. So incredible is it, and yet so widespread, that the excavator's own proud account of it may be repeated. He says:

> In order that our deep digging might be satisfactorily carried out, an extensive system of levelling was necessary. The levels of every building and of every wall were therefore taken, especial attention being paid to door-sills and pavements as being for purposes of stratification the most important parts of a building. In addition, both the locus and level of every object found, whether it was regarded at the time as important or not, were noted in order not only to correlate each object with the building in which it was found, but also to facilitate the study of the development of art and technique. As some thousands of objects were unearthed in the sections that we excavated, it may be thought that this procedure was unnecessarily laborious. This, however, was not the case. The levelling instruments were set up early in the morning and remained in position all day; and it was quite a simple matter to take the level of each object directly it appeared.

It was, however, admitted that this method was not wholly free from complexity; that there were

> limitations to the deductions to be drawn from the levels at which objects are found. For instance, if a jar or a seal lies either below or at some distance

above a pavement or door-sill, it is difficult to decide to what period it belongs. We, therefore adopted the rule that all objects found in or near the foundations of a building be assigned to the period of that building rather than to the previous phase, unless they actually rested on the remains of a pavement of earlier date; for it is more than probable that they were dropped or left behind when the foundations were being made.

The chapters on the pottery and other finds in the excavator's subsequent report include page after page of elaborate but insignificant tables based on this procedure.

In other words, be it repeated, the so-called "stratification" of the Indus valley civilization, one of the major civilizations of the ancient world, was dominated, not by local observation, but by the level of the sea nearly 300 miles away! This mechanical classification can only be categorized as the very parody of scientific method. It bears little more relationship to scientific archaeology than astrology bears to astronomy.

To appreciate its utter absurdity, we need only recall that, except perhaps at the earliest level of a site (hardly ever adequately explored), an ancient city in the East is never level. Very rarely is a city completely destroyed and completely rebuilt at one moment and at one horizon. Normally, a house is reconstructed or replaced as it decays, or at the whim of its owner. The town as a whole is constantly in a state of differential destruction and construction. Individual building-sites rise above their neighbors; the town-site itself rises and assumes the contour of a hill; buildings on its slopes are contemporary with buildings on its summit. A doorway or a potsherd may be found at one spot 10 feet below a doorway or a potsherd of precisely the same date at another spot. Such differences, of vital importance to the scientific interpretation of the site, are ironed out and obliterated by the bench-level. If it be necessary to illustrate further the grievous fallacy of this method, two diagrams (Fig. 4) may serve. They are self-explanatory.

Yet, for all the obvious absurdity of the datum-line system just described, the substitution of so-called "levels"—whether abstract building levels or purely arbitrary depth-lines—for factual stratification dies hard. It recurs, for example, in a revised edition (1950) of A *Manual of Archaeological Field Methods* prepared by a leading American university. There, as sturdily as ever, thrives the old outworn system, with its mechanical "unit-levels," governed not by changes of soil but by "the length of the shovel-blade (6 to 12 inches)." True the word "stratification" is not unknown to the authors. It represents a phenomenon, they admit, which "may be visible in the walls of the excavation"; but, we are assured, "any stratigraphy of artifact types and animal bones will appear after a study has been made and need not bother the excavator in the field" [*sic*]. The notion of peeling off the successive strata in conformity with their proper bed-lines, and thus ensuring

Figure 4. Diagrams Illustrating the Stratification of a City-mound (below) and the Fallacy of Recording by Mechanical Levels (above).

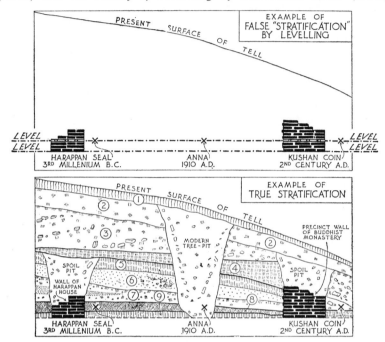

the accurate isolation of structural phases and relevant artifacts, is not even considered.

Enough of criticism; let us turn to a more positive aspect of the matter. The preparation for the record of the section begins with the first spadeful dug. From the outset, the strata are carefully observed, distinguished, and *labelled* as the work proceeds. It is, of course, as the work proceeds that "finds" are isolated and recorded, and their record is necessarily integral with that of the strata from which they are derived. The supervisor must therefore make up his mind clearly from moment to moment as to the limits and nomenclature of his strata; and his decisions, whether ultimately approved or modified, must be susceptable to accurate delineation, if only for the subsequent correlation of his "finds." In other words, both he and the spectator or the future reader must know exactly what he thinks he is doing.

I have found in practice that there is only one foolproof method of ensuring this. The successive layers must be defined and clearly labelled as they come to light. By labelling I meant the actual pinning of a label by a nail or peg into the side of the trench in (preferably on the top edge of) each layer. The label bears the number of the layer within a circle (I reserve encircled numbers for this purpose, to avoid all risk of confusion with numbers having other connotations), supplemented by a name: for example "lower brown," "red clay," "porridge"—it matters not what, so long as a distinctive word or phrase is used to emphasize and cross-check the differentiation. Numbers may on occasion be erroneously duplicated, but the addition of a name avoids risk of confusion. And incidentally the use of a name tends to give individuality to a layer and helps the mind in a pictorial reconstruction of the section.

Accordingly, I like to see my sections plastered from head to foot with orderly arrays of labels, which serve three main purposes: they demand clear and decisive thought on the part of the supervisor who invents them, they show on the ground and on the drawing precisely what his small-find labels mean, and they make it possible for the director or a substitute-supervisor to understand at once the diagnosis up to date. Incidentally, they enable that diagnosis to be checked—always with the proviso that any material alteration in it will probably mean either a relabelling of the relevant "finds" or at least a recording of the original as well as the corrected diagnosis. As a general guide to the young, it is wiser to insist upon the over-stratification than the under-stratification of a section in the first instance: it is easy subsequently to group layers and their contents but it will never be safe to subdivide them.

Now a word as to systems of numbering. Layers or strata it is obviously necessary to number downwards from the top of a cutting, so that the numbers are mostly in the reverse order of accumulation, the latest (top-most) layer being layer 1. This somewhat illogical procedure is unavoidable since it is necessary to give layer-numbers to small-finds as they come to light, without waiting for the completion of the section. The same disability does not apply to *cultures*, which emerge as recognizable entities at a later stage of the work and are not used for labelling purposes. Here the logical system can, and certainly should, be followed: namely, to number the earliest culture or phase as number I, with II, III, etc., in sequence above them.

STRATIGRAPHY AND SERIATION

Relative dating rests on two basic archaeological techniques, stratigraphy and seriation. JOHN HOWLAND ROWE's paper is a clear exposition of the principles of both methods. He concludes that the best results can be obtained by a combination of stratigraphy with seriation.

📖 A friend whom I regard as an archaeologist of great ability recently remarked that "a properly conducted stratigraphic analysis carries a higher degree of credibility than the best of seriations." I have heard similar statements often enough before so that it seems to me probable that the view expressed has some currency in the archaeological profession.

The statement quoted has the merit of recognizing that there are more and less credible stratigraphic studies and more and less credible seriations. Beyond this point, however, the argument is questionable. I should like to maintain that, within the conditions under which each of the methods is applicable, the right kind of seriation, properly done, carries the same degree of conviction as a good stratigraphic study. Both stratigraphy and seriation have their limitations which must be understood in evaluating results achieved by either method. The general difference, perhaps, is that it is easier to do a bad seriation than a bad stratigraphic analysis.

The principles of stratigraphy were first worked out in geology in the eighteenth century, and the method was adopted by archaeologists when it was already fully developed. Hence, some of the insights into stratigraphic theory provided by the development of the idea have escaped the attention of many archaeological users of it. Stratigraphic interpretation depends on two principles ("laws"), as pointed out by Stamp (1934:2-3) and Neaverson (1955: 1):

1. THE LAW OF SUPERPOSITION (Lehmann's principle, 1756). In any pile of deposition units in which the top and bottom of the pile can be identified,

"Stratigraphy and Seriation" by John Howland Rowe, *American Antiquity* 26, No. 3 (1961) 324-330. Reprinted by permission of the author and the Editor of *American Antiquity*. For basic accounts of seriation, see James Deetz, *Invitation to Archaeology* (New York: Doubleday & Company, 1967), and James A. Ford, "Mound Builders of the Mississippi," *Scientific American* 186, No. 3 (March 1952).

the order of succession from bottom to top gives the order of deposition. This principle indicates to the observer the order of particular units in a particular outcrop or site. Its geological application is explained by Dunbar and Rodgers (1957: 110–1, 289). In archaeological work the units observed may be lenses of refuse, buildings, burials, pits and hearths as well as more or less horizontal layers. The first archaeological use of this principle appears to have been made by Thomas Jefferson in 1782 (Jefferson 1787: 156–162; Fraser 1935).

2. THE LAW OF STRATA IDENTIFIED BY FOSSILS (Smith's principle, 1796; Fenton and Fenton 1952: 70–83; Adams 1954: 268–276). In a given outcrop or site, the deposition units can be distinguished from one another by contrasts in the features of the fossils or artifacts which they contain and by the frequency with which such features occur. Two deposition units in different sites which contain the same features in the same proportions are assumed to be contemporary. This principle makes it possible to interpret a sequence of deposition units as a sequence of biological or cultural units. The first archaeological use of Smith's principle appears to have been made by Georg Christian Friedrich Lisch in a book review (Lisch 1847).

Superposition alone is not stratigraphy, and the observation of superposition has virtually no archaeological significance unless the cultural contents of the deposition units are contrasted. Jefferson understood superposition, but he had no notion of stratigraphy.

The Law of Superposition has no exceptions, and it is this fact which gives stratigraphy its high reputation for credibility in present-day archaeology. There are, however, certain conditions in which the order of deposition of the units at a particular site may not reflect accurately the order of cultural succession.

1. MIXING OF UNITS. Mixing of units may occur as a result of erosion, plowing, burrowing, or any digging operation which turns over the earth leaving it still in place, such an earlier excavation in search of antiquities or building stones. It may also occur as a result of the use of sloppy excavation techniques by the archaeologist. Some mixing of adjacent units inevitably takes place when a site with complex layering is excavated by arbitrary blocks.

There is nothing in the principles of stratigraphy which enables the archaeologist to distinguish mixed units from unmixed ones. The distinction is usually made in one or both of two ways. The first is mechanical. If two fragments of the same object are found at greatly different depths, mixing is strongly indicated. This situation occurred, for example, in some of Wendell C. Bennett's pits at Huari (Bennett 1953: 90). The second method of detecting mixed units is comparative. If certain features which occur together in a deposition unit at one site, or one part of a site, are found to occur separately at other sites or other parts of the same site, mixing in the first case is indicated. It may be impossible to identify mixing in the first excavation in an unknown area.

How seriously mixing affects the stratigraphic interpretation depends on whether the analysis is done in terms of presence and absence of features or in terms of frequencies of taxonomic types. I have contrasted these two approaches in an earlier paper (Rowe 1959). If the analysis is done in terms of presence and absence, the existence of mixed deposition units will prevent the investigator from distinguishing as many successive phases of culture as he would have been able to distinguish with un-mixed units. The order of the units that can be distinguished is not affected, however. If the analysis is done in terms of type frequencies mixing may even produce a situation which can be interpreted as giving an order the reverse of the true one.

The best example of a reversal of order attributable to mixing is found in Bennett's excavations at Huari, already cited. Bennett dug 15 pits at Huari, in all of which he found pottery which he classified in four "style groups" of a taxonomic nature: Wari, Ayacucho, Acuchimay, and Huarpa. He only found one of these "style groups" in isolation; that was Huarpa, which occurred by itself in the bottom of his Pit 4 isolated from the rest of the deposit by 50 cm. of "washed stone and gravel" (Bennett 1953: 33). Above this sterile layer all four style groups were found together, and this mixture, in different proportions, was found in all the other pits. In spite of the fact that there was mechanical evidence of mixture in the other pits, as we have noted, Bennett chose to seek indications of sequence in them by calculating the frequencies of the style groups in his arbitrary levels. He also treated the surface collection from the area of each pit as if it were a unit of superposition. All four style groups occurred from top to bottom of the pits, except, of course, in Pit 4, and there was no clear pattern in their fluctuations. However, Huarpa sherds were more frequent in all the surface units than in the levels below, and under the influence of this evidence Bennett decided that Huarpa was the latest of the style groups. This decision forced him to explain the situation in Pit 4 as a case of reversed stratigraphy. Subsequent work in the Huari area by Dorothy Menzel and me in 1958 suggests that the correct order was that given by Pit 4 which Bennett rejected. The associations of styles at other sites indicate that Huarpa must have been earlier than Wari, Ayacucho and Acuchimay rather than later. The situation at Huari which confused Bennett can be explained on the basis of certain peculiarities of Huarpa pottery. This style includes very large bowls with heavily thickened rims, usually having some simple painted decoration around them. Sherds deriving from these rims are almost indestructible and remain on the surface even when plowing and trampling have reduced most other sherds to virtually unrecognizable fragments. It was differential wear, not lateness of date, which made Huarpa sherds so abundant in Bennett's surface collections.

2. FILLING. A fill is a deposition unit laid down for the purpose of altering the ground level. If the material for the fill is taken from an earlier midden, the result may be a "reverse stratigraphy" in which the cultural order does not correspond to the deposition order (for examples, see Heizer 1959: 328–343). Filling is common wherever monumental architecture is found but may occur even without it. Sometimes the fill differs in texture and structure from undisturbed midden, but fill does not necessarily have any formal distinguishing characteristics. The cultural material in a unit of fill may correspond to a single cultural unit; if it does, the rules for detecting mixing will not necessarily detect filling. Only other evidence of sequence will solve the problem.

3. COLLECTING. We usually make the assumption, in interpreting archaeological associations, that the date of use of an object is, for all practical purposes, the same as its date of manufacture. This assumption may not always be warranted. There are numerous ethnographic examples of the systematic collection and re-use of ancient objects (grinding stones, pottery vessels, jewelry, amulets), and some archaeological examples have been recorded (Lathrap 1956: 24). As archaeological chronologies become more refined we can expect cases of collecting to be identified with greater frequency. It may take work at many sites and very careful attention to stylistic contrasts in order to make a certain identification in such cases.

Mixing, filling, and collecting are situations which set limitations to the effectiveness of stratigraphic analysis as a way of establishing cultural sequences. A single stratigraphic excavation will not provide certainty as to the order of cultural succession unless all three of the limiting possibilities can be definitely eliminated. There are certain sites at which these possibilities can be eliminated, but the degree of certainty attainable depends as much on the situation in the ground as it does on how carefully the stratigraphic analysis is conducted. Stratified sites are rare everywhere, and ones that will yield an absolutely certain cultural sequence are even rarer.

It cannot be emphasized too strongly that the principle of superposition offers absolute certainty only of the sequence of deposition units at a particular site. The cultural sequence for the area may or may not be the same as the sequence of deposition units at the site studied; it will usually take more evidence than can be secured from one stratigraphic excavation to determine the cultural sequence with certainty.

Let us turn now to a consideration of seriation. Seriation is the arrangement of archaeological materials in a presumed chronological order on the basis of some logical principle other than superposition. The units seriated may be individual specimens of a particular kind (pottery vessels, stone axes) or units of archaeological association, such as grave lots or single deposition units of refuse, such as might be found in a "one period" site. The logical order on which the seriation is based is found in the combinations of features of style or inventory which characterize the units, rather than in the external relationships of the units themselves. Hence, seriation involves a detailed study of style and inventory, with attention to the associations of features on individual specimens and in the units of archaeological association.

There are two types of seriation, distinguished by the principles of ordering on which they depend. We can call these types *evolutionary seriation* and *similiary seriation*, the latter term meaning "seriation by resemblance." Evolutionary seriation is done by assuming a universal rule of cultural or stylistic development, such as, for example, that development is always from simple to complex, or that artistic style always develops from realism to conventionalization. The rule which is assumed defines the relevance of the features to be studied and gives both the direction and the order of the development. No points of reference already fixed in time are needed. The credibility of the results depends, of course, entirely on the credibility of the universal rule by which the seriation is accomplished. Unfortunately, none of the rules which have been used so far for evolutionary seriation has any valid claim to universality. If approximately correct results have been achieved now and then by evolutionary seriation, it is no more than a coincidence. Until a rule of development is discovered which really does have universal applicability, evolutionary seriation is nothing but a waste of time.

Similiary seriation is quite a different matter. It is based on the assumption that, within a given cultural tradition, change in culture in general and change in style in particular are both usually gradual processes. On this assumption, objects or cultural units which are close to one another in time can be expected to resemble each other more, at least in certain features, than objects or cultural units which are further apart in time; as General Pitt-Rivers said, "like fits on to like" (Fox-Pitt-Rivers 1875: 308). No assumptions are made about the nature or direction of the changes taking place. This type of seriation was first done by John Evans in 1849 (Evans 1850).

The statement that change in a cultural tradition is usually gradual is one of the most general statements that can be made about human behavior. It appears to be valid within certain limitations which must be understood. There are two types of situations which may lead to sudden and substantial changes in a cultural or artistic tradition: strong outside influence suddenly felt, and archaism, the deliberate imitation of earlier style or custom. Both of these situations result in change which is not gradual in the sense of the general statement. Since similiary seriation depends on the assumption of gradual change, the credibility of its results depends on our ability to recognize the types of situations which do not fit the assumption, and to do so before or during the process of seriation. We shall come back to this problem after discussing some other conditions for successful seriation.

In order to obtain a sequence by similiary seriation, at least one extreme of the sequence must be known at the start of the project, since no assumption is being made about the order in which changes take place. In the New World the known extreme is often the style or cultural unit which was contemporary with European contact. If we can assume that all phases of the cultural tradition which are later than the time of contact will show some indication of European influence, we can consider that all cultural units which show no signs of such influence are earlier than the phase which we know to be contemporary with contact. The culture of the time of contact then becomes a known extreme from which the cultural units which are assumed to be earlier can be seriated back into the past by arranging them in an order of decreasing similarity to the known extreme. This type of argument enabled Francisco L. Cornely to make a highly credible seriation of five pre-contact cultural units in the Elqui Valley in northern Chile (Cornely 1950, 1956: 79–93).

Under the conditions generally prevailing in the New World, it is usually a safe assumption that cultural units later than the time of contact will show some evidence of European influence. It is not safe to assume, however, that each individual object made after the time of contact will show such influence; not uncommonly relatively few post-contact objects of native manufacture show any European influence at all. Cornely's assumption would therefore not justify an attempt to seriate unassociated objects using European contact as the later extreme of the sequence and identifying the contact by stylistic criteria. When both extremes are known and the materials to be seriated are of such a nature that it is possible to assume that they belong somewhere in the gap we have optimum conditions for a successful and credible seriation.

Another factor which affects the credibility of the results of seriation is the way the ordering is done. Two different methods of seriational ordering are in current use: ordering by type frequency and ordering by continuity of features and variation in themes.

The method of ordering by type frequency is applicable only to refuse deposits and to objects which occur abundantly in refuse; potsherds are usually used. Standard samples are taken from the refuse, usually by collecting all sherds found in blocks of refuse of arbitrary dimensions. The sherds are then classified in formal types, and the frequency of each type is calculated for each refuse sample. Each refuse sample can be considered to be characterized by the presence of certain particular types in certain particular percentages. Ordering is done by arranging the refuse samples in such an order that the frequency of each pottery type shows a pattern of gradual increase to a maximum popularity and then gradual decrease to disappearance. This method should give the correct chronological order of the refuse samples if the following conditions are met:

1. The sherd samples are large enough so that the type frequencies reflect popularity rather than chance occurrence. It may be doubted that a sample of any type consisting of less than ten sherds gives a fair indication of the popularity of the type.

2. The span of time represented by each refuse sample is relatively short.

3. The patterns of frequency in the samples are such that they can be arranged in an order in which there are few sudden jumps. If there are long spans of time not represented in the samples this condition may not be met.

Up to this point I have been assuming that the units being seriated are excavated refuse units, perhaps from a number of different small sites no one of which shows stratigraphic differences. J. A. Ford maintains, however, that surface samples from unexcavated sites can be seriated in the same way as excavated units, and even that a single seriation can be made using both surface and excavated samples (Phillips, Ford, and Griffin 1951: 219–233; Ford 1949). The use of surface samples for type frequency seriation introduces two further assumptions which are not involved in the seriation of excavated refuse units. The first assumption is that the frequencies of types in surface collections are not affected by differences in the nature of the site; for example, that the surface of a refuse deposit with looted burials in it will give the same type frequencies as a contemporary refuse deposit without burials. The second assumption is that surface sherds are subject to the same kind and degree of "natural selection" on all the sites compared, so that frequencies would not be altered by differences of weathering, plowing, trampling, pot-hunting, or prior collecting. Ford apparently feels that these assumptions are justified by the fact that his seriation of surface samples from lower Mississippi Valley sites gave nearly the same sequence which Phillips arrived at by stratigraphic analysis. I am not sufficiently familiar with the archaeology of the lower Mississippi Valley to compare field conditions there with those in Peru, where I have worked, but I would certainly be very reluctant to make these two assumptions about Peruvian surface collections in the light of the surface conditions which I have observed at Peruvian sites. The results of Bennett's excavations at Huari, which we have already reviewed, reveal the danger of including both surface and excavated samples in a single seriation.

The second method of seriational ordering now in use is the method of ordering by continuity of features and variation in themes. Because this method is based on observations of presence and absence rather than frequency, it involves fewer sampling problems than the method of ordering by type frequency, and hence it can be applied to a wider range of materials, including rare and unassociated specimens as well as materials found in some kind of archaeological association. The units of discussion are features and themes, defined by contrast in the particular materials to be studied. It is unnecessary, and even undesirable, to use types as the units of this kind of seriation. Continuity of features and variation in themes are two complementary principles of ordering which provide checks on one another and should be used together, although it would be theoretically possible to use either one separately.

Ordering by continuity of features rests on the assumption that the occurrence of features of style in time is not random, but that most features have a continuous span of existence. A feature is introduced, used for a while, and then dropped. Naturally, not all features can be expected to show this ideal pattern of distribution; a feature which has been used earlier in a sequence may reappear because it is reinvented, because it is reborrowed from another tradition, or because its use is deliberately revived. Furthermore, the investigator rarely controls a sample of material sufficiently large to document the complete span of existence of every significant feature. Nevertheless, the assumption that most features will show this pattern of distribution is defensible. In seriating on this assumption the objects or associated lots to be ordered are arranged in that sequence for the largest number of features. Since there are always some features which do not show the assumed pattern of distribution, it is important to study enough features so that the exceptions will fall in a minority. Some very inaccurate seriations have been made by archaeologists who were in too much of a hurry and relied on three or four features which turned out to be among those which did not have continuous spans of existence. The larger the sample and the more features studied, the greater will be the reliability of a seriation by continuity of features.

The precision with which an individual specimen can be dated by observing the features associated on it will depend on the number of features the observer is able to distinguish on it and the length of their spans of existence. Generally speaking, the more elaborately a specimen is decorated, the more precisely it can be dated.

In ordering by variation in themes, the investigator selects some complex feature or theme which is found in several variations in the material he is studying, and he makes an arrangement of the variations in order of similarity with reference to the known extremes. In seriating pottery, for example, the profiles of food bowls might be taken as a theme, and the variations in bowl profiles used to establish a tentative ordering. Variations in the proportions of bottle spouts might provide another basis for ordering. If representational or geometric designs are present, variations in some unit of design can be seriated. In Nasca pottery designs, for example, a common figure is a man with an elaborate costume wearing a mouth mask and a forehead ornament. The variations in the way the forehead ornament and the hair are shown have proved to be sensitive chronological indicators for this style.

The important point is that the variations contrasted must be variations on the same theme, alternate ways of meeting the same technical or artistic problem. It makes no sense to treat one theme as a variation on another; for example, to treat bowls as a variation on the same theme as bottles and ask whether bowls were earlier than bottles or vice versa. The shapes were made for different purposes, and presumably people used both bowls and bottles of some kind at any given time.

A seriation of variations on one theme will give only a tentative order for those specimens or association units in which the particular theme occurs. The variations in other themes must then be studied to see if the tentative order also gives a series of gradual changes for these. Errors in the tentative order are revealed by discrepancies in the seriation of other themes, and the tentative order can be modified accordingly. The more different themes have been studied, the greater the confidence the seriational order merits.

If the seriation is done with specimens which were collected under such conditions that their archaeological context is known, the data of the archaeological associations can be used to relate the sequences of different themes to one another. When a bowl with a certain profile is found repeatedly in grave lot association with a jar with a certain curve in the neck the two varieties must be at least in part contemporaneous, even though they are decorated in very different ways. If the seriation has to be done with unassociated pieces, there will always be some pieces which cannot be seriated, because they do not share enough themes with the pieces on which the seriation is based.

In practice it is usually easier to make the original ordering by studying variations in themes and then to check it by charting the spans of existence of a substantial number of features. A minimum of 100 is recommended. The reverse procedure is also possible, however.

Now we can come back to the problem of the degree to which sudden outside influence and archaism, the situations which do not fit the assumption of gradual change, can be recognized and allowed for in a seriational study. In both cases the problem is different depending on whether the ordering is done by type frequencies or by studying continuity of features and variations in themes.

In ordering by type frequencies, sudden outside influence should be reflected in the sudden popularity of certain new types, probably correlated with an equally sudden decline in the proportion of old types. The same effect would be produced by a gap in the record, however, and there is nothing in the theory of seriation which would guide the investigator to the correct interpretation. Archaism, if it were common enough to show up at all in the sherd counts, would produce a curve showing two peaks of popularity for some of the types. If no allowance were made for the possibility of archaism the investigator would be likely to force certain samples into the wrong place in the sequence.

In ordering by continuity of features and variations in themes, specimens showing sudden outside influence could probably not be seriated in the same sequence with earlier pieces. If the earlier tradition survived at all, however, there would be certain themes discoverable in which gradual change did take place, and these themes could be used as the basis of the ordering. The problem could probably not be handled without some evidence, in the form of archaeological associations, of what kinds of pieces were contemporary with one another.

Archaistic specimens in which the archaism affects only a few features can be identified without much difficulty in ordering by continuity of features if enough features are studied. Such specimens can also be distinguished in some cases by the presence of anomalies in the combinations of theme variations they show. Really good imitations of earlier pieces cannot be identified by seriational methods alone, but they can be detected readily enough if archaeological associations of contemporaneity are available.

We can conclude that both methods of ordering are vulnerable to errors resulting from sudden outside influence and archaism, but that the difficulties can be avoided in the method of seriation by continuity of features and theme variation by checking the seriational order against archaeological associations of contemporaneity, such as grave lots or deposition units of refuse.

To sum up the comparison of stratigraphy and seriation, it appears that there are several different ways of doing both, and that the chances of attaining credible results depend on the nature of the archaeological evidence available, the alternative method chosen, and the degree to which the theoretical limitations of the method are kept in mind in the course of the work. There is one type of seriation, namely similary seriation in which the ordering is done by continuity of features and theme variation, which can give results fully as credible as the best stratigraphic analysis, provided that associations of contemporaneity are used as well as unassociated specimens.

If the investigator has the time and the choice, he can profitably combine the methods by excavating a stratified site, making a stratigraphic analysis of the materials found, and then doing a parallel seriational analysis of the same materials. Since the limitations of the two methods are different, each provides a check on the other. If the results agree, the maximum credibility has been attained.

The common belief that stratigraphic analysis always gives more credible results than seriation rests in part on misunderstanding of the limitations of the two methods, in part on the professional bias of most archaeologists in favor of settling all problems by excavation, and in part on the fact that examples of deficient seriational studies come readily to mind. Our review does not confirm this common belief, but it does suggest that there may be more different ways to be wrong in seriation than there are in stratigraphic analysis.

Bibliography

Adams, F. D.
   1954 *The Birth and Development of the Geological Sciences.* New York: Dover Publications.
Bennett, W. C.
   1953 "Excavations at Wari, Ayacucho, Peru." *Yale University Publications in Anthropology,* No. 49. New Haven.
Cornely, F. L.
   1950 "Prehistoria del territorio Diaguita chileno (provincias de Coquimbo y Atacama)." *Publicaciones de la Sociedad Arqueológica de La Serena, Boletin,* No. 5, pp. 3–18. La Serena.
   1956 *Cultura Diaguita chilena y cultura de El Molle.* Editorial del Pacifico, Santiago.
Dunbar, C. O., and John Rodgers
   1957 *Principles of Stratigraphy.* New York: John Wiley and Sons; London: Chapman and Hall.
Evans, John
   1850 "On the Date of British Coins." *The Numismatic Chronicle and Journal of the Numismatic Society,* Vol. 12, No. 4, pp. 127–137. London.
Fenton, C. L., and M. A. Fenton
   1952 *Giants of Geology.* Garden City: Doubleday.
Ford, J. A.
   1949 "Cultural Dating of Prehistoric Sites in Virú Valley, Peru." *Anthropological Papers of the American Museum of Natural History,* Vol. 43, Part 1, pp. 29–89. New York.
Fox-Pitt-Rivers, A. H. L.
   1875 "On the Principles of Classification Adopted in the Arrangement of His Anthropological Collection, now Exhibited in the Bethnal Green Museum." *The Journal of the Anthropological Institute of Great Britain and Ireland,* Vol. 4, pp. 293–308. London.
Fraser, A. D.
   1935 "Thomas Jefferson as Field Archaeologist." *The Four Arts,* Vol. 2, No. 3, pp. 3–4, 15. Richmond.
Heizer, R. F. (editor)
   1959 *The Archaeologist at Work; A Source Book in Archaeological Method and Interpretation.* New York: Harper and Brothers.
Jefferson, Thomas
   1787 *Notes on the State of Virginia,* second English edition. John Stockdale, London.

Lathrap, D. W. (editor)
    1956 An Archaeological Classification of Culture Contact Situations. In "Seminars in Archaeology: 1955," Robert Wauchope, editor. Pp. 1–30. *Memoirs of the Society for American Archaeology*, No. 11. Salt Lake City.
Lehmann, J. G.
    1756 *Versuch einer Geschichte von Flötz-Gebürgen, betreffend deren Entstehung, Lage, darinne befindliche Metallen, Mineralien und Fossilien.* . . . Berlin: Klütersche Buchhandlung.
Lisch, G. C. F.
    1847 "Der Verein für Lübeckische Geschichte." *Allgemeine Zeitschrift für Geschichte,* Band 7, pp. 377–381. Berlin.
Neaverson, Ernest
    1955 *Stratigraphical Palaeontology; A Study of Ancient Life Provinces,* second edition. Oxford: Clarendon Press.
Phillips, Philip, J. A. Ford, and J. B. Griffin
    1951 "Archaeological Survey in the Lower Mississippi Alluvial Valley, 1940–1947." *Papers of the Peabody Museum, Harvard University,* Vol. 25. Cambridge.
Rowe, J. H.
    1959 "Archaeological Dating and Cultural Process." *Southwestern Journal of Anthropology,* Vol. 15, No. 4, pp. 317–324. Albuquerque.
Stamp, L. D.
    1934 *An Introduction to Stratigraphy (British Isles),* second edition. London: Thomas Murby & Co.

THE LAW OF ASSOCIATION

One of the earliest methods for the relative dating of archaeological sites, the principle that objects in a burial are those which were in use at the time, was first stated by a Dane, J. J. A. Worsaae, in 1843. The following paper by JOHN HOWLAND ROWE discusses the history and use of Worsaae's Law, and points out many problems that the researcher must be prepared to meet in order to apply this law correctly.

🔁 Worsaae's Law is the principle that the objects accompanying a burial are in most cases things which were in use at the same time. This principle forms the basis of all use of grave associations for dating purposes

"Worsaae's Law and the Use of Grave Lots for Archaeological Dating" by John Howland Rowe, *American Antiquity* 28, No. 2 (1962) 129–137. Reprinted by permission of the author and the Editor of *American Antiquity.*

in archaeology, but its implications have received little attention in the literature of the field. It has some important limitations, and there is one way in which it can be extended. A discussion of these matters and of the ways in which the principle of grave association can be used for dating may increase its value for archaeological interpretation.

The story of how Worsaae's Law came to be formulated is an interesting one and contributes to our understanding of its significance. The principle under discussion was first stated in 1843 by the Danish archaeologist Jens Jakob Asmussen Worsaae in a book entitled *Danmarks Oldtid opylst ved Oldsager og Gravhøie,* a title which may be rendered "Denmark's past elucidated by means of antiquities and burial mounds." The book was widely read in Denmark and was translated into German in 1844 and English in 1849. The English translation, done by William J. Thoms, was retitled *The Primeval Antiquities of Denmark;* it scarcely does justice to the original, being undistinguished in style and frequently inaccurate in detail. The difference in title is symptomatic; Worsaae's reference to burial mounds in the title of the original was intended to call attention to his use of archaeological associations as well as objects taken in isolation, this use being his major original contribution; the point is lost in the English title.

Worsaae's book is exactly what the Danish title suggests, a study of Denmark's past in the light of archaeological evidence. Its sections on method and theory are relatively brief, and in order to see the significance of what Worsaae was doing we need to look at the historical context of his work.

Between 1818 and 1820 C. J. Thomsen organized the collections of the Museum of Northern Antiquities in Copenhagen according to the theory that the use of iron for tools was preceded by the use of bronze, and that before bronze was known implements were made of stone (Hermansen 1935, 1941). It was the first time that anyone had tried to use this theory to classify and date a collection of archaeological specimens, although the theory itself was not new, as Thomsen was well aware.

The theory of three successive stages in the materials used for tools came to be called the Three Age System, the stages in it being called Stone Age, Bronze Age, and Iron Age. This theory had been more or less current among European antiquarians since the latter part of the seventeenth century, although only sporadic attempts were made to apply it to actual objects (Müller 1897–98, 1:230–234; Stemmermann 1934:122–129). As used by the antiquarians, the theory of the three stages in materials for tools was not just an inference from the idea of progress. Greek and Roman writers preserved the tradition that bronze was used for tools and weapons before iron, and the antiquarians cited their testimony. The philosopher poet Lucretius also argued on logical grounds that there must have been a time before men knew how to use metal of any kind when weapons consisted of stones and the branches of trees (Müller 1897–98, 1:228–230). Observant travellers, such as William Dampier, called attention to the fact that there were still people in America and other remote parts of the world who knew no metal working and made their tools and weapons of stone. This contemporary use of stone for implements was taken to confirm the speculation of Lucretius.

There was important religious opposition to the theory of the Three Ages, however. According to Genesis 4:22 bronze and iron working were introduced together by Tubal-cain, who lived before the Flood, and in the minds of the devout biblical authority always outweighed the testimony of pagan writers. An attempt was made to resolve the contradiction by saying that the knowledge of metal working was no doubt lost at the time of the Flood, so that mankind had to start over again, but this argument was not very convincing (Goguet 1778, 1:298). It was the growth of religious rationalism in the 18th century which cleared the way for a wider acceptance of the Three Age theory. By the time of Thomsen's boyhood it had even penetrated the school history books of Denmark (Suhm 1776; Petersen 1938:10–11).

Thomsen was not a field man himself, and the specimens he worked with in the Museum of Northern Antiquities were mostly not accompanied by archaeological data. Thomsen classified them first by material and technique and then began to look for style differences. By the time he published his results, in 1836, he had worked out enough of a style sequence for Denmark so that he could assign objects of bone, wood, and pottery to the appropriate age and distinguish bronze objects made in the Iron Age from ones which belonged to the Bronze Age proper (Bibby 1956:11). Using the sequence of materials suggested by the Three Age theory as a framework, he had developed a general cultural sequence for the Danish area (Petersen and Thomsen 1836). It was an original achievement of a very high order.

Worsaae's contribution was to confirm and extend Thomsen's sequence by the use of archaeological associations. He did so in a series of excavations in Danish burial mounds carried out between 1839 and 1841, noting that implements appropriate to each of Thomsen's Three Ages were found consistently in different tombs. He also in effect reduced Thomsen's sequence to a series of predictions of what kind of objects should be found together in graves, and he found the associations the predictions called for. It was the first use of grave associations to solve a chronological problem. This achievement becomes even more impressive when we note that Worsaae was an eighteen-year-old student in 1839, and that his general book on Danish archaeology appeared when he was 22. As Johannes Brønsted says, "He felt himself to be, and indeed was, in the scientific field, a young Heaven-stormer, rich in ideas, independent, unbound by dogmas and prejudices, nor, to quote his own statement in his biography, 'free from self-assurance and conceit.' " (Bronsted 1944:304, translated for the author by R. H. Lowie). Fortunately, he was also right.

Worsaae's own statement of his use of archaeological associations occurs on pp. 60–61 of *Danmarks Oldtid* and may be translated as follows:

> To establish as reliable and complete a picture as possible of the earliest settlement and most ancient circumstances of our native land, it is not sufficient to be concerned only with antiquities which have been removed from the earth. It is indispensable also to study and compare *the sites where the antiquities are most commonly found,* because otherwise many of the most important problems will not be solved at all or will be resolved in a very unsatisfactory manner. Thus, in the preceding pages we should scarcely have been able to refer the antiquities mentioned to three successive ages if experience had not taught us that antiquities which belong to different ages are also regularly found separately.
>
> Not all places where discoveries are made will be considered here in the the same manner, however. Many antiquities are dug up in peat bogs, for example, but who would care to affirm that the objects found in the peat had lain in the very same place ever since the time they were used? Furthermore, who could determine whether or not they might have become mixed with more recent objects thrown into the bog or lost there? Consequently, it is not the places where antiquities can be found accidentally which deserve to be the subject of a more detailed description for the purpose mentioned, but rather our ancient stone structures and burial mounds; for, with regard to the burials themselves, we know that they regularly contain not only the bones of the dead but also many of their weapons, implements and ornaments which were buried beside them in antiquity. Here, therefore, we can in general expect to find together those things which were originally used together at one time.
>
> Furthermore, burial mounds frequently serve to elucidate the circumstances of pagan antiquity. They are the most trustworthy sources of information on the burial customs which gradually succeeded one another and, because they are fixed monuments which can be destroyed but not shifted from their original locations, they provide, from their position and distribution, particularly noteworthy evidence regarding the earliest settlement of the various districts. One should not, of course, insist on concluding too much from a single burial mound taken by itself, but by combining many observations from all parts of the country we gradually find out what the burials have in common and what their peculiarities are, and we learn thereby to group the different kinds of burials into distinct classes and to assign them to some extent to different times. The importance of this procedure is far reaching (translated by J. H. Rowe with the aid of the German version).

The ancient stone structures referred to in this passage are megalithic monuments. Many of Worsaae's elders regarded these structures as altars, but he had argued in an earlier paper, published in 1839, that they were the remains of tombs.

The key sentence, in which the principle of the contemporaniety of grave goods is stated, is clear and carefully worded: "Here (i.e., in burials), therefore, we can in general expect to find together those things which were originally used together at one time." This statement, after a hundred and twenty years, still remains the best one we have on the subject. How generally is Worsaae's principle applicable?

Worsaae's generalization is based on a number of assumptions, only one of which is made explicit in his discussion. The one he mentions is that the ancients buried objects with their dead; his statement implies that it was general knowledge in his time that the ancients did so. This knowledge was based on reports of pagan antiquity by Greek and Roman writers. As that philosophical physician, Thomas Browne, said in 1658,

> Now that they accustomed to burn or bury with them, things wherein they excelled, delighted, or which were dear unto them, either as farewells unto all pleasure, or vain apprehension that they might use them in the other world, is testified by all Antiquity (Browne 1658:23).

Worsaae, of course, was writing a book about the archaeology of Denmark, not a general account of archaeology everywhere. For his purposes it was sufficient to know that a custom of burying objects with the dead had been widespread in pagan Europe. To justify the application of his principle in other areas, however, we need evidence that such a custom was practiced elsewhere in the world as well. Evidence that it was practiced elsewhere is provided in some abundance by early travel accounts and more recent ethnographic descriptions. The custom of burying objects with the dead was not universal, but it was very common.

Another assumption, which Worsaae did not mention, is that it was customary to place objects beside the dead only at the time of burial and not at a variety of times earlier and later. The objects found in a given grave are supposed to be contemporary with one another because they are all contemporary with the burial of the occupant. One case has been reported, however, in which it was customary to renew objects buried with the dead periodically over a long period, and Worsaae's Law clearly does not apply under such circumstances. This case has more than local interest, for if there is one area where Worsaae's Law does not always apply there may be others also.

The area in question is the sierra of ancient Peru. In a paper entitled "On the Relative Antiquity of Ancient Peruvian Burials," published in 1904, Adolph Bandelier cited historical evidence that, in this area, tombs were opened annually for the renewal of the clothing and food offerings accompanying the burials. In spite of the efforts of the Spanish authorities to suppress pagan rites, some native communities maintained this practice for a hundred years after the Spanish conquest. Bandelier summarizes the situation as follows:

> The cloth with which all the corpses (ancient and modern) were covered was *periodically renewed, as late as the middle of the seventeenth century.* The fact that food and drink also were replaced from time to time implies, that the vessels found along with the bodies *are no longer those originally buried with them* (Bandelier 1904:224; emphasis Bandelier's).

This is a fair enough statement, except that the last phrase is a little too strong. The food vessels may have been replaced when the food offerings were renewed, but it is also possible that the original vessels were reused. The uncertainty only makes the archaeological problem even more complicated, however.

An archaeological field study of the results of a periodical renewal of burial offerings would be most interesting, but there is real doubt that it would now be possible. The historical documents which Bandelier cites refer to burials made above-ground in masonry structures or in caves or under overhanging boulders, such burials serving the purpose of keeping the bodies of the dead dry, clean, and relatively accessible for ceremonies and offerings. Because they were accessible the tombs were also conspicuous, however, and enormous numbers of them have been looted. The only ones which have been found intact and reported are the burials under overhanging boulders at Machu Picchu (Eaton 1916). This site, however, was occupied for such a short period that we could hardly expect to trace the effects of the renewal of burial offerings in its tombs. There may be no untouched above-ground burials left in the parts of the country which have been continuously settled.

From the point of view of archaeological dating the crucial question is how long the renewal of offerings continued after the original burial in these tombs. If it was not continued for more than about 25 years the effects of the renewal would not be distinguishable in an archaeological study, because the amount of stylistic change accumulated in such a short time would be too small to be recognized. If the renewal continued for much longer than 25 years it would have a serious effect on archaeological interpretation.

In the Peruvian sierra it is possible that the renewal of offerings in some burials continued for as much as two centuries. Genealogies of certain important families were preserved in the male line for as much as eight generations, and the tombs of the ancestors were probably remembered as well (Hernández Príncipe 1923). Unfortunately, our historical sources do not explain whether offerings were renewed in the tombs of the most remote ancestors as well as in those of recent ones, but there is no reason to suppose that they were not. In ordinary families less attention was paid to genealogy, and no doubt the period in which offerings were renewed was shorter.

The implication of the Peruvian case of the renewal of offerings is that objects found in the same burial should not be assumed to be contemporary with the burial and with one another unless and until the burial customs of the time and place have been investigated and evidence has been found to indicate that offerings were not renewed. It may be possible, for example, to argue that the tombs were opened only once. Masonry tombs are usually closed by walling up the entrance and, if the fill of the entrance has been torn out and replaced several times, traces of the work should be visible. In the case of underground burials, there may be traces of each disturbance in the soil. Most soils, other than clean, dry sand, are altered in color and consistency with each disturbance, because the different layers are mixed in varying proportions.

The renewal of offerings seems not to have been generally practiced on the Peruvian coast. Burials on the coast were usually made in the ground and were rarely marked in any permanent fashion on the surface, so that they would have been very difficult to relocate after an interval. Furthermore, food offerings are occasionally found at or near the surface over such burials, indicating that it was not considered necessary to place them in the tomb itself (Uhle 1944:90–91). In ancient Egypt also offerings for the dead were deposited outside of the burial chamber.

Even where the renewal of burial offerings is not customary, it may happen in certain exceptional circumstances. An interesting example in Greece has been reported by George E. Mylonas. The men who made Burial Gamma 10 in the west cemetery at Eleusis during the Late Geometric period accidentally dug into an earlier burial, smashing the skull. They stopped, changed the direction of their digging to avoid further damage, tried to reassemble the broken skull, and placed a handsome pitcher beside it as an offering. The later pitcher thus came to accompany the earlier burial (Mylonas 1961:62 and Fig. 10). This case caused no confusion in archaeological dating, because the excavation was done with sufficient care so that the sequence of events could be read from the evidence in the ground.

There is still another assumption underlying Worsaae's Law which remains to be examined. The objects accompanying a burial are presumed to be ones which were owned or used by the occupant or his friends at the time of his death. Even though they may have been made at different times, they represent the choice of objects existing in people's houses at the time the burial was made. There may, however, be special circumstances in which objects that were not in use at the time a burial was made were nevertheless deposited with the body. Such a possibility was suggested by Max Uhle to explain an anomalous situation in the cemetery at Soniche in the Ica valley on the Peruvian coast. Grave Tf-1 in this cemetery can be dated to the early Colonial period, because it contained some European glass beads. It was dug into the fill of a deeper burial of the Inca period which had been looted. Certain objects in the Inca style of a sort not usually found in Colonial burials were associated with Grave Tf-1. Uhle suggested that the makers of this grave dug into the Inca period burial by accident and removed certain objects from it which they added to the burial they were making (cf. Rowe 1961a:323). Regardless of whether or not Uhle's explanation of the associations in this particular burial is correct, the situation he suggests is one which could certainly occur.

The situation envisioned by Uhle is not likely to have occurred very often, however, and any excavator who is aware that it could occur should be able to recognize it by applying the same reasoning Uhle used. The archaeologist would only face real trouble if the practice of furnishing later burials with objects looted from earlier ones became customary, but as far as I am aware no actual case in which it did so has ever been reported. In this hypothetical case, of course, no use of grave associations for chronological purposes could be made.

The basis for arguing that the objects found in a grave were in use at the same time is, of course, their association with one particular burial. If the bodies of many individuals are found in the same tomb it is necessary to ask whether they all represent one burial or whether they were placed in the tomb at different times. There is usually some evidence in the relationship of bodies and objects to one another on the basis of which the distinction can be made. There are a number of different circumstances in which two or more individuals may be buried together at the same time. The commonest, perhaps, is the simultaneous death of a mother and child or even a whole family. The retainers of a king or other important person may be slaughtered to accompany him in the tomb, as in the famous Royal Tombs of the Early Dynastic period at Ur. The victims of a massacre are also frequently buried together. The objects accompanying multiple burials of these types are just as likely to have been in use at the same time as the objects accompanying a single body.

The burial of several individuals in the same tomb but at different times may reflect a practice of burial in family vaults or the reuse of an earlier tomb by later people. In either case the objects accompanying each burial represent a separate chronological unit, and if they cannot be distinguished the tomb provides little evidence for dating.

Burial in family tombs was a common practice in the Old World before 1000 B.C. For example, such tombs are found in Palestine throughout the Bronze Age (Kenyon 1960:122–123, 189–190, 198); in Mesopotamia during the time of the Third Dynasty of Ur (Woolley 1928:160–161); in England, Scotland, and Denmark in the Bronze Age (Keiller and Piggott 1938:129–131); and in Mycenaean Greece in Late Helladic times (Mylonas 1948:76–77). All these cases reflect similar attitudes toward the dead, no respect being shown the bodies after decomposition. The remains of earlier burials were swept to the sides of the tomb to make room for each new one. Only the objects accompanying the latest burial in such a tomb can be related to a particular body.

It may, of course, happen that all the burials in a family vault are made within a few years of one another, the time difference between the earliest and the latest being too small to be reflected in the style of the offerings, but there is usually no way to determine the span of use of a family tomb before the chronological significance of style differences has been determined. No reliable inference can be drawn from the number of individuals present. A husband and wife may die forty years apart, or twenty members of a single family may be carried off by an epidemic in a matter of days.

The reuse of earlier tombs is also not uncommon. This practice is reported for Palestine in the Middle Bronze Age (Kenyon 1960:189) and Greece in the Geometric Period (Mylonas 1961:61). Bandelier was told of modern burials in ancient tombs in the Bolivian sierra (Bandelier 1904: 225). It may be easier to sort out the associations in a tomb which has been reused than in a family vault; the time interval between earlier and later burials is likely to be greater, resulting in greater contrast in the selection and style of the offerings.

Our discussion of the assumptions underlying Worsaae's Law has brought out a number of limitations which affect it. These limitations can be summarized by saying that the law applies to those cases in which the association of objects with a single burial can be recognized, renewal of offerings over a long period was not customary, and objects placed in graves were supposed to be ones in current use. In order to control these limitations it is necessary to determine the burial customs prevailing at the time and place involved, usually a relatively simple archaeological problem if any considerable number of burials can be studied. With a reasonable body of evidence available the pattern of custom usually emerges clearly, the exceptions can easily be identified, and their special significance can be studied. Under the conditions here specified Worsaae's Law is generally applicable.

It is also possible to suggest an extension of the principle. Worsaae's wording was very cautious, and he only asserted that objects associated with the same burial were in *use* at the same time. We can go further and argue that, in most cases, objects associated with the same burial were also *made* at the same time, or at least within a few years of one another.

There is nothing novel about this extension; Worsaae himself probably assumed contemporaneity of manufacture as well as contemporaneity of use when he relied on grave associations for dating, even though he did not say so, and many subsequent archaeologists have done the same. Probably W. M. F. Petrie was the first to argue explicitly for contemporaneity of manufacture as well as use (Petrie 1904:150–151).

It is, of course, most unlikely that the objects found together in a grave were all made in the same month or even in the same year, and there is no question of assuming such close contemporaneity. When an archaeologist says that certain objects were made at the same time he means that they were made within the span of the same primary time unit in his relative chronology. Archaeological dating is done by reference to changes in style, so the length of the primary time units depends on the thoroughness of the style analysis on which the chronology is based. There is, however, a limit set by the fact that, in any given year, some craftsmen will be working in a more advanced style and others in a more conservative style. The experience of Classical archaeologists suggests that periods of 25 to 30 years are the shortest time units which dating by style permits (compare Rowe 1959:317).

What is the likelihood that all the objects in a single grave were made within 25 years of the time of burial? This question can be answered best by discussing the possibility that objects older than 25 years may be included. We can classify such older objects as heirlooms and antiques. An heirloom in this sense is an object of moderate age, perhaps 25 to 75 years, which could have come into the possession of the deceased through being handed down in the family. An antique, on the other hand, is an object of greater age, presumably collected by the deceased or one of his relatives. Once collected, of course, an antique can also be handed down as an heirloom, but it would be difficult to recognize this situation from archaeological evidence.

We have ethnographic reports of cultures in which heirlooms are unknown, because personal property is not inherited but destroyed or buried with the owner. The inheritance of personal property makes its accumulation easier, however, and people who value luxury goods are likely to treasure heirlooms. We should expect to find some preservation of heirlooms in many cultures throughout the world. On the other hand, at any given time the proportion of heirlooms to objects of recent manufacture is not likely to be high because of wastage from use and accidental destruction.

Jewelry and metal weapons, being both durable and highly valued, are perhaps the objects most likely to be handed down from one generation to another, with utilitarian pottery at the other extreme. George Foster, who interviewed housewives in Tzintzuntzan, Mexico, regarding the "life-expectancy" of pottery vessels, estimated that cooking and eating vessels in daily use in that town last an average of one year. The only heirloom vessel he reported was an enormous olla with a capacity of 45 liters; it was between 40 and 50 years old and had been handed down for three generations (Foster 1960).

Antiques may be collected for a variety of reasons. Interest in them may be purely practical, as when later occupants of an area collect mortars from archaeological sites to save themselves the trouble of manufacturing new ones. Antiques may be associated with mythology and used in religious or curing ceremonies, as polished stone axes were in Classical and mediaeval Europe. In other times and places they may be collected simply out of respect for the ancients and admiration of their work (compare Rowe 1961b:326). In any case, as archaeologists have good reason to know, antiques are not easy to find, and we can expect them to be rare everywhere in comparison with recently made objects.

It is the rarity of heirlooms and antiques which makes it possible to recognize them when they appear in tombs. If a particular variety of bowl is common in earlier burials and occurs very rarely in later ones, the later occurrences can be considered to reflect the transmission of heirlooms or the collection of antiques, depending on the time difference involved. No one who has studied any considerable number of ancient grave lots can fail to be struck with the high degree of consistency of style which the great majority of such lots displays. It is only when the grave lots available are so few and so poor that no clear pattern of consistency emerges that there is real danger of confusing heirlooms and antiques with recently made pieces.

If Worsaae's Law is acceptable even with the extension that objects accompanying the same burial were made as well as used at the same time, with only rare exceptions, we can next ask how this principle can be used for archaeological dating. There are two situations to consider, the first being that in which no stylistic sequence has yet been established for the area and the problem is to make one, while the second is that in which a stylistic sequence is available and the problem is to apply it.

Grave association itself provides no evidence for sequence at all but only evidence of contemporaneity. In order to use objects found in grave association for constructing an archaeological chronology, some external evidence of sequence is necessary. Such evidence may be provided by the stratigraphic relationships of the burials themselves, as, for example, when a later burial cuts into an earlier one; by the occupation sequence in a stratified habitation site; or by seriation in order of stylistic similarity where at least one end of the sequence is known. Worsaae used the stone-bronze-iron sequence proposed by Thomsen as his evidence of sequence. In any case, the procedure to be followed is to use the evidence for sequence to set up a hypothesis that certain stylistic changes occurred in a certain order. Grave associations can then be used to test the hypothesis. The hypothesis should imply that certain features will not occur together because they occupy different places in the sequence. If such features are associated repeatedly in grave lots, the hypothetical sequence is defective and needs to be modified. Systematic lack of association of the features, on the other hand, supports the hypothesis. What is supported, of course, is not the order of the sequence but only the validity of the stylistic units or phases that make it up. This is the crucial problem, however; it is very unusual in archaeology to establish valid stylistic units and get them in the wrong order. On the other hand, if the units of a hypothetical sequence are invalid the order is very likely to be wrong as well.

Worsaae's procedure, summarized earlier, provides an excellent example of the use of grave associations to check a proposed chronological scheme. Another example may provide further clarification. In 1948 Rafael Larco Hoyle published the outline of a hypothetical sequence for the Moche pottery style from the north coast of Peru. The proposed sequence consisted of five phases, each characterized by a distinctive variant of the stirrup-shaped bottle spout which is common in this style. Larco published no evidence by which his hypothesis could be tested, however. In 1950 it occurred to me that the 33 Moche grave lots in the University of California Museum of Anthropology could be used to test Larco's idea. I studied these grave lots with the assistance of Dorothy Menzel and found that some grave lots contained bottles attributable to only one of Larco's phases, according to the criterion of spout shape which he had suggested, while other lots included bottles attributable to two phases. In all cases in which there were bottles attributable to two of Larco's phases in the same grave lot, however, the two phases were adjacent ones in the proposed sequence. I found no case in which the spout shapes characteristic of two nonadjacent phases occurred in the same lot, or in which spout shapes of more than two phases occurred together. It seems reasonable to suppose that there had been transitions between the phases, and that the grave lots containing spouts corresponding to two adjacent phases belonged in the transitions. I therefore concluded that the Moche grave associations supported the validity of Larco's phases.

The University of California grave lots provided no check on the order of the Moche phases, but we were able to turn to the evidence of seriation on this point. The pottery of the first phase of Larco's sequence was most like the pottery of the style which we knew to have immediately preceded Moche, while some pieces of the last phase showed the influence of a style which we knew to be generally later. Between the two extremes the phases were arranged in order of similarity.

A stylistic sequence is established first in a limited category of objects; in the example just cited the basic sequence applied only to pottery bottles with one particular variety of spout. The next problem is to extend the sequence to other kinds of objects until it can be used as a basis for discussing cultural change. In our example the sequence had first to be extended to other shapes of pottery vessels, and work by Dwight T. Wallace and Carleton I. Calkin contributed to the solution of this problem. To some extent the inclusion of other shapes in the sequence could be achieved by careful stylistic analysis, but differences .in shape in pottery are often associated with differences in decorative style, even in the work of a single potter, and many pieces could only be assigned to a phase on the evidence of grave associations. After a sufficient number of pieces had been assigned to phases the sequence of changes in other pottery categories could be worked out.

There happened to be little besides pottery preserved in the Moche grave lots in Berkeley. If there had been more we should have gone on to make chronological studies of metal work, small carvings, textiles, tools, and whatever else there was; we have, in fact, used grave associations for this purpose on the south coast, where preservation conditions are somewhat better.

These examples from personal experience could be supplemented from the literature of archaeology, but not as extensively as one could wish. Although thousands of grave associations have been recorded in different parts of the world, and many archaeologists have attempted to use them for dating, there are remarkably few discussions of the way in which the evidence of associations was used and the assumptions on which the procedure was based. Furthermore, the evidence itself is seldom available. Reports in which grave associations are adequately illustrated and discussed are still rare, and many museums make no effort to keep associated lots together, either in their catalogues or in their study rooms. It is no exaggeration to say that there is still little appreciation of the value of grave associations in archaeology today. This discussion of the principles involved in their use is presented with the hope that it will stimulate interest in a valuable aid to archaeological dating.

Bibliography

Bandelier, Adolph Francis Alphonse
    1904   "On the Relative Antiquity of Ancient Peruvian Burials." *Bulletin of the American Museum of Natural History,* Vol. XX, Article XIX (June 16) pp. 217–226. New York.
Bibby, Thomas Geoffrey
    1956   *The Testimony of the Spade.* New York: Alfred A. Knopf.
Brønsted, Johannes
    1944   "Worsaae, Jens Jacob Asmussen 1821–85, Arkaeolog." *Dansk Biografisk Leksikon,* Vol. XXVI, pp. 303–313. København: J. H. Schutz Forlag.

Browne, Thomas
 1658 *Hydriotaphia, Urne-buriall, or a Discourse of the Sepulchrall Urnes lately Found in Norfolk. . . .* London: Hen. Brome.
Eaton, George Francis
 1916 "The Collection of Osteological Material from Machu Picchu." *Memoirs of the Connecticut Academy of Arts and Sciences,* Vol. V. New Haven.
Foster, George McClelland
 1960 "Life-expectancy of Utilitarian Pottery in Tzintzuntzan, Michoacán, Mexico." *American Antiquity,* Vol. 25, No. 4 (April) pp. 606–609. Salt Lake City.
Goguet, Antoine Yves
 1778 *De l'origine des loix, des arts et des sciences, et de leurs progrès chez les anciens peuples.* Paris: Knapen, Libraire-Imprimeur. 6 Vols.
Hermansen, Victor
 1935 "C. J. Thomsens første Museumordning; et Bidrag til Tredelingens Historie." *Aarbøger for nordisk Oldkyndighed og Historie udgivne af det Kgl. nordiske Oldskrift-Selskab,* 1934, 1. Halvbind, pp. 99–122. København.
 1941 "C. J. Thomsen and the Founding of the Ethnographical Museum. Ethnographical Studies, Published on the Occasion of the Centenary of the Ethnographical Department, National Museum. *Nationalmuseets Skrifter, Etnografisk Raekke,* I, pp. 11–27. København.
Hernández Príncipe, Rodrigo
 1923 "Mitología andina." *Inca; revista trimestral de estudios antropológicos,* Vol. 1, No. 1, eneromarzo, pp. 25–68. Lima.
Keiller, Alexander, and Stuart Piggott
 1938 "Excavation of an Untouched Chamber in the Lanhill Long Barrow." *Proceedings of the Prehistoric Society,* n.s., Vol. IV, Part 1 (Jan.–July) pp. 122–131. Cambridge.
Kenyon, Kathleen Mary
 1960 *Archaeology in the Holy Land.* New York: Frederick A. Praeger.
Müller, Sophus Otto
 1897–98 *Nordische Altertumskunde, nach Funden und Denkmälern aus Dänemark und Schleswig gemeinfasslich dargestellt.* Strassburg: Karl J. Trübner. 2 vols.
Mylonas, George Emmanuel
 1948 "Homeric and Mycenaean Burial Customs." *American Journal of Archaeology,* Vol. LI, No. 1 (January-March) pp. 56–81. Menasha.
 1961 *Eleusis and the Eleusinian Mysteries.* Princeton: Princeton University Press.
Petersen, Carl Sophus
 1938 *Stenalder, Broncealder, Jernalder; Bidrag til nordisk Arkaeologis Litteraerhistorie, 1776–1865.* København: Levin & Munksgaard, Ejnar Munksgaard.
Petersen, Niels Matthias, and Christian Jürgensen Thomsen
 1836 *Ledetraad til nordisk Oldkyndighed.* Det Kongelige nordiske Oldskrift-Selskab, København.
Petrie, William Matthew Flinders
 1904 *Methods & Aims in Archaeology.* London: Macmillan and Co., Limited; New York: The Macmillan Company.
Rowe, John Howland
 1959 "Archaeological Dating and Cultural Process." *Southwestern Journal of Anthropology,* Vol. 15, No. 4. (Winter) pp. 317–324. Albuquerque.
 1961a "The Chronology of Inca Wooden Cups." *Essays in Pre-Columbian Art and Archaeology,* by Samuel K. Lothrop and others, pp. 317–341. Cambridge: Harvard University Press.
 1961b "Stratigraphy and Seriation." *American Antiquity,* Vol. 26, No. 3 (January) pp. 324–330. Salt Lake City.
Stemmermann, Paul Hans
 1934 *Die Anfänge der deutschen Vorgeschichtsforschung. Deutschlands Bodenaltertümer in der Anschauung des 16. u. 17. Jahrhunderts.* Inaugural-Dissertation zur Erlangung der Doktorwürde einer hohen philosophischen Fakultät an der

Ruprecht-Karls Universität zu Heidelberg. Handelsdruckerei C. Trute, Quakenbrück i. Hann.

Suhm, Peter Frederik
1776   *Historien af Dänemark, Norge og Holsten udi tvende Udtog til den studerende Ungdoms Bedste.* København.

Uhle, Max
1944   "The Aims and Results of Archaeology." *University of California Publications in American Archaeology and Ethnology,* Vol. 46, No. 1, pp. 54–100. Berkeley and Los Angeles.

Woolley, Charles Leonard
1928   *The Sumerians.* Oxford: The Clarendon Press.

Worsaae, Jens Jakob Asmussen
1839   "Efterretning om Undersögelsen af to Steendysser i Veibye Sogn." *Annaler for nordisk Oldkyndighed udgivne af det Kongelige nordiske Oldskrift-Selskab,* 1838–1839, pp. 170–176. København.

1843   *Dänmarks Oldtid oplyst ved Oldsager og Gravhoie.* Selskabet for Trykkefrihedens rette Brug, København.

1844   *Dänemarks Vorzeit durch Alterthümer und Grabhügel beleuchtet.* Aus dem dänischen übersetzt von N. Bertelsen. København: Verlag von C. A. Reitzel, Universitätsbuchhändler.

1849   *The Primeval Antiquities of Denmark.* Translated, and applied to the illustration of similar remains in England, by William J. Thoms. London and Oxford: John Henry Parker.

POLLEN ANALYSIS

The study of fossil pollen (palynology) is of interest for a number of reasons. First, it enables the archaeologist to reconstruct the types of vegetation surrounding an archaeological site; second, it is invaluable in the study of paleoclimate; third, and most important, pollen analysis is a reliable method of relative dating for archaeological sites found in polliniferous localities. In this paper by JANE GRAY and WATSON SMITH, these and other uses of palynology are discussed and explained.

▣ For centuries it has been recognized that many plants produce in enormous abundance microscopic structures called *pollen* or *spores*. Because

"Fossil Pollen and Archaeology" by Jane Gray and Watson Smith, *Archaeology,* 1962, pp. 16–26. Reprinted from *Archaeology,* Vol. 15, No. 1, copyright, 1962, Archaeological Institute of America, with the permission of the Editor of *Archaeology,* and the authors, Jane Gray, Museum of Natural History, University of Oregon, Eugene, Oregon, and Watson Smith, Peabody Museum, Harvard University, Cambridge, Massachusetts.

of their small size, their buoyancy, and special adaptations for dispersal, they are disseminated through a wide range of environments and may be recovered from sedimentary deposits. These factors, together with their remarkable diversity and their chemical stability, which enables them to endure under favorable conditions for millions of years, make pollen analysis, or palynology, one of the most useful and rapidly developing new sciences, with ramifications in geology, paleontology, archaeology, biology and medicine.

Palynology offers such diverse pathways of investigation as stratigraphic correlation, the location of ancient shore lines, the reconstruction of ancient environments, the study of plant evolution, phylogeny and taxonomy, the determination of times of forest clearance and the introduction of agriculture by Early Man, and the dating of artifacts.

The special usefulness of pollen analysis to archaeology rests upon its success in dating evidence of human activity preserved in pollen-bearing strata. Its application depends upon three hypotheses: that the pollen content of successive sedimentary strata reflects vegetational conditions at the time of their deposition; that objects found there were deposited at approximately the time that the sediments were laid down; and that the lower strata are older than the upper.

What is pollen? The word means fine dust or flour. Botanically, it is a mass of microscopic single-celled structures produced by seed-bearing plants. Pollen is the male element, carrying the sperm to the female element so that fertilization may be effected. A newly formed pollen grain, called a microspore, has a single nucleus. This divides several times, and when released from the plant the pollen grain is multinucleate and is called a male gametophyte.

The "lower," so-called free-sporing plants (including ferns, club mosses, horsetails and others) do not produce pollen but bear reproductive bodies called spores. Among some free-sporing plants two kinds of spores (microspores and megaspores) are released. Typically, megaspores are larger than microspores (some are visible to the naked eye) and are produced in fewer numbers.

The pollen grains of seed-plants, including those having flowers (*angiosperms*) as well as those bearing cones (*gymnosperms*), correspond to the microspores of the free-sporing plants. The term "microspore" may refer both to pollen grains and to small spores, and both are included in pollen analysis.

For the pollen analyst the critical stage in the life-cycle of the plant follows release of the microspores. Some fulfil the purposes for which nature intended them—fertilization and dispersal; many are destroyed by oxidation, but others settle into depositing sediments where oxygen is absent and endure almost unaltered for millions of years. Small spores

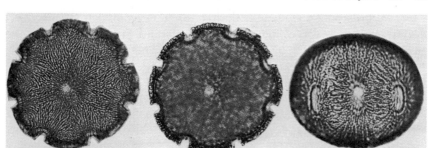

Pollen of the Phlox family. *Left:* polar view showing details of the striate sculpture pattern of the exine; *middle:* optical cross-section showing elements of the outer exine layer; *right:* equatorial view of three of the eight elongate pores. Pollen photographs, unless otherwise indicated, were taken by Jane Gray.

were dominant or very abundant through the first several hundred million years of geologic time. Megaspores are seldom encountered in sediments less than sixty million years old (the geologically young strata!). Fossilized pollen grains, especially of angiosperms, are dominant only in the younger strata, and probably reflect the recent evolution of this group of plants, which now forms most of the world's vegetation.

The wind-pollinated (anemophilous) plants produce enormously greater amounts of pollen than the animal-pollinated (zoöphilous) plants, which frequently are adapted to pollination by a particular animal. Thus most of the pollen preserved in sediments was wind-borne.

Among the wind-pollinated plants are all conifers and many hardwood trees and herbaceous plants. The spores of free-sporing plants are also wind-borne. Although insect-pollination prevails among angiosperms as a whole, the world's major vegetation types—forest and grassland— are almost wholly wind-pollinated, especially outside the tropics.

Several years ago the German scientist Pohl published some interesting figures on pollen production, based both on careful calculations and on estimates. Pine, for example, may produce 1,500,000 grains per male cone, juniper 400,000, oak 41,000 per tassel, maple 8000 per flower. Differences in absolute pollen production must be considered in interpreting differences in fossil pollen frequencies. Some genera with abundant pollen are naturally over-represented in sediments, while others with sparse pollen production leave an inadequate picture of their abundance.

Pollen output may also be expressed as the total pollen productivity of a forest, or as total counts of deposited pollen. The spruce forests of Sweden are said to produce 75,000 tons of pollen annually—about 1,000,000,000,000,000,000,000 or 10^{21} grains. In Britain the aerobiologist

Hyde records pollen settling at the rate of 5000 grains per square centimeter per year, which would amount to something on the order of 50-100 grains per cubic millimeter of accumulating sediment.

Current pollen research is built on discoveries made in the early nineteen hundreds, when Swedish scientists were pioneers in the study of bog stratigraphy. The discovery of plant fragments (such as tree trunks, seeds and pine cones) in various bog levels enabled them to reconstruct the vegetation and climate of Sweden since the last glaciation. The splendid preservation of fossil pollen among the other plant remains in the peat stimulated the imagination of the botanist H. G. Lagerheim and the young geologist Lennart von Post, his student. Although Lagerheim laid the groundwork in pollen analysis, it was von Post who achieved the full potential of the method. He found that by assembling data on the *kind* and *number* of grains from samples at different stratigraphic levels in bogs, the history of climatic change could be determined more sensitively than by the use of plant fragments preserved in the bogs.

Previously the importance of quantitative data had not been fully appreciated; only the occurrence and distribution of pollen types had been noted. Since frequency analysis is the basis of all modern pollen work, von Post's discovery was of the greatest importance. This work was preceded by about 250 years of pollen study, most of it descriptive. The foundation for modern pollen morphology was laid largely by the nineteenth-century German scientists Fritzsche, von Mohl and Fischer, as well as by the seventeenth-century microscopists Malpighi and Grew. Fossil microspores observed in ancient sediments in the 1830s and in subsequent years were treated more or less as paleobotanical curiosities.

Thousands of years ago pollen and plant fertilization played a part in the life of peoples who had no idea of pollen's microscopic appearance or its scientific value. For example, the Assyrians, around 885 B.C., depicted the symbolic fertilization of the date palm in a series of sun-baked brick mural reliefs. Since the date palm provided "food and drink, shelter and furniture, and materials for his crafts" (J. B. Stearns and D. P. Hansen, *The Assyrian Reliefs at Dartmouth* [Dartmouth, 1953] page 3), the Assyrians practiced hand-pollination to insure fertility and superior yields. Thus they recognized sexuality in plants nearly three thousand years before it was understood to the satisfaction of modern biologists.

The success of fossil pollen research depends on a fortunate combination of features: first, most pollen and spores possess a stable, chemically inert outer wall (exine) which resists deterioration and the action of chemical reagents necessary to extract it from the rock matrix; second, the exine has diagnostic features which are inherited, so that pollen and spores, at least for the last sixty million years of earth history, can be linked taxonomically with living genera. Pollen of alder or birch, for instance, can be traced back for millions of years without appreciable change.

For pollen identification, analysts rely upon certain observable features: apertures (kind, number, arrangement and structural modifications), sculpture pattern (surface design) and wall structure. The apertures consist of pores and furrows (*colpi*); these may be breaks in the exine, but are usually places where the exine is thinned and structurally modified. The pore is typically round; the furrow is usually long and boat-shaped. The apertures serve two purposes: they permit the exit of the pollen tube (which carries the sperm nucleus to the egg nucleus) and they allow volumetric and shape changes of the grain with change in water content of the protoplasmic contents. Living pollen grains do not have a fixed size or rigid shape, but because their small size reduces the effect of gravity they do tend toward spherical symmetry. Grains may have one to many furrows, one to many pores, or pores and furrows may be associated, giving a composite aperture. Some grains lack apertures but have thin, flexible walls to compensate.

Typically, gymnosperms have grains without apertures, or with only one furrow or one pore, and many, especially among the large pine family, have double wings which aid in wind dispersal. Some flowering plants such as lilies, palms, grasses (monocotyledons) also have pollen without apertures or with a single furrow or pore, but their sculpture pattern is distinct from that of the gymnosperms. However, the great mass of flowering plants (dicotyledons) is characterized by grains with three apertures, occurring as pores, furrows, or pores enclosed by furrows.

With the best light microscope and magnifications of 1000 diameters, the exine is seen to consist of two different layers. At this magnification the inner layer appears homogeneous; the outer is made up of elements of different geometric shapes. These build up the structural details of the wall and form the sculpture pattern of the grains as seen from above.

Pollen characters depend on heredity and on environment. Grains of closely related genera and species tend to be similar, but the environment molds pollen characters through natural selection and through the contact stresses imposed on the grains during their formation. Pollen of a wind-pollinated genus may have a thin exine and no apertures, as compared with that of a closely related but insect-pollinated genus with thick, elaborately ornamented exine. Contact stresses can alter the number of apertures; a normally three-furrowed grain may sometimes have four, five or six furrows. To attribute pollen characters specifically to heredity or to environmental influences is difficult.

Spores usually have distinctive aperture patterns which distinguish

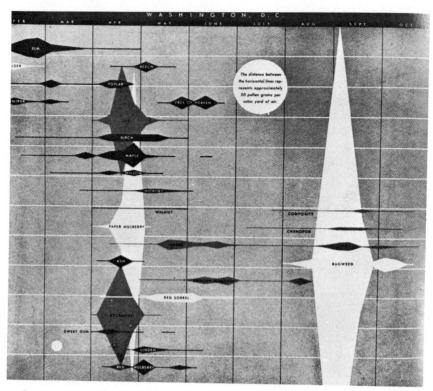

Quantitative pollination calendar for Washington, D.C. Most of the genera and families represented are entirely wind-pollinated. Chart from Botanical Research Department, Abbott Laboratories.

them from pollen grains. These serve as bursting points when the spore germinates during growth of the gametophyte.

Although it is theoretically possible to determine the natural affinities of most pollen and spores less than sixty million years old, in practice the level to which identifications can be carried varies tremendously. Identifications of plant microfossils are satisfactorily made only by comparisons with modern microspores whose plant sources are known. Even in recent sediments, certain large, ecologically variable genera such as oak, pine and birch can seldom be identified to species by their pollen. Among fossil grains only a few million years old, it is generally impossible to establish identities below the genus level. Some large groups such as the sunflower, pea, rose and grass families have pollen so similar within the family that identification may be possible for only a few genera. Fossil pollen and spores more than sixty million years old are largely from extinct genera, but even when their botanical affiliations are uncertain they may be grouped in distinct morphological units.

Fossil pollen occurs in many types of sediments, of differing ages and of varying degrees of lithification. Included are marine, lacustrine, swamp and alluvial deposits; soils, middens and cave deposits, including coprolites; fossilized sand dunes, and even glacial ice and salt deposits. Environmental conditions especially favorable to good pollen preservation and recovery demand a heavy local pollen rain and a slow to moderately slow sedimentation rate. Sediments most promising for pollen recovery are often fine-grained and dark in color from their organic content. Excessive weathering or leaching of sediments and the heat and pressure of geological activity destroy pollen or result in poor preservation.

Since pollen and spores may circulate in the atmosphere over the entire earth, it is theoretically possible to find them even in deep sea sediments. But the concentration lessens seaward from the source of production, and grains that are water-borne into the sea also tend to settle out, along with mineral particles of about the same size, before they are carried great distances. Marine sediments within twenty to thirty miles of the shore are usually the richest repositories of pollen and spores.

The pollen worker collects his samples directly from exposed sediments or from buried strata by means of hand-operated boring devices or by rotary core drills. Sediments exposed in road cuts, railroad cuts or naturally trenched stream walls provide some of the more accessible sources. It is always necessary to expose a fresh, unweathered surface before the sediments are collected, and to take care that the samples are not contaminated with fresh pollen.

Peats in bogs and certain lake sediments are most commonly collected by hand-operated boring devices, designed to penetrate the sediment without compressing or destroying its sequence. Deeply buried consolidated sediments or a continuous section hundreds or thousands of feet thick can be taken by well-drilling equipment, giving a solid drill-core. Samples for analysis are taken at intervals varying from a few inches to as much as fifty to one hundred feet.

Sediments must always be given some kind of treatment, usually chemical, in order to extract the pollen. The aim is to remove the mineral content of the sediment and any organic detritus that would conceal the grains. Following extraction, a sample of the pollen-rich residue, usually stained and mounted in glycerine or glycerine jelly, is put on a microscope slide. The analysis consists of a methodical examination of the pollen. Each pollen and spore type is tabulated until the desired number of grains is counted (at least 200, and generally 500 to 1000).

Since it is seldom possible to compute the absolute number of pollen grains shed, the analyst determines the relative frequency of each pollen type counted. The pollen frequencies in each stratigraphic level constitute what is called a *pollen spectrum*. A stratigraphic series of spectra constitutes a *pollen diagram*, which presents visually the results of the analysis. The reasons for any vegetational change depicted may be climatic change, soil change, plant evolution or other factors.

The pollen found in sediments was first mixed in the atmosphere and then sifted down to earth, more or less uniformly. It will represent the surrounding vegetation with varying degrees of accuracy, depending on a number of factors such as the volume of pollen production and release by different plants, pollen dispersal capacities, plant blooming periods, differential pollen preservation, wind direction and velocity, volume, velocity and source of water flowing into the sedimentary basin, and so on. But within these limitations the preserved pollen rain provides a reasonably good picture of the regional, wind-pollinated vegetation, usually within a radius of less than 20–30 miles.

In northwestern Europe pollen analysts have established a detailed vegetational history covering the entire time span since the end of the Pleistocene or Glacial age. This sequence was put together from separate pollen diagrams from many sites. Two earlier Swedish botanists, Blytt and Sernander, had characterized a system of post-glacial climatic periods in accordance with the dominant vegetational types found in each, and these were later verified by pollen studies. By the study of the pollen sequence from a particular deposit of peat or other sediments, it has become possible to place it in its appropriate position in the Blytt-Sernander series and thus to establish its relative age.

For precise calendrical dating some single universal datum is essential, but an ideal one has not been found. Various partial bases are used, such as the correlation of vegetational changes with fluctuations in the level of the Baltic Sea, and the direct association of pollen-bearing peat deposits with varves or with certain glacial moraines. In addition, objects datable by association with other cultures have been used to provide absolute dates for the strata in which they were found. By extrapolation, corresponding dates may then be assigned to similar strata elsewhere.

A striking variation of the use of a modified varve chronology in conjunction with pollen spectra was applied by Max Welten, who investigated a small lake in Switzerland that had been almost filled over a long period of time. In some places Welten found what he believed to be a yearly periodicity of fine chalk deposition caused by influx of mineral-rich water in early summer, alternating with organic mud from late autumn and early winter. By counting the layers he inferred a chronology which fixed the date of the sudden extension of the Mixed Oak Forest of Blytt and

1		2	3			4		5	6	7		8
Chronology		Ice Stages	Stages of Baltic Basin			Blytt-Sernander Climatic Periods		Vegetation	Fauna	Archaeology		Economy
C14 Dates	Varve Dates		Land		Water							
600 B.C.	0	Post Glacial	Emergence		Modern Baltic Sea	Sub-Atlantic	IX	Beech Increase, Pine Revertence	Domestic Cattle Domestic Sheep Swine	Historic	Neolithic	Settled Agriculture Herding Hunting Fishing
	2000 B.C.					Colder & Wetter		Pine Increase, Mixed Forest Decrease, Grass & Heather Spread Weeds & Cereals of Cultivation	Domestic Horse Red Deer Roe Deer Wild Pig Dog Beaver Bear	Iron Age		
						Sub-Boreal	VIII			Bronze Age		Extensive Forest Clearance Shifting Agriculture Herding, Hunting Fishing
3000 B.C.						Warm, Dry, Continental				Neolithic		
	4000 B.C.		Submergence		Littorina Sea	Atlantic	VII	Mixed-Oak Forest (Oak, Elm, Lime, Alder)	Aurochs Elk Red Deer Roe Deer Wild Pig Beaver Bear Dog	Ertebolle	Neolithic	Hunting Fowling Fishing Gathering
5500 B.C.						Warm Maximum Moist, Oceanic						
	6000 B.C.				Ancylus Lake	Boreal	VI	Hazel Maximum Pine Decrease, Oak-Forest Starts		Maglemose		
7000 B.C.		Feniglacial				Rising Temp. Dry, Continental						
	8000 B.C.				Yoldia Sea	Pre-Boreal	V	Pine-Beech For.				
8300 B.C.		Fenno-Scandian End Moraine				Rising Temp. Cool	IV	Beech-Pine For.	Aurochs Elk Reindeer Bison Wild Horse Alpine Horse	Lyngby		
9300 B.C.	10000 B.C.		Submergence			Arctic (Upper Dryas)	III	Tundra Flora		Ahrensburg		
						Cold						
	12000 B.C.	Gotiglacial			Baltic Ice-dammed Lake	Alleröd Oscillation	II	Park Tundra Birch Forest	Irish Deer Elk Beaver Bear	Hamburgian		
						Warmer						
13900 B.C.	14000 B.C.	Late Glacial				Sub-Arctic (Older Dryas)	Ic	Tundra Flora	Reindeer		Upper Paleolithic	
	16000 B.C.	Baltic End Moraine				Arctic	Ib	Park Tundra	Reindeer?			
	18000 B.C.	Daniglacial			Ice Recession	Cold	Ia	Tundra Flora	Reindeer			
		Brandenburg Moraine										

Late Glacial and post-Glacial chronology of northern Europe, correlating geological, paleobotanical, paleontological and archaeological data. The specific contributions of palynology are shown in columns 4 and 5, and much of the basis for column 7 is derived from pollen-analysis of sediments containing archaeological specimens. Chart compiled by the authors after Clark, Movius, Deevey, Nilsson and Godwin.

Sernander's Atlantic period (Zone VII) at about 5400 B.C. By a correlation of the pollen sequences with those from nearby sites which contained artifacts he estimated that agriculture (shown by the presence of pollen from cultivated plants) was introduced about 2700 B.C. and that the Neolithic period ended about 1800 B.C. This is in fairly close agreement with other estimates derived from quite different data.

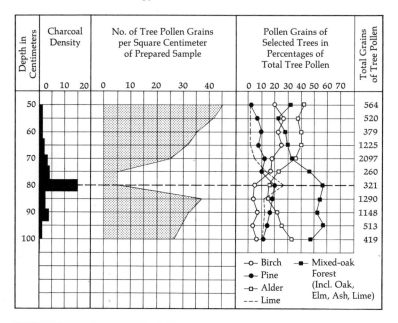

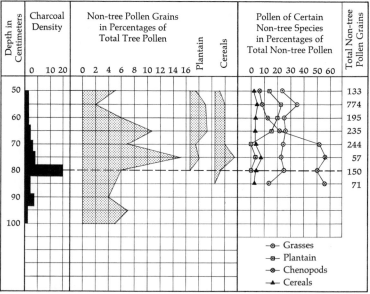

Pollen diagram for the upper levels at Ordrup Mose in Denmark (after Iversen). Horizontal dashed line indicates introduction of agriculture. At this level the charcoal density is abnormally high, total tree pollen is very low, total non-tree pollen is relatively high, and plantain and cereal pollen first appear

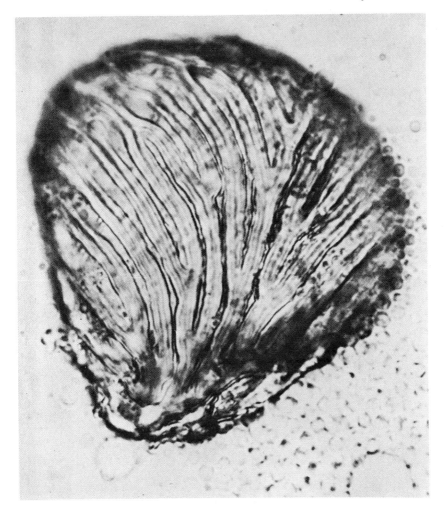

This shell-like spore, seen here in dorsal view, belongs to a member of an ancient and venerable order of ferns widespread in early geologic times, and now confined almost entirely to tropical and subtropical regions. Although its distinctive aperture is not visible, its anastomosing surface pattern immediately distinguishes it from pollen grains of gymnosperms and flowering plants. Photograph by L. M. Cranwell.

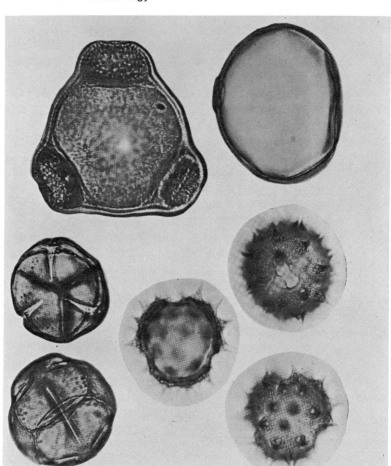

Top, left: Pollen of the Evening Primrose family. The grain in polar view has three very large protruding pores located at the angles of the grain. The two layers of the exine can be clearly distinguished.

Top, right: The simplicity of grass pollen contrasts sharply with the pollen of many dicotyledons. The single pore, slightly thickened at the rim (shown here in cross-section), and the smooth exine are characteristic of all grass pollen.

Bottom, right: Pollen of the Sunflower family. *Center,* grain in polar view, optical cross-section showing construction of solid-headed spines; *above,* equatorial view, looking into one elongate furrow, with its large, centrally located "lip-shaped" pore; *below,* grain in polar view, at high focus.

Bottom, left: Pollen of the Heath family. Each unit consists of four united grains. The furrows extend across the contact, being shared by two grains. All pollen and spores go through a tetrad stage in their development; members of the Heath family are among the very few groups in which the grains remain united at maturity.

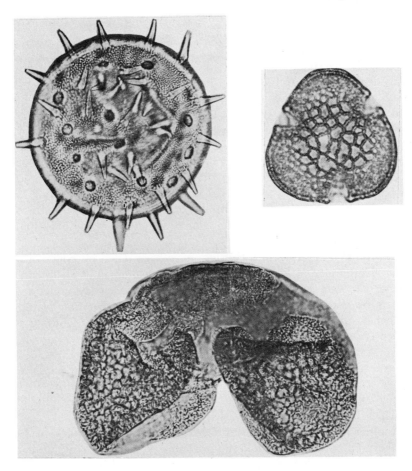

Top, left: Pollen of the Mallow family (*Hibiscus*). Numerous small, round pores are scattered over the grain surface. The very large solid spines are characteristic of many mallows. Photograph by L. M. Cranwell.

Top, right: Pollen of the genus *Fremontia.* The triangular shape of the grain in polar view, the position of the three shortened furrows midway between the apices and the coarse reticulum of the exine, which diminishes toward the equator of the grain, immediately distinguish this dicotyledenous pollen grain.

Bottom: Pine pollen. The two large wings attached to the dorsal side of the grain conceal the single furrow. This general pollen type occurs in fir, spruce, *Podocarpus* and true cedar.

An example of the use of dated objects in fixing the age of the deposits in which they were found was provided at the Federsee site in Swabia. The sequence of deposition showed first a moss peat without pollen—a thoroughly glacial phase. Then came muds with pine pollen but no cultural deposits; then an increase of hazel, oak, elm, poplar and alder, with Mesolithic artifacts; then a later Mixed Oak Forest with Neolithic objects; and finally a maximum of beech forest with Bronze Age remains dating about 800 b.c. The earlier levels were dated by interpolation between two bracketing dates established on geological grounds, the late glacial climax, about 18,000 b.c., and the time of maximum solar radiation, about 8000 b.c.

Organic deposits containing artifacts may sometimes be dated precisely by radiocarbon analysis, and the date of a particular pollen spectrum established in this manner may be applied to similar pollen spectra in other localities, at least within the same general region. This has been done at many British sites.

Two important cultures in Holstein have been dated by pollen analysis —the Hamburgian at Meiendorf and the Ahrensburgian at Stellmoor. The former site was a reindeer hunters' settlement which lay under several meters of peat resting on varved clay. The pollen spectrum placed the settlement in a treeless, post-glacial phase with a variety of tundra grasses, which is referred to as Early Dryas, and the implements were of Magdalenian (i.e., Upper Paleolithic) character. At Stellmoor a Hamburgian component occurred just at the beginning of a birch-pine-willow phase, while above it came a period of pine dominance indicating a drier interval, known as the Allerød Oscillation, followed by a second birch-pine phase in which lay the Ahrensburg (early Mesolithic) component.

Another Mesolithic culture, termed Maglemosian, was widespread over northern Europe. Sites at Müllerup in Denmark, elsewhere in Scandinavia, at the Dogger Bank in the North Sea and in England have been dated on pollen evidence to the Boreal or late Pre-Boreal periods.

A still later Mesolithic horizon known as the Ertebølle has been ascribed on pollen evidence to the Atlantic and early Sub-Boreal periods, a significant fact because it shows the survival of a Mesolithic people along the ancient shores of the Baltic Sea well into what were Neolithic times elsewhere. In England the most significant archaeological pollen applications have been made in the Fenlands, where Maglemosian (Mesolithic) bone harpoons were found in early Boreal deposits. At Peacock's Farm in Cambridgeshire there were three levels of occupation: Late Mesolithic in the Boreal period, Mesolithic early in the Atlantic period, and Early Bronze late in the Atlantic period.

Pollen analysis has also been used successfully to date sledge-runners and skis from Finnish and Swedish bogs, and wooden causeways in England and Central Europe. It was used to date a sixty-foot ship at Hjortspring, in Jutland, to about 400 B.C. A timbered village in submerged peat at Biskupin, Poland, was dated by pollen analysis at about 700 B.C.

Not many actual human remains have been dated by pollen analysis; an exception is the well preserved body of a man found at Tollund in Denmark under seven feet of peat. He had been buried about the beginning of our era.

One of the most dramatic applications of pollen analysis to archaeological interpretation was made by Professor J. Iversen in Denmark.* Although it is probable that Paleolithic and Mesolithic man had little influence on the vegetation where he lived and that forest development during those times can be ascribed wholly to natural causes, Iversen's researches documented Neolithic man's dominance over his local environment. Observing pollen diagrams from several sites dating to the transition from Atlantic to Sub-Boreal (ca. 2500 B.C.), Iversen noticed that just when alder, birch, pine and Mixed Oak Forest were at their maxima, pollen values for elm decreased markedly, as did those for ivy, while ash pollen increased, indicating a change to drier and more continental conditions. Immediately afterward the pollen curves show a striking and peculiar change: oak, linden, elm and ash all decline suddenly and steeply. Along with this change there occurs a layer of charcoal, above which the forest trees again gradually increase, although birch and alder increase most rapidly and hazel reaches a pronounced maximum. Closely connected with falling or minimum tree-pollen curves is the sudden rise, almost three-fold, of herb and shrub pollen, including small but sustained quantities of pollen of cultivated plants and a continuous record of plantain and wormwood, both of which are weeds associated widely with human disturbance of natural vegetation.

The inference is strong that these conditions indicate the introduction of agriculture by Neolithic people, who came into the northern forests soon after the climatic change, cleared the forests with axe and fire, and cultivated cereals. Strong evidence against explaining these phenomena by climatic change is provided by the decline of all forest tree-pollen almost in equal proportion and not selectively, followed by a typical forest regeneration with rapid reestablishment of pioneer species (alder, birch, hazel), and the simultaneous appearance of plantain, wormwood and cereals which point to the presence of human agriculturists, who probably also set the fires as a means of clearing the land.

To determine whether Neolithic man could have felled large areas of forest trees, Iversen and his colleagues experimented on similar trees with actual Neolithic axes, and proved beyond doubt that such a feat was easily

* See Chapter Five, pages 161–168 in this volume.

within the ability of small groups of men even so meagerly equipped. They then burned the area, and observed that the subsequent changes in vegetation closely simulated those of the Neolithic as evidenced in the pollen diagrams. What Iversen first saw in Denmark has been noted at numerous other sites in northern Europe and the British Isles, so that the introduction of agriculture over the entire area, probably at about the same date, is now well established.

Much pollen analysis has also been done in other parts of the world, although its application to archaeology has been limited. In North America several factors have militated against its success. Except in New England and the Maritime Provinces nothing like the forest history of northern Europe occurs, and even there the changes appear to have been less definitive. Furthermore, few or no surviving remains of distinctive archaeological horizons have been found in North America in contexts susceptible to the establishment of an orderly sequence related to climatic successions. The earlier and more highly evolved cultures all flourished in the semiarid West or in the Middle American tropics, where no long-sustained sequences of sediments bearing both pollen and artifacts have been discovered.

In Europe much of the success of pollen analysis in archaeological contexts is due to the fact that during the Boreal period Maglemosian sites were scattered over the whole of the north European plain, including the British Isles. The people were fishers and hunters who lived on or near bogs and left their distinctive implements in strata that are susceptible to pollen dating. Other European cultures have been fitted into this scheme by relationship to the Maglemosian. Nothing like this seems to have occurred in North America. Some significant studies of pollen in North American sites have indeed been made, for example at the Boylston Street fishweir in Boston, in the Klamath Lake area of Oregon, in the Valley of Mexico and at other places. The results have not yet been definitive or susceptible of wide application, but they provide a beginning with which future findings can be associated.

It should be strongly emphasized that some pollen studies which at present do not seem to relate directly to human prehistory may very likely become of great significance when human remains or the remains of animals killed by man are found in alluvial deposits, in caves or in other contexts which can be dated by pollen content. Every archaeologist should remember the importance of preserving soil or peat adhering to excavated objects, and should restrain his natural (and otherwise worthy) impulse toward precipitate cleaning of his specimens. Even though the pollen content of the soil or peat may not at present be datable, there is every reason to expect that a chronology will eventually be worked out and that the samples will become very useful.

Pollen analysis is, of course, an independent field of research, but many of its results, when properly interpreted by an expert, can be of great value to the archaeologist, and it will undoubtedly be used increasingly in the future in conjunction with other methods to expand and enlighten our understanding of the past.

RADIOCARBON DATING

Certainly the best known form of absolute dating is radiocarbon or carbon 14 dating. This method, which has now been refined to the point where it is useful for dating organic remains up to sixty thousand years old, was developed by the noted physicist WILLARD F. LIBBY. This early paper by Libby describes the process in detail and lists some classic examples of its use.

▣ Radiocarbon dating had its origin in the curiosity about the possible effects that cosmic rays might have on the earth and particularly, of course, on the earth's atmosphere. We were interested in testing whether any of the various effects which might be predicted could actually be found and used. In the initial attack the problem seemed rather difficult, for our ignorance of billion-volt nuclear physics was so abysmal at the time we began this research in 1946, and still is so abysmal, that it is nearly impossible to predict with any certainty the effects of the collisions of the multibillion-volt primary radiation with air.

FORMATION OF RADIOCARBON

In 1939, just before the War, Professor Korff and others discovered that the cosmic rays produced neutrons in their initial collisions with the air. The neutrons were found by sending counters, designed to be sensitive to neutrons, up to high altitudes. They were found to have an intensity which corresponded to several neutrons being generated for each square centimeter of the earth's surface per second. That is, the primary intensity of

"Radiocarbon Dating" by Willard F. Libby, *American Scientist* 44 (1956) 98–112. Reprinted by permission of the author and the Board of Editors of the *American Scientist.*

the cosmic radiation would be only perhaps one-tenth of the intensity of the secondary neutrons produced. Now, whereas it was extremely difficult to predict the types of nuclei that might be produced by the billion-volt primaries, the neutrons being secondaries were in the million-volt energy range and therefore subject to laboratory test. So at this point the question was, "What will million-volt neutrons do if liberated in the air?" The answer to this question was already available—in fact Professor Korff noted in one of the papers announcing the discovery of the neutrons that the principal ways in which the neutrons would disappear would be to form radiocarbon. The reaction involved is a simple one. Oxygen is essentially inert to neutrons but nitrogen is quite reactive. Nitrogen 14, the abundant nitrogen isotope, reacts to form carbon 14 with the elimination of a proton, the cross-section for this reaction in the thermal energy range being about 1.7 barns (10^{-24}cm^2), which is a large cross-section. In higher energy ranges it still has an appreciable cross-section for the formation of carbon 14 by this reaction and is larger than any oxygen reactions throughout the range. Another reaction occurs, probably with nitrogen 14, in a high energy range to form another radioactivity in which we have also been interested; that is tritium, the isotope of hydrogen of mass three, and carbon 12. Both carbon 14 and tritium are produced in the atmosphere by the cosmic radiation. The amount of tritium produced is small as compared with the amount of carbon 14 produced. It is possible that part of the tritium we do find is produced by the billion-volt reaction and not by the neutron mechanism. But the total tritium produced amounts to only a fraction of a percent of the carbon 14 produced. So the neutrons form carbon 14 essentially quantitatively.

Knowing that there are 2.4 neutrons formed per square centimeter per second, and assuming that the cosmic rays have been bombarding the atmosphere for a very long time in terms of the lifetime of carbon 14, (carbon 14 has a half life of about 5600 years) to form carbon 14, we can see that if the cosmic rays have been bombarding the earth in essentially their present intensity for 10 or 20 thousand years, we can expect that a steady-state condition has been established, in which the rate of formation of carbon 14 is equal to the rate at which it disappears to form nitrogen 14. This allows us to calculate quantitatively how much carbon 14 should exist on earth, for the production rate of 2.4 neutrons per square centimeter per second must be equal to 2.4 carbon 14 atoms formed per square centimeter per second, and must be equal to 2.4 carbon 14 disintegrations per square centimeter per second. Now the specific disintegration rate of carbon 14 is 1.7×10^{11} disintegrations per second per gram, and this means that for each square centimeter of the earth's surface there must be $(2.4/1.7) \times 10^{-11}$ grams of carbon 14 stored on the earth, or some 72 metric tons total for the entire earth's surface. The production mechanism

Figure 1.   Schematic Showing Carbon 14 Production Mechanism.

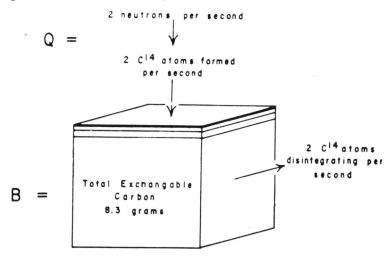

$$\text{Specific Activity} = \frac{Q}{B} = 15 \text{ min}^{-1} \text{ gm}^{-1}$$

is illustrated by the schematic diagram, Figure 1. We made this figure with two carbon atoms being made per second per cm^2 on the average, though the correct number is 2.4. They go into a mixing reservoir with about 8.3 grams of carbon and this gives the observed specific activity.

MEASUREMENT TECHNIQUES AND THE
NATURAL DISTRIBUTION OF RADIOCARBON

The next question of course is, "Where would we expect to find this radioactive material?" Carbon 14 is about as radioactive as radium in terms of its rate of disintegration. This is quite a large amount of radioactivity and our first question was, why hasn't it been noticed? It is obvious, after a moment's thought, that it hadn't been seen because it is diluted with ordinary carbon. The dilution process is one which is easily predicted. We know that the carbon 14 is produced in the highest layers of the atmosphere. If the neutron intensity is measured as a function of altitude it is found that it reaches a maximum at about 9 meters of water equivalent, that is, at about one meter of water below the top of the atmosphere. If we plot on a logarithmic scale, the neutron intensity against the depth of the atmosphere the curve, as determined by Dr. Yuan and Professor Ladenberg at Princeton, is as shown in Figure 2. The fall off at the top is quite interesting. This is due to the escape of neutrons from the earth

Figure 2. Neutron Intensity Variations with Altitude.

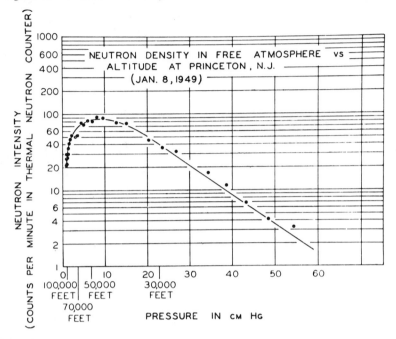

which have been produced near the top of the atmosphere. But the neutrons which do not escape from the earth correspond to the area under this curve and the mean altitude of production is about 30,000 feet. So the neutrons are produced and disappear, that is the carbon 14 is produced, at about 30,000 feet. The carbon 14 atoms are formed with an energy of some 40,000 electron volts, carbon atoms moving through the air with a very high velocity. We do not know all of the details of this type of hot-atom chemistry as applied to this particular problem, but assumed in the first stages of the work, apparently correctly, that the radiocarbon is burned to radioactive carbon dioxide in the atmosphere. It is then mixed by the winds with the inert carbon dioxide in the atmosphere and enters the biosphere by the photosynthetic process. That is, the plants live off carbon dioxide in the atmosphere and the animals live off the plants, and at death, a good part of their carbonaceous material forms carbon dioxide to return to the atmosphere. This mixing cycle insures that the carbon 14 produced by the cosmic rays will be mixed uniformly throughout the biosphere, provided the turnover time for the biosphere is short as compared to the lifetime of radiocarbon. Radiocarbon has such a very long lifetime that this seems certain to be true.

Various estimates of the turnover time for the lifecycle have been made. They range from a few hundred to values as high as 1000 years but none of them approach the lifetime of radiocarbon. For these reasons we expected to find that all living things would be radioactive with the cosmic ray produced radiocarbon, and that their radioactivity would be uniform because of the adequacy of mixing.

There was one question which worried us a bit and that is connected with the fact that the cosmic rays themselves varied in intensity with latitude. The intensity of the neutron producing component at the latitude of Chicago is about four times the intensity at the equator, as shown in Figure 3,* according to the measurement of Dr. Simpson and his coworkers. The question therefore was whether the northerly and southerly mixing effects would be adequate to assure a uniform radiocarbon assay for living material all over the earth's surface in view of the strong variation of the production rate. However when it is realized that the carbon 14 atoms in any organism have on the average been up in the air 8 or 9 times during their average lifetime of 8000 years (the *half* life is 5600 and the *average* life 8000), it seemed to be extremely probable that such a latitudinal variation of radiocarbon assay for biological matter would be of negligible magnitude. This we found to be true. All living organisms seem to have the same specific radiocarbon content; that is, the same amount of radiocarbon per gram of contained carbon.

The amount of material in the biosphere determines the concentration. Now it is not only the biosphere which dilutes the radiocarbon but the dissolved carbonaceous material in the oceans which can exchange carbon with the atmospheric carbon dioxide does so also. In fact this is the larger part of the diluting carbon reservoir, as we show in Figure 4. For each square centimeter of the earth's surface, there are about 7.25 gm of carbon dissolved in the ocean in the form of carbonate, bicarbonate, and carbonic acid. The biosphere itself contains about 0.33 gm per square centimeter of surface. The estimate for this is rather uncertain; however, the inorganic carbonate content of the sea is quite accurately known and since it is the major component of the total carbon reservoir, it allows us to predict with some certainty what the specific radioactivity of living organic matter should be. That is to say, when we add all these small items to the 7.25 gm of the inorganic carbon in the sea, the 2.4 carbon 14 atoms disintegrating every second should be contained in 8.3 gm of carbon and so the specific activity of living carbon should be that number. We find this to be true to within about 10%. Dr. Rubey, the eminent geologist, for entirely different reasons, made an analogous estimate of the reservoir and as you see we agree to about 5% (Figure 4).

* Figure 3 is omitted.

Figure 4. *Carbon Reservoir Makeup.*

| | EXCHANGE RESERVOIR (g C/cm²) | |
	ANDERSON AND LIBBY	W. W. RUBEY
Ocean "carbonate"	7.25	6.95
Ocean, dissolved organic	0.59 ⎫	
Biosphere	0.33 ⎭	0.78
Atmosphere	0.12	0.125
Total	8.3	7.9

This is interesting for it means the following: the present intensity of the cosmic radiation (unless there have been canceling errors in our calculations) corresponds to the average intensity over the last 8000 years. It says also that the ocean is mixed nearly perfectly to its bottom depths in 8000 years. This we know because we took all of the dissolved carbon in the sea. These conclusions could be false if errors in two quantities so different as the intensity of the cosmic rays and the mixing rate of the sea should happen just to cancel one another. Being so unrelated, we believe this to be very unlikely and conclude that the agreement between the predicted and observed assays are encouraging evidence that the cosmic rays have indeed remained constant in intensity over many thousands of years. Now you understand that we are in the radiocarbon dating business as soon as that is said, for it is clear from the set of assumptions that I have given that organic matter, while it is alive, is in equilibrium with the cosmic radiation; that is, all the radiocarbon atoms which disintegrate in your body are replaced by the carbon 14 contained in the food you eat, so that while you are alive you are part of a great pool which contains the cosmic ray produced radiocarbon. The specific activity is maintained at the level of 16 disintegrations per minute per gram by the mixing action of the biosphere and hydrosphere. You assimilate cosmic ray-produced carbon 14 atoms at just the rate that the carbon 14 atoms in your body disappear to form nitrogen 14. At the time of death, however, the assimilation process stops abruptly. There is no longer any process by which the carbon 14 from the atmosphere can enter your body. Therefore at the time of death the radioactive disintegrative process takes over in an uncompensated manner and according to the radioactivity decay law after 5600 years the carbon that was in your body will show half the specific carbon 14 radioactivity that it shows while you are alive. Since we have evidence that this has been true for thousands of years, we should expect to find that a body 5600 years old would be one-half as radioactive as a present-day living organism. This appears to be true. Measurements of old mummies have shown this to be so within the experimental errors of measurement.

The research on radiocarbon dating consisted of several stages. In the first place we had to demonstrate that the expected radioactivity of living material actually existed. At that time we had no measurement techniques sufficiently sensitive to detect the radioactivities involved. They are quite low levels of radioactivity. Later we developed methods for the measurement but at that time we did not have such methods. So we used methods of concentrating the isotopes of carbon. Such an apparatus had been built by and was being used by Dr. Aristide von Grosse, then of the Houdry Process Corporation at Marcus Hook, Pennsylvania. He was concentrating the carbon 13 isotopes for medical tracer purposes and was very glad to try to concentrate some biological methane for our crucial test. We had to use biological as contrasted with petroleum methane for we had at this point arrived at a distinction between living and dead organic chemicals. We had dead methane and living methane in the sense that oil methane from oil wells in which the oil has been long buried would be expected to be entirely free from radiocarbon while the methane made from disintegration of living organic matter should contain 16 dpm per gram of radiocarbon. The task was to take this living methane and concentrate it in the isotope separation column and to see whether the enriched product was radioactive. Happily for our research it was found to be so and in about the expected amount.

The second stage of the research was the development of methods of measurement which were sufficiently sensitive so that we could avoid the use of a ten thousand dollar thermal diffusion isotope column and many thousands of dollars of operating expense to measure the age of a single mummy. Obviously it would have been an impractical method of measuring archaeological ages if this phase of the research had been unsuccessful. The method developed involves measuring the radioactivity of solid carbon itself. We convert the samples by chemical methods into elementary carbon—a type of lampblack. This lampblack is placed on the inner surface of the wall of a Geiger counter where it itself becomes the wall. This is possible because lampblack is an electrical conductor. In this way a maximum count rate is achieved.

The Geiger counter itself was shielded from the background radiations in order to accentuate the carbon 14 count. Figure 5 shows the instrument used for measurement. There are more sensitive methods that have now been developed, but this one was very useful. I found it possible, with one assistant burning the samples and producing the lampblack, to make about 300 measurements just in odd moments while other research was going on. It was a matter of starting the counter and reading it at intervals. The counter runs night and day the year round. This is a rather simple way of doing it, though not quite as sensitive as some of the newer methods. The radioactive materials in the earth were shielded out by the

Figure 5.   Screen Wall Counter.

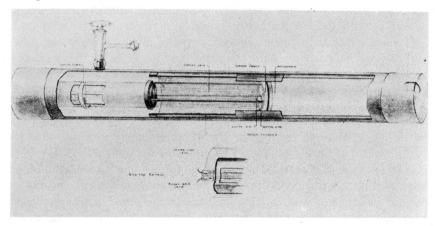

use of a thick layer of non-radioactive iron or lead, and the cosmic rays which cannot be shielded by any reasonable thickness of solid material were excluded by the use of an anti-coincidence principle, as we called it. This method consisted simply of surrounding the Geiger counter containing the radiocarbon with a ring of Geiger counters which were arranged in tangentially close contact, shown in Figures 6 and 7, so that no cosmic ray could pass between them. The shielding counters then were wired in such a way that whenever one of them fired, the inter counter with the carbon dating sample in it was turned off for a very small fraction of a second. In this way we eliminated from the record the counts due to the penetrating cosmic rays. We could do this with impunity for the reason that the carbon 14 radiation—the radiation emitted by carbon 14 when it becomes nitrogen 14—is not penetrating and would not kick off one of the shielding counters. In these ways it was possible to eliminate over 99% of the background. We were then able to measure directly the radioactivity of living carbon and of the ancient samples back to an age of about 25,000 years.

You lose a factor of 2 for each 5600 years. So after about 25,000 years the intensity is so low that it is difficult to measure it with any accuracy by this method of measurement unless one takes particular care. Our normal measurement technique is to count the sample for about 48 hours. This is an arbitrary figure selected for reasons of convenience. In two cases we measured samples for as long as three months. These were cases in which very important archaeological points were involved—the correlations of the calendars of the Mayas in Central America and of the Babylonians in Asia Minor with our own Christian Calendar. Since that time the counter development has progressed considerably in other laboratories. The data on the natural abundance of radiocarbon in the earth was pre-

Figure 6.   End View of Counter with Shielding.

Figure 7.   Side View of Counter with Shielding.

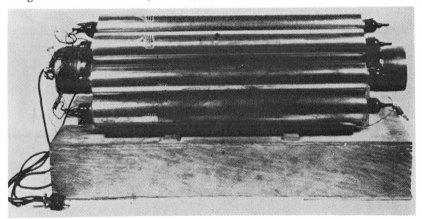

Figure 8.   Geographical Distribution of Modern Samples.

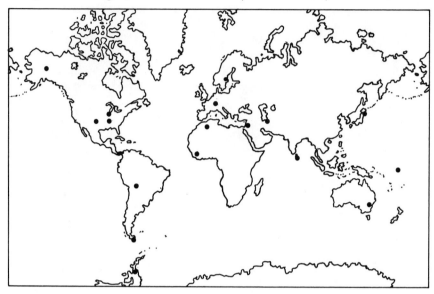

sented by Dr. E. C. Anderson for his doctoral thesis at the University of Chicago. We proceeded, after developing the method of measurement, to make as thorough a measurement as we could of the present-day abundance of radiocarbon in the various species and at various spots over the earth's surface. Figure 8 shows the spots on the earth's surface where we took modern samples. They are pretty well scattered over the earth's surface except for Soviet Russia. Figure 9 is a tabulation of the data for these samples. You see no appreciable difference in any of them. They go from the South Pole to not quite the North Pole.

Our whole research was supported generously by the Viking Fund of New York City (now the Axel Wenner-Gren Foundation), the United States Air Force, the Geological Society and the Guggenheim Foundation.

DATING BY THE RADIOCARBON TECHNIQUE

After the assay of the natural occurrence of radiocarbon, the next stage was to see whether we had a method of dating mummies. We had a decay curve drawn which predicted with no unknown factors, no adjustable constants, the specific activity of ancient mummies. And so the question was to see whether it worked. The first thing we had to do, of course, was to get the mummies. This was done by enlisting the cooperation of the American Anthropological Association and the American Geological Society (the geologists have been quite interested in the results of this dating). A committee of advisors was appointed to select the samples for us and to help us collect them. These distinguished gentlemen worked very hard for several years, assisting and collecting the samples and advising Dr. James Arnold and myself. Dr. Arnold was principal collaborator, in the development of the dating work. The research consisted of two stages. The first shock Dr. Arnold and I had was that our advisors informed us that history extended back only 5000 years. We had thought initially that we would be able to get samples all along the curve back to 30,000 years, put the points in, and then our work would be finished. You read books and find statements that such and such a society or archeological site is 20,000 years old. We learned rather abruptly that these numbers, these ancient ages, are not known; in fact, it is at about the time of the first dynasty in Egypt that the last historical date of any real certainty has been established. So we had, in the initial stages, the opportunity to check against knowns, principally Egyptian artifacts, and in the second stage we had to go into the great wilderness of prehistory to see whether there

Figure 9.   Measured Activity of Terrestrial Biosphere Samples.

ACTIVITY OF TERRESTRIAL BIOSPHERE SAMPLES

SOURCE	GEOMAGNETIC LATITUDE	ABSOLUTE SPECIFIC ACTIVITY (dpm/g)
White spruce, Yukon	60°N.	14.84 ± 0.30
Norwegian spruce, Sweden	55°N.	15.37 ± 0.54
Elm wood, Chicago	53°N.	14.72 ± 0.54
Fraximus excelsior, Switzerland	49°N.	15.16 ± 0.30
Honeysuckle leaves, Oak Ridge, Tenn.	47°N.	14.60 ± 0.30
Pine twigs and needles (12,000 ft. alt.), Mount Wheeler, New Mexico	44°N.	15.82 ± 0.47
North African briar	40°N.	14.47 ± 0.44
Oak, Sherafut, Palestine	34°N.	15.19 ± 0.40
Unidentified wood, Teheran, Iran	28°N.	15.57 ± 0.31
Fraximus Mandshurica, Japan	26°N.	14.84 ± 0.30
Unidentified wood, Panama	20°N.	15.94 ± 0.51
Chlorophora excelsa, Liberia	11°N.	15.08 ± 0.34
Sterculia excelsa, Copacabana, Bolivia (9000 ft. alt.)	1°N.	15.47 ± 0.50
Ironwood, Majoro, Marshall Islands	0°	14.53 ± 0.60
Unidentified wood, Ceylon	2°S.	15.29 ± 0.67
Beech wood, Tierra del Fuego	45°S.	15.37 ± 0.49
Eucalyptus, New South Wales, Australia	45°S.	16.31 ± 0.43
Seal oil from seal meat from Antarctic	65°S.	15.69 ± 0.30
Average		15.3 ± 0.1

were elements of internal consistency which would lead one to believe that the method was sound.

In the prehistoric period our committee set up a network of problems which were designed to check, in as many ways as possible, points of internal consistency. They set out about a dozen major projects, and we collected samples from each of these projects and worked hard and measured them. The measurements are still going on. At the present time, in our laboratory in Chicago, we have completed about five hundred radiocarbon dates. Other laboratories in this country and Europe are dating. There is a very prolific laboratory in the Geological Survey here in Washington. Dr. Suess has finished over 200 dates by an improved technique which he developed in which the carbon is counted not as solid but as acetylene gas. This seems to be a superior and more sensitive method of measurement. There are other methods that have been developed in Europe using carbon dioxide gas.

Figure 10 is a curve of the results for samples of known age. The curve is drawn from Dr. Anderson's work on the modern assay and the known half life of radiocarbon. These are the knowns which were given us by our committee and which we measured. The uncertainties of measurement are indicated by the arrows; they have varying lengths depending upon the length of time involved and size of sample and the way the counter was working. The oldest one is the very first dynasty in Egypt and was a piece of charcoal. The next point was a piece of wood from a roof beam. The point marked Zoser was the very first sample we measured. It had an unfortunately large error. We had a very small sample and it discouraged us a little bit. The point marked Sesostris is a very interesting sample. It is a part of the deck of a funeral ship that was placed in the tomb of this King Sesostris of Egypt. It was stored in the Chicago Museum of Natural History. The ship is about 20 to 30 feet long and 6 feet high, and is quite an imposing object. They sawed a great hole in the deck and gave us a board. We needed only a little chunk about the size of an ounce, so if you visit the museum, you'll see a hole in that deck from where our sample came. The next point is the heart wood of one of the largest redwood trees ever cut. The tree was about 3000 years old when it was cut. This is an interesting point as it shows that, in the redwood at least, the sap is not in chemical equilibrium with the inner portions of the tree; in other words, the carbon in that central wood was deposited there about 3000 years ago though the tree itself was cut just a few years ago. The point marked Tayinat is a house in Asia Minor which was burned in 675 B.C. This was a door beam in the house. The next point is a mummy coffin from another Egyptian King, and next is a manuscript of the book of Isaiah which was found in Palestine shortly after the War, or, more correctly, it is the linen wrappings in which this manuscript was found.

Figure 10. Measured Samples of Known Age.

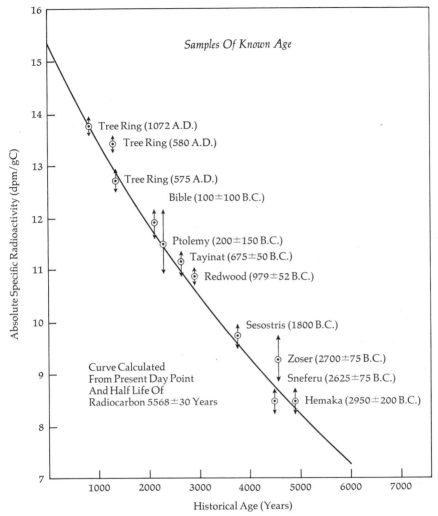

Historical Age (Years)

The other points on the curve are samples of wood which were dated by the Douglas Tree Ring Counting Technique.

Figure 11 shows us the most important single general result in the prehistoric period. That is the time at which the last ice sheet covered the northern part of this and the European continent. The classic site for this, the Mankato glaciation, is the Two Creeks forest bed in northern Wisconsin. It is a spruce forest which was growing luxuriantly. The outer twenty rings of the trees in this forest are thinner indicating that the climate had suddenly become colder. The trees were all pushed in a given direction

Figure 11.   Measured Dates of Latest Glaciation.

LATEST GLACIAL AGE

NORTH AMERICA	YEARS
Two Creeks: wood and peat from Two Creeks Forest Bed, Manitowoc Co., Wisc. Underlies Valders Drift. Spruce forest pushed over and buried by last ice sheet	
Sprucewood, Wilson, Mass.	10,877 ± 740
Tree root, Bretz, Chicago	11,437 ± 770
Peat in which root was found, Bretz, Chicago	11,097 ± 600
Sprucewood, Horberg & Bretz, Chicago	12,168 ± 1500
Peat, Horberg & Bretz, Chicago	11,442 ± 640
Average	11,404 ± 350

GERMANY

German Alleröd: Zone IIb, northwest Germany. Firbas, Germany	11,044 ± 500

ENGLAND

Alleröd I: peat, Hawks Tor, Cornwall. Late glacial, Zone II. Godwin, Cambridge	9,861 ± 500
Godwin: lake mud, Neasham, near Darlington, Zone II. Blackburn & Godwin, England	10,851 ± 630

IRELAND

Irish Mud: lake mud, Knocknacran, County Monoghan, Late glacial Zone II. Mitchell, Dublin	11,310 ± 720

and covered with glacial debris. Apparently the glacier just moved down on the forest, pushed it over and covered it. There's no scarcity of wood; we used various portions of different trees, as well as the peat from the soil in which the trees were growing. All of the numbers from these different samples agreed at a date of about 11,400 years for the time that the forest had been killed by the advancing glacier. In Germany and in other parts of Europe analogous phenomena exist. Some of the results from the Radiocarbon Dating Laboratory in Copenhagen checked this number to within two or three centuries. Thus it appears that on the basis of radiocarbon the last glaciation occurred about 11,000 years ago, and occurred simultaneously in both Europe and North America.

At the present time those of us interested in the validity of the method are waiting to see whether the geologists and archaeologist find the results palatable. We know of no serious proportion of the dates which are not internally consistent. However, there are questions which can be asked about, for example, the cosmic rays. The argument that I gave you was restricted to about 8000 years, and so the question of whether the cosmic rays were at the same intensity 40,000 years ago (some of these new methods will go back that far) is a pertinent one. Also, the question of whether the amount of material in the carbon reservoir has remained constant is an equally pertinent question. For the quantity which we are interested in is the specific radioactivity, which is the ratio of the cosmic radiation to the amount of carbon in the reservoir, or, in other words, the ratio of the intensity of the cosmic rays to the amount of carbon in the ocean. We know that during the Ice Ages there was an abrupt change in the ecology of the earth and a considerable amount of water, perhaps as much as 200 or 300 meters, was deposited on the land in the form of ice so that the depth of the sea was changed; however, the mean depth of the sea, 3600 meters, is such that this is a small percentage. The ocean at the present time has an average temperature of $0°C$ so it couldn't have been much colder. It is therefore likely that this disturbing influence probably was not serious. There are various other points of doubt that can be tested; for example, if you pick up an ancient piece of charcoal (charcoal incidentally is one of our very best types of sample, since it is inert chemically and is very common) how do you know that the carbon atoms in that sample are the carbon atoms which were present in the original piece of wood? We can make the chemical argument that it is very difficult to imagine replacing the carbon atom in a graphite-type lattice with one from carbon dioxide. It would be easy to burn part of it but that isn't the question. The question is replacing the carbon atoms in an ancient piece of charcoal or wood, or cloth, or flesh, etc. It isn't a question of the decay of the sample to form some lower and degraded products, it is a question of whether the molecular structure in the sample has had its carbon atoms replaced. All we know from the laboratory tests on these replacement reactions, and from organic chemistry in general, would indicate that in these giant molecules the carbon atoms are very difficult to replace. The carbon is practically impossible to replace by ordinary chemical reactions. So, from chemical reasoning, we would say that it is very likely that the charcoal has the same atoms, if you make certain that the only carbon you measure in the sample is carbon in the charcoal and not dirt that was in the cracks and interstices or was absorbed. So we are very careful in making measurements on the charcoal and the samples of wood or cloth or whatever material we may use (and we have used all sorts of material from human hair to animal feces, including even limestone, or seashells; sometimes these results are not quite as promising as the results on organic matter) to see that extraneous carbon is not introduced.

SUMMARY OF OTHER ARCHAEOLOGICAL RESULTS

We determined many dates from various archaeological sites scattered over the world. Material from Egypt beginning in the prehistoric and continuing through the historic period was measured. Egyptian history starts at the first dynasty about 4800 years ago. This was the period when they first built the great pyramids. Obviously, there were people there before. In fact granaries in which grain still exists and which the Egyptian farmers had used are found left by the early farmers. We measured portions of these original grains and found them to be about 6300 years old. In other words, the agricultural society lived prior to the first dynasty by about 1500 years. Measuring the hair from human bodies buried in the desert sand gave evidence of continuous occupation from the time of the farmers which I have just described down to the time of the pyramids. These bodies were found in various places all over Egypt, and have been used by the archaeologist in setting up a relative chronology. These samples were extremely valuable, for they were the prime materials used by the archaeologists in their original researches in Egyptian archaeology.

In Iraq we measured what is supposed to be the oldest known village in the world, a place called Jarmo. The result was 6600 years, or 4600 B.C. The time of Hammurabi, the Babylonian King, has been measured also. There was an uncertainty about the Babylonian calendar, in its relation to the Christian calendar. The Babylonians had a very good calendar but there was an uncertainty of about 300 years—which I understand was due to the identification of a particular eclipse—in the correlation of it with our own calendar. We had a portion of a house about 4000 years old that was dated accurately on the Babylonian calendar. An accurate measurement of this particular piece of wood should fix the Babylonian calendar relative to the Christian calendar. Fortunately, there were just two or three alternative results which were allowed; that is, the uncertainty was such that if we fixed it within a century, it would be possible to distinguish clearly between the various alternatives, and the Babylonian calendar would then be relatively accurately fixed, within a matter of days, relative to the Christian calendar. On this sample we spent three months of measurement. The result agreed, I am pleased to say, with the one the scholars thought to be most likely. Also in Iraq we have found the oldest evidence of man that we have measured. It is a cave in which a campfire had been built and which, to our limits of sensitivity, contained no radiocarbon. In other words, the charcoal in this cave in Iraq had been produced by a campfire which had been built more than 25,000 years earlier.

In Afghanistan we measured artifacts from a Bronze Age site which had been established in Afghanistan. There were no records in Afghanistan for the archaeologists to tie to. It developed that the appearance of the Bronze Age in Afghanistan was contemporaneous essentially, within our error of measurement, which is two or three centuries normally, with that in Lebanon and other parts of the Middle East.

In France we have a considerable number of interesting samples. The main story about the Mediterranean base is that when the ice sheet moved south in Northern Europe, the people moved south ahead of it, and so one finds no lack of evidence of the human occupation around the Mediterranean basin as far back as the radiocarbon technique will go. One of the most striking sites from which we had samples was the famous Lascaux caves in Southern France which were discovered during the German occupation. These caves were opened accidentally, I believe, during that time and were found to contain most remarkable colored paintings. We had charcoal picked laboriously from the soil of the floor of this cave which dated at 15,000 years. There is some evidence that this charcoal itself is younger than the paintings. These people preceded the last ice age and they painted these beautiful pictures, which I think rival those in many museums.

All of Northern Europe and England was covered by the ice, essentially at the same time, so the oldest Englishman is as old as the oldest Dane and so on, because the glacier is a very clean broom and sweeps everything clean. We do not find any evidence of human beings in England older than about 10,000 years. This is also the oldest American we have ever seen—the oldest Dane—the oldest Irishman, etc.—and they are all contemporaneous. We find that this is true of the North American continent for some strange reason; that is, we have never seen a man of North or South or Central America older than this Ice Age. This may be accidental; I do not know enough about archaeology to be certain about it but I know this is true of the samples we have measured. In Europe there is abundant evidence of people that are pre-glacial. There is one very strange thing about the American situation and that is that the Westerners are older than the Easterners. The oldest site we have any measurements on in New England is an ancient fishweir of fabulous construction under the Boston Commons which had, I think, 16,000 stakes hand hewn. It is now well submerged. It was discovered when constructing the foundation for a large building. This material is about 5000 years old. New York State, New England, Kentucky, Alabama, all of them at the deepest level, according to our results are contemporary at about 5000 years, the time of the first Egyptian dynasty. However, in Nebraska and several places in Nevada, Texas, Oregon, and Washington we find 10,000-year-old men. We find them in the very southern tip of South America at 9000 years. We find them in New Mexico, although there's probably a little more uncertainty about that state. The Oregon sample was particularly remarkable. There was found a shoe store in a cave with 300 pairs of shoes in it that are 9300 years old. It was covered by the eruption of an ancient volcano—and the archaeologist, Dr. L. S. Cressman, who furnished the samples said the only thing he could say about it was that it was an ancient shoe store. The shoes are woven sandals made of grass rope, beautifully woven with a decorative strap across the instep—a slip-on sandal that you would be very glad to wear as slippers. They are about normal size.

Crater Lake in Oregon was formed about 6600 years ago. It was made by a giant eruption of an ancient mountain called Mt. Mazama. The eruption covered the whole countryside with lava—and as a result there was no scarcity of material for it burned the forest. We had 100 pounds of beautiful charcoal. We find evidence of human occupation throughout the Northwest, running from the time 10,000 years ago continuously down to the present. There is one fabulous sight in Western Utah at Wendover, Utah, right on the state line. It is a cave, overlooking the Great Salt Lake Flats, in which 15 feet of garbage was found at its mouth. At the bottom of the garbage collection was beach sand (this was 120 miles from the present lake shore and about 100 feet higher than the present lake). In the beach sand were bits of driftwood and other artifacts which were dated at 11,000 years. Strangely enough there were also bits of sheep droppings there that were dated the same age. Above this are signs of human occupation in which the earliest date is about 10,000 years and which runs apparently continuously down to the present. Dr. Jennings who discovered and excavated the site has given us samples from various depths in this deposit. It's the only archaeological site that I ever visited and I'll never forget it. One can make a cross-section through this and can see 10,000 years of history written in garbage.

Finally, various miscellaneous points: we have a 4300-year-old graveyard near Sacramento, California. The Indians learned to cultivate corn about 2700 years ago both in Arizona and in Peru. The Mayan calendar is dated relatively to the Christian calendar; the older of the two possible dates for the Mayan calendar is the one confirmed. There's a fabulous dwelling place in Peru where the Indians lived about 4300 years ago and which they abandoned about 2000 years ago when the garbage got so high they couldn't climb up on it anymore. There is an old house in Japan that is 4300 years old. There is an ancient town in Southern Rhodesia, a completely walled city, for which there is no history. We measured it and found it to have been built about 500 A.D. or about 1500 years ago. We measured a large number of samples from Africa but I know practically nothing about the archaeology. I can't even describe it, except to say that there are evidences of very ancient man in South Africa, and evidences that South Africa was never glaciated. . . .

CHAPTER FOUR

🙢🙢🙢🙢🙢🙢🙢🙢🙢🙢🙢🙢🙢🙢

Archaeological Excavation

A passage on the strategy of excavation
is followed by the reconstruction of
a prehistoric battle through
careful excavation and interpretation
of the data uncovered.

THE STRATEGY OF EXCAVATION

*SIR MORTIMER WHEELER, the doyen of Old World field
archaeologists, has done more than anyone to introduce meticulous
standards of excavation into prehistory. In this classic passage on
the strategy of digging, he discusses the evidence to be obtained by
vertical and horizontal trenching, two basic approaches to site
investigation.*

▣ . . . From time to time the question arises: shall stress be laid (in some
particular program of work) upon horizontal or upon vertical excavation?
By "horizontal excavation" is meant the uncovering of the whole or a large
part of a specific phase in the occupation of an ancient site, in order to
reveal fully its layout and function. By "vertical excavation" is meant the
excavation of a restructed area *in depth,* with a view to ascertaining the
succession of cultures or of phases and so producing a time-scale or
culture-scale for the site. The two procedures are of course complementary,
not antagonistic, and the excavator may be expected to attempt, if rarely
to achieve, both methods of approach. But in a great majority of instances,
a priority has to be determined, having regard to the state of current
knowledge and the resources available.

Let us consider the nature of the evidence which the two methods may
be expected to supply. Vertical excavation alone, while supplying a key

From *Archaeology from the Earth* by Sir Mortimer Wheeler, published by the Clarendon Press,
Oxford, 1954, pp. 126–129. Reprinted by permission of the author and the publisher. Photographs courtesy of Sir Mortimer Wheeler and the Society of Antiquaries of London.

Vertical excavation—Maiden Castle, England.

to the length of an occupation, to its continuity or intermittency, and to some part of its cultural equipment, cannot be expected to reveal save in the most scrappy fashion the significant environment—economic, religious, administrative—of a human society. In other words, it leaves us in the dark as to those very factors which fit a past culture or civilization into the story of human endeavor and so make its recovery worthwhile. It is the railway time-table without a train. On the other hand, the extensive horizontal excavations which were in effect the normal practice before stratification was adequately understood generally produced an abstraction—often a very confused and misleading abstraction—unrelated with any sort of precision to the sequence of human development. They were trains without a time-table. The trains sometimes ran vigorously enough, but we knew not when they were running or where they started, or their intermediate stopping-places, or their destination.

At certain stages of research both these incomplete methods may have a substantive value; indeed, they are themselves stages in the progress of research. I am not, for example, of those who scorn the horizontal excavation (in the nineties) of the Roman town of Silchester. True it was dug like potatoes, without a shadow of the scientific nicety of the contemporary excavations in Cranborne Chase; and the resultant plan is the uncritical synthesis of a varying urban development through more than three centuries. But it gave at once, and with a rough accuracy, the general impression of a Romano-British town such as fifty years of subsequent and often more careful work have failed to equal. More exact vertical and horizontal digging on both this and other similar sites has indeed begun to reveal the sociological evolution essential to our historical perspective; but who among these later and wiser excavators has not constantly referred back with profit to the crude, primitive assemblage of Silchester?

So also elsewhere. The Glastonbury lake-village, excavated uncritically with results that are often infuriatingly baffling, has nevertheless given us the complete layout of a small Early Iron Age settlement and so enabled us to assess in broad terms the social and economic significance of such a settlement as no exacting and partial probing could have rendered possible. For that, even in moments when the evidence in detail completely fails us, we may be properly thankful. And let us for a moment look further afield. One of the most dramatic and revealing of all excavated cities is prehistoric Mohenjo-daro, beside the Indus in Pakistan. Technically the methods adopted by a succession of excavators there became almost an international scandal, and neither Professor Piggott nor I have been at pains to spare the lash. But the primary marvel of the great Indus city is not that it did (or did not) develop in such-and-such a fashion between, let us say, 2500 and 1500 B.C., *but that it existed at all* in the remarkable form that extensive, if disproportionately summary, excavation has revealed to us. Its house-walls, towering accumulatively above our heads, its long straight streets, its lanes, its elaborate drainage system, its citadel —these and other things in bulk re-create a whole phase of human society even though in detail they fail to analyze it for us. Analysis—by careful vertical digging—should, of course, have accompanied all this summary horizontal clearance; but there can be no question that Mohenjo-daro takes its place as the representative of one of the great civilizations of the ancient world in some measure by virtue of the crimes of its explorers.

And since we have arrived in Pakistan, let us take again one more familiar example from that land. For a thousand years the city of Taxila stood upon successive sites in the northern Punjab, and one of these sites, of the first centuries B.C.–A.D., was extensively cleared by Sir John Marshall so that a considerable portion of a remarkable rectangular town-plan was ultimately revealed. The clearance did not conform with modern technical standards, and in fact more than one phase is represented without discrimination in the published plan. Nevertheless, the outstanding interest of Parthian Taxila is the general character of its buildings and their relation to a street-grid without known analogy in this part of Asia. Had the excavator concentrated on vertical digging on this deep site he would have given us valuable information for which we are still waiting; but he could scarcely have given us also the picture which we owe to him of a teeming city with its streets and temples, its palaces and its shops. He would have

Horizontal or grid excavation—Maiden Castle, England.

given us a useful catalogue but not, as in fact he has, a vivid chapter of social history.

The four examples of horizontal digging which I have given—Silchester, Glastonbury, Mohenjo-daro, and Taxila (Sirkap)—are not very happy in that none of them was excavated with adequate skill. Technically, they all belong to the pre–Pitt-Rivers era, though Pitt-Rivers had in fact established his methods before any of them began. Needless to say, it must not be inferred that horizontal excavation is necessarily summary and unscientific! Ideally, the excavation of a town-site would begin with vertical digging, sufficient to establish the time- or culture-sequence, and would proceed to the careful horizontal digging of sucessive phases, one at a time. Obviously the process cannot be reversed, and at the three sites mentioned, only the careful vertical excavation of areas not yet touched can partially replace the squandered evidence. A better example of horizontal excavation on a small scale is provided by Little Woodbury near Salisbury, where Dr. Gerhard Bersu cleared the greater part of an Iron Age farmstead and was able to reconstruct both its architecture and its economy. The site was a shallow one, and the technical problem was incomparably simpler than on a deeply accumulative town-site; nevertheless, it is chastening to reflect how little of the real meaning of Little Woodbury could have been re-covered merely by vertical samples of it.

With the proviso, then, that all horizontal digging must proceed from clear and comprehensive vertical sections, the question of priority is fundamentally not in doubt. Careful horizontal digging can alone, in the long run, give us the full information that we ideally want. Vertical dig-ging will, by itself, serve a valuable purpose in establishing the geographical distribution of a culture and its time-relationship with other cultures from place to place; but this evidence still derives its ultimate significance from a knowledge of the social environment of the cultures concerned. . . .

A PREHISTORIC BATTLE

*The reconstruction of the past from archaeological data requires
imagination, insight, and sound excavation technique combined with
impeccable recording. Maiden Castle is an Iron Age hill-fort in
southern England, which was sacked by the Romans in the first
century B.C. SIR MORTIMER WHEELER was able to portray the sacking of
the settlement in great detail by skillful inference from archaeological
data. His description is a classic example of the use of small finds to
reconstruct the past.*

THE EARLY ROMAN PERIOD (*c.* A.D. 43–70)

And so we reach the Roman invasion of A.D. 43. That part of the army of
conquest wherewith we are concerned in Dorset had as its nucleus the
Second Augustan Legion, whose commander, at any rate in the earlier
campaigns, was the future Emperor Vespasian. Precisely how soon the
invaders reached Maiden Castle can only be guessed, but by A.D. 47 the
Roman arms had reached the Severn, and Dorset must already have been
overrun. Suetonius affirms that Vespasian reduced "two very formidable
tribes and over twenty towns (*oppida*), together with the Isle of Wight,"
and it cannot be doubted that, whether or no the Durotriges (as is likely
enough) were one of the tribes in question, the conquest of the Wessex
hill-fort system is implied in the general statement. Nor is it improbable
that, with the hints provided by the mention of the Isle of Wight and
by the archaeological evidence for the subsequent presence of the Second
Legion near Seaton in eastern Devon, a main line of advance lay through
Dorset roughly along the route subsequently followed by the Roman road
to Exeter. From that road today the traveller regards the terraced ramparts
of the western entrance of Maiden Castle; and it requires no great effort
of the imagination to conjure up the ghost of Vespasian himself, here
confronted with the greatest of his "twenty towns." Indeed, something
less than imagination is now required to reconstruct the main sequence
of events at the storming of Maiden Castle, for the excavation of the

From *Maiden Castle* by Sir Mortimer Wheeler, Society of Antiquaries of London (1943), pp.
61–68. Reprinted by permission of the author and the Society of Antiquaries. Photograph
courtesy of Sir Mortimer Wheeler and the Society of Antiquaries. Footnotes and references
are omitted.

eastern entrance has yielded tangible evidence of it. With only a little amplification it may be reconstructed as follows.

Approaching from the direction of the Isle of Wight, Vespasian's legion may be supposed to have crossed the River Frome at the only easy crossing hereabouts—where Roman and modern Dorchester were subsequently to come into being. Before the advancing troops, some 2 miles away, the sevenfold ramparts of the western gates of Dunium towered above the cornfields which probably swept, like their modern successors, up to the fringe of the defenses. Whether any sort of assault was attempted upon these gates we do not at present know; their excessive strength makes it more likely that, leaving a guard upon them, Vespasian moved his main attack to the somewhat less formidable eastern end. What happened there is plain to read. First, the regiment of artillery, which normally accompanied a legion on campaign, was ordered into action, and put down a barrage of iron-shod ballista-arrows over the eastern part of the site. Following this barrage, the infantry advanced up the slope, cutting its way from rampart to rampart, tower to tower. In the innermost bay of the entrance, close outside the actual gates, a number of huts had recently been built; these were now set alight, and under the rising clouds of smoke the gates were stormed and the position carried. But resistance had been obstinate and the fury of the attackers was roused. For a space, confusion and massacre dominated the scene. Men and women, young and old, were savagely cut down, before the legionaries were called to heel and the work of systematic destruction began. That work included the uprooting of some at least of the timbers which revetted the fighting-platform on the summit of the main rampart; but above all it consisted of the demolition of the gates and the overthrow of the high stone walls which flanked the two portals. The walls were now reduced to the lowly and ruinous state in which they were discovered by the excavator nearly nineteen centuries later.

That night, when the fires of the legion shone out (we may imagine) in orderly lines across the valley, the survivors crept forth from their broken stronghold and, in the darkness, buried their dead as nearly as might be outside their tumbled gates, in that place where the ashes of their burned huts lay warm and thick upon the ground. The task was carried out anxiously and hastily and without order, but, even so, from few graves were omitted those tributes of food and drink which were the proper and traditional perquisites of the dead. At daylight on the morrow, the legion moved westward to fresh conquest, doubtless taking with it the usual levy of hostages from the vanquished.

Thereafter, salving what they could of their crops and herds, the disarmed townsfolk made shift to put their house in order. Forbidden to refortify their gates, they built new roadways across the sprawling ruins, between gateless ramparts that were already fast assuming the blunted profiles that are theirs today. And so, for some two decades, a demilitarized Maiden Castle retained its inhabitants, or at least a nucleus of them. Just so long did it take the Roman authorities to adjust the old order to the new, to prepare new towns for old. And then finally, on some day towards the close of the sixties of the century, the town was ceremonially abandoned, its remaining walls were formally "slighted," and Maiden Castle lapsed into the landscape among the farm-lands of Roman Dorchester.

So much for the story; now for its basis. First, scattered over the eastern end of Maiden Castle, mostly in and about the eastern entrance and always at the same Romano-Belgic level, were found upwards of a dozen iron arrowheads of two types: a type with a pyramidal point, and the simple flat-bladed type with turn-over socket. Arrowheads occurred at no other Iron Age level, but both types are common on Roman military sites where *ballistae* but not hand-bows are to be inferred. There, then, in the relatively small area uncovered, are the vestiges of the bombardment.

Secondly, the half-moon bay which represents the Iron Age B adaptation of the Iron Age A barbican, close outside the portals of the eastern entrance, was covered with a thick layer of ash associated with the postholes of three or more circular or roundish huts. In and immediately below this ash were quantities of late Belgic or "Belgicizing" pottery. In the surface of the ash was similar pottery with scraps of pre-Flavian Samian. There are the burned Belgic huts, covered by the trodden vestiges of the continued post-conquest occupation for which more tangible evidence will be offered shortly.

Thirdly, into this ash a series of graves had been roughly cut, with no regularity either of outline or of orientation, and into them had been thrown, in all manner of attitudes—crouched, extended, on the back, on the side, on the face, even sitting up—thirty-eight skeletons of men and women, young and old; sometimes two persons were huddled together in the same grave. In ten cases extensive cuts were present on the skull, some on the top, some on the front, some on the back. In another case, one of the arrowheads already described was found actually embedded in the vertebra, having entered the body from the front below the heart. The victim had been finished off with a cut on the head. Yet another skull had been pierced by an implement of square section, probably a ballista-bolt. The last two and some of the sword-cuts were doubtless battle-wounds; but one skull, which had received no less than nine savage cuts, suggests the fury of massacre rather than the tumult of battle—a man does not stay to kill his enemy eight or nine times in the melee; and the neck of another skeleton had been dislocated, probably by hanging. Nevertheless, the dead had been buried by their friends, for most of them were accompanied by bowls or, in one case, a mug for the traditional food and

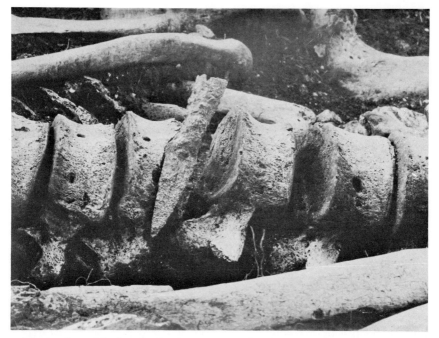

The battle at Maiden Castle. An iron arrowhead embedded in the backbone of a skeleton buried in the battle cemetery at the site.

drink. More notable, in two cases the dead held joints of lamb in their hands—joints chosen carefully as young and succulent. Many of the dead still wore their gear: armlets of iron or shale, an iron finger-ring, and in three cases bronze toe-rings, representing a custom not previously, it seems, observed in prehistoric Britain but reminiscent of the Moslem habit of wearing toe-rings as ornaments or as preventives or cures of disease. One man lay in a double grave with an iron battle-axe, a knife and, strangely, a bronze ear-pick across his chest. The whole war cemetery as it lay exposed before us was eloquent of mingled piety and distraction; of weariness, of dread, of darkness, but yet not of complete forgetfulness. Surely no poor relic in the soil of Britain was ever more eloquent of high tragedy, more worthy of brooding comment from the presiding Spirits of Hardy's own *Dynasts.*

The date of the cemetery was indicated by a variety of evidence. Most obvious is the Roman arrowhead embedded in the vertebra, but other associated relics point to the same conclusion. The seventeen pots put into the graves at the time of burial are all of that Wessex "Romano-Belgic overlap" class which has long been recognized at Jordan Hill, Weymouth, and elsewhere. The gear with one of the skeletons included, as has been remarked above, a Roman "ear-scoop," the use of which may or may not have been understood more clearly by its Belgic possessor than by the modern antiquary; at least it implies Roman contacts which, in Wessex, appear not long to have anticipated the Roman Conquest. One grave, moreover, contained a late British coin, and though it was impossible to say safely whether the coin was inserted at the interment or was incorporated in the loose ash into which the grave was cut, at least it was dropped within a very short time of the event. And finally, the materials included in the strata which "bracket" the cemetery are themselves, as noted above, sufficient to indicate a date at the end of the pre-Conquest period.

There, then, is the climax of the more human side of the story of conquest. But on the structural side the evidence for that event and for its sequel is no less vivid. On the topmost Belgic road-metal, in both portals of the eastern entrance but particularly in the southern, excavation revealed the tumbled stones from the massive walls that had formerly flanked the entrances. Here and there the fallen stones lay overlapping, like a collapsed pack of cards, in the sequence in which they had formerly stood as a vertical wall. With them was no cascade of rampart-earth such as might have implied a fall through subsidence, even could one presuppose the coincidence of the simultaneous fall of every part of the structure; the walls had been deliberately pulled down and no attempt had been made to replace them. But that was not all. Over the debris in each portal a new road had been built, metalled like the Belgic roads now buried beneath them. The new roads partially covered the surviving bases of the flanking walls, showing that the condition of these today is identical with their condition at the time of the road-building and confirming the permanence of the structural ruin. No provision of any kind was made in the new scheme for a gate; not a single post-hole was associated with the new road, and indeed the mutilated rampart-ends would have provided a poor setting for a fixed barrier. The implications of all this are evident. The entrance had been systematically "slighted" and its military value reduced permanently to a minimum; but traffic through it did not cease, no interval occurred in the continuity of the occupation.

That this dramatic episode should be ascribed to the Roman invader is proved by a liberal supply of associated evidence. The road-surface underlying the tumbled sidewalls in each portal is the last of a series of three or more which are all interleaved with British coins of the late "south-western" type, and with the coins were Belgic or cross-bred "BC" sherds, and fragments of Roman amphorae. Samian pottery was not found in these levels. On the other hand, in and on and beside the new road-surface which was laid down *over* the fallen walls, Samian sherds began to occur with some freedom. Where identifiable, these sherds are mainly of pre-Flavian type or fabric, and, in the whole of the eastern entrance, only *two* Samian sherds (both of them from the surface-soil) are later than the Flavian period. A detailed analysis, by Dr. T. Davies Pryce and Mr. J. A. Stanfield, . . . may here be summarized . . . :

Samian sherds from the eastern entrance
Datable fragments are assignable as follows:

To the pre-Flavian period	45
To the Nero-Vespasian period	9
To the Flavian period	4
To the Antonine period	2

Many small fragments, which do not admit of approximate dating, appear to be pre-Flavian.

Dr. Pryce concludes that the Samian from the entrance "indicates a definite occupation in the pre-Flavian period. The evidence for its continuation into the Flavian period is slight." It should be emphasized that seventeen of these Samian sherds, all ascribed by Dr. Pryce to the time of Claudius and Nero, were found embedded either in the road-metal of the new road in the southern portal (where the structural evidence was clearest) or in the layer of trodden mud upon its surface. On the other hand, the two Antonine sherds were both, as already remarked, in mixed topsoil.

Two conclusions emerge from this structural and ceramic evidence. First, the destruction of the sidewalls of the entrance occurs exactly between the Belgic and the Claudian occupation of the site: i.e., at the moment of the Roman invasion. Secondly, the occupation of the site continued, in spite of this interruption, to the beginning of the Flavian period, i.e., to *c.* A.D. 70, whereafter a break supervened. Other evidence amplifies this result.

A test-section cut through the rampart between the portals of the entrance revealed one of the large post-holes of the Belgic palisade or revetment. The post, like its equivalents on site E, had been about a foot in diameter, and its socket was 4 ft. deep. At a depth of 2 ft. in the filling of the socket (and 4 ft. from the present surface) occurred a Samian sherd of distinctively early fabric, and in the same filling were two bronze scales of a Roman cuirass. These objects indicate that the socket was empty in early Roman times, and the complete uniformity of the filling indicates rather the uprooting of the post than its gradual decay. There is at least a strong probability that the slighting of the entrance was accompanied by a removal of the stockade along the rampart.

Further, on sites L and Q, on the summit of the eastern knoll within the camp, a considerable quantity of Samian pottery was brought to light. The sherds . . . from the main occupation may be considered in summary here. . . . On this site, the thick layer of Belgic occupation passed, without structural division, into the early Roman, and its topmost portion contained Samian pottery. This has been examined by Dr. Pryce, who reports that every sherd is Flavian or pre-Flavian, with a strong predominance of the latter: the evidence for occupation actually within the Flavian period is "very meagre." In other words, the evidence here—and, it may be added, elsewhere in Maiden Castle—tallies exactly with that of the eastern entrance.

The picture is now complete in outline. Disarmed at the Roman Conquest, Maiden Castle remained in use for about a quarter of a century after the invasion, a pre-Roman city still in all essentials, partaking only a little of the cultural equipment of its conquerors. The picture is a reasonable and convincing one. The first generation of Roman rule was preoccupied with the subjugation of the difficult hill-countries of the north and west, with the development of mining areas, the planning of arterial roads, the founding or development of those few towns which had an immediate military or commercial function. Dorset offered, it is true, iron ore on a modest scale; but between Sussex and the Mendips there was little mineral wealth to attract the Roman prospector in the first flush of conquest. Wessex could wait. There was no urgent need to upset the traditional economic basis of the urbanized peasantry which crowded the downlands. To do so would have been to court added political difficulties at a time when difficulties were already manifold. It was better that, under surveillance, the Wessex farmers should for a time (and doubtless in return for the periodical payment of just or unjust dues) be allowed to maintain themselves in the fashion which they knew. The removal or, alternatively, the ennoblement of their rulers would rob them of independent leadership. A few police-patrols would do the rest.

Here, too, the evidence fits comfortably into place. The famous little Roman fort set in a corner of the Iron Age town on Hod Hill near Blandford—some 20 miles from Maiden Castle—has not been scientifically excavated, but pottery and other objects have been recovered at various times from it or its immediate vicinity. This material includes many Roman weapons and some Samian pottery dating from the time of Claudius and Nero. The occupation, in other words, was something more than transitory, and would appear to have lasted approximately from the time of the Roman invasion to c. A.D. 60 or a little later. With this supposition the comparatively elaborate plan of the Roman earthwork agrees: it is not that of a mere "marching camp," But rather that of a "semi-permanent" work possessing some of the attributes of a permanent fort. At its strategic point above the valley of the Stour, this little Roman hill-fort was a fitting center for the policing of a part of the native hill-town region during the interval between conquest and romanization.

The period of guarded *status quo* came to an end, it seems, in the reign of the actual conqueror of Maiden Castle. Under Vespasian and Domitian, notably in the governorship of Agricola, the systematic development of the civil life of Roman Britain was at last undertaken throughout the lowland region. Hitherto such development had been in a large measure opportunist; it now became an avowed part of the official policy for the final and complete subjugation of the provincials. Towns were rebuilt in the comfortable Roman fashion or were newly founded; and among the new foundations—if the available evidence is representative—would appear to have been Dorchester, Durnonovaria or Durnovaria of the Itinerary. Of seventy-five Samian sherds from Dorchester, examined by Dr. Pryce in the Dorchester Museum, four or less are likely to be earlier than Vespasian. The proportions of early and late sherds, on a comparison of the groups from Dorchester with those from the main occupation of Maiden Castle, are thus approximately reversed; and, on the evidence, it may be affirmed provisionally that the occupation of the two sites is complementary. Dorchester begins where Maiden Castle ceases, i.e., *c.* A.D. 70. The sequence is doubtless significant. In Gaul under Augustus the process of romanization had entailed the removal of the more inaccessible hill-populations to new Roman cities founded under official auspices in the valleys. In Britain it is reasonable to suppose that, in the equivalent regime of the Flavians, a similar procedure was followed: that Flavian Caerwent, for example, became the Roman focus for the little native towns of Llanmelin and Sudbrook, that Uriconium was (then if not earlier) the heir of the *oppidum* on the Wrekin, and similarly that Roman Dorchester inherited something of the population and the prestige of Maiden Castle. Certain it is, at least, that after the beginning of the Flavian period the eastern entrance of Maiden Castle fell into disuse. A layer of humus 7–9 in. deep was found to overlie the early Roman road-surfaces, implying that the site was, at the end of the first century A.D., as overgrown as in modern times. When we come to examine the final phase of Maiden Castle, it will be seen that this layer of barren mould intervenes between the first- and the fourth-century levels, so that its context is not open to doubt. In the second and third centuries A.D. Maiden Castle had reverted to downland or to tillage.

Of the actual moment of the official abandonment of the site, a vestige may indeed be recognized with some probability at the fruitful eastern entrance. Reference has been made in a preceding section to the stone-faced platform or bastion on the western flank of the southern causeway cut through the original barbican in phase IV (*c.* end of first century B.C. or beginning of first century A.D.). As excavated in 1936, this revetment was preserved to a maximum height of five courses; but the remainder of the wall still lay piled up alongside, upon the metalling of the roadway. The evidence compelled certain inferences:

(i) The wall had been *deliberately* pulled away from the bank which it revetted, for the bank itself stood firm and had not fallen forward with the masonry, as would have been the case if the latter had been thrust outwards by pressure from the bank.

(ii) The wall had not been demolished for the reuse of its stonework, since the fallen stones lay untouched where they had fallen.

(iii) The fallen stones lay on, and in contact with, the actual metalling of the road: i.e., they had fallen when the road was still in use and unencumbered with the covering of wind-blown earth which (as experience shows) accumulates within a month on exposed surfaces at Maiden Castle.

(iv) Both the road and the adjacent city went out of use immediately after the fall, since the debris blocked a good half of the roadway and—an important point on a stoneless site where stone is proportionately valuable —had not been appreciably plundered for its useful building-material.

It is fair to infer that this important and striking structural feature of the entrance had been "slighted" deliberately at the precise moment when the population was finally moved down from the ancient city to the new Roman town which must now have been prepared in the valley below. It is not difficult to imagine something of the pomp and circumstance with which this revolutionary incident in the history of the region was carried out—the solemn procession of civic and religious authorities, perhaps with some rather anxiously important emissary of the provincial government in attendance; and the ultimate ceremonial defacement of a work which had already, a generation previously, received its first and more drastic disarming at the moment of conquest—the earlier slighting carried out, perhaps, at the actual order of Vespasian, commander of the Second Legion, and the later slighting under the remote eye of Vespasian, now emperor of Rome.

CHAPTER FIVE

𐃏𐃏𐃏𐃏𐃏𐃏𐃏𐃏𐃏𐃏𐃏𐃏𐃏𐃏𐃏

Prehistoric Economies

Economic archaeology has been a neglected field
until recent years, when the importance of
ecology, environment, and economy in interpreting
prehistoric culture change was finally realized.
The extracts in this chapter are drawn
from several areas of the world, and show
a variety of approaches to economic evidence.
Most of them are little known papers,
although Iversen's is a classic example of
the application of palynology to archaeology
and has been widely quoted in
archaeological literature.

A PALEO-INDIAN BISON KILL

Economic evidence from archaeological sites drawn from animal
bones and organic remains is normally incomplete. Occasionally,
however, the archaeologist is able to make astonishingly complete
reconstructions of life in the past, especially at butchery sites.
JOE BEN WHEAT's article is a succinct description of a bison-kill
site in Colorado and gives a vivid impression of the excitement of
a game drive.

When one thinks of American Indians hunting buffaloes, one usually visualizes the hunters pursuing a herd of the animals on horseback and killing them with bow and arrow. Did the Indians hunt buffaloes before the introduction of the horse (by the Spanish conquistadors in the sixteenth century) and the much earlier introduction of the bow? Indeed they did. As early as 10,000 years ago Paleo-Indians hunted species of bison that are now extinct on foot and with spears. My colleagues and I at the University of Colorado Museum have recently excavated the site of one such Paleo-Indian bison kill dating back to about 6500 B.C. The site so remarkably preserves a moment in time that we know with reasonable certainty not only the month of the year the hunt took place but also such details

135

Site of the kill is 140 miles southeast of Denver. It is named the Olsen-Chubbuck site after its discoverers, the amateur archaeologists Sigurd Olsen and Gerald Chubbuck.

as the way the wind blew on the day of the kill, the direction of the hunters' drive, the highly organized manner in which they butchered their quarry, their choice of cuts to be eaten on the spot and the probable number of hunters involved.

The bison was the most important game animal in North America for millenniums before its near extermination in the nineteenth century. When Europeans arrived on the continent, they found herds of bison ranging over vast areas, but the animals were first and foremost inhabitants of the Great Plains, the high, semiarid grassland extending eastward from the foothills of the Rocky Mountains and all the way from Canada to Mexico. Both in historic and in late prehistoric times the bison was the principal economic resource of the Indian tribes that occupied the Great Plains. Its meat, fat and bone marrow provided them with food; its hide furnished them with shelter and clothing; its brains was used to tan the hide; its horns were fashioned into containers. There was scarcely a part of the animal that was not utilized in some way.

This dependence on big-game hunting probably stretches back to the very beginning of human prehistory in the New World. We do not know when man first arrived in the Americas, nor do we know in detail what cultural baggage he brought with him. The evidence for the presence of man in the New World much before 12,000 years ago is scattered and controversial. It is quite clear, however, that from then on Paleo-Indian hunting groups, using distinctive kinds of stone projectile point, ranged widely throughout the New World. On the Great Plains the principal game animal of this early period was the Columbian mammoth [see "Elephant-hunting in North America," by C. Vance Haynes, Jr.; *Scientific American*, June, 1966]. Mammoth remains have been found in association with projectile points that are usually large and leaf-shaped and have short, broad grooves on both sides of the base. These points are typical of the complex of cultural traits named the Clovis complex; the tool kit of this complex also included stone scrapers and knives and some artifacts made of ivory and bone.

The elephant may have been hunted out by 8000 B.C. In any case, its place as a game animal was taken by a large, straight-horned bison known as *Bison antiquus*. The first of the bison-hunters used projectile points of the Folsom culture complex; these are similar to Clovis points but are generally smaller and better made. Various stone scrapers and knives, bone needles and engraved bone ornaments have also been found in Folsom sites.

A millennium later, about 7000 B.C., *Bison antiquus* was supplanted on the Great Plains by the somewhat smaller *Bison occidentalis*. The projectile points found in association with this animal's remains are of several kinds. They differ in shape, size and details of flaking, but they have some characteristics in common. Chief among them is the technical excellence of the flaking. The flake scars meet at the center of the blade to form a ridge; sometimes they give the impression that a single flake has been detached across the entire width of the blade. Some of the projectile points that belong to this tradition, which take their names from the sites where they were first found, are called Milnesand, Scottsbluff and Eden points. The last two kinds of point form part of what is called the Cody complex, for which there is a fairly reliable carbon 14 date of about 6500 B.C.

Paleo-Indian archaeological sites fall into two categories: habitations and kill sites. Much of our knowledge of the early inhabitants of the Great Plains comes from the kill sites, where are found not only the bones of the animals but also the projectile points used to kill them and the knives, scrapers and other tools used to butcher and otherwise process them. Such sites have yielded much information about the categories of projectile points and how these categories are related in time. Heretofore, however, they have contributed little to our understanding of how the early hunters actually lived. The kill site I shall describe is one of those rare archaeological sites where the evidence is so complete that the people who left it seem almost to come to life.

Sixteen miles southeast of the town of Kit Carson in southeastern Colorado, just below the northern edge of the broad valley of the Arkansas River, lies a small valley near the crest of a low divide. The climate here is semiarid; short bunchgrass is the main vegetation and drought conditions have prevailed since the mid-1950s. In late 1957 wind erosion exposed what appeared to be five separate piles of bones, aligned in an east-west direction. Gerald Chubbuck, a keen amateur archaeologist, came on the bones in December, 1957; among them he found several projectile points of the Scottsbluff type. Chubbuck notified the University of Colorado Museum of his find, and we made plans to visit the site at the first opportunity.

Meanwhile Chubbuck and another amateur archaeologist, Sigurd Olsen, continued to collect at the site and ultimately excavated nearly a third of it. In the late spring of 1958 the museum secured permission from the two discoverers and from Paul Forward, the owner of the land, to complete the excavation. We carried out this work on summer expeditions in 1958 and 1960.

The Olsen-Chubbuck site consists of a continuous bed of bones lying within the confines of a small arroyo, or dry gulch. The arroyo, which had long since been buried, originally rose near the southern end of the valley and followed a gently undulating course eastward through a ridge that forms the valley's eastern edge. The section of the arroyo that we excavated was some 200 feet long. Its narrow western end was only about a foot and a half in depth and the same in width, but it grew progressively deeper and wider to the east. Halfway down the arroyo its width was five feet and its depth six; at the point to the east where our excavation stopped it was some 12 feet wide and seven feet deep. At the bottom of the arroyo for its entire length was a channel about a foot wide; above the channel the walls of the arroyo had a V-shaped cross-section.

Today the drainage pattern of the site runs from north to south. This was probably the case when the arroyo was formed, and since it runs east and west it seems certain that it was not formed by stream action. Early frontiersmen on the Great Plains observed that many buffalo trails led away from watering places at right angles to the drainage pattern. Where such trails crossed ridges they were frequently quite deep; moreover, when they were abandoned they were often further deepened by erosion. The

Bones of bison unearthed at the Olsen-Chubbuck site lie in a long row down the center of the ancient arroyo the Paleo-Indian hunters utilized as a pitfall for the stampeding herd. The bones proved to be the remains of bulls, cows and calves of the extinct species *Bison occidentalis.* Separate piles made up of the same types of bones (for example, sets of limb bones, pelvic girdles, or skulls) showed that the hunters had butchered several bison at a time and had systematically dumped the bones into the arroyo in the same order in which they were removed from the carcasses. In the foreground is a pile of skulls that was built up in this way.

similarity of the Olsen-Chubbuck arroyo to such historical buffalo trails strongly suggests an identical origin.

The deposit of bison bones that filled the bottom of the arroyo was a little more than 170 feet long. It consisted of the remains of nearly 200 buffaloes of the species *Bison occidentalis*. Chubbuck and Olsen unearthed the bones of an estimated 50 of the animals; the museum's excavations uncovered the bones of 143 more. The bones were found in three distinct layers. The bottom layer contained some 13 complete skeletons; the hunters had not touched these animals. Above this layer were several essentially complete skeletons from which a leg or two, some ribs or the skull were missing; these bison had been only partly butchered. In the top layer were numerous single bones and also nearly 500 articulated segments of buffalo skeleton. The way in which these segments and the single bones were distributed provides a number of clues to the hunters' butchering techniques.

As the contents of the arroyo—particularly the complete skeletons at the bottom—make clear, it had been a trap into which the hunters had stampeded the bison. Bison are gregarious animals. They move in herds in search of forage; the usual grazing herd is between 50 and 300 animals. Bison have a keen sense of smell but relatively poor vision. Hunters can thus get very close to a herd as long as they stay downwind and largely out of sight. When the bison are frightened, the herd has a tendency to close ranks and stampede in a single mass. If the herd encounters an abrupt declivity such as the Olsen-Chubbuck arroyo, the animals in front cannot stop because they are pushed by those behind. They can only plunge into the arroyo, where they are immobilized, disabled or killed by the animals that fall on top of them.

The orientation of the skeletons in the middle and lower layers of the Olsen-Chubbuck site is evidence that the Paleo-Indian hunters had initiated such a stampede. Almost without exception the complete or nearly complete skeletons overlie or are overlain by the skeletons of one, two or even three other whole or nearly whole animals; the bones are massed and the skeletons are contorted. The first animals that fell into the arroyo had no chance to escape; those behind them wedged them tighter into the arroyo with their struggles. Many of the skeletons are sharply twisted around the axis of the spinal column. Three spanned the arroyo, deformed into an unnatural U shape. Ten bison were pinned in position with their heads down and their hindquarters up; an equal number had landed with hindquarters down and heads up. At the bottom of the arroyo two skeletons lie on their backs.

The stampeding bison were almost certainly running in a north-south direction, at right angles to the arroyo. Of the 39 whole or nearly whole skeletons, which may be assumed to lie in the positions in which the ani-

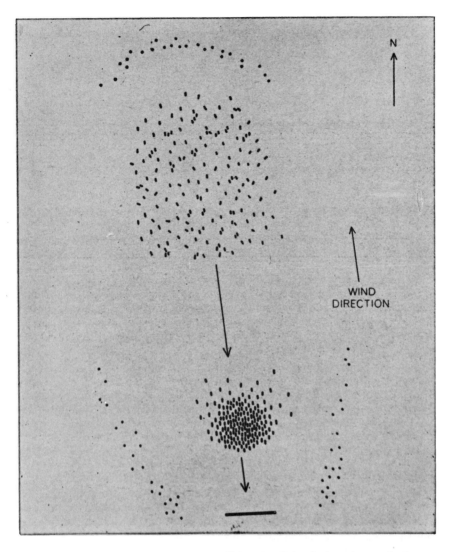

Bison stampede was probably set off by the Paleo-Indian hunters' close approach to the grazing herd from downwind. Projectile points found among the bones of the animals at the eastern end of the arroyo (*bottom*) suggest that some hunters kept the bison from veering eastward to escape. Other hunters probably did the same at the western end of the arroyo.

mals died, not one faces north, northeast or northwest. A few skeletons, confined in the arroyo's narrow inner channel, face due east or west, but all 21 animals whose position at the time of death was not affected in this

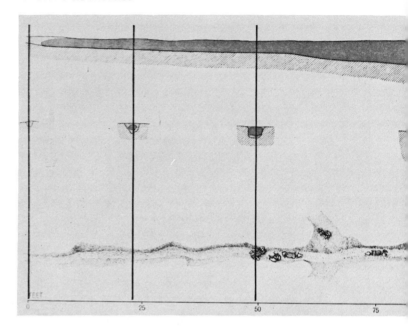

Section and plan of the Olsen-Chubbuck site show how the remains of the
dead and butchered bison formed a deposit of bones that lined the center
of the arroyo for a distance of 170 feet (top). One part of the site had been
excavated by its discoverers before the author and his associates began work
in 1958; this area is represented by the 20-foot gap in the deposit. The
shallow inner channel at the bottom of the arroyo can be seen in the plan
view (*bottom*); outlines show the locations of 13 intact bison skeletons.

manner faced southeast, south or southwest. The direction in which the
bison stampeded provides a strong clue to the way the wind was blowing
on the day of the hunt. The hunters would surely have approached their
quarry from downwind; thus the wind must have been from the south.

We have only meager evidence of the extent to which the stampede,
once started, was directed and controlled by the hunters. The projectile
points found with the bison skeletons in the deepest, most easterly part
of the arroyo suggest that a flanking party of hunters was stationed there.
It also seems a reasonable inference that, if no hunters had covered the
stampede's western flank, the herd could have escaped unscathed around
the head of the arroyo. If other hunters pursued the herd from the rear,
there is no evidence of it.

Even if the hunters merely started the stampede and did not control it
thereafter, it sufficed to kill almost 200 animals in a matter of minutes.
The total was 46 adult bulls and 27 immature ones, 63 adult and 38 im-

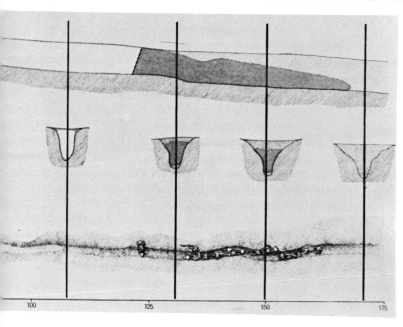

mature cows and 16 calves. From the fact that the bones include those of calves only a few days old, and from what we know about the breeding season of bison, we can confidently place the date of the kill as being late in May or early in June.

As we excavated the bone deposit we first uncovered the upper layer containing the single bones and articulated segments of skeleton. It was soon apparent that these bones were the end result of a standardized Paleo-Indian butchering procedure. We came to recognize certain "butchering units" such as forelegs, pelvic girdles, hind legs, spinal columns and skulls. Units of the same kind were usually found together in groups numbering from two or three to as many as 27. Similar units also formed distinct vertical sequences. As the hunters had removed the meat from the various units they had discarded the bones in separate piles, each of which contained the remains of a number of individual animals. In all we excavated nine such piles.

Where the order of deposition was clear, the bones at the bottom of each pile were foreleg units. Above these bones were those of pelvic-girdle units. Sometimes one or both hind legs were attached to the pelvic girdle, but by and large the hind-leg units lay separately among or above the pelvic units. The next level was usually composed of spinal-column units. The ribs had been removed from many of the chest vertebrae, but ribs were still attached to some of the other vertebrae. At the top of

Bison skull and stone point lie in close association at one level in the site. The projectile point (*lower left*) is of the Scottsbluff type. The bison skull, labeled 4-F to record its position among the other bones, rests upside down where the hunters threw it.

nearly every pile were skulls. The jawbones had been removed from most of them, but some still retained a few of the neck vertebrae. In some instances these vertebrae had been pulled forward over the top and down the front of the skull. When the skull still had its jawbone, the hyoid bone of the tongue was missing.

Like the various butchering units, the single bones were found in clusters of the same skeletal part: shoulder blades, upper-foreleg bones, upper-hind-leg bones or jawbones (all broken in two at the front). Nearly all the jawbones were found near the top of the bone deposit. The tongue bones, on the other hand, were distributed throughout the bed. About 75 percent of the single foreleg bones were found in the upper part of the deposit, as were nearly 70 percent of the single vertebrae. Only 60 percent of the shoulder blades and scarcely half of the single ribs were in the upper level.

The hunters' first task had evidently been to get the bison carcasses into a position where they could be cut up. This meant that the animals had to be lifted, pulled, rolled or otherwise moved out of the arroyo to some flat area. It seems to have been impossible to remove the bison that lay at the bottom of the arroyo; perhaps they were too tightly wedged together. Some of them had been left untouched and others had had only a few accessible parts removed. The way in which the butchering units were grouped suggests that several bison were moved into position and cut up simultaneously. Since foreleg units, sometimes in pairs, were found at the bottom of each pile of bones it seems reasonable to assume that the Paleo-Indians followed the same initial steps in butchering that the Plains Indians did in recent times. The first step was to arrange the legs of the animal so that it could be rolled onto its belly. The skin was then cut down the back and pulled down on both sides of the carcass to form a kind of mat on which the meat could be placed. Directly under the skin of the back was a layer of tender meat, the "blanket of flesh"; when this was stripped away, the bison's forelegs and shoulder blades could be cut free, exposing the highly prized "hump" meat, the rib cage and the body cavity.

Having stripped the front legs of meat, the hunters threw the still-articulated bones into the arroyo. If they followed the practice of later Indians, they would next have indulged themselves by cutting into the body cavity, removing some of the internal organs and eating them raw.

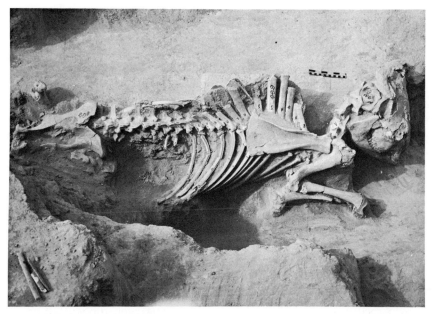

Intact skeleton of an immature bison cow, uncovered in the lowest level of the arroyo, is one of 13 animals the Paleo-Indian hunters left untouched. The direction in which many bison faced suggests that the stampede traveled from north to south.

This, of course, would have left no evidence among the bones. What is certain is that the hunters did remove and eat the tongues of a few bison at this stage of the butchering, presumably in the same way the Plains Indians did: by slitting the throat, pulling the tongue out through the slit and cutting it off. Our evidence for their having eaten the tongues as they went along is that the tongue bones are found throughout the deposit instead of in one layer or another.

The bison's rib cages were attacked as soon as they were exposed by the removal of the overlying meat. Many of the ribs were broken off near the spine. The Plains Indians used as a hammer for this purpose a bison leg bone with the hoof still attached; perhaps the Paleo-Indians did the same. In any case, the next step was to sever the spine at a point behind the rib cage and remove the hindquarters. The meat was cut away from the pelvis (and in some instances simultaneously from the hind legs) and the pelvic girdle was discarded. If the hind legs had been separated from the pelvis, it was now their turn to be stripped of meat and discarded.

After the bison's hindquarters had been butchered, the neck and skull were cut off as a unit—usually at a point just in front of the rib cage— and set aside. Then the spine was discarded, presumably after it had been completely stripped of meat and sinew. Next the hunters turned to the neck and skull and cut the neck meat away. This is evident from the skulls that had vertebrae draped over the front; this would not have been pos- sible if the neck meat had been in place. The Plains Indians found bison neck meat too tough to eat in its original state. They dried it and made the dried strips into pemmican by pounding them to a powder. The fact that the Paleo-Indians cut off the neck meat strongly suggests that they too preserved some of their kill.

If the tongue had not already been removed, the jawbone was now cut away, broken at the front and the tongue cut out. The horns were broken from a few skulls, but there is little evidence that the Paleo-Indians broke open the skull as the Plains Indians did to take out the brain. Perhaps the most striking difference between the butchering practices of these earlier Indians and those of later ones, however, lies in the high degree of or- ganization displayed by the Paleo-Indians. Historical accounts of butchering by Plains Indians indicate no such efficient system.

In all, 47 artifacts were found in association with the bones at the Olsen- Chubbuck site. Spherical hammerstones and knives give us some idea of what constituted the hunter's tool kit; stone scrapers suggest that the bison's skins were processed at the site. A bone pin and a piece of the brown rock limonite that shows signs of having been rubbed tell some- thing about Paleo-Indian ornamentation.

The bulk of the artifacts at the site are projectile points. There are 27 of them, and they are particularly significant. Most of them are of the

Scottsbluff type. When their range of variation is considered, however, they merge gradually at one end of the curve of variation into Eden points and at the other end into Milnesand points. Moreover, among the projectile points found at the site are one Eden point and a number of Milnesand points. The diversity of the points clearly demonstrates the range of variation that was possible among the weapons of a single hunting group. Their occurrence together at the site is conclusive proof that such divergent forms of weapon could exist contemporaneously.

How many Paleo-Indians were present at the kill? The answer to this question need not be completely conjectural. We can start with what we know about the consumption of bison meat by Plains Indians. During a feast a man could consume from 10 to 20 pounds of fresh meat a day; women and children obviously ate less. The Plains Indians also preserved bison meat by drying it; 100 pounds of fresh meat would provide 20 pounds of dried meat. A bison bull of today yields about 550 pounds of edible meat; cows average 400 pounds. For an immature bull one can allow 165 pounds of edible meat, for an immature cow 110 pounds and for a calf 50 pounds. About 75 percent of the bison killed at the Olsen-Chubbuck site were completely butchered; on this basis the total weight of bison meat would have been 45,300 pounds. The *Bison occidentalis* killed by the Paleo-Indian hunters, however, was considerably larger than the *Bison bison* of modern times. To compensate for the difference it seems reasonable to add 25 percent to the weight estimate, bringing it to a total of 56,640 pounds. To this total should be added some 4,000 pounds of edible internal organs and 5,400 pounds of fat.

A Plains Indian could completely butcher a bison in about an hour. If we allow one and a half hours for the dissection of the larger species, the butchering at the Olsen-Chubbuck site would have occupied about 210 man-hours. In other words, 100 people could easily have done the job in half a day.

To carry the analysis further additional assumptions are needed. How long does fresh buffalo meat last? The experience of the Plains Indians (depending, of course, on weather conditions) was that it could be eaten for about a month. Let us now assume that half of the total weight of the Olsen-Chubbuck kill was eaten fresh at an average rate of 10 pounds per person per day, and that the other half was preserved. Such a division would provide enough fresh meat and fat to feed 150 people for 23 days. It seems reasonable to assume that the Paleo-Indian band was about this size. One way to test this assumption is to calculate the load each person would have to carry when camp was broken.

The preserved meat and fat, together with the hides, would have weighed about 7,350 pounds, which represents a burden of 49 pounds for each man, woman and child in the group (in addition to the weight of whatever other necessities they carried). Plains Indians are known to have

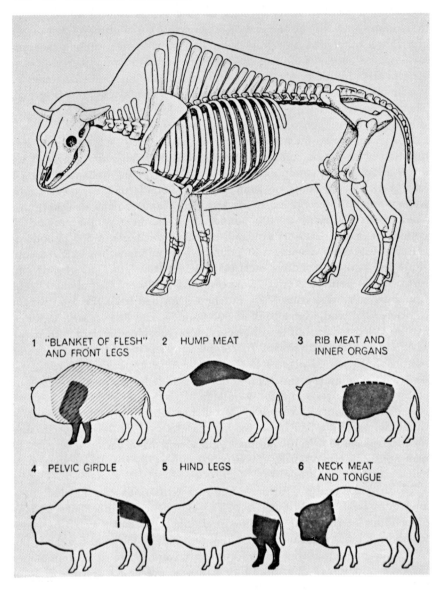

1 "BLANKET OF FLESH" AND FRONT LEGS 2 HUMP MEAT 3 RIB MEAT AND INNER ORGANS

4 PELVIC GIRDLE 5 HIND LEGS 6 NECK MEAT AND TONGUE

Butchering methods used by the Paleo-Indians have been reconstructed on the dual basis of bone stratification at the Olsen-Chubbuck site and the practices of the Plains Indians in recent times. Once the carcass of the bison (*skeleton at top*) had been propped up and skinned down the back, a series of "butchering units" probably were removed in the order shown on the numbered outline figures. The hunters ate as they worked.

borne loads as great as 100 pounds. Taking into account the likelihood that small children and active hunters would have carried smaller loads, a 49-pound average appears to be just within the range of possibility.

A band of 150 people could, however, have eaten two-thirds of the kill fresh and preserved only one-third. In that case the fresh meat would have fed them for somewhat more than a month. At the end the meat would have been rather gamy, but the load of preserved meat per person would have been reduced to the more reasonable average of 31 pounds.

One possibility I have left out is that the Paleo-Indians had dogs. If there were dogs available to eat their share of fresh meat and to carry loads of preserved meat, the number of people in the group may have been somewhat less. In the absence of dogs, however, it seems improbable that any fewer than 150 people could have made use of the bison killed at the Olsen-Chubbuck site to the degree that has been revealed by our excavations. Whether or not the group had dogs, the remains of its stay at the site are unmistakable evidence that hunting bands of considerable size and impressive social organization were supporting themselves on the Great Plains some 8,500 years ago.

DOMESTIC ANIMALS AND AGRICULTURE

Domestic animals and their grazing habits exercised a profound effect on the prehistoric environment, and in turn were affected by forest clearance and the development of agriculture. CHARLES F. W. HIGHAM's analyses of European domestic animals have been skillfully combined with evidence from other sources to reconstruct the economic prehistory of Switzerland. The quoted passages summarize some of his conclusions.

📖 The assessment of prehistoric methods and aims of stock rearing depends on the availability of modern comparative bone samples. These samples should derive from animals of known sex and breed, and where

From "Stock Rearing as a Cultural Factor in Prehistoric Europe" by Charles F. W. Higham, *Proceedings of the Prehistoric Society* 33, No. 6 (1967) 99–103. Reprinted by permission of the author and the Prehistoric Society. Footnotes are omitted.

possible, of age and plane of nutrition. Two such samples have been collected for bovine, and one each for sheep and goats. By establishing the degree of variance and extent of sexual dimorphism for given measurements from specific anatomical bones, it has been possible to order potential reasons for the distribution of corresponding prehistoric bones in terms of their plausibility. The application of statistical methods of study to prehistoric faunal samples has thus provided information of direct relevance to the prehistorian.

Younger Cortaillod faunal samples are both large and numerous. Analysis has shown that the aims of the stock rearers at all sites examined bear the stamp of a common tradition. All Cortaillod sites were situated in a similar physical and floral environment, yet their economy was no slavish upshot of environmental dictat: three other prehistoric cultures, each displaying similar technological abilities, adapted the composition of their herds to the same environment in quite different ways. As soon as different environmental conditions were encountered however, the stock rearing aims of the Michelsberg and Horgen Cultures, as seen in the relative numerical importance of each domestic species, changed both radically and logically.

Pollen studies have provided information basic to an understanding of man's effect on the environment. The examination of technological processes and critical artefact types, in particular the axe, reveal a correlation between technological proficiency and the intensity of forest clearance. Results of faunal studies suggest that the aims of stock rearing integrated with the agricultural methods and technological attainments of prehistoric societies in Switzerland.

Welten's assessment of the Cortaillod pollen spectra as being indicative of agriculture undertaken in small forest clearings holds also for the Michelsberg Culture occupation of Thayngen-Weier. Increases in charcoal fragments in Cortaillod pollen samples during the earliest phase of occupation suggests strongly that fields were created by burning part of the forest cover, a situation which allows their agriculture to be described as *Brandwirtschaft*. Such a method entails a constant search for virgin soil, and is reflected in the short occupation phases of Egolzwil 3, Thayngen-Weier and the Burgäschi Lake sites.

While Cortaillod and Michelsberg Cultures were in part contemporary, and both occupied lakeshore or riverine sites in the lowlands, there was hardly any territorial overlap between their settlements. Moreover, not only their technological capabilities, but also the essential elements of their respective economies were similar. Thus at Ehrenstein and at the Cortaillod sites which have been considered, a substantial number of bovines were killed when under a year of age. Such an attitude towards bovine husbandry clearly integrates with hoe-agriculture in forest plots:

there is no evidence for the maintenance of or need for working oxen from the settlements of either culture.

The mutually exclusive territorial distribution of the Michelsberg and Cortaillod Cultures is extremely unlikely to result from chance alone. The similar levels of technology and economic attitudes of the two cultures have been observed: it is tempting to view such distributions as the result of the contemporaneous presence of two groups of farmers deploying similar abilities and attributes.

Both those cultures were superseded by the Horgen Culture. While its origins remain obscure, it would appear as feasible to see the Horgen Culture as a westward extension of the Pfyn and Jevisovice Groups, as it would be to view it as an eastward extension from France. Although there is insufficient evidence to permit a detailed reconstruction of the Horgen economy, Childe's derogatory assessment of this culture's abilities appears to be premature. Despite Childe's claim, hunting did not increase significantly over the levels recorded for the Younger Cortaillod Culture, and in some cases, was considerably less. Moreover, the evidence for a woollen textile industry, combined with that for a relative increase in the numbers of swine kept by this culture, may well indicate a more rational utilization of environmental resources than was hitherto the case. Therefore, although the definition of the factors underlying the spread of the Horgen Culture requires further faunal samples and evaluated pollen spectra, it is asserted that an unsophisticated approach to arts and crafts need not necessarily accompany an unsophisticated economy.

The westward expansion of the Corded Ware Culture has commonly been ascribed to migrations of warrior nomad pastoralists. Moreover, recent palynological investigations of Standvoetbeker Culture burial mounds in Holland have shown that the degree of forest clearance undertaken just prior to the construction of the mounds was considerably greater, in the Drenthe area at least, than was the case for the Megalithic Funnel-Necked Beaker Culture.

It should be noted, however, that not only pasture indicators, but also the fraction of cereal pollen increased over levels recorded for the Funnel-Necked Beaker Culture. Furthermore, the presence of furrows under the Corded Ware Culture burial mound of Aldrupgaarde, as well as the presence of grain impressions on the corded ware itself, suggest strongly that agriculture, aided by the ox-drawn ard, played a prominent role in the Corded Ware economy. A widespread cultural complex combining the knowledge of ox traction, the ard and copper metallurgy in association with evidence for intensified forest clearance and establishment of pastureland in addition to cereal fields, was clearly of crucial importance in the early economic history of Central Europe. A picture of efficient mixed farmers who by means of the ard developed a more productive economy than was practiced by their predecessors, is held to be a more accurate assessment of the Corded Ware Culture than that of bands of warrior nomads.

The features apparent in the Corded Ware Culture economy are paralleled at Arbon Bleiche, where increased forest clearance and the establishment of pastureland attest a more efficient economy than any of those documented for the Middle Neolithic period. By conditioning the local vegetation to fit their requirements, the Early Bronze Age farmers were able to overwinter more cattle and sheep, and ensure thereby a greater supply of food, hides and basic raw materials than was available during the Neolithic Period. Moreover, a continuation of ard agriculture would have led to increased agricultural productivity. Thus, by fostering food bearing trees and creating pastureland, an environment was developed which permitted an expansion of human population.

The fraction of pasture indicators in the Zug Sumpf pollen spectrum reflects yet more forest clearance than was the case for the Early Bronze Age. Nevertheless, the surviving areas of woodland would have enabled the inhabitants to utilize the resources of both forest and pasture. Moreover, the present interpretation of the Late Bronze Age stock rearing attitudes reveals an integration with the economy as a whole: a number of adult oxen were maintained for draught purposes, while the increased fraction of sheep may well reflect their [foaling] as well as wool-bearing qualities. Indeed, the distribution of the Urnfield Culture over so much of Central Europe may be seen as a direct result of the sophisticated way in which the potentialities of bronze were exploited for the development of an economically effective symbiosis between flora and fauna.

The assertion that stock rearing and agriculture absorbed the greater part of the energy, time and skill of the prehistoric farmer in Switzerland necessitates a consideration of the limiting factors exercised by the environment upon his activities. Modern farming in the Alpine Foreland is restricted by the relatively severe climate, and the influence of altitude and aspect on land use. Viticulture flourishes on the sunny northern margins of Lake Neuchâtel, but forest and rough pasture are found on the higher hillsides and on northward facing slopes. Moreover, the growing season for crops shortens markedly with even slight increases in altitude. Aspect, in that it determines both the degree of insolation and the composition of the natural vegetation cover, is a crucial factor in modern farming, and imposes strict controls on potential land use.

Because of its relatively high altitude, spring comes late to the Alpine Foreland. This lengthens the period of winter feeding for stock, and emphasizes the importance of sown grasses in providing adequate winter fodder. To the prehistoric peasant, a further limiting factor not found today was the all-pervading forest. Raising sheep in a damp forested environment is fraught with difficulties. Apart from the natural antipathy of sheep to woodland, animals are particularly susceptible to blow-fly attacks in warm humid weather, to foot-rot and the ravages of the liver-fluke. Bovines, like sheep, would have found feeding in the mixed oak forest limited, and in the beechwoods, impossible. Consequently, any diminution in the forest cover and creation of pasture would have encouraged the proliferation of herbivores. Any prehistoric society or tribe which not only encouraged stock rearing and agriculture by removing or reducing limiting factors in the environments, but also conditioned the composition of its herds to the resulting culture-influenced landscape, would have promoted its chances for survival by increasing economic productivity.

In considering the Swiss prehistoric farming sequence in the light of the above principle, it is clear that all societies discussed positioned their settlements where aspect and altitude favored their activities. All but Eschner Lutzengüetle bordered piedmont lakes, where the relatively low altitude, and presence of rich easily worked lacustrine soils of a southerly aspect, encouraged agriculture. Furthermore, the proximity of large bodies of water resulted in climatic amelioration, and the provision of vital supplies of early spring fodder in the form of waterplants. The mixed oak forest, which existed near all sites, would have provided herbaceous undergrowth for supplementing the requirements of grazing stock, as well as acorns for foraging swine. Prehistoric activity appears to have been funneled into a restricted territory, in which unexploited land was at a premium.

The absence of pastureland around neolithic settlements necessitated the collection of wasteland hay for feeding stock during the winter. At the same time as the first metal tools became available, however, pastureland was established to an increasing extent, and the foggage system of grazing, in which animals were allowed access to fields where grass had been left to grow long during the summer, would have shortened the period of winter feeding. Consequently, more bovines could have been over-wintered with less expenditure of effort.

The destruction of forest was thus synonymous with the removal of a major limiting factor imposed upon the prehistoric farmer in Switzerland. If human activity is seen as but one element in a series of dynamic and changing biotopes, then it becomes increasingly relevant to the prehistorian to define the economic aims, and methods by which they were achieved, of successive prehistoric societies. In the period when mixed farming had superseded hunting and gathering in the Aare Valley and its tributaries, human aspirations integrated with the limiting factors of the environment and developing technological ability to produce a distinct pattern of economic evolution. In this sense is stock rearing a cultural factor in Prehistoric Europe.

PREHISTORIC DIET IN NEW ZEALAND

The reconstruction of prehistoric diet is a comparatively new field of research, and one which requires extremely critical assessment of archaeological data. WILFRED SHAWCROSS's account of the dietary habits of a New Zealand coastal population is an excellent example of the use of economic evidence. The Galatea Bay site lies on an offshore island of the North Island of New Zealand, and dates to within the last 500 years.

It has not been possible to obtain any clear evidence for the age of the site, owing to the absence of a suitable assemblage, or, for that matter, any corresponding sequence to which it might be related. However, the presence of cannibalism and the absence of European goods, indicates that it is likely to be no later than Proto-historic, which is itself in New Zealand terms a rather variable quantity. Theoretically, no early limit need necessarily be put on its age, though the absence of Moa, relative absence of rocky shore shellfish and the specialized nature of the site may be quoted as negative evidence against an early age. The one fishhook may well be a late form, and the relatively thin soil which has accumulated on top of the midden suggests a recent age. Lastly, in an important and as yet unpublished study of the fishhooks of Murihiku, Mr. Jan Hjarnø observed the scarcity of later, prehistoric fishhooks in that area prior to a final line-fishing efflorescence. A distinct possibility exists that this decrease of line-fishing may correspond to a high development of net fishing. The early European explorers, notably Captain Cook, commented on the remarkable development of nets in New Zealand, Cook describing such a net as five fathoms deep and 400 long. Augustus Hamilton (1908) and Elsdon Best (1929) illustrate a wide and highly-developed range of nets from more recent times. It may thus be that the virtual absence of hooks from the site can be explained by the use of net-fishing. The estimated sizes of the sub-fossil snapper were examined in an attempt to find evidence for the mode of fishing, but the results were inconclusive, as the smallest fish was about 300 grams and the most frequent sizes

From "Prehistoric Diet and Economy on a Coastal Site at Galatea Bay, New Zealand" by Wilfred Shawcross, *Proceedings of the Prehistoric Society* 33, No. 7 (1967) 125-130. Reprinted by permission of the author and the Prehistoric Society. Footnotes and references are omitted, and figures renumbered.

Figure 1. Frequency Distribution Curves of the Measurements of Vertebrae, Dentaries, Premaxillaries and Maxillaries of the Subfossil Fish-bones from the Galatea Bay Site.

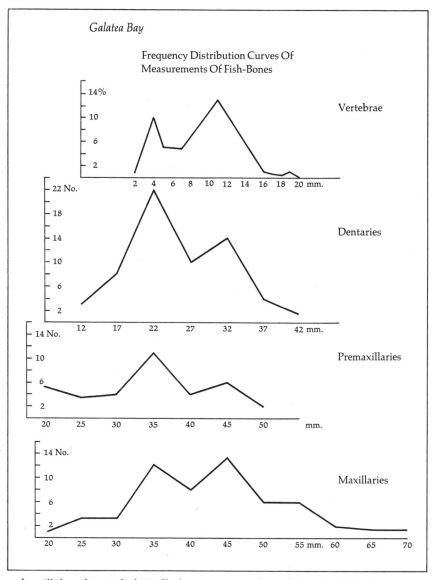

It will be observed that all the curves are bimodal and that both peaks closely coincide for each bone. The scales for the jawbones are all the same, as these bones are of approximately the same size, whereas the scale of the vertebrae, which are much smaller, has been increased.

correspond to those caught in modern times by both methods. Likewise, the bimodal distribution curve of size group frequencies (Fig. 1) is more likely to be a reflection of the structure of the living populations than of the selective effects of hooks. Finally, if net-fishing was the method employed at this site two things need to be explained. The first is the absence of the net sinkers and the second is the relatively small size of the community. For line-fishing is still today a much more individualistic activity than the more cooperative work required by netting. On the other hand these objections could be met if we suppose that the netting was a cooperative venture among the men of the separate families occupying the various adjoining bays of Ponui Island. In this light, the menfolk would be out on the water fishing from their canoes while the women remained in the family group ashore, gathering food, particularly shellfish. Augustus Hamilton gives an eyewitness account of this latter activity, carried out by three women. These would wade out into deep water, where they held one of their number upside down under the surface while she scraped the shellfish into a basket for as long as her breath lasted.

The reconstruction of the diet of the Galatea Bay (Fig. 2) community has, up to this point, been based entirely upon the available, visible evidence. However, there are good grounds for supposing that this is incomplete. In the first place, documentary evidence copiously describes the use of such animal foods as crayfish, crabs and sea-urchins, and, much more important, vegetable foods, including seaweeds and other wild products, particularly fern root (*aruhe*), the rhizome of *pteris aquilina* and cultivated crops, of which the sweet-potato is generally considered to have been the one of greatest importance. However, because of the readily decomposible nature of these foods there is never any direct archaeological evidence for them. This is sharply at variance with other areas of the world, as for example, California, where R. Ascher, having calculated that nearly 2,000 kilograms of meat protein were represented by a particular midden, was then able to assume a much larger quantity of vegetable protein, on the basis of the relatively small number of animals other than shellfish and, more directly, because of the large numbers of milling stones. On the other hand, Grahame Clark was able to ignore for practical purposes the importance of vegetable foods at the large mammal-hunting camp of Star Carr. In the case of New Zealand the importance of plant foods is well enough documented, but impossible to quantify alongside the sea animal foods, certainly until the results are available from considerably more research, which is at present under progress. Therefore, it is only possible to make a number of very generalized statements: first, it is unlikely that the forest and bush were capable of supporting other than very small numbers of people, in spite of the impression to the contrary which might be gained from such authorities as Elsdon Best. The plant foods of the forest which Best described, principally the *hinau, karaka*

*Figure 2.   Graphic Representation of the Kinds and Quantities of Food
Represented in the Excavated Part of the Galatea Bay Midden.*

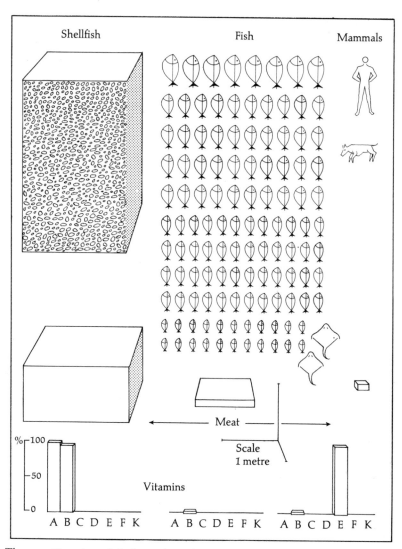

The constituents and their products have been drawn approximately to scale
and are in three vertical columns, showing the volume of shellfish on the
top left, the number of fish in the center and the mammals on the right.
Below these quantities are representations of the approximate wet volumes
of meat produced from these three sources. The lowermost line shows in a
simplified manner the relative importance of each food source in terms of the
total supply of vitamins, but it should however be noted that though the
mammals would appear to supply the entire amount of vitamin E, this is in
fact a relatively insignificant quantity.

and *kahikatea* berries, are not distributed in such large and readily replenishible quantities throughout the bush as to be able to occupy more than a very subsidiary role in the diet of a community; probably more important was their role as a minimal food supply for travellers. It is worth pointing out here that the economic importance of the New Zealand forest should not be thought of on equal terms with such areas, well known for their relative richness, as Southern California. On the other hand, the fern root, which grows in open areas, was . . . of fundamental importance in the economy, for which [Best] cites a great body of early documentary evidence. It would also seem that the fern root was far more generally important than *kumara* (sweet-potato), owing to the soil and climatic restrictions on the latter's cultivation. It is therefore not possible to arrive at more than a very general estimate that the plant foods would supply an amount of energy probably equal to that derived from animal foods, though the range of variation could lie between nothing and double that quantity. A similar level of generalization must be approached in trying to estimate the total quantity of midden which formerly existed and of which only a part has been excavated. On two sides the midden has well-defined boundaries, abutting the steeply rising sides of the valley. On the third side it may be seen to be thinning out; on the fourth side an unknown amount has been eroded away by the sea. Once again, the most reasonable estimate will be that the excavated part represents about half the original site, though, because it is obvious that a certain amount is still unexcavated, the minus error cannot equal the estimated addition. These two further estimates will bring the total energy inferred for the occupation to 12,000,000 $\pm$ 9,000,000 calories, which represents either 4,444 $\pm$ 3,155 man/days or 692 $\pm$ 699 days for the family group.

SEASONALITY

. . . Earlier . . . evidence was brought forward that this site had been occupied during the summer only, and must have been abandoned for part of the year: the dentition of the snapper demonstrated the season and the absence of their body parts suggested that these had been dried and taken elsewhere. This raises two questions. The first is how far we should modify the values in length of occupation or size of population so far obtained to take account of this discontinuous occupation and the storage of food for another season. The second is why there should be such a seasonal movement and where the winter quarters might be.

Clearly seasonal occupations, during which a food surplus was being created for the lean season by storage methods, complicates any estimate of the length of occupation or community size on quantities of food represented on the site, for the food debris represents a surplus of unknown quantity beyond the immediate needs of the community. In the analysis made above of the relative frequencies of the different parts of the snapper bodies, it was concluded that about three-quarters of the number had their dried bodies taken elsewhere. But this is in fact no guide, because it is impossible to tell either whether the surplus would represent the total needed by the community during the seasons in which it was absent from the site or if it was augmented by other food gathering activities during the lean season, or, again, for how great a proportion of the year the community spent its time at Galatea Bay gathering its surplus. These variables allow a wide range of interpretations, but they may conveniently be reduced to five broad possibilities:

(1) The Galatea Bay site represents the virtually continuous occupation by a community throughout the year. But this is unlikely on several grounds, chiefly those proposed in previous sections, that the fish appear to have been caught at a particular season, while their selective representation of body parts, indicating a technique of food preservation, both of which correspond to ethnographic accounts of seasonal movements of the Maori.

(2) The possibility of an occupation over nine months, with an absence of perhaps three months during the lean season, can also be ruled out on the grounds that the dentition of the fish appears to last for only a much shorter period in the state of exfoliation. And it would seem even more unlikely that fishing would only go on for a strictly limited period during an extended occupation of a coastal site.

(3) The seasonality could consist of approximately half the year spent on the coast, accumulating a sufficient surplus to support the population for the other half of the year elsewhere. But the argument against this must be that there would be no point in abandoning this locality where, after all, fish may be caught throughout the whole year, for another locality where, it must be assumed, there are no food supplies at all. This is a strong argument against the supposition that the amount of food prepared at seasonal sites, like Galatea Bay, for storage was sufficiently large to tide the community over a long, otherwise foodless period.

(4) Judging by the observations made above the choice is reduced to about three months of the year, which might be interpreted in one way if a relatively insignificant surplus was produced at the time, leaving the remaining nine months of the year to be spent elsewhere, at one or more different locations, during which food consumption and supply remained about equal. This could well have been the case, reflecting a purely hand-to-mouth economy, dangerously susceptible to any unforeseen failure of supply, but it would also indicate a state which is not associated with Maori culture. Under these conditions communities would have been small and thinly dispersed and incapable of developing the economic surpluses which must have been necessary for the practice of warfare, building of fortifications, and for the existence of such vigorous forms of Maori Art as wood-carving, which is certainly prehistoric. Therefore, while there were, no doubt, instances when this would have been the correct interpretation, another must be sought.

(5) It is reasonable to assume that the stimulus for seasonal movement was an economic one, though it must be admitted that possibly some of the reasons why the modern New Zealander migrates to the coast in the summer may have worked in the past. However, if an economic reason is looked for, it has already been pointed out that life on the coast would be capable of providing at least a continuous supply of food, in which case there must have been some more powerful reason for drawing the population away from this source for a good part of the year, yet not for the whole year. The reason must be that adequate food-producing activity could only be carried out elsewhere. This leads to the final interpretation of the seasonality of the Galatea Bay site, which is thought to be the correct one, namely that the location was occupied for perhaps three months of the year, during which a modest surplus was stored, and that for the remainder of the year the community lived elsewhere, for six or more months of which it was perhaps engaged in other food gathering and preparing activities, maybe adding further preserved foods, which when combined with those prepared at the fishing camp were sufficient to tide the community over the leanest season as well as providing a surplus for trade, warfare, or other activities.

If the argument for the site being occupied for only a short summer season of about three months, and that during this time only a relatively small proportion of the food was preserved (it being supposed that the drying of the fish was preferred to that of shellfish, though no doubt both were so preserved), and if the estimated size of the community based on Captain Cook's evidence is also accepted, then it may be readily calculated that the site could not have been occupied for more than six successive years. This would be the maximum, assuming that no significant surplus was preserved, but as it seems certain that preservation was being carried out, the probable answer would be a year or two less. This short period of reoccupations would find confirmation in the analysis of the size group frequencies of the snapper (Fig. 1); because, if the site had been regularly reoccupied over many years the frequency curves would reasonably be expected to conform to a normal curve, instead of which they are distinctly bimodal, which can only be understood to represent a few fish populations.

Turning to the final question, posed earlier in the paper, on why there was seasonal movement and where the occupation for the rest of the year might be, the first part will already have been seen to have been answered. The economic reason, and it would be fruitless to speculate on any other kind of reason, must be that other, presumably inland localities were important sources of food. It may be added that "inland" need not be taken to mean far inland. A cursory examination of the most thorough field surveys of sites which have so far been published, notably that by Dr. A. G. Buist, of North Taranaki, indicates that about 90 percent of sites are within three miles of the coast, while the majority of the remainder are close to large rivers or lakes. It is probable that the inland sites would be close to patches of land suitable for cultivation, or open, fern-covered land. On the Auckland isthmus, at a distance of about thirty kilometers from Galatea Bay, there were extensive areas of good volcanic soil, represented by market gardens today, though fast disappearing under building developments. But these soils are missing, closer to the site, and they are probably too far distant for the island community to have exploited them. Otherwise, the mainland closer to the site, or the large island of Waiheke, or Ponui itself, appear to present rather similar conditions of quite high, broken ground, probably mainly covered by forest and with occasional, rather small patches of alluvial soil. Certainly the coastlines of the mainland, Waiheke and Ponui itself were extensively, if not necessarily densely, settled as is shown by the number of beach, stream sites and fortified *pa* still visible.

POLLEN ANALYSIS AND PREHISTORIC AGRICULTURE

Pollen analysis has already been summarized in an earlier chapter, and Gray and Smith mention the use of palynology to detect man's influence on prehistoric vegetation. To Danish botanist JOHANNES IVERSEN goes the credit for first recognizing that pollen diagrams reflect the radical vegetational changes resulting from slash and burn agriculture. He followed up his original work with an account of Stone Age forest clearance published in Scientific American *some years later (1965, 194:36–41). A passage from his earlier publication, a good example of scientific deduction from palynological data, is reprinted here.*

▣Following upon the final glacial period the vegetation in Denmark at first developed according to the same laws as those governing events in the inter-glacial periods; all changes were merely an expression of altera-

From *Land Occupation in Denmark's Stone Age* by Johannes Iversen, Danmarks Geologiske Undersøgelse, Copenhagen (1941), II Raekke, No. 66, pp. 20-26. Reprinted by permission of the author and the Danish Geological Institute.

tions in climate and other natural factors. The primitive cultures of the Early Stone Age could have but little effect on the forest growth. The hunters had their paths as the animals their tracks; and just as the vegetation around bird colonies receives its character from the manure supplied to it, that in the immediate vicinity of Mesolithic settlements was characterized by midden plants. Man's influence on the vegetation did not extend far; the virgin forest closed in a few paces outside the settlement, and there nature alone determined what was to grow.

All this went through a radical change with the introduction of farmer culture to the country. Then, and not before, the forest picture began to be altered by man, and there can be no doubt that the changes thus brought about were just as profound and just as interesting as those which earlier were associated with climatic and other purely natural causes. It would therefore be anticipated a priori that they would be clearly identifiable in the pollen diagrams.

In pollen diagrams the Danish Late Stone Age begins at a place close to zone border VII–VIII, after Jessen's zonal divisions of the diagrams. This must mean that farmer culture started at about this time and it would be a very attractive task to find its traces in the pollen-floristic development of these strata. With this in view I have made a careful analysis of material from particularly suitable localities in various parts of the country. In order to bring new elements to light I have also made systematic counts of less common types of pollen (pollen of cereals, weeds, *Hedera, Viscum*, etc.), which provide information just as valuable as the pollen of the trees. This has entailed the counting of much greater quantities of pollen than otherwise, a time-consuming labor but one that has also been to the benefit of the other pollen curves, the statistical uncertainty having thus been reduced to a minimum.

On the basis of some selected pollen diagrams from Zealand, Funen, East and Middle Jutland I shall now examine one by one the various phases in the aforesaid critical stage of the vegetation development round about zone border VII–VIII and at the same time endeavor to grasp their nature. . . .

It is in the middle of the Oak Period. For about two thousand years *Quercus, Ulmus* and *Tilia* together have formed the high forest; there was a little *Pinus* in poor soil; *Alnus* grew especially in wet places with a little *Betula. Viscum album* was a common parasite on those trees that make suitable hosts, and flowering *Hedera helix* climbed wherever it could obtain a hold and was of a luxuriance seen nowadays only in southern and western Europe.

Then occurred some rather inconspicuous but important changes in the forest picture. *Fraxinus excelsior*, which formerly had played only an unimportant role, increased in frequency at the expense of *Ulmus*, whose curve fell rapidly. The curve for *Hedera* describes exactly the same course as the *Ulmus* curve; it falls abruptly, and above this level *Hedera*, even in *per mille* diagrams, no longer forms a continuous curve. In most cases the *Quercus* curve displays a slight rise. These small pollen-floristic changes can scarcely be connected with human interference; for even if one might at a pinch explain the decline of *Ulmus* as the result of the attentions of domestic animals, the simultaneous decline of *Hedera* can no more be explained in this fashion than the increase of *Fraxinus*. As the same course of development can be shown to have taken place all over the country, in parts both fertile and unfertile, it is reasonable to assume a climatic cause. One factor alone, the marked decline of flowering *Hedera*, gives an indication as to the direction in which the climate must have changed. *Hedera* is distinctly an Atlantic plant, partial to warm summers and mild winters, that is to say a climate which from early times has been connected with the "Atlantic Period" of the post-glacial age. As that very period must, according to the theory, have extended over the time during which *Hedera* was so common in Denmark, followed by the more continental "sub-Boreal Period," whose cold winters must have been inimical to *Hedera's* growth, it seems the obvious thing to do to connect the fall in the *Hedera* curve with the change from "Atlantic" to "sub-Boreal" climate. Consequently, in our pollen diagrams I have laid the border between these two climatic periods where the *Ulmus* curve falls, this being simultaneous with the decline of *Hedera*. If then we place the zone border VII–VIII at this point, we find that Zone VII corresponds to the Atlantic period and Zone VIII to the sub-Boreal, thus obtaining perfect concordance between the classical scheme of climatic periods after the Ice Age (Blytt, Sernander, Hartz) and the pollen-floristic division according to Jessen. In Norwegian diagrams (from Jaeren) the border between the Atlantic and sub-Boreal climatic periods was similarly drawn . . . by Faegri . . . and although a comparison between Norwegian and Danish diagrams is rendered difficult by the natural differences between these two regions, Faegri's border seems to be in full conformity with the one described above. . . .

Just above the zone border VII–VIII as plotted here, i.e., in the beginning of the sub-Boreal Period, the curves in most Danish pollen diagrams describe a very peculiar course which bears witness of a remarkably sudden change in the composition and state of the forests. The elements of the high forest, *Quercus*, *Tilia*, *Fraxinus* and *Ulmus* undergo a distinct but contemporary decline, while *Betula* reveals a transitory, *Alnus* a more lasting increase in pollen frequency, and at the same time the *Corylus* curve reaches a very pronounced maximum. What is the significance of this conspicuous minimum in the curve for the "Oak Mixed Forest" (*Quercus* + *Tilia* + *Fraxinus*)? Can it be the expression of a temporary lowering of the temperature?

There are various arguments against that interpretation. It must be realized that this climatic decline must have been of a sudden and actually a catastrophic character to depress the curves of the Oak Forest so abruptly and violently, and this would be incompatible with the rapid advance of the hazel. Nor is there any apparent decline in *Viscum*, though its thermal requirements are greater than those of *Quercus* and *Tilia*. It would also need some explaining why it was *Betula* and *Alnus*, but not the *Pinus*, that profited from the altered conditions. On the contrary, the pollen of *Pinus* as a whole declines in frequency in this zone. The hypothesis fails entirely when we have to explain the important fact that the phase is initiated with a sudden increase in the pollen of herbaceous plants.

In order to circumvent these difficulties, one might postulate a climatic change of another character than a general decline. A lowering of the ground-water level as a consequence of a very dry period would cause birch and alder to move out over marshy areas previously occupied solely by fern plants. This would explain the increase of *Betula* and *Alnus* pollen and the relative decrease in that of the other trees. Here again, however, the increase in the pollen frequency of the herbs forms an obstacle, and the explanation must be dropped.

There remains the influence of man. It seems reasonable to place the minimum in the curve of the Oak Mixed Forest in connection with forest clearance. Originally my idea was this: the clearance chiefly affected the Oak Forest of the high ground, whereas the marsh forests with their alder and birch escaped. Accordingly, the latter trees must display a relative increase in the diagrams. Doubtless this phenomenon did assert itself, but it cannot be the whole explanation. In the diagrams from salty fjord deposits this form of curve is handsomely developed, though there are no marsh forests at the borders of salt fjords.

On the other hand, we arrive at a natural and satisfactory explanation of the courses of the various pollen curves if we assume that the pollen-floristic changes express the vegetation developments in a region where land-tilling people have occupied the land and cleared this dense primeval forest with axe and fire. Now as this explanation requires that fire was largely made use of, it would be natural to expect that traces of it could be found. I recollected a suspicious, sharply delimited stratum of charcoal in Ordrup Mose just under the problematic zone, and subsequently embarked upon a precise and complete analysis of the sample series that had been collected. The result seemed to affirm my supposition that there was some connection between this charred layer and the minimum in the curve of the Oak Mixed Forest, and I shall now go through the diagram from that aspect.

During the Litorina transgression Ordrup Mose was a fjord in the Øresund; the charred layer was near the upper edge of a thick deposit of saltwater gyttja (gyttja = organic mud). On the extreme left of Fig. 1

is a silhouette representing the frequency of charcoal fragments in slides from the deposit just under the charcoal layer, from that layer itself and from the deposits overlying it. It will be seen that the substratum to the fire-deposit also contains some charcoal; this is only natural, as the section lies in the immediate vicinity of the well-known large Mesolithic Bloks-bjerg Settlement, whose primitive inhabitants still seem to have been in occupation when the new farming people took the area into possession and forced them out. On the left of the pollen diagram there are also silhouettes to indicate the changes in the pollen numbers of various trees per square centimeter of slide; in contrast to what is the case with the pollen diagram, which exhibits only the relative changes in pollen frequency, we are here told something of the absolute pollen density in the various gyttja deposits. Finally, on the right of the pollen diagram there are frequency curves for herbaceous plants calculated in proportion to the total quantity of tree pollen.

How then did the vegetation react to the fire clearance? The curves for pollen density show that immediately over the fire deposit there was a sudden and unprecedented decline in the pollen of all kinds of trees. This conspicuous poverty of pollen cannot be accidental, as every one of 34

Figure 1. Pollen Diagrams at Ordrup Mose, Denmark.

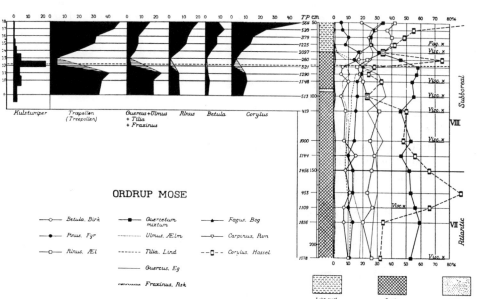

Left: proportion of pollen per square centimeter of preparation. *Right:* relative percentage of pollens in stratigraphic order (TP, tree pollen; depths in centimeters).

samples from the marine series, 4 meters thick, under the fire deposit contained a considerable and apparently quite uniform pollen density. The clearance fire evidently encompassed the whole of the forest in the neighborhood of Bloksbjerg, and it affected all trees alike. Consequently the pollen diagram exhibits no great change: the relative frequency ratio between the tree pollens is pretty much the same.

Judging by all appearances the fire deposit was laid down in the course of some few years. It consists mainly of charcoal, and its thickness is no more than a hundredth part of the whole marine series. Thus we have a chance of following the succession of plant growth after the clearance fire. In the fire deposit the pollen frequency of the herbaceous plants suddenly rises threefold. This relative increase corresponds very well to the above mentioned simultaneous decline in the absolute tree-pollen frequency, and we must therefore assume that it is only a consequence of this decline. Already in the same analysis (Fig. 1, left) the forest regeneration begins. *Betula* and *Alnus* appear quickest, and therefore these trees record a considerable relative advance in the pollen diagram; it is principally this fact that causes the abrupt fall in the curves of the Oak Mixed Forest.

The explanation is quite simple. *Betula* and *Alnus* have a much greater power of dispersal than *Quercus*. Their seeds form regularly every year in large quantities, they are small and light and carry far on the wind, whereas the heavy fruits of the oak spread only slowly; therefore, in contrast to *Quercus*, *Betula* and *Alnus* are able to spring up immediately wherever suitable conditions for germination prevail. In addition, *Betula* and *Alnus* flower and fructify when they are only ten or twelve years old, whereas *Quercus* is 30–40 years old before it does so. This means that *Betula* and *Alnus* may produce some generations before the oak has even reached maturity. The significance of this is obvious. Like *Quercus*, *Corylus* has a poor power of dispersal, but on the other hand it reaches maturity before *Betula* and *Alnus*. These two circumstances may perhaps explain the curious features of its curve.

The tree that profited most from the clearance fire was *Betula*; shortly after the land occupation it reached a higher frequency than ever since the Birch-Fir Period. This is very interesting, for nowadays too it is mainly *Betula* that makes its appearance after a forest fire. The great dispersal and early maturity of this tree is not the sole explanation, however; after ordinary forest clearances in fertile regions *Betula* does not usually appear. The fact is that its seed germinates only when the soil conditions are favorable. On ashy soil, however, these conditions are exceptionally favorable.

The uppermost analysis in the diagram reveals a decline in the *Betula* curve. This is not accidental; all diagrams with a marked minimum on the curve of the Oak Mixed Forest show that *Betula* flourishes only for a short time. The birch is the tree requiring most light, it cannot tolerate shade, and it only gets a chance when the forest is cleared of other trees. The birch is the pioneer among our trees, and the brief *Betula* maximum above the charcoal deposit is therefore very significant.

Throughout the foregoing the expression "clearance fire" has been employed. But the question arises of whether the vegetal development evidenced by the pollen flora might not just as well have occurred as the result of a natural forest conflagration.

In the first place one might answer that natural forest fires occur almost exclusively in conifer forests; indeed, it requires a good deal of effort to make a foliferous forest burn. This is a negative argument only, but fortunately we have much positive evidence to show that agriculture was brought to the region just at the time when the fire occurred.

As we have seen, the pollen frequency of herbaceous plants rises immediately after the fire. A "non-tree pollen diagram" plotted on the pollen of herbaceous plants and heather, shows that in the main it is chiefly the same plants as those that were growing there earlier, first and foremost *Chenopodiaceae* and *Gramineae*. But next we find for the first time some pollen of plantain (*Plantago*), not, be it noted, of the salt-marsh plant *Plantago maritima*, but of the weeds *Pl. major* and *Pl. lanceolata*. The pollen of these two plants is to be found in all our diagrams as soon as we come to the "land occupation phase"; this is its first appearance, but thereafter it has a continuous curve up to the present day. Apparently *Plantago* came to Denmark together with the first farmers in the same manner as it has since followed the European all over the world, wherever he has settled. *Plantago* has been called "the white man's trail" by the American Indians; the trail of the Neolithic conquerors is the *Plantago* pollen in our diagrams. In Ordrup Mose the course of the *Plantago* curve is typical; it starts where the Oak Mixed Forest begins to fall, and reaches its maximum where the other is at the minimum. Side by side with *Plantago* a common weed was *Artemisia cf. vulgaris;* its pollen was found in large quantities, and in historic times too it was a greatly detested field weed, one that became of minor importance only with the era of modern deep ploughing.

It is a familiar fact that in the Late Stone Age a good deal of cereal cultivation took place, and therefore it was to be expected that cereal pollen would also be demonstrable in the fire deposit. Firbas showed that the pollen of cultivated cereals is larger than that of "the wild grasses," *Elymus arenarius* alone having pollen as large. If nevertheless one finds hardly any cereal pollen in Stone and Bronze Age deposits, where *Plantago* pollen often occurs in large quantities, the reason must in part be that barley and wheat, the cereals that were cultivated in those ages, are self-fertilizing and give off scarcely any pollen. Notwithstanding this unfavorable circumstance there was some cereal pollen in the strata directly overlying the fire horizon—not much, it is true, but sufficient to prove that cereals were cultivated.

Further evidence of the arrival of farmer people is provided by the finding of a bone which Dr. M. Degerbøl identified as the tibia of a domestic cow. With the aid of a little gyttja picked out of the hollows in the bone it was possible to date it with fair accuracy. It belongs to the lower part of the lake marl, i.e., just in the Oak Mixed Forest minimum. This closes the chain of evidence.

HUNTER-GATHERERS AT GWISHO

The Gwisho hot springs on Lochinvar Ranch in Central Zambia, south central Africa, were the locale for several hunter-gatherer camps some 4,000 years ago. The archaeological sites consist of low mounds; the bottom levels are in a waterlogged state, lying below the water table of the springs. Many organic materials, including wood, bone, and vegetable foods, were recovered during the excavations. These brief extracts by BRIAN M. FAGAN from the forthcoming monograph on Gwisho B describe the seeds and fruit found at the site, and summarize the economy of the settlement. The extracts show the type of information that can be obtained from vegetable foods and about their role in the economy, as well as illustrate the use of controlled analogy from modern hunter-gatherers at an approximately similar economic level. Those used are the !Kung bushmen from the Dobe area of Botswana, southern Africa.

THE VEGETAL REMAINS

A total of 9,996 macroscopic vegetal remains have been identified from Gwisho B. A negligible amount of material was found at C, mainly Hyphaene nuts, and unidentifiable fragments.

The specimens were in soft condition, and preserved in plastic bags before being gradually dried out in the laboratory. Identification of the

"The Economic Evidence" by Brian M. Fagan from *The Hunter-Gatherers of Gwisho* by Brian M. Fagan and Francis Van Noten. (In preparation 1970.) Footnotes are omitted.

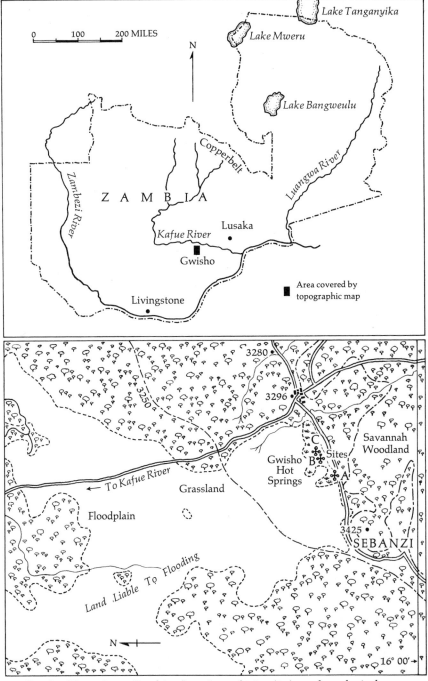

Gwisho Hotsprings, Zambia. Location of site (*top*), and ecological zones (*bottom*).

various types was made easier by the enormous quantities of material in a limited number of categories. The identifications have been made as follows:

SPECIES	NUMBER	% OF TOTAL
Bauhinia	4339	55.29%
Hyphaene	3190	40.65
Gourd	158	2.00
Adansonia digitata	48	.61
Scelocarya caffra	45	.56
Strychnos pods	38	.48
Swartzia	11	.14
Parinaria (Mobula)	8	.10
Nymphaea	4	.05
Cyperus fulgens	3	.03
Commiphora	2	.02
Amblygogonocarpus pods	1	.01
Total identifiable fragments	7847	100.00%
Total unidentifiable fragments	2153	
Grand Total	9996	

The stratigraphical data for the seeds is given in the tables (not included here). Most of the specimens come from the waterlogged levels of trench II, 8–13, with some isolated material from the lower levels of II, IV, and VI, where, once again, waterlogged conditions pertain. The data is too incomplete for meaningful conclusions on stratigraphical changes to be drawn. *Hyphaene* nuts and *Bauhinia* were overwhelmingly dominant at all levels, great concentrations of their fruit occurring in trench II, where most of the wooden implements and other organic materials were found.

CHARACTERISTICS OF THE VEGETAL REMAINS

Bauhinia sp. is a shrub prized for its fruit and roots, the former generally coming into season during the period from October to February. Its distribution is ubiquitous, the species being common in the Lochinvar region at the present time. *Bauhinia* is a staple diet of !Kung bushmen. Its consumption rate varies with the abundance of the shrub. The species also has wide medicinal properties.

Hyphaene ventricosa, or ivory palm, is widespread in Zambia and is especially common in the Choma-Namwala area. Seed kernels of this species are the dominant vegetal remains found in the sites. *Hyphaene* is found commonly in the Gwisho area today. The fruit has many economic uses. Bushmen today relish the milk from the seed, while Bantu-speaking peoples make use of the palm for matting, rope, basketry, and thatching. The food value of *Hyphaene* is not high; it does not form an important part of !Kung diet today.

Gourd (Lagenaria sp.) is used by Bushmen for containers; the exact species used at Gwisho could not be identified. Its use here is predictable, but surprisingly few fragments were found.

Adansonia digitata (Baobab) is well known for its economic value. The tree is comparatively common at Lochinvar, and the fruit ripens in February and July. The fruit is a highly favored part of !Kung diet, being prized especially during the winter months. Baobab is surprisingly rare at Gwisho B, but was evidently eaten regularly.

Scelocarya caffra (Morula) is a common tree in lower-lying and hotter areas of Zambia, with fruit that ripens in March and April. The nut makes a delectable food, but is small and crumbles easily; for this reason, the !Kung do not eat the nuts often. They are comparatively rare finds at Gwisho, perhaps because of their crumbly nature. The Morula tree has an important role in subsistence, for its leaves form the food of a species of beetle used in the manufacture of arrow poison.

Strychnos sp. is widespread in Zambia. Its fruit, which ripens towards the end of the calendar year, is generally edible. Both Lee and Silberbauer agree that this species of shrub has less attraction to the !Kung, being regarded as a supplementary food.

Swartzia Madagascariensis, a small- or medium-sized deciduous tree, is widespread in the Southern Province of Zambia. The pods of *Swartzia,* which ripen in June, are used to make an arrow poison by !Kung bushmen. The pod is roasted, the rind scraped away, and a portion of the pulp is ground up and added to a sticky mess prepared from a nontoxic fibrous root. *Swartzia* is sometimes used as a fish poison in Zambia. The presence of this species in the Gwisho deposits is of particular significance, for it provides indirect evidence of the use of poison for hunting and fishing. The pods are not eaten in Zambia today, although they have some medicinal applications.

Parinari curatellifolia (Mobula) is an evergreen tree with fruit which ripens in July and August. The fruit is widely eaten in Zambia, and is also used by Bantu peoples to make a fermented liquor.

Nymphaea is recorded as being used as a famine food in South and West Africa. This shrub is an insignificant element in the Gwisho collections, and is a "rare food" among the !Kung.

The three remaining species are insignificantly represented. The bulbs of *Cyperus fulgens* are a supplementary food among the !Kung, while *Commiphora,* another plant, has wide medicinal uses as well as being employed as a fish and arrow poison in the Congo and Ethiopia. *Amblygogonocarpus* provides useful timber, and the trees grow in abundance near the Kafue Flats.

All the vegetal remains from the sites which can be regarded as regular food sources are common in the area today. The number of *Hyphaene* and

Bauhinia are dominant, the latter being an obviously primary food source, as it is currently among the !Kung. Somewhat more surprising is the abundance of *Hyphaene* kernels in the waterlogged levels. We can only conclude that either the hunters of Gwisho relied more heavily on the species than their !Kung counterparts do, or that the kernels were introduced into the site by some other agency, perhaps even dropping onto the camp site from trees which at that time grew near the springs.

The range of species represented in the Gwisho collections is small, relative to the large number of seeds recovered from the deposits. We may conclude that the inhabitants drew their vegetable diet from a comparatively small range of species, even if their botanical knowledge was comprehensive, perhaps supplementing it with the regular use of a large number of vegetable foods.

Gabel, the previous excavator at Gwisho, records dominant *Hyphaene* from Gwisho A, together with large quantities of Morula (*Scelocarya caffra*) and also the flat seeds of the Musaule (*Guibourtia coleosperma* [Berth]). The Musaule yields an edible, red pulpy fruit which ripens from June to August. This species, common on Lochinvar, was not found at Gwisho B or C.

There is little comparative data on the food-collecting habits of the late Stone Age people of Central Africa in archaeological literature. Cooke has recorded numerous Morula nuts in the deposits at Pomongwe Cave in the Matopo Hills, while *Musuku* fruit were found at Nachikufu, a species now plentiful in the vicinity. But the large collection of vegetal remains from the Gwisho sites has provided a much more complete picture of Late Stone Age gathering habits than has hitherto been obtained north or south of the Zambezi.

[After a discussion of the animal bones found at Gwisho, the economy is summarized.]

THE GWISHO ECONOMY

The fragmentary faunal and vegetal remains from Gwisho B and C do not allow a complete reconstruction of the economic habits of the inhabitants. However, some general conclusions can be drawn, especially in the light of Lee's important account of !Kung bushmen ecology.

Buffalo, warthog, lechwe, zebra, and impala were the dominant species captured by the Stone Age hunters of Gwisho. The faunal list as a whole includes a wide variety of mammals, all of which are found within a comparatively short distance of the site today. Four distinct ecological zones are found near the sites: woodland, the hot-spring environment itself, grassland with some thorn tree cover, and the Kafue Flats. The faunal remains include animals from each of these zones. Bushbuck, Kudu, haartebeeste, grysbuck, duiker, and impala are all species that flourish in the woodland and in the hinterland away from the Flats. On the other hand, lechwe, zebra, and wildebeest are well represented, indicating there was by no means a total dependence on one zone or another. Pig bones are abundant in the remains, and they frequent the hot-spring areas. The Gwisho hunters seem to have exploited all the zones, even if the preponderance of mammal remains tends toward woodland and hinterland species. The lechwe traces, although frequent, are not dominant. The Flats are over seven miles from the springs, which means the herds of lechwe are far from the site for much of the year, except when the waters of the Kafue are high. Unfortunately, the fragmentary faunal remains cannot reveal whether the hunters killed lechwe only at certain times of the year. The hinterland and woodland provided plentiful supplies of game, without the necessity of travelling to the Flats for lechwe meat. Skulls, horn cores, and many teeth testify that carcasses were carried to the settlement, and probably for no great distance. We may speculate that the lechwe was probably hunted when the waters of the Kafue were at their maximum extent and the plains species tended to congregate nearer the hot springs.

One of the most interesting features of the faunal collection is the concentration on medium- and large-sized species. This is in contrast to Iron Age sites on the Batoka Plateau and even to the Sebanzi site, where smaller antelope were preferred in spite of the hunting advantage gained through use of iron-tipped bows and arrows. An even higher degree of hunting selection is suggested by the Gwisho data on warthog mortality, studied by Graham Child, who indicates there was a preference for mature specimens.

Comparable data from other Late Stone Age sites is scanty. The Mumbwa Wilton fauna contains a wide variety of bovidae, but the sample is too small for valid comparison. Wells has detected traces of hunting selection in South African Late Stone Age caves, but few other examples appear in archaeological literature.

In an environment where game is plentiful, and abundant supplies of meat can be obtained without much trouble both from the chase and from scavenger kills, hunters might be expected to exploit those species that give a large yield of meat per kill. Lee shows that the amount of meat provided by a kudu is equivalent to that from 20 steenbuck, a convincing argument for the pursuit of larger antelope. Hunting larger game has other implications, too. The large surplus of meat from a big species is liable to go bad quickly unless either dried (a rare habit among !Kung bushmen) or shared between the families at the camp, or with people living at the camp, or with people living elsewhere. Such a pattern is, as Lee points out, ecologically adaptive.

Most of the mammals whose jaws survive in the deposits are mature or prime beasts. The samples are too small to allow firm conclusions, but adult beasts appear to have played an important role in the meat diet.

Mammals represent the highest percentage of animals in the Gwisho deposits. If modern practice reflects the past, various species may have been tabooed or subject to restrictive eating by certain members of the camp. But small mammals, such as rodents, are conspicuous by their rarity. Only two cane rats were found, while rodent bones are relatively more common in the smaller Sebanzi Iron Age collections. Birds are uncommon, and the surviving remains are probably confined to those species which could be readily snared. The tortoise and leguaan are rare, and frogs and other invertebrates are absent. Preservation conditions are so perfect that we can hardly argue that rodent bones have not survived. A possible explanation may be the abundance of larger game animals which precluded the necessity of eating smaller creatures. Small mammals are not eaten by the !Kung, for they feel there is too little meat per carcass to bother catching them.

The vegetal remains also display a marked selection of species. Twelve species of fruit or seed are preserved in the collections from Gwisho B. Of these, two, *Hyphaene* and *Bauhinia,* are the most abundant.

The criteria by which the !Kung select their vegetable foods are probably applicable to the Gwisho hunters. All the major species represented at the site are abundant in the area, and their seasons are comparatively long. With an abundant meat diet—and flesh is regarded as the most desirable food by Bushmen—there would be little incentive to broaden the base of the plant quest, except under exceptional conditions. The archaeological finds represent, of course, only a small proportion of the vegetable resources available to, and used by, the Gwisho people. But the three species found in overwhelming dominance are all well-known food species, and their frequency at Gwisho B presumably results from systematic and long-term exploitation of this small part of the wide spectrum of total vegetable species available to the inhabitants.

The Gwisho hunters had a potentially very broad subsistence base, which they exploited on a very selective basis. The archaeological evidence for the food quest at Gwisho is limited by factors of preservation; it is difficult for us to establish how sophisticated their economic strategy was.

PREHISTORIC TRADE

*Trade, which formed a vital part of prehistoric economy, has become
a major field of archaeological research. The interdependence of
prehistoric communities for raw materials and luxuries led to the
development of complicated bartering networks and trade routes
which are reflected in the archaeological record by finds of objects
of foreign origin in sites far from their source. Europe was an area
of intensive trade in both raw materials and exotic ornaments during
prehistoric times. GRAHAME CLARK published an economic study of
prehistoric Europe some years ago, and this extract gives an idea of
the flourishing trade in stone axes during Neolithic times, and of the
use of distribution maps in prehistory.*

By far the most important trading activity of the Stone Age in northwestern Europe to leave traces in the archaeological record was the commerce in finished or partly finished tools, most commonly axe and adze
blades, made from raw materials of superior quality and limited distribution. Although based fundamentally on the virtues of certain materials,
it should be stressed that this was nevertheless a trade in more or less
completely manufactured objects. The precise stage to which the work
was carried varied. Sometimes, as in Denmark, one finds hoards of bars
of flint—for instance those from Alslev, near Logumkloster, and Purland,
Vallo—evidently roughed out at such surface spreads of flint as that in
the Stevns district; but more often the blades were finished up to the
point at which they were ready for polishing. A moment's reflection will
show why trade took this form. No one who has watched flint or stone
being flaked need be reminded of the high proportion of waste. Transport
of the raw material in its natural state would therefore have involved the
carriage of a large proportion of useless matter. The obvious alternative
was to remove the waste at the mine or quarry and trade the product.
This implies that the most important single tool among most later Stone
Age communities, the blade of axe or adze, was not produced on a domes-

tic basis, unless from cheap and inferior kinds of flint or stone, but was manufactured in bulk by professional knappers working at the sources of the most desirable raw materials. These knappers were maintained in part no doubt by other members of their immediate families, but in some measure they lived on the proceeds of exchange.

One of the most significant facts about this trade is that it was carried on by hunter-fishers in just the same way as by farmers, and indeed it sometimes passed from one to the other. The closest parallels among modern primitive peoples are to be sought among food-gathering groups in parts of Australia, where until quite recently the tougher stones needed for ground axes were obtained from quarries in the mountains. These would generally be owned and operated by the tribe in whose territories they were situated or by a family within the tribe. The quarry for axe-blades at Mt. William, near Lancefield, southeast Australia, was owned by one Billi-billeri, who lived with his family on the site and split the rock needed for the whole Wurunjeni community. When a neighboring tribe needed a fresh supply of stone, messages would be sent offering articles in exchange for a stipulated quantity of the material and later a party would be sent to camp near the quarry. Anyone caught stealing the stone was liable to get involved in a fight with Billi-billeri and his family, but as a rule a barter transaction would be arranged and so trade in this essential raw material would eventuate.

Some of the most interesting stone axe factories in prehistoric Europe, those on the island of Bomlo off the southwest coast of Norway, were certainly active in pre-neolithic times in that part of the world; indeed the indications are that, although the neolithic Vepestad people continued to make stone axes on the island, the main trade, which extended over much of Jaeren on the mainland, was conducted by the mesolithic Nøstvet people. In this case quarry and factory were separated by the open sea, the raw material having to be quarried from the side of a small rocky islet called Hespriholmen, and carried by boat to the factories on Bømlo, which are situated at the head of a small fjord still used as a port for shipping from the mainland. The Bømlo industry illustrates in a very striking fashion that the sea, so far from being an obstacle to prehistoric trade, served to link quarry, factory and market.

Further evidence that trade in objects made from localized but keenly sought after stone was carried on among hunter-fishers is to be found in Finland and the East Baltic area. The material from which the traded adzes, gouges, chisels and ornaments were made, the so-called Olonetz green slate, was apparently roughed out close to the village of Suoju, near Petrosavodsk in Eastern Carelia, where great quantities of splinters and waste have been found. As the map shows (Fig. 1), finished objects made

Figure 1. Trade in Objects Made from Olonetz Green Slate.

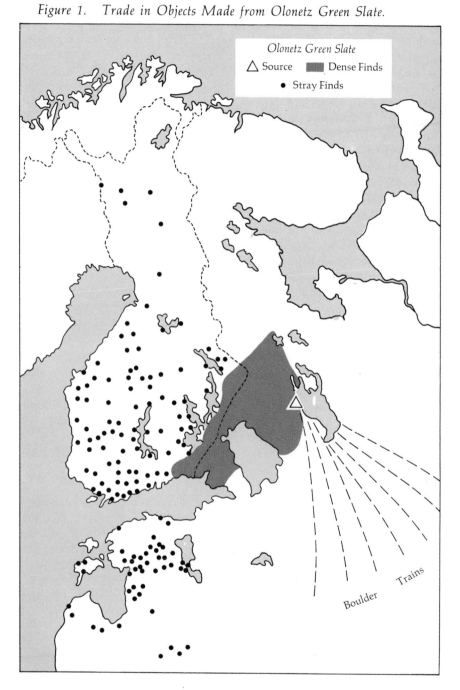

from this material abound in contiguous parts of Carelia and of southwest Finland and isolated finds occur both in Esthonia and over the greater part of Finland up to beyond the Arctic Circle. It is particularly to be noted that no finds have been made in the region southeast of Lake Onega, over which erratics of the "green slate" were deposited by the Pleistocene ice-sheet. This only goes to confirm that one is here concerned with the export of finished objects from workshops in the Petrosavodsk area.

Over much of northwestern Europe the trade in axe and adze blades of stone was carried on by neolithic farmers. Where flint of good quality was available in the chalk or in residual deposits, this might also be traded in the form of more or less completed tools. Although one can often recognize flint axes or adzes in lowland Britain as the products of mine-factories, it has not yet proved possible to verify this by objective means, still less to determine the actual mine involved. Style of workmanship, distinctiveness of raw material and absence of native sources of supply, though, are all clues, which in combination can give fairly sure results. Examples of such include thick-butted axes from south Germany and Switzerland and gouges from northern Scandinavia, all of grey flint from the west Baltic area. The color and texture of the flint of Grand Pressigny, combined with the technique by which blades were struck from long prepared cores, makes it comparatively easy to recognize products of the factories. Another easily recognizable material is the conspicuously banded flint from eastern Galicia and southern Kielce in Poland. As a rule it was traded in the form of thick-butted axes, but it was also used for sickle-blades, knives and scrapers. The flint was traded over the territories of the semi-nomadic herdsmen, whose culture is defined by their characteristic globular amphorae, from the Carpathians to the Baltic and from the Niemen to the Elbe and the Saale (Fig. 2). Since Baltic amber is distributed fairly widely over the same territory and is commonly associated with the banded flint in graves, it may well be that the two commodities were exchanged.

In the case of stone, petrological determinations have already yielded important results, even though the method is still only in process of being applied and in some countries has hardly been used. Mention has already been made of the trade between certain west Norwegian islands and the mainland of Jaeren, which flourished mainly in mesolithic times. In addition it has long been known that axes made from grorudite, a material from the immediate area of Oslo, were traded over much of the eastern part of the country, and quite recently it has been shown that axes of Vestland type made from west Norwegian schist were traded across the Skagerrak to Vendsyssel in northern Jutland. Evidence is cited in a later paragraph for the trading of stone axes from the Taunus to the Cologne area, and instances might be multiplied.

Figure 2. Trade in Banded Flint from Eastern Galicia and Southern Kielce.

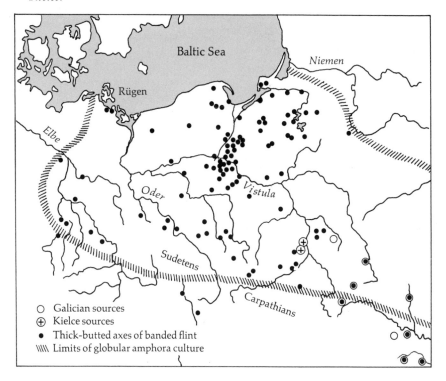

The most thorough investigations so far undertaken are those now in progress in Britain. The first step was the identification at Windmill Hill, Avebury, and at other sites, mostly in Wessex, of axes made of augite granophyre from the workshops of Graig Lwyd in North Wales, a type of stone which can often be recognized at a glance, particularly when fractured. Systematic investigation by petrologists of slices cut from a large number of prehistoric axes has not only extended the range of the Graig Lwyd trade to Cambridgeshire and northwards to East Lothian (Fig. 3), but has revealed the presence up and down the country of the products of a number of axe factories including the well-known ones at Stake Pass, Langdale, Cumberland and at Tievebulliagh near Cushendall, Antrim, and on Rathlin Island. Some of the results already obtained, such as the spread of axes from Trenow and other unidentified sites in Cornwall over the southwestern counties of England, are not unexpected, but others, notably the export of axes from Stake Pass through Wessex to the neighborhood of the Dorset coast, as well as westwards to the Isle of Man and north-

Figure 3. Trade in Stone Axe and Adze Blades from Factories in North Ireland, the Lake District and North Wales.

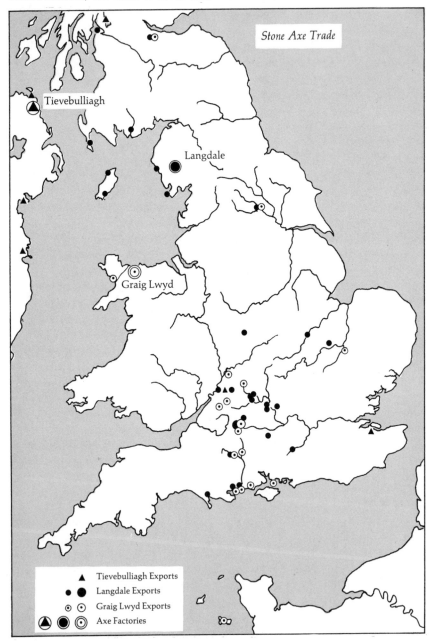

wards to East Lothian, and the trading of North Irish products as far afield as Sittingbourne in Kent and of Prescelly stone to Antrim are more surprising. It is evident that trade activities within Great Britain were a good deal more complex than other sources would have led one to expect. As was the case in Scandinavia, commerce was by no means confined to the interior, but struck boldly out across the sea, a point brought out particularly clearly by the North Irish trade, by the occurrence of an axe from Graig Lwyd on Jersey, and by the fact that a third of the stone axes from the neolithic house at Ronaldsway in the Isle of Man were made from stone obtained from Stake Pass. Further, there is evidence, unfortunately not yet confirmed by scientific determinations of the raw materials, that certain highly polished axes of "jadeite" were imported to Britain from Brittany. Their form, triangular, with pointed butt and thin section, resembles a type common in Brittany, made apparently from the same material, which almost certainly occurs naturally in the peninsula. It may be noted that, although comparatively rare in Britain and extending northwards into Scotland, there are marked concentrations of these axes both in the Channel Islands and in the Southampton district.

Historically it is significant that the axe-trade in Britain was opened up by the predominantly hunter-fisher groups, which spread in from the east during the later stage of the neolithic settlement, rather than by the western neolithic farmers. Much remains obscure about the way in which the trade was actually organized. Strong grounds have already been advanced for thinking that the extraction of the raw material and its shaping into axes and kindred tools was carried out by specialists, who for some part of the year at least would have been solely engaged on these activities. The question arises how their products were distributed. Was this achieved, as in central Australia, by visits to the mines and quarries of representatives of communities needing to replenish their stores? To what extent was the trade carried on through a number of intermediaries, the axes passing from hand to hand through many different territories before being taken into use by some remote community? And how far was the commerce in the hands of merchants, who, drawing their supplies from the workshops, travelled around and disposed of them direct to consumers?

As will be shown later, there is little doubt that in so far as it extended into the coniferous zone, over territories occupied by hunter-fishers, the axe trade was organized by merchants who maintained trading posts well beyond their own homeland. On the other hand, it is difficult to believe that the circulation of axes among farming communities at a similar level of culture could have provided a sufficient livelihood to merchants and it is significant that, apart from Scandinavia, one does not find large concentrations of merchandise buried in the soil. Numerous small hoards of unused and often unpolished flint axes are of course common, but these are rightly interpreted as personal possessions buried for safety, votive offerings, or in the case of those buried with the dead as provision for the next world. Such hoards do, on the other hand, show that unused axes were regarded as a form of wealth and it is conceivable that among peoples to whom they were almost a technological necessity they would have formed a convenient medium of exchange. It may well be, therefore, that axes were distributed over extensive areas in the ordinary course of barter. The great distances over which the axes travelled, particularly in the case of those from Langdale and Tievebulliagh or Rathlin Island, show that the distribution can hardly be explained alone in terms of visits to the workshops by representatives of the consumers, though such visits must have occurred and may help to explain the rather flimsy traces of settlement on the part of several different groups at such a site as Easton Down in Wiltshire.

Trade in the well-known yellow wax-colored flint from Grand-Pressigny in southern Touraine falls into the same category as the axe-trade in the sense that it comprised artefacts rather than unworked blocks of raw material. This is shown by the absence in the export areas of cores and by the presence over the whole area of distribution of traits, such as shallow, oblique, parallel flake-scars, characteristic of the Grand Pressigny workshops. The most specialized type, and one that was also widely diffused, is a blade having one face pressure-flaked and subsequently polished over part of its surface. A great part in the diffusion of the flint was evidently played by rivers: from Touraine the trade spread downstream to Morbihan and upstream, across to the Paris basin and so by way of the Aisne and the Oise, into Belgium and Holland, and further, round the bend of the river into the Bourbonnais, eastwards to the Saône and on through the Belfort gap into Switzerland as far as Lake Constance. The sea played a much less important role than in the axe trade, and though Grand-Pressigny flint reached Jersey and even Guernsey, it is doubtful whether it crossed the English Channel. As might be expected of trade objects, blades and other forms of Grand-Pressigny flint penetrated the territories of several distinct cultures. It is found on the settlements of the people who made decorated Chassey pottery and it was also current among the Seine-Oise-Marne neolithic people, who buried it with their dead in the characteristic gallery graves and chalk-cut grottoes. The trade reached its greatest extent at the end of neolithic times and during an early stage of the Bronze Age: Grand-Pressigny flint seems first to have entered Switzerland in any quantity, with corded ware; in Jersey it was common at the Pinnacle site, which also yielded bell beaker pottery and a flat copper axe; and a typical blade, with one face flaked and polished, from a secondary burial in barrow III at Emmen in Gelderland, dates from the Early Bronze Age.

CHAPTER SIX

◫◫◫◫◫◫◫◫◫◫◫◫◫◫◫◫

Artifacts

The stone implements, potsherds, iron
artifacts, and other tools of prehistoric man
are the raw material of archaeology,
from which the past is reconstructed.
But the classification of these artifacts
and the concept of type are two of the
most controversial subjects in archaeology.
The papers that follow are a cross-section
of the basic literature on the first subject.
Consideration of the concept of type
controversy is omitted. For this subject, see
J. A. Ford, "On the Concept of Types,"
American Anthropologist 56 (1954) 42–53.

CLASSIFICATION OF ARTIFACTS

*Artifact classification involves the placing of all artifacts in a
collection site within a single set of classes based upon attributes
that reflect the customs and concepts of the manufacturers. In this
paper IRVING ROUSE divides classification into two varieties, analytic
and taxonomic, and describes the concepts upon which each is
based, as well as its uses.*

🔲 A number of recent papers, such as Phillips (1958), Wheat, Gifford, and
Wasley (1958), and Sears (1960), have been concerned with particular
methods used by archaeologists to classify artifacts. The present paper is
instead an attempt to survey the range of current methods. It is intended
to differentiate the various methods, to discuss their theoretical basis, and
to assess their relative utility.

According to the dictionary (Nielson, Knott, and Earhart 1940: 496), the
word classification refers to "the act of assigning [artifacts] to a proper
class." If the class is a new one, it will have to be defined by listing the
criteria used to form it and will also have to be given a name or a number.
If pertinent classes had previously been established, it will be enough to
determine that the new artifacts have the criteria diagnostic of one of the
classes, and to give them the name of that class.

Classification, like statistics, is not an end in itself but a technique by

"The Classification of Artifacts in Archaeology" by Irving Rouse, *American Antiquity* 25,
No. 3 (January 1960) 313–323. Reprinted by permission of the author and the Editor of
American Antiquity.

means of which to attain specified objectives, and so it must be varied with the objective. The main opportunity for variation comes in selecting the criteria which are to be considered diagnostic of one's classes. In my experience, archaeologists select these criteria to meet one of two alternate objectives: either to form modes or to establish types. If modes are the objective, the classification is called "analytic" (Whiteford 1947). If, instead, the purpose is to form types, then the classification becomes "taxonomic" (Phillips 1958). I shall discuss these two kinds of classification in turn.

ANALYTIC CLASSIFICATION

By the term "mode" is meant any standard, concept, or custom which governs the behavior of the artisans of a community, which they hand down from generation to generation, and which may spread from community to community over considerable distances (Rouse 1939). Such modes will be reflected in the artifacts as attributes which conform to a community's standards, which express its concepts, or which reveal its customary ways of manufacturing and using artifacts. Analytic classification focuses on these attributes and, through them, attempts to get at the standards, concepts, and customs themselves. In effect, it attempts to read such modes out of the artifacts.

Not all the attributes of the artifacts are indicative of modes. Some attributes will instead express personal idiosyncracies of the artisans. A unique design, which occurs only once, may be cited as an example. Other attributes fall within the realm of biology, chemistry, or physics rather than culture. The atomic structure of artifacts is an obvious example. The white color of shell artifacts is another. This whiteness does not appear until after the artifacts have been in the ground for some time, it is as prevalent among natural as among worked shells, and hence it must be considered a purely biological trait which has no part to play in cultural studies.

Analytic classification, then, must single out modes, which are cultural, and exclude those traits which are purely biological, chemical, or physical. One way to do this is to examine a collection in terms of the artisan's procedure, starting first with the materials he used, continuing with his techniques of manufacture, and then considering shape, decoration, and uses. At each stage in the procedure one may find that the artisan had some choice of standards or customs (Fig. 1). This makes it possible, for example, to divide a given collection into one or more series of classes on the basis of the materials used. One can then redistribute the same specimens into other series of classes on the basis of techniques, elements of shape and decoration, and uses (Fig. 2). Each class will have one or more diagnostic attributes, and those attributes will be indicative of a single mode.

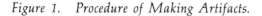

Figure 1. *Procedure of Making Artifacts.*

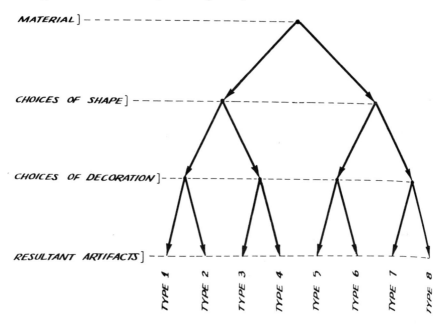

For example, an archaeologist may take a collection of potsherds and divide it into two classes, one consisting of sherds with inclusions of grit and the other, of sherds with inclusions of shell. He thereby determines that the potters had two alternative customs of tempering their vessels, one with pieces of stone and the other with pieces of shell. Then, he may pick out the sherds which are from rims and regroup them into a second series of classes, each characterized by a different set of rim attributes. In this case, he will have established a series of standards to which the potters conformed in making rims. He may repeat this process of reclassification with other aspects of material, shape, decoration, and use, ending up, as I have done in the case of my Antillean collections, with as many as 80 modes of material, shape, and decoration (Rouse 1939, 1941, 1952).

It is not necessary, of course, to be so systematic and all-inclusive as this in doing analytic classification. Various authors have concentrated upon technology (Matson 1942), upon shapes (Black and Weer 1936), upon designs (Amsden 1936), or upon uses (C. S. Ford 1937). The important point is that the author be interested in establishing independent modes and not in studying the manner in which those modes are combined on the artifacts.

Figure 2.   *Example of the Analytic Approach to Classification.*

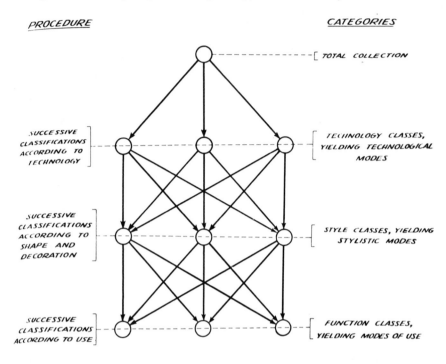

The modes may be of two kinds: (1) concepts of material, shape, and decoration to which the artisans conformed and (2) customary procedures followed in making and using the artifacts. In the case of conceptual modes, the archaeologist need only designate one or more attributes of his artifacts to be diagnostic of each class, but in the case of procedural modes he must also infer behavior of the artisans from the diagnostic attributes. The process of inferring procedural modes has been well described and illustrated by other authors (Osgood 1942; Thompson 1958).

Once modes have been set up—whether conceptual or procedural—and their diagnostic attributes have been determined, one may identify these modes on new artifacts simply by looking to see whether the proper diagnostic attributes are present, without actually grouping and regrouping the artifacts. Many archaeologists (Waring and Holder 1945, Fig. 1) have found it helpful to make drawings of the more complex conceptual modes, such as rim profiles or designs, to assist in identification.

TAXONOMIC CLASSIFICATION

We have seen that analytic classification concentrates on the attributes of the artifacts which indicate modes. Taxonomic classification is instead concerned with those attributes which indicate types (Gladwin and Gladwin, 1930, 1931, 1933; Haury 1936; Sayles 1936). As in the case of analytic classification, the attributes indicative of types must be chosen for their cultural significance (Gifford 1960). Indeed, if the archaeologist is being completely logical, he should first do analytic classification in order to form modes and should then classify taxonomically in terms of those modes, instead of going back again to the original attributes. In such a case, for example, he will use the technique of incision as a criterion for taxonomic classification, rather than the attribute of incised lines. In order to simplify the following discussion, I will assume that the archaeological taxonomist does work in terms of modes rather than raw attributes, in which case a type may be defined as a complex of modes which is diagnostic of a certain class of artifacts and which serves to differentiate that class from all other classes.

There are several different ways of classifying a collection to form types. The most systematic one is to divide the specimens into two or more classes on the basis of one set of modes, for example, of materials; then to subdivide each class on the basis of another set of modes, such as shapes; and to continue this process until all the artifacts of the same kind have been separated into a single sub-subclass (Fig. 3). Another way is to work intuitively by simply sorting and resorting the artifacts until they end up in relatively homogeneous classes (Krieger 1944, Fig. 25). A third is to work statistically, for example, by noting the taxonomically significant modes of each artifact on a punch card and sorting out the cards according to the most frequent combinations of modes (Shepard 1956: 322–332). In all cases the end result is the same: a single series of classes or subclasses rather than the successive series which result from analytic classification (compare Figs. 2, 3).

In all cases, the classifier must decide how many modes he is to consider diagnostic, that is, how many are going to end up in the type. He must select more than one, since by definition a type consists of two or more modes. On the other hand, he cannot expect to use all the modes; to do so would result in too large a number of types, especially if the artisan was permitted choices of modes during the course of the manufacture of the artifacts (Fig. 1). The proportion of modes which it is practicable to use as the criteria for taxonomic classification varies with the complexity of the artifacts and with the number of alternatives open to the artisan. Simple artifacts with few alternatives, for example, no decoration, can be classified in terms of almost all their modes, whereas complex artifacts with many alternatives, such as elaborately decorated pottery, require selection of only a few modes from among many. The type "stone ball" may be cited as an example of the former extreme; here the three diagnostic modes, use of stone, grinding, and spherical shape, are practically the only ones which

Figure 3.   *Example of the Taxonomic Approach to Classification.*

PROCEDURE   CATEGORIES

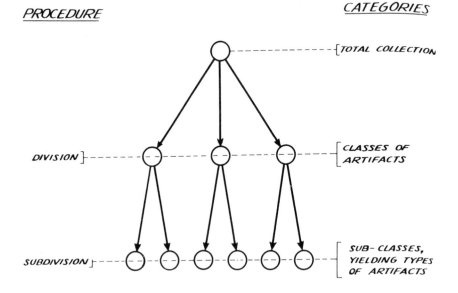

can be analyzed from the specimens. Pottery types illustrate the other extreme; for example, Ritchie and MacNeish (1949: 99, Fig. 36), in their study of pre-Iroquoian pottery, explicitly limited the diagnostic modes they used to rim profiles, designs, and decorative techniques, excluding all the other modes which were analyzable from the sherds.

The personality of the taxonomist may also have an effect upon the number of modes which he selects to be diagnostic. If he is a "lumper," he will group the artifacts into large and inclusive classes, each of which will contain so much variation that relatively few of its modes can be considered diagnostic. If, on the other hand, he is a "splitter," he will establish many more classes, there will be less variation within each class, and as a result the ratio of diagnostic to non-diagnostic modes will be considerably higher.

The current tendency on the part of some archaeologists to subdivide pottery types into varieties (Gifford 1960) seems designed to meet this problem. It permits one to select a relatively small number of diagnostic modes for one's types and thereby to satisfy the lumper, and at the same time to define varieties in terms of larger numbers of diagnostic modes, thus satisfying the splitter as well.

The distinction between diagnostic modes, which form part of the type or variety, and non-diagnostic modes, which do not, is frequently obscured by the practice of "describing types" (Ford and Willey 1949: 71–78). In the terminology of the present paper, such descriptions amount to a presentation of the modes analyzable from the artifacts of each class. Some of these modes will be diagnostic and, as a result, form part of the type; but others—and in many cases the majority—will not. Ritchie and MacNeish (1949: 100–116) provide a good example. In the case of each type, these authors specify only three "diagnostic features" and then proceed to list a much larger number of other modes of "paste," "surface finish," "decoration," and "forms." The latter modes are not part of the type, as the word is used in the present paper.

The selection of modes has a qualitative as well as a quantitative aspect. The taxonomist must decide not only how many but also what kinds of modes are to be considered diagnostic of his classes and hence constituents of his types. Our colleagues in biology solve this problem by selecting the diagnostics which best show the course of organic evolution. We archaeologists are not so consistent. In the case of pottery and sometimes also projectile points, we select those modes which best indicate differences in time and space (Ford and Willey 1949: 40). Otherwise, we tend to select modes which best express the intrinsic nature of the artifacts (Rouse 1952: 327–329). This difference is reflected in the names of our types, for example, "Glades Plain" in the case of pottery and "semilunar knife" in the case of stonework—or "problematical form" when the nature of the artifact is not known.

This difference must be kept in mind if we are to think clearly about classification. It leads me to make a distinction between (1) historical types, whose modes have been selected, consciously or unconsciously, for their time-space significance and (2) descriptive types, composed of modes referring primarily to the nature of the artifacts.

Once types have been established—whether they are historical or descriptive—they may be used to identify new artifacts without the necessity of actually grouping the artifacts into classes. One need only determine that the new artifacts have the modes comprising a certain type and then apply the name of that type. This is easy enough to do if the types are simple. In the case of more complex types, containing a greater number of diagnostic modes, it has sometimes proved helpful to establish a key to assist in comparison. As in biology, such a key consists of a list in outline form of the modes comprising all of the types. To identify an unknown artifact, one need only trace it down through the key by means of its modes (Colton and Hargrave 1937: 36–41; Colton 1952, 1955).

Another device to assist in the identification of new material is the "type artifact(s)." Not to be confused with an artifact type, this consists of the most typical artifact(s) in a class. To identify unknown artifacts or to check identifications made by means of a key, one may compare the unknown artifacts with the type artifacts and thereby, in effect, assign them to the classes typified by those artifacts (Osgood 1942: 22–25).

Modes vs. Types

We have now distinguished the two principal ways in which archaeologists classify artifacts, analytic and taxonomic. Analytic classification is done by forming successive series of classes, focusing on different features of the artifacts. Each class is characterized by one or more attributes which indicate a procedure to which the artisan conformed, such as a technique of manufacture, or a concept which he expressed in the artifacts, such as an element of shape or decoration. Each custom or concept constitutes a mode.

Taxonomic classification is done by formulating a single set of classes, which differentiate the artifacts in one's collection according to type. Each taxonomic class is characterized by two or more modes, selected from among the total number of modes obtainable by means of analytic classification. The modes diagnostic of each class constitute its type.

Types, then, consist of selected modes. We have seen that the nature of the selection will vary from type to type depending upon the complexity of the artifacts, the number of alternatives which the culture offered to the artisans, the personal inclination of the taxonomist (whether he is a "lumper" or a "splitter"), and the purposes for which he plans to use the types.

To put this in another way, modes are inherent in one's collection. If two archaeologists analyze the same collection and do an equally good job of it, they should produce the same modes (Taylor 1948: 129–130). Types, on the contrary, are imposed on the collection. If two taxonomists classify the same collection and decide, for whatever reason, upon different diagnostic modes, they will produce different types (Brew 1946: 46). The mode, therefore, is a natural unit of cultural study, whereas the type is an arbitrary one.

It does not follow from this that types are any less demonstrable than modes. An archaeologist can validate types equally well by grouping them into classes and demonstrating that the artifacts of each class share the same diagnostic modes. The point is that he can then regroup the artifacts according to another set of diagnostic modes and thereby produce other types which will have equal validity.

It should not be implied, either, that a type consists merely of the sum of its constituent modes. The fact that all these modes recur from artifact to artifact gives them a reality above and beyond that of the individual modes.

We have distinguished two kinds of modes: (1) conceptual modes, consisting of ideas and standards which the artisans expressed in the artifacts and (2) procedural modes, consisting of customs followed by the artisans in making and using the artifacts. Conceptual modes are directly indicated by the attributes of the artifacts whereas procedural modes have to be inferred from the attributes. Hence, the distinction between the two is primarily a matter of relative reliability.

Two kinds of types have likewise been distinguished: (1) historical types, formed in order to establish differences of time and space, and (2) descriptive types, formed in order to express differences in the nature of the artifacts. There may be some overlapping between these two, but generally they will be distinct, because the modes comprising each will have been chosen for different reasons. Here, we have a good example of the arbitrary nature of types.

A comparison with ethnology may perhaps help to clarify these distinctions. One of the things an ethnologist does in studying material culture is to ask or observe how his informants make and use their artifacts. Such observations enable the ethnologist to distinguish various techniques of manufacture and uses of the artifacts. In the terminology of the present paper, the latter are procedural modes.

It is likewise possible for the ethnologist to ask his informants to identify the various parts of their artifacts. If the informants go on to distinguish different kinds of handles, for example, or if the ethnologist himself does so, they will be producing the units here called conceptual modes.

A third possibility is for the ethnologist to ask his informants to identify the artifacts as complete objects by saying, for example, that they are "knives" or "scrapers." If either the informant or the ethnologist goes on to define the resultant categories by listing the modes diagnostic of each, he will be producing the units which we have termed descriptive types.

Finally, the informants may refer to certain artifacts as being "old-" or "new-fashioned" and to others as being of a local or foreign style. If either the informant or the ethnologist should define these categories by listing their distinctive modes, he would be producing what are here called historical types.

In other words, the ethnologist as well as the archaeologist may do both analytic and taxonomic classification. The ethnologist, however, is able to do so with the assistance of informants, whereas the archaeologist is forced to rely entirely upon his own judgment and experience in formulating modes and types.

UTILITY OF THE METHODS

Brew (1946: 65) has observed that "we need more rather than fewer classifications, different classifications, always new classifications, to meet new needs." If Brew is correct, we ought to be able to list the needs for classification in archaeology and to state the kinds of classification which best meet each need. The remainder of the paper will be devoted to this task. It will be done in terms of the products of our two kinds of classification, conceptual and procedural modes and historical and descriptive types.

IDENTIFICATION OF ARTIFACTS. There is probably no professional archaeologist who has not, at one time or another, had an amateur come up to him, take an artifact out of his pocket, and ask for an identification. When the amateur does this, he expects to be answered in terms of descriptive types, that is, to be told that the artifact is a "knife" or a "scraper," for example. If the artifact is a potsherd, the professional will probably answer instead in terms of historical types, calling it "Sebonac Stamped," for example. In my experience the latter answer is not so satisfying to the amateur. He does not understand it, unless he is unusually sophisticated, and tends to look upon it as an affectation of the professional. The amateur is probably right in this, insofar as he is interested purely in identification and not in the historical significance of the potsherd. It would be more appropriate for the professional to identify the sherd descriptively as "a fragment of a cooking pot" instead of terming it "Sebonac Stamped."

Interest in such descriptive identification is, of course, not limited to amateurs. The professional must do it in cataloguing his artifacts and in preparing museum exhibits, where specimens are grouped according to types. Descriptive identification is also basic to several more academic pursuits of the archaeologist, which are discussed below. It is fortunate that taxonomy has not lost prestige among archaeologists as it has in the other natural sciences, for it is a vital part of our research.

DETERMINATION OF THE CULTURE OF A COMPONENT. Following the lead of Taylor (1948: 197), I would suggest that, when archaeologists determine the culture of a component, that is, of a culturally homogeneous site unit, they would do well to conform to ethnographic practice. As already indicated, ethnographers handle their collections in two different ways: (1) they identify the artifacts, usually in terms supplied by their informants, and (2) they discuss the manufacture and use of the artifacts (Thompson 1958: 65–146). From the standpoint of the present paper, (1) corresponds to descriptive types and (2) to the modes produced by means of analytic classification. (Ethnographers seem to emphasize procedural modes, but many of them also pay some attention to conceptual modes.) Accordingly, I would suggest that the best way to determine and present the culture of a component is in terms of descriptive types and of procedural and conceptual modes. I doubt that historical types are necessary for this particular purpose, so long as the descriptive approach is applied to pottery and projectile points as well as to other kinds of artifacts, since the historical types will overlap the descriptive types, and anyway they are designed for a different purpose.

The descriptive types and modes will, of course, suffice only to present the material culture of the component. They must be combined with other traits and complexes inferred from the non-artifactual content of the component, for example, the settlement pattern, in order to establish the total culture of the component. The various types, modes, and other traits may simply be listed or they may. be grouped into culturally meaningful categories. For example, Fairbanks (1942: 228–229) has organized them about the activities of the people inhabiting the Stallings Island component, in accordance with the concept of activity proposed by Linton (1936: 397).

CLASSIFICATION OF COMPONENTS TO FORM CULTURES. Many archaeologists find it advisable to group their components into cultures, known variously as foci, phases, complexes, industries, or styles. This requires a form of taxonomic classification. The common practice is to compare the components in terms of their "traits" and, as in the taxonomic classification of artifacts, to select certain traits to be "determinants" of each culture (Cole and Deuel 1937: 207–223). When one examines such determinants from the standpoint of the present paper, one finds that they consist of varying combinations of procedural and conceptual modes and of descriptive and historical types. The four appear to be used indiscriminately, without thought as to which units, if any, would be more suitable. To my knowledge, the only author who has attempted to discriminate among the various kinds of determinants is Phillips (1958: 123–124), who advocates the use of types as the primary basis for classifying components but would supplement them with modes.

Phillips does not distinguish among the various kinds of types and modes but, if the suggestions made above for the presentation of the culture of a component are correct, it would be appropriate to use descriptive types and both kinds of modes. Personally, I would hesitate to state categorically, as Phillips does, that types should be given priority over modes. I suspect that this will depend on the nature of the cultures being studied. In fact, I can conceive of cases in which modes might suffice by themselves. I do not believe that it would do merely to use single modes, but types are not the only available kinds of combinations of modes. It has been possible, for example, to establish structural relationships among modes, such as Amsden's (1936) correlation of "design vocabulary" and elements of shape. Such structural relationships have proved to be effective as determinants in other branches of anthropology, for example, in the classification of folktales (Propp 1958), and I wonder whether they might not work better in the classification of some archaeological components than typological complexes of modes, whether selected for their historical or their descriptive significance.

Alternatively, there may well be cases in which neither types nor modes are the best criteria to use in classifying components. Non-artifactual traits, such as settlement patterns and means of subsistence, may sometimes prove to be superior.

In any case, I am certain that artifact types alone cannot provide an adequate basis for the classification of components, if only because they do not cover enough of the culture of the components. For example, Brew (in Tax and others 1953: 245) has argued that there is no such thing as a Folsom culture (complex) because practically nothing is known of it but the Folsom type of projectile point. Even assuming that we have only the one type of point, the situation looks better when viewed in terms of modes and non-artifactual traits, for we know the kinds of material used; the techniques of manufacture; distinctive elements of shape; a characteristic, if assumed use; and something about the means of subsistence. All these are separate traits which Brew obscured by limiting himself to the type concept.

DATING OF COMPONENTS AND CULTURES. Historical types are unquestionably the most effective kind of unit to use in dating components and cultures. The fact that their constituent modes have been selected for time-space significance makes them superior to descriptive types; and the fact that they consist of multiple modes gives them greater reliability than individual modes. This is true whether the types are used as "time markers" with which to correlate strata (components) in the manner of paleontology or are studied in terms of their relative popularity in a more purely archaeological fashion (Heizer 1958: 112–113, 114–115).

DEFINITION OF CULTURAL PERIODS. By the same token, historical types should be most suitable for defining local cultural periods. J. A. Ford's various chronological studies may be cited as examples; his lettered "time scale" and the correlated periods are measured against the frequency changes of pottery types (Phillips, Ford, and Griffin 1951, Figs. 17–21). If, on the other hand, one wishes to work with chronology on a regional, multi-areal basis, modes are likely to be more practicable, whether used singly or in combinations, since they tend to have a broader distribution than types (Cruxent and Rouse 1959).

STUDIES OF CULTURAL DISTRIBUTION. Following J. A. Ford's lead (1952: 319), I would suggest that modes are the best unit to use in studying cultural distributions. One may trace their persistence and their relative popularity through time (Rouse 1939, Fig. 6) or their diffusion from area to area (Wendorf 1953: 163–170). By so doing, one will not only be able to reconstruct the histories of the individual modes but also one will find that certain modes tend always to occur together and hence to form discrete historical complexes. Some of these complexes will correspond to types, that is, they will consist of the same modes as those comprising types, but other complexes will cut across the types. The structural relationships discussed above provide one example. The "traditions" and "horizon styles" of Peruvian archaeology are another (Willey 1945).

An archaeologist who studies the distributions of individual modes, then, will be in a position to reconstruct the histories of those modes and also the histories of types and of non-typological complexes of modes. On the other hand, the archaeologist who studies only the distributions of types will be unable to get at the histories of the other kinds of units. Southwestern archaeology, where it is customary to concentrate on the distribution of types (Colton and Hargrave 1937, Fig. 1), is a case in point. Several authors (Rouse 1954: 223) have commented on the lack of horizon styles in the Southwest. This may well be a peculiarity of the culture history of the Southwestern area, but there is also a possibility that it reflects failure on the part of Southwestern archaeologists, in their preoccupation with types, to trace the distribution of enough individual modes.

STUDIES OF CULTURAL CHANGE. If one is interested in the problem of how one complex (whether typological or not) or one culture has changed into another, modes are again the proper unit to use. As Barnett (1953: 185) has put it,

> In order to understand the innovative process, we must be prepared to analyze ideas in any fashion and without limit . . . so that we may follow the ramifications of recombination as they actually occur. We cannot deal with the gross stereotyped wholes [i.e., types] only. . . . We must treat conventional ideas, such as those of tables and men, merely as more or less stable organizations of experience that can be torn down and reassembled in the wink of an eye.
>
> In all the sciences we have come to expect very detailed analyses of data for purposes of classification. This lead, however, has not been followed by students of [culture change]. . . . In trying to understand invention it is common practice to deal with such gross units as automobiles and buggies or [pottery types] and spinning wheels. The attempt to understand one of these complex wholes in terms of the whole of another will give us no insight into their true relationships. We must view the inception of each one in terms of an analysis of its component parts.
>
> The linguists long ago recognized this necessity, and students of linguistic change do not hesitate to break down sentences, words, parts of words, and parts of these parts. . . . There can be no question that linguists are far ahead of the rest of us in their understanding of the mechanics of cultural change.

Barnett might have added that archaeologists are also accustomed to do analysis and to study culture change in terms of the resultant modes. Gladwin's (1957: 282–284) final report on Southwestern archaeology may be cited as an example. Linguists cannot claim sole credit for this kind of approach, nor to have produced the only significant results from it.

CONCLUSIONS

In the foregoing section I have attempted to indicate some of the situations in which it is better to use modes, resulting from analytic classification, or types, resulting from taxonomic classification. I do not pretend to have fully covered the subject; rather I have intended to call attention to it as a problem which deserves the consideration of archaeologists. Too many of us, in my experience, fail to discriminate between modes and types, treating them as equivalent units and substituting one for the other whenever it is convenient to do so (Webb and Snow 1945: 16–28). We need to think more about when the various kinds of modes, types, or combinations thereof will be the most effective units to use.

This paper has likewise been intended to call attention to the way in which analysis and taxonomy complement each other as methods of classification. I think we should beware the tendency of some archaeologists to become preoccupied with one to the neglect of the other.

As already indicated, taxonomic classification has received particular emphasis in the American Southwest. We appear at the moment to be witnessing the diffusion of certain Southwestern taxonomic developments to the Southeast (Phillips 1958) and Mesoamerica (Smith, Willey, and Gifford 1960). I do not criticize this diffusion; indeed, I would recommend that it be expanded to include other Southwestern taxonomic devices, such as the key and the type artifact.

On the other hand, I share with Sears (1960) the belief that the analytic approach likewise needs to be strengthened and applied more widely. We need more studies of individual modes and of their non-typological combinations, such as the recent work of Wasley (1959) in the Southwest.

The fact is that both analytic and taxonomic classification must be done in order to make a full study of any collection. Neither, by itself, will supply a complete picture of the culture of the collection, nor will either be able to furnish all the data needed to formulate cultures or to reconstruct culture history.

Bibliography

Amsden, C. A.
    1936 The Structural Analysis of Pottery Design. In his "An Analysis of Hohokam Pottery Design," *Medallion Papers*, No. 23, pp. 1–17. Gila Pueblo, Globe.
Barnett, H. G.
    1953 *Innovation: the Basis of Cultural Change.* New York: McGraw-Hill.
Black, G. A., and P. Weer
    1936 "A Proposed Terminology for Shape Classification of Artifacts." *American Antiquity*, Vol. 1, No. 4, pp. 280–294. Menasha.
Brew, J. O.
    1946 The Use and Abuse of Taxonomy. In his "Archaeology of Alkali Ridge, Southeastern Utah," *Papers of the Peabody Museum, Harvard University*, Vol. 21, pp. 44–66. Cambridge.
Cole, Fay-Cooper, and Thorne Deuel
    1937 *Rediscovering Illinois: Archaeological Explorations in and around Fulton County.* Chicago: University of Chicago Press.

Colton, H. S.
  1952 "Pottery Types of the Arizona Strip and Adjacent Areas in Utah and Nevada." *Museum of Northern Arizona, Ceramic Series,* No. 1. Flagstaff.
  1955 "Check List of Southwestern Pottery Types." *Museum of Northern Arizona, Ceramic Series,* No. 2. Flagstaff.
——, and L. L. Hargrave
  1937 "Handbook of Northern Arizona Pottery Wares. *Museum of Northern Arizona, Bulletin,* No. 11. Flagstaff.
Cruxent, J. M., and Irving Rouse
  1959 "An Archeological Chronology of Venezuela." *Pan American Union, Social Science Monographs,* No. 6. Washington.
Fairbanks, C. H.
  1942 "The Taxonomic Position of Stalling's Island, Georgia." *American Antiquity,* Vol. 7, No. 3, pp. 223–231. Menasha.
Ford, C. S.
  1937 "A Sample Comparative Analysis of Material Culture." In *Studies in the Science of Society,* edited by G. P. Murdock. 225–246. New Haven: Yale University Press.
Ford, J. A.
  1952 "Measurements of Some Prehistoric Design Developments in the Southeastern United States." *Anthropological Papers of the American Museum of Natural History,* Vol. 44, Pt. 3. New York.
——, and G. R. Willey
  1949 "Surface Survey of the Virú Valley, Peru." *Anthropological Papers of the American Museum of Natural History,* Vol. 43, Pt. 1. New York.
Gifford, J. C.
  1960 "The Type-Variety Method of Ceramic Classification as an Indicator of Cultural Phenomena." *American Antiquity,* Vol. 25, No. 3, pp. 341–347. Salt Lake City.
Gladwin, H. S.
  1957 *A History of the Ancient Southwest.* Portland, Maine: Bond, Wheelwright.
Gladwin, Winifred, and H. S. Gladwin
  1930 "Some Southwestern Pottery Types, Series I." *Medallion Papers,* No. 8. Gila Pueblo, Globe.
  1931 "Some Southwestern Pottery Types, Series II." *Medallion Papers,* No. 10. Gila Pueblo, Globe.
  1933 "Some Southwestern Pottery Types, Series III." *Medallion Papers,* No. 13. Gila Pueblo, Globe.
Haury, E. W.
  1936 "Some Southwestern Pottery Types, Series IV." *Medallion Papers,* No. 19. Gila Pueblo, Globe.
Heizer, R. F. (editor)
  1958 *A Guide to Archaeological Field Methods.* Third revised edition. Palo Alto: National Press.
Krieger, A. D.
  1944 "The Typological Concept." *American Antiquity,* Vol. 9, No. 3, pp. 271–288. Menasha.
Linton, Ralph
  1936 *The Study of Man.* New York: Appleton, Century.
Matson, F. R.
  1952 "The Contribution of Technical Ceramic Studies to American Archaeology." *Prehistoric Pottery of the Eastern United States,* No. 2, pp. 1–7. Ann Arbor.
Neilson, W. A., T. A. Knott, and P. W. Earhart (editors)
  1940 *Webster's New International Dictionary of the English Language.* Second edition. Springfield: G. and C. Merriam Co.
Osgood, Cornelius
  1942 "The Ciboney Culture of Cayo Redondo, Cuba." *Yale University Publications in Anthropology,* No. 25. New Haven.

Phillips, Philip
  1958 "Application of the Wheat–Gifford–Wasley Taxonomy to Eastern Ceramics."
    American Antiquity, Vol. 24, No. 2, pp. 117–130. Salt Lake City.
——, J. A. Ford, and J. B. Griffin
  1951 "Archaeological Survey in the Lower Mississippi Alluvial Valley, 1940–1947."
    Papers of the Peabody Museum, Harvard University, Vol. 25. Cambridge.

Propp, V.
  1958 "Morphology of the Folktale." *Publications of the Indiana University Research
    Center in Anthropology, Folklore, and Linguistics*, No. 10. Bloomington.

Ritchie, W. A., and R. S. MacNeish
  1949 "The Pre-Iroquoian Pottery of New York State." *American Antiquity*, Vol. 15,
    No. 2, pp. 97–124. Menasha.

Rouse, Irving
  1939 "Prehistory in Haiti: A Study in Method." *Yale University Publications in
    Anthropology*, No. 21. New Haven.
  1941 "Culture of the Ft. Liberté Region, Haiti." *Yale University Publications in
    Anthropology*, No. 24, New Haven.
  1952 "Porto Rican Prehistory." *The New York Academy of Sciences, Scientific Survey
    of Porto Rico and the Virgin Islands*, Vol. 18, Nos. 3–4, pp. 307–578. New York.
  1954 "On the Use of the Concept of Area Co-Tradition." *American Antiquity*, Vol.
    19, No. 3, pp. 221–225. Salt Lake City.

Sayles, E. B.
  1936 "Some Southwestern Pottery Types, Series V." *Medallion Papers*, No. 21. Gila
    Pueblo, Globe.

Sears, W. H.
  1960 "Taxonomic Systems and Eastern Archaeology." *American Antiquity*, Vol. 25,
    No. 3, pp. 324–329. Salt Lake City.

Shepard, A. O.
  1956 "Ceramics for the Archaeologist." *Carnegie Institution of Washington, Publication*,
    No. 609. Washington.

Smith, R. E., G. R. Willey, and J. C. Gifford
  1960 "The Type-Variety Concept as a Basis for the Analysis of Maya Pottery."
    American Antiquity, Vol. 25, No. 3, pp. 330–340. Salt Lake City.

Taylor, W. W.
  1948 "A Study of Archeology." *Memoirs of the American Anthropological Association*,
    No. 69. Menasha.

Tax, Sol, L. C. Eiseley, Irving Rouse, and C. F. Voegelin (editors)
  1953 *An Appraisal of Anthropology Today*. University of Chicago Press, Chicago.

Thompson, R. H.
  1958 "Modern Yucatecan Maya Pottery Making." *Memoirs of the Society for Ameri-
    can Archaeology*, No. 15. Salt Lake City.

Waring, A. J., Jr., and Preston Holder
  1945 "A Prehistoric Ceremonial Complex in the Southeastern United States."
    American Anthropologist, Vol. 47, No. 1, pp. 1–34. Menasha.

Wasley, W. W.
  1959 "Cultural Implications of Style Trends in Southwestern Pottery: Basketmaker
    III to Pueblo II in West Central New Mexico." MS, doctoral dissertation,
    University of Arizona, Tucson.

Webb, W. S., and C. E. Snow
  1945 "The Adena People." *The University of Kentucky Reports in Anthropology and
    Archaeology*, Vol. 6. Lexington.

Wendorf, Fred
  1953 "Archaeological Studies in the Petrified Forest National Monument." *Museum
    of Northern Arizona, Bulletin*, No. 27. Flagstaff.

Wheat, J. B., J. C. Gifford, and W. W. Wasley
  1958 "Ceramic Variety, Type Cluster, and Ceramic System in Southwestern Pottery
    Analysis." *American Antiquity*, Vol. 24, No. 1, pp. 34–47. Salt Lake City.

Whiteford, A. H.
  1947 "Description for Artifact Analysis." *American Antiquity*, Vol. 12, No. 4, pp. 226–237. Menasha.
Willey, G. R.
  1945 "Horizon Styles and Pottery Traditions in Peruvian Archaeology." *American Antiquity*, Vol. 11, No. 1, pp. 49–56. Menasha.

THE DIMENSIONS OF ARCHAEOLOGY

In the following concise and well reasoned paper, ALBERT C. SPAULDING deals with the empirical data of archaeologists' artifacts, which may be studied in terms of three dimensions: form, space, and time. The dimension of form consists of artifact attributes that are subject to statistical analysis. The dimension of space is seen as the context of artifacts within a site, and time is manifested in absolute or relative scales. The relationships between these three dimensions are strongly defined, and the need for their being kept separate is emphasized.

 This paper is an attempt to describe clearly the fundamental operations of archaeology on its empirical data. Behavioral inferences may creep in, but they will be evidence of weak-mindedness. The goal is most definitely not a lecture on how archaeology ought to be done; it is rather a description of what is done when exposition is incisive, economical, and convincing. The topic is particularly suitable for a volume honoring Leslie White, whose major work has been the systematic exposition of interrelationships of cultural phenomena. A great gain would result if my purpose could be realized fully: questions of fact would be sharply separated from questions of theory, thus pointing accurately to those topics on which factual data are needed and providing a guide for research along the most effective lines. Since all the matters discussed here are essentially common knowledge, I have not provided any references.

"The Dimensions of Archaeology" by Albert C. Spaulding in Gertrude E. Dole and Robert L. Carneiro: *Essays in the Science of Culture in Honor of Leslie A. White*, pp. 437–456. Copyright 1960 by Thomas Y. Crowell Company. Reprinted by permission of the author and the publisher.

METHOD OF ANALYSIS

I assume that on an elementary level we cannot improve on the concepts that are successful in other branches of science, especially in the physical sciences, which enjoy a long tradition of enviable precision and clarity, at least when viewed from the outside. These sciences can be thought of as studying the interrelationships of the dimensions appropriate to their specified subject matter. The subject of mechanics, for example, is physical objects, and the dimensions in terms of which the objects are considered are length, mass, and time. Classical mechanics can be defined economically as the study of the interrelationships of length, mass, and time exhibited by physical objects. Thermodynamics, on the other hand, can be considered a more complicated science because it deals with temperature in addition to the three dimensions of mechanics. A dimension can be thought of as an aspect or property of the subject matter which requires its own special measuring device. There are invariable rules for operating with dimensions (the examples given are not logically independent), of which we can mention:

1. The units of discrete dimensions do not possess additive properties. Any formulation of the type $L + T = x$ or $L = T$ (feet plus minutes equals x, or feet equals minutes) or "the artifact is older than it is heavy" is meaningless.

2. Ratios of discrete dimensions, usually called rates, are meaningful, familiar examples being miles per hour or pounds per cubic foot.

3. Concepts involving more than one application of the measuring instrument can be meaningful. Thus area is length squared, and volume is length cubed.

4. Dimensional equations must be homogeneous, that is, the same dimensions must appear on both sides of the equation. However, dimensionless numbers may be introduced into such equations.

SUBJECT MATTER AND DIMENSIONS
OF ARCHAEOLOGY

It seems quite clear that the subject matter of archaeology is artifacts, using this term in its broadest sense as any material expression of human cultural activity and adding the qualification that I am concerned here with prehistoric artifacts. Although deciding whether or not a particular object is an artifact may be difficult, I will treat the artifact as given in this discussion for reasons of economy. The dimensions of artifacts which will be considered here are form (in the sense of any physico-chemical property of the artifact), temporal locus (meaning the dating of prehistoric events as inferred from artifacts, specifically the time of manufacture, period of use, and time of deposition of an artifact or a class of artifacts), and spatial locus (the position of the artifact in the three dimensional world). There is, I believe, general agreement that archaeologists are always concerned with these properties of artifacts, and there is an implication that archaeology can be defined minimally as the study of the interrelationship of form, temporal locus, and spatial locus exhibited by artifacts. In other words, archaeologists are always concerned with these interrelationships, whatever broader interests they may have, and these interrelationships are the special business of archaeology.

All of the rules for operation with dimensions apply to form, time, and space, and certain theoretical formulations can be dismissed at once on this basis. A statement of the type "the focus concept contains more of form than it does of time (or space)" is equivalent to the dimensional equation $F + T = x$, which is dimensionally heterogeneous and hence meaningless. Presumably what is involved here is a statement of the idea that a group of artifact assemblages having a high degree of formal resemblance to each other will usually or invariably show a compact clustering in time and in space, or in dimensional terms

$$\left[\frac{F_1}{T_1} = \frac{F_2}{T_2} \right].$$

The dimensional equation (put in brackets to indicate that it is not algebraic) states that a systematic relationship holds between degree of formal resemblance and length of time span; since form and time appear on both sides of the equation, it is homogeneous and can be given a determinate meaning. This illustration is intended to show that reasoning in terms of dimensional analysis can be something more than a sterile formality: it can be a safeguard against unclear thinking or exposition. The dimensional equation also points directly to a very real archaeological problem: if we are to substitute real data for the symbols of the equation, then we must develop objective scales for our dimensions.

THE FORMAL DIMENSION. It is plain that the formal dimension cannot be dealt with by the application of any simple kind of scale, although it is a useful concept for broad theorizing. In practice formal descriptions and comparisons are made by analyzing artifact form into a number of discrete attribute systems: color, chemical composition, weight, various lengths (and the length relationships which describe shape), and so on. These attribute systems can be treated as dimensions in their own right, and from this point of view the formal dimension is a class of dimensions. I will not attempt more than a glance at some of the obvious characteristics of formal attributes.

Formal attributes can be divided into two classes, quantitative attributes (or measurements) and qualitative attributes. Quantitative attributes, weight and length for example, vary continuously, and they can be measured by ordinary scaling devices divided into equal units. Artifacts can be compared absolutely in terms of these measurements, that is, the difference between two artifacts can be expressed in equal units of the appropriate scale (x is 25 pounds heavier than y). Relative comparisons are also possible (x is twice as long as y) if the zero point of the scale is not arbitrary. To borrow an example from another dimension, it cannot be said that Hopewell is twice as old as Middle Mississippi because the age relationship is merely a function of an arbitrarily chosen reference point in time. Quantitative attributes can be described neatly in scale units, and the numerical properties of the measurements lend themselves to straightforward statistical description and inference.

Qualitative attributes cannot be described and compared by means of any familiar scaling device. They are thought of as discrete properties of artifacts, and the scale applied is no more than a notation of presence or absence. Recognition of the qualitative attributes of an artifact seems to be largely intuitive. The observer has a personal knowledge of human musculature and sensory apparatus and of the properties of materials, and he can judge at once that the addition of a pair of side notches to a flint projectile point represents a discrete segment of the total behavior involved in making the point. Qualitative attributes which are mutually exclusive can be grouped into a dimension; thus the projectile point may be made from white flint, argillite, or some other material. This grouping provides a three-position scale within the dimension of material for describing the point and for classifying a collection of points.

In an ultimate sense, the distinction between quantitative and qualitative attributes tends to break down because any real measuring instrument must be divided into discrete steps, however small they may be. Nevertheless, the distinction remains in practice; the fineness of recorded measurements is limited only by the precision of the measuring instrument and the nature of the number system in which the records are kept, but the nature of the attribute itself limits the observation of the qualitative attribute. It is sometimes possible to transform ostensibly qualitative attributes into continuously variable properties, as when personal judgments of shades of color are replaced by measurements with physical apparatus, and the resulting gain in objectivity may prove to be valuable. However, the essentially discrete nature of many attributes is plain enough to make such a translation superfluous for many purposes, and a wholesale attempt to replace with measurements the current presence-or-absence observation of recognized attributes would have no utility. No one questions the reasonableness or objectivity of describing a vessel as having four strap handles and contrasting it with other vessels having two or no strap handles.

The distinction between quantitative and qualitative attributes is operationally relevant in a fundamental archaeological problem, the preparation of an attribute list for the formal description of a collection of artifacts. The very nature of quantitative attributes ensures that no two artifacts will yield exactly the same measurement, but it is necessary to discriminate between the unimportant and presumably random variation expected of products made by hand from materials which are not uniform and the culturally meaningful variation resulting from significantly differing models held by the makers of the artifacts. The problem can be attacked by listing in order the individual values of some measurement (say projectile point length) in a collection. If the list seems to show a pronounced clustering of values around a central point with progressively fewer values toward the extremes of the observed range, the conclusion ordinarily reached will be that the variation is of the random type. If, on the other hand, there are two or more values around which the measurements cluster, then two or more categories will be distinguished, and each can be thought of as a separate qualitative attribute such as "large" and "small." The problem is purely statistical, although in many instances it can be solved by inspection rather than by formal statistical curve fitting.

Qualitative attributes are by definition those properties of artifacts which are already recognized as representing discrete segments of behavior, and accordingly they can be placed on the attribute list without further analysis. Subsequent study may show that a supposed qualitative attribute can in fact be split into two or more meaningful classes; for example, a description of a motif as an incised triangle may disguise a significant difference between large and small or scalene and isosceles triangles. Conversely, some distinctions may be quite objective but turn out to have a sharply limited utility for the purpose of describing significant variations in patterns of attribute association. Thus triangles, rectangles, or circles might appear as decorative elements on a group of otherwise identical pots, and on this basis it would make sense to group them as a class of geometrical decorative elements. These qualifications are essentially secondary, however, and do not override the basic distinction of continuity *versus* discontinuity which is the root of the quantitative-qualitative division.

Techniques for recognizing formal attributes logically precede the next problem, that of studying artifact interrelationships in terms of formal attributes. For this problem, the recognized attributes serve as linking constants from artifact to artifact: they are the units whose presences and absences constitute similarity or difference. In some respects attributes are analogous to linguistic phonemes. They represent minimal units of meaningful behavior; they are taken to be constant for comparative and descriptive purposes; and they are articulated to form the artifact, which can be regarded as the minimal independent unit of material culture. In the simplest terms, the problem is what to do with a collection of artifacts and a list of formal attributes which the artifacts exhibit. There appear to be three possibilities in ordering a collection of artifacts with respect to their formal attributes:

1. The collection can be characterized by tallying each appearance of every attribute recognized.

2. The particular combination of attributes exhibited by each artifact can be listed, and the list can be condensed by grouping and tallying identical combinations.

3. The artifacts can be classified in terms of attribute clusters; this is accomplished by mathematical manipulation of the data provided by Types 1 and 2. This process is referred to here as cluster analysis.

Classification of Type 1 results in a number of classes having no relationship to one another except that imposed by the nature of the attribute systems. The description offered by such a classification is of the general type: red pots, 50, other colors, 50; grit tempered pots, 35; sand tempered pots, 65; bowls, 30; jars, 30; plates, 40; and so on. Tallies in sets of mutually exclusive attributes must sum to the total number of artifacts, but no other relationship is expressed. The information on relationships furnished by the physical association of attributes on the individual artifacts is wasted; we are told in the example that 35 of the 100 pots are grit tempered, but we do not know how many grit tempered pots are red.

Classification of Type 2 requires a list of all observed attribute combinations as the categories within which the individual specimens are tallied. It contains all the information presented by the attribute count plus full information on attribute association. The categories of combinations divide the entire collection according to one principle so that there is no question of which of two or more possible piles a specimen belongs to. In short, it is a complete descriptive classification which wastes no information, although its completeness is, of course, relative to the adequacy of the underlying attribute list. However, some unexploited analytic possibilities involving the relationships of attribute and attribute combination frequencies remain, and these are dealt with by the Type 3 classification.

Classification of the third type, cluster analysis, is dependent on the data of the second, and it is specifically concerned with such questions as how many of the red jars are grit tempered. Its basic feature is the comparison of the observed count for each attribute combination with the count expected on a hypothesis of attribute independence. These comparisons result in a rating on a continuous scale for each attribute combination along the lines of less than expected, about the same as expected, and more than expected. The reasoning involved is more easily exemplified than stated abstractly. Calculation of the expected tally for a particular combination under the hypothesis of independence uses only the attribute frequencies. In the example given, we can ask how many red grit tempered jars can be expected if these attributes are independent. In the total of 100 pots, 50 are red, 35 are grit tempered, and 30 are jars; if these attributes have no tendency to stick together, we can calculate that

$$\frac{50}{100} \times \frac{35}{100} \times \frac{30}{100} \times 100 = 5.25$$

red grit tempered jars will be expected. The observed tally for the combination can range from 0 to 30 pots under the conditions specified. If the tally is actually 0, it would appear that the combination was avoided by the maker of the pots; a tally of 5 or 6 would suggest that the combination was neither avoided nor sought after; and a tally of 25 or 30 would indicate a strong tendency to group the three attributes. The last case illustrates what is meant here by an attribute cluster—a strong positive association of two or more attributes. I have ignored for the sake of clarity the sampling uncertainties which are so troublesome in real problems.

So far as I can see, classification with respect to attribute clusters exploits fully the formal information presented by a collection of artifacts since it interrelates the entire list of discriminated attributes in terms of both attribute frequency and attribute combination frequency. In my opinion, it also offers an explicit, operationally useful model of the relationships comprised under the concept of artifact type. A distinctive cluster of attributes is the consistent pattern central to the idea of type in both ordinary usage and discussions in archaeological literature. Cluster analysis is simply a full-dress exposition of the reasoning implied in the shorthand statement that type classifications are accomplished by putting together the artifacts that look alike. It is important to note that cluster analysis does not create clusters when they are not implied by the empirical data, it does not of itself explain the cultural meaning of the clusters (or lack of them) revealed by the analysis, and it will not necessarily assign every artifact to a typological pigeon hole: some artifacts may be genuinely intermediate between two clusters and others may be aberrant hangers-on of a reasonably well-defined type. It is equally important to realize that artifact types are not necessarily the most convenient and economical units for investigating possible systematic formal relationships in a set of collections; for this purpose simple attribute or attribute combination relative frequencies may serve as well.

When a formal analysis of two or more collections has been completed, comparisons in terms of the attribute list, the attribute combination list, and the type list are possible. These orders of comparison provide increasingly sensitive scales of similarity. Thus on a presence-or-absence basis two components may have identical attribute lists but not identical attribute combination lists, and they may have identical attribute combination lists but not identical artifact types.

Still more sensitive comparisons are possible when category frequencies (reduced to proportions so as to provide standard values for collections of varying sizes) are considered. Obviously it may be possible to detect valid differences between two collections on the basis of attribute frequencies even though both possess the same list of attributes. Somewhat less obvious is the fact that two collections may differ in attribute combination frequencies although they have the same attribute list, identical attribute frequencies, and identical attribute combination lists. This situation is illustrated in Table 1, in which three sets of attributes are symbolized by letters and subscripts with a total of 100 specimens and the following frequencies assumed for two collections:

A_1	35	B_1	50	C_1	25
A_2	65	B_2	50	C_2	75
	100		100		100

Comparison of attribute combination frequencies is, in fact, the most sensitive possible because the combination tallies are a complete enumeration of the formal empirical data. Comparisons of type frequencies in the sense of the type concept used here would not add information to the formal likeness scale because any difference in the attribute clusters must be a reflection of differences in combination frequencies. The artifact type has no special value for formal comparison, although it does express objectively relationships inherent in or implied by the data. The attribute associations (or lack of them) revealed by cluster analysis are already contained, so to speak, in the attribute combination tallies. Cluster analysis brings

Table 1.   *Variation in Attribute Combination Frequencies in Two Collections*

	COLLECTION I						COLLECTION II				
	A_1		A_2				A_1		A_2		
	B_1	B_2	B_1	B_2	Total		B_1	B_2	B_1	B_2	Total
C_1	15	8	1	1	25	C_1	3	2	9	11	25
C_2	10	2	24	39	75	C_2	15	15	23	22	75
Total	25	10	25	40	100	Total	18	17	32	33	100

into the open relationships which in many cases do not by any means leap to the eye from a simple inspection of the combination tallies; its purpose is to provide a basis for a culturally significant interpretation of differences in combination frequencies by ordering already existing data in a new way. It provides an escape from the dilemma of regarding everything as arbitrary (in which case "arbitrary" is robbed of any definite meaning) or neatly packaged (which is manifestly not true).

Overall characterization and comparison of collections of artifacts can be conducted at a still more generalized level at which the entire body of empirical formal data is replaced by a single number. Ranking in terms of complexity is a familiar example. The basis for judging that, for example, a Hopewell assemblage is more complex than a Lamoka assemblage is usually not the result of a formal calculation, but it is plain that a simple comparison of the number of attributes, attribute combinations, or types in the two entities would support the judgment. If one were willing to assume that any attribute has about the same complexity as any other attribute, an attribute count would offer an objective measure of formal complexity. A second kind of overall characterization can be made in terms of the degree of attribute clustering shown by a collection. This sort of characterization in nonmathematical idiom takes the form of describing a collection in some such terms as rigidly stylized as opposed to unconstrained or imaginative. Possible mathematical devices to objectify judgments of this sort need not concern us in detail. A very simple example would be the ratio of observed attribute combinations to possible attribute combinations, and more complex statements based on contingency tables could be worked out.

THE SPATIAL DIMENSION. Scaling of artifact loci is a familiar operation. It means no more than the application of a yardstick in the three ordinary directions of space to produce the latitude, longitude, and depth measurements which define a point uniquely. Spatial attributes in this sense are given; the measuring instrument can be applied directly to the artifact *in situ*, and the resulting measurement can be recorded and analyzed with the aid of all the techniques appropriate to a continuous variable.

There are, however, certain circumstances under which spatial units are given special meaning. These are the cases where artifacts occur in some sort of container, and there is consequently a relationship between them which goes beyond mere propinquity. The container may be culturally produced, examples being the grave goods of a single burial, a group of artifacts in a cache or storage pit, or the contents of a room in a pueblo. Here the entire collection of associated artifacts becomes a descriptive and comparative unit, and the spatial interrelationships of the component artifacts are presented in a formal description of the unit as a sort of superartifact. The container may be provided by natural action—a single gravel lens in a stream deposit, a stratum of debris sealed by a layer of volcanic ash, and so on—or it may be the result of combined cultural and natural activity, as in the case of strata produced by the abandonment of a site, development of an erosion surface, and reoccupation. These situations do not differ theoretically from that of the culturally produced container; the component artifacts again become a special unit of association, and for many purposes the significant spatial measurement may be simply whether a given artifact is within or outside of the container. When these special association units are present, spatial observations are interpreted in the light of the physical laws of superposition and intrusion applied to the contents of the entire unit. On the other hand, when visible strata or other boundaries yielding association units within an archaeological deposit are not present, the analysis of spatial relationships becomes an example of the general case. Thus the interpretation of vertical relationships in a massive deposit is a function of the actual vertically scaled position of each artifact.

Aside from these examples of special association, space scaling yields a set of coordinates on a continuously variable scale as another sort of attribute for each artifact, and collections of artifacts are characterized by lists of coordinate sets. One of the primary results of the analysis of such data is so obvious that it is usually thought of as simple observation rather than analysis. This result is the recognition of the very strong tendency for artifacts to occur in tight spatial clusters, that is, in archaeological sites. The site is ordinarily taken to be a given, and the assemblage of artifacts from a site is the customary unit of description and comparison. In many cases the vertical component is treated as if it were negligible; indeed, there is no other course for surface collections or thin deposits. If adequate vertical segregation is present, however, the site may be divided into two or more assemblages.

Actual techniques for analysis of the spatial coordinates of artifacts need not be described in full detail for the purposes of this paper. When strata or other boundaries giving immediately observable units are not present, the deposit can be divided into arbitrarily defined blocks for cluster analysis along the general lines discussed earlier. Excavations are often arranged to give such blocks immediately on the assumption that measuring the individual artifact coordinates would produce needlessly refined data. Such techniques in effect transform the quantitative space attributes into qualitative attributes for ease of control and statistical manipulation. It is possible to work directly with the individual coordinates treated as continuous variables if the underlying information is available and if it is judged that the expected gain in precision justifies the additional work. Finally, assemblages can be described and compared in terms of overall size and configuration.

THE TEMPORAL DIMENSION. Time itself is a continuum sensed as a succession of events. There are two types of time scales, relative and absolute. Relative time scaling is simply ranking an event as before or after some other event. Absolute time scaling means placing an event with respect to a sequence of events which are thought to occur at regular intervals and which are given a standard designation by reference to an arbitrarily chosen point. Our absolute scale is, of course, the calendar. As I noted above, all calendars are reckoned from an arbitrary starting period so that in a strict sense relative comparisons in terms of the calendar (x is twice as old as y) are not possible, although absolute comparisons (x is 500 years older than y) are. We can also make absolute and relative comparisons of time intervals between events and in consequence can make rate-of-change comparisons in relative terms. These aspects of chronology suggest that some confusion might be avoided if we adopt the term "time ranking" for the major type of time scale called "relative" above and generally referred to as relative chronology.

Since time scaling refers to events, not things, it is apparent that the temporal attributes of a prehistoric artifact must be prehistoric events whose occurrence is implied by the formal and spatial attributes of the artifact. The prehistoric events usually thought of as archaeologically significant—the targets of chronological inference—are the manufacture and primary deposition of the artifact. In most instances no serious question is asked about the time interval separating these two events; the general uncertainties of chronological scaling are such that the interval can be treated as negligible without serious difficulty. When the unit considered is a spatial cluster (an assemblage) of artifacts, as is usually the case, the question becomes still more complicated because a large number of events is involved. Here the goal is to define the assemblage so that the events represented by the component artifacts form a sufficiently tight cluster in time to permit the inference that no marked cultural changes took place during the time interval between the first and last events implied.

An equally plain consequence of the nature of chronological attributes is the fact that they cannot be observed directly in the way that formal and spatial characteristics can. All chronological judgments are inferences made by interpreting spatial and formal attributes in the light of physical, biological, or cultural principles. We have mentioned above the physical principles of superposition and intrusion, which allow spatial attributes to be transformed into temporal ranking. Similarly, measurement of radioactivity permits an estimate of absolute chronology based on a formal property of the artifact. These and other noncultural principles are of the highest importance because they provide a method of studying culture change over time without prior assumptions about the nature of cultural change. In short, they offer raw material for the construction of cultural theories. On the other hand, chronological judgments obtained by application of culturally derived theories of change merely illustrate what is meant by the theories; the judgments will be sound if the theories are sound and are applied correctly, but they will not be independent contributions to cultural theory. Thus one can arrange a group of assemblages in order of formal complexity of some class of artifacts common to all and infer that this arrangement is also a chronological ordering, but this procedure demonstrates nothing about formal changes in time because the ordering is a product of a prior theory about such changes.

A few remarks about chronological periods are probably in order here because of some apparent confusion in the literature and in archaeological discussions. It seems plain enough that a chronological period can be defined uniquely only by specifying unique sequent events for its boundaries in time. Nevertheless, examples of time periods defined by criteria which are actually an ambiguous succession of events are by no means unknown, and they have led to misunderstandings. Such "cultural periods" seem to have their origin in the observation that a number of assemblages in some geographical area have several artifact types in common while a number of other assemblages are characterized by quite different sets of types. In symbolic terms, there are ABCD sites (letters standing for types) and EFGH sites, and, since the spatial factor is limited, the observer falls into the habit of thinking of an ABCD period and EFGH period without further analysis. Sooner or later, however, a CDEF assemblage turns up, and it becomes apparent that something is wrong with the supposed chronological division. The new assemblage belongs to both or neither of the two original periods, and a new scheme is called for. This difficulty could have been avoided at the outset by more careful definition delineating a true division of time. If it is known that type A appeared before type E, then the periods could have been defined as: (1) from the appearance of type A to the appearance of type E, and (2) after the appearance of type E. Any assemblage having either E or A (or both E and A) can be placed in this scheme without ambiguity, and the periods can be subdivided if accumulating information makes it desirable.

INTERRELATIONSHIPS OF DIMENSIONS

The study of the interrelationship of the formal, spatial, and temporal properties of artifacts presupposes an independent scaling of each dimension considered. I have discussed in a very general way the characteristic scales and some of the scaling problems associated with each dimension, and I wish to consider now how the result of simultaneous classification in two or more dimensions leads to certain familiar archaeological concepts. The possible relationships are form-space, form-time, space-time, and form-space-time.

FORM-SPACE. In the discussion of the formal characterization of collections of artifacts, it was asserted that artifact types could be defined solely on the basis of clusters of formal attributes. A minimum cluster is a close association of two formal attributes. But if we replace the intentionally vague concept of collection with the more restricted idea of assemblage (a spatial cluster of artifacts thought to represent something approaching a point in time), it may be possible to show a close association of a formal and a spatial attribute. Suppose that the problem at hand is a typological description of a group of vessels which are substantially identical except for the presence or absence of incised decoration on the lip, and suppose further that the collection consists of a number of assemblages. If an assemblage tally shows that plain and incised lips rarely or never occur in the same assemblage, then it would appear reasonable to recognize the two classes of vessels as distinct entities, and there is no objection to calling them artifact types. A cluster of a formal and a spatial attribute exists when the assemblage is treated as a unit of association.

Even within a single assemblage, it might be possible to show formal-spatial clustering and hence types if the special association units are considered as, for example, when the vessels with incised lips appear only as grave furnishings. Moreover, examination of the actual coordinates of the spatially segregated form variants can yield information for further inferences about the prehistoric behavior underlying the empirical data. The two types of vessels could be northern and southern or upstream and downstream variants, for example. Even the absence of any systematic arrangement of coordinates has definite implications for inferential reconstructions of behavior. A systematic time difference can be treated in the same manner; a cluster of a formal and a temporal attribute also provides satisfactory evidence for an artifact type.

A second level of form-space synthesis results from treating the assemblage as a unit of association of artifact types. The reasoning is very similar, perhaps identical, to that employed in discussing the concept of artifact type, with the assemblage playing the part of the artifact and the artifact type that of the attribute. The problem is to classify a group of assemblages with respect to their formal attributes (artifact types) so as to reveal the degree of clustering of artifact types, that is, to investigate the problem of assemblage typology. The essential raw material is a list of the artifact type combinations exhibited by each of the assemblages of the group being investigated. The method of investigation involves the familiar computing of an expected number of assemblages for various artifact type combinations under a hypothesis of independence and comparing the expected tally with the observed tally. As before, a substantial excess of observed over expected indicates a strong association of at least two artifact types, and this strong association defines a type of assemblage—a culture type. The culture type defined in this manner—as a group of assemblages possessing in common two or more artifact types having a strong positive association—seems very close to the old archaeological concept of "a culture," and it has the same faults and virtues. Specifically, it is noncommittal as to the number or nature of the artifact types forming the characterizing cluster. In fact, it implies no more than the existence of some sort of distinctive cultural entity, and the component assemblages might be virtually identical through a long list of complicated artifact types or they might barely fulfill the minimum requirements. It is plain that subclasses or subculture types can exist within a culture type. There is useful work for such concepts as the phase or the ranked (according to complexity of identifying criteria) scale of the McKern system.

A higher order of space-form relationship can be derived from the spatial position and formal typology of assemblages. If the loci of the assemblages comprising a culture type form a geographical cluster, then the area occupied by the cluster is a culture type area. Repeated examples of such culture type areas would lead to recognition of a principle of spatial coherence of the component assemblages of a culture type. Finally, the spatial clustering of culture type areas themselves can be investigated to discover whether or not there is repeated association of such areas with one geographical region. A geographical region that does show such a cluster of clusters can be considered an archaeologically defined culture area, one in which some factor is at work to produce a culturally distinct region independently of the particular types of culture characteristic of any given time period. The possibility of this kind of analysis has apparently never occurred to the archaeologists who argue that the culture area concept has no value to archaeology because variation in time inevitably produces more than one culture type in any area.

The foregoing discussion of space-form relationships is a more or less mechanical approach to some possible formulations in keeping with aims of this paper. I think it safe to hazard, however, that all archaeologists would agree to the general proposition that artifact form does in fact vary systematically in space. The relationship is a direct one: artifacts or assemblages which are formally close tend strongly toward spatial closeness. The explanation for this phenomenon is obvious, but it is drawn from observations of living cultures, not from the data of archaeology: most formal similarities are the result of person-to-person transmission of ideas and objects, and space is a barrier to this transmission. The converse of the relationship, that artifacts or assemblages which are formally distant tend strongly to be spatially distant, is no better than half true. Space is not the only barrier to transmission; time is equally effective. Hence, we expect two assemblages that are very much alike formally to be close both in space and in time. Two assemblages that are very different formally are expected to be distant in space, distant in time, or distant in both space and time.

The existence of a systematic relationship between formal similarity and spatial locus does not necessarily imply that there is any simple ratio of formal likeness to spatial distance (the time effect having been removed) which can describe the relationship adequately. If such a relationship did exist, cluster analysis would not indicate any special relationship of formal similarity to any bounded area. Similarities across all possible boundaries would be as great as similarities within boundaries. Indexes of likeness between assemblages would simply decrease at a regular ratio from any arbitrarily chosen starting point, or, if one conceded the spatial coherence of the component assemblages of a culture type, indexes of likeness of culture types would decrease at a regular rate. I am quite willing to argue that such a simple relationship does not represent adequately the empirical data. Formal similarities do tend to knot up in space, and culture areas are objectively demonstrable phenomena, not arbitrary descriptive conveniences. The explanation is again obvious, and again it is drawn from outside the limits of strictly archaeological observation. From the standpoint of human behavior, space is not a simple matter of x and y coordinates, of barriers to communication completely described in terms of miles. The real world not only presents special impediments to communication in the form of mountains, oceans, and the like, it also poses special problems of technological and social adaptation in the form of distinctive ecological areas.

FORM-TIME. Since time is not a directly observable artifact attribute, form-time relationships have necessarily been dealt with to some extent in the remarks on time scaling. The discussion here will consist of listing some assertions about the nature of form-time relationships and examining the empirical implications of the assertions. These assertions are that artifact form exhibits serial correlation, that formal innovations tend to cluster on the time scale, and that formal change through time tends to be unidirectional.

The principle of serial correlation of form implies that, other things being equal, there is an inverse relationship between the formal resemblance between two artifacts, assemblages, or culture types and the amount of time separating them. Put in a slightly different way, the best prediction of the formal characteristics of the material culture of a society for next year is that they will not differ much from the situation this year. The archaeological technique of seriation is a direct application of this principle; when a group of assemblages is arranged in order of formal likeness, the assemblages are also ranked in time. If a simple, consistent ordering in an index of likeness matrix or a graphic representation is not achieved, it is taken to mean that some factor other than time (sampling difficulties, spatial variation, and so on) is also represented. Evidence from living societies and stratified archaeological deposits offers ample testimony of the general correctness of the principle, and, so far as I know, there is no serious question of its applicability to time ranking.

The existence of clustering of formal innovations on the time scale is not so easily demonstrated, although the idea seems to be widely accepted and is implicit in many formulations. In the context of historic and proto-historic studies, the concept of cultural revolutions is a clear example. The view of cultural dynamics underlying the concept is that a typical mode of cultural change is the achievement of a key invention—a sort of quantum advance—followed quickly by a number of functionally related auxiliary innovations. The short periods of rapid change would be separated by relatively long periods of comparative quiescence, although not of total cultural stagnation, of course. If one accepts the view that social systems are devices for operating technological systems (as I do), there is a clear implication that the character of key inventions is technical; they are directed toward the natural environment and have a generative relationship to changes in social organization. This view is important to archaeology because archaeological data yield much fuller information on technological matters than they do on social systems. The empirical implications of such a developmental theory are clear enough: assemblages formally transitional between sequent and sharply distinctive culture types should be rare, and assemblages well within the formal boundaries of culture types should be relatively abundant. I think that the actual data do show this condition, and I suspect that the principle holds good for relationships of less spectacular dimensions than those of the grand culture types. It is this clustering tendency which makes the ambiguously defined "culture period" a useful concept in spite of its logical imperfections. The several events marking the opening or closing of the period are in fact clustered in time so that most assemblages do not seem to belong to two periods.

Unidirectionality of formal changes through time is simply the idea of cultural evolution. In strictly archaeological terms, sequent culture types in one region would be expected to show greater numbers of artifact types, not only through more formalized and more varied combinations of some stock of attributes but also through the addition of new attributes to the available list. One would also expect the sites of later culture types to be more numerous (or at any rate larger) than those of the earlier ones. These expectations are a translation into formal evidence of the behavioral concept that culture change is in the main rational: technological devices are modified and reorganized so as to increase productivity, and innovations are accepted if they are demonstrably superior with respect to productivity. Hence change tends strongly to be unidirectional. It is quite true that backsliding can occur, but it would be expected only under unusual circumstances such as climatic change. A change from an agricultural to a hunting and gathering economy in a restricted area can be imagined easily and it would not be difficult to suggest plausible explanations, but it is practically impossible to imagine circumstances short of total world disruption which would cause the abandonment of agriculture everywhere. The concept of a stage of cultural development is a combination of the ideas of unidirectionality and the key invention mode of change; there are stair-steps in culture change, and the steps lead consistently upward.

SPACE-TIME. Time to space relationships, form being constant, are not the subject of much analysis in archaeology. Probably the most familiar generalization is that underlying the age-area concept. It is expected that the area of distribution of an artifact type will increase through time, and under some conditions a more widely distributed type is judged to have been invented earlier than a less widely distributed type. Judgments of this sort are necessarily precarious because of ecological and other conditions which can limit the spread of a type. No one expects snowshoes to be as widely spread as the use of fire, whatever their respective dates of first appearance may be. A few other remarks can be made about space-time relationships. If we consider the time-space distribution of artifacts as such, it is apparent that distribution increases in space through time, at least until the entire world is inhabited, and that space is more thickly studded with artifacts as time goes on. In short, both the quantity and the area of distribution of artifacts increases through time.

FORM-SPACE-TIME. The interrelationships of form, space, and time taken together have been foreshadowed by the discussion of the relationships of pairs of these dimensions. In a very broad sense, space and time are both expressible in terms of formal distance; the formal differences between two assemblages may be associated with either spatial distance or temporal difference or with both. If we assume that the rate of formal change has been constant in both dimensions, the interrelationship would be another example of the Pythagorean theorem. Plotting time on the vertical and space on the horizontal axis, the formal distance between a pair of points (representing two assemblages) on the graph would be the square root of the sum of squares of the time and space scales. From a dimensional point of view, such an operation implies that we have reduced time and space to the same dimension measured by a common scale calibrated in units of formal distance.

CONCLUSION

I have tried to make the common operations of archaeology somewhat more explicit than is frequently the case in archaeological discussions. The method used has been a translation of customary terminology into that of technically simpler and more elegant sciences, and the result has been a gain in precision and generality at the expense of realism. Certainly, to take an obvious example, there is a substantial discrepancy between my facile assumption of objective formal scales and the actual job of comparing the collections of artifacts from two assemblages. The question is whether or not such ideal formulations serve any useful purpose.

The answer is that these ideal formulations are implicit in actual archaeological research in any case, and there is no useful purpose served by not making them explicit. Indeed, failure to analyze the dimensional implications of statements about relationships has permitted formulations that are manifestly meaningless. Similarly, one may deny the possibility of objective formal scales, but the universally accepted judgment that Middle Mississippi culture is more complex than that of Indian Knoll inescapably implies that such scales are employed, however imperfect they may be. The sterile argument as to whether or not such scales exist can be replaced by a profitable discussion of ways and means to increase the sensitivity of formal scaling. The measure of success of any archaeological formulation is the degree to which it approaches the ideal, and the ideal is indispensable as an indicator of the direction and distance of the goals of archaeological research.

STATISTICAL ANALYSIS

*Archaeologists are often confronted with large quantities of data
from which they must identify the trends that will allow them to
arrive at a proper interpretation. Thus the use of statistical
techniques in archaeology has proved an invaluable aid to research.
The following paper by ALBERT C. SPAULDING, a pioneer in
the use of statistical analysis, deals with the methods for identifying
artifact types, most notably the use of chi-squared tests.*

🔁 Within recent years there appears to have been an increasing awareness on the part of archaeologists that certain statistical techniques offer economical methods of extracting information of cultural significance from archaeological data. The discussions of Kroeber (1940), Robinson (1951), and Brainerd (1951) have appeared in *American Antiquity,* and the last two even evoked a comment (Lehmer, 1951). In addition to these papers, which are primarily devoted to exposition of method, a considerable number of special applications can be found in the literature. Archaeological research inevitably brings the researcher face to face with the problems of ordering and comparing quantities of data and of sampling error. There seems little doubt that the best approach to these problems involves a search of statistical literature for appropriate methods.

The discussion which follows is an attempt to apply certain statistical methods to the discovery and definition of artifact types and to suggest other applications to related problems. No effort has been made to explain such important statistical concepts as population, random sample, sampling error, and so on; these explanations are the proper function of textbooks, and any paraphrasing here would be presumptuous. I am indebted to Paul S. Dwyer, Consultant in the Statistical Research Laboratory of the University of Michigan, for reading and commenting on an earlier version of the manuscript.

The artifact type is here viewed as a group of artifacts exhibiting a consistent assemblage of attributes whose combined properties give a characteristic pattern. This implies that, even within a context of quite similar artifacts, classification into types is a process of discovery of combinations of attributes favored by the makers of the artifacts, not an arbitrary procedure of the classifier. Classification is further an operation which must be carried out exhaustively and independently for each cultural context if the most fruitful historical interpretations are to be made. It is the primary purpose of this paper to argue that with the aid of suitable statistical techniques the degree of consistency in attribute combinations can be discovered in any meaningful archaeological assemblage provided sufficient material is at hand, and hence that valid types can be set up on the basis of analysis of material from one component.

Wholesale acceptance of these views entails modification of a widely held concept of typology which has been clearly expressed by Krieger (Krieger, 1944; Newell and Krieger, 1949). Under this concept, the method employed to demonstrate the existence of a valid type is a site-to-site comparison to show consistency of the identifying pattern, range of variation,

"Statistical Techniques for the Discovery of Artifact Types" by Albert C. Spaulding, *American Antiquity* 18, No. 4 (April 1953) 305–313. Reprinted by permission of the author and the Editor of *American Antiquity.* Tables are renumbered.

and historical relevance. In the absence of a method for investigation of consistency and range of variation within the site, this is indeed the only convincing technique available for validation of a proposed type. On the other hand, the presence of an adequate method for investigating consistency and range of variation within the site obviates a comparative study so far as the questions of the existence and definitive characteristics of a type are concerned. Historical relevance in this view is essentially derived from the typological analysis; a properly established type is the result of sound inferences concerning the customary behavior of the makers of the artifacts and cannot fail to have historical meaning. This is not meant to imply that corroborative evidence from the other sites would not be welcome in the case of a dubious type, i.e., one which is on the borderline of probability owing to a deficient sample or lack of clear evidence of attribute clustering, nor is it meant to imply that the classifier is relieved of the responsibility of avoiding synonymy. Finally, it is not intended to assert that artifact types are the only useful units of attribute association for site-to-site comparison; numerous examples of good comparative work with body sherds are sufficient refutation of such an assertion, although the common practice of failing to distinguish between kinds of body sherds and types of vessels is a stumbling block in understanding the cultural meaning of a comparison. It should be pointed out that this discussion owes much to the expositions of Rouse (1939: especially 9–23), Krieger (1944), Newell and Krieger (1949: 71–74), and Taylor (1948: especially 113–130).

The customary technique of classification consists of inspection and segregation of obtrusive combinations, or occasionally of attempting to describe all of the observed attribute combinations on an equal basis. Categories resulting from both of these methods are called "types," although they are not exactly comparable. Both methods fail to yield surely artifact types in the sense in which the term is used here. In the first case, segregation of obtrusive combinations, the cultural implications of the data are usually not exhausted, although under favorable circumstances all of the types may be discovered and described. In the second case, description of all combinations, the problem of typology is not faced at all; some of the "types" described will in all probability consist of combinations habitually avoided by the makers of the artifacts. Questions of typology arise, of course, only in a situation where a considerable variety exists within a group of generally similar artifacts—it is obvious that a stone projectile point and a pottery vessel belong in two separate artifact types. But within a group of similar artifacts the propriety of division into more than one type may be anything but obvious. It follows from the concept of the type adopted here that a pronounced association of two attributes is the minimum requirement for the demonstration of the existence of an artifact type, since two is the smallest number which can be considered an assemblage.

Application of this concept to concrete material can be illustrated by a few simple examples. Inspection of a collection of 100 vessels which represent all the pottery from a component results in the noting of the following attributes: smooth surface, cord wrapped paddle stamped surface, grit tempered paste, and shell tempered paste. The question to be answered is whether the vessels represent one or two pottery types with respect to these attributes. The data necessary to answer the question are the frequencies of vessels in each of the four possible categories into which two pairs of alternatives can be grouped, here smooth surface and grit temper, smooth surface and shell temper, cord wrapped paddle stamped surface and grit temper, and cord wrapped paddle stamped surface and shell temper. Table 1 presents these frequencies in 2 x 2 form under the assumption that the count in each category is 25 vessels.

Table 1.   Four-Cell Frequencies with No Association of Attributes

	GRIT TEMPER	SHELL TEMPER	TOTAL
Stamped Surface	25	25	50
Smooth Surface	25	25	50
Total	50	50	100

It is evident by inspection that the 100 vessels cannot be separated into two types under these circumstances. The cord wrapped paddle stamped vessels are equally divided with respect to grit temper and shell temper, the same is true of the smooth surfaced vessels, and conversely both the shell tempered and the grit tempered vessels are equally divided with respect to surface finish. A mathematical statement to the same effect can be obtained by applying the simple and useful four-cell coefficient of association described by Kroeber (1940). If the upper left cell is designated a, and the upper right cell b, the lower left cell c, and the lower right cell d, the coefficient of association for the attributes grit temper and cord wrapped paddle stamped surface would be computed as

$$\frac{(a + d) - (b + c)}{a + b + c + d} = \frac{(25 + 25) - (25 + 25)}{25 + 25 + 25 + 25} = \frac{0}{100} = 0.$$

The same result would follow for the other three pairs. The opposite situation would be that of Table 2. Here there are plainly two types with respect to the traits considered, a cord wrapped paddle stamped and grit tempered type and a smooth surfaced and shell tempered type. The com-

Table 2.   Four-Cell Frequencies with Perfect Association of Attributes

	GRIT TEMPER	SHELL TEMPER	TOTAL
Stamped Surface	50	0	50
Smooth Surface	0	50	50
Total	50	50	100

puted coefficient of association for the attributes grit temper and cord wrapped paddle stamped surface is

$$\frac{(50 + 50) - (0 + 0)}{50 + 0 + 50 + 0} = +1.0,$$

and the same coefficient would be obtained for the shell tempered, smooth surfaced category. On the other hand, the calculation for the smooth surfaced, grit tempered category shows

$$\frac{(0 + 0) - (50 + 50)}{0 + 50 + 0 + 50} = -1.0,$$

and this is also true of the cord wrapped paddle stamped, shell tempered category.

The discussion of four-cell coefficients has been introduced chiefly to illuminate the concept of the two attribute association as the minimum requirement for the establishment of an artifact type, although the simple four-cell coefficient of association and its more sophisticated relatives are by no means to be ignored as working methods under the proper conditions. One of the serious deficiencies of the four-cell coefficient is its failure to consider the vagaries of sampling, since a conservative interpretation of the material from any archaeological component requires that it be considered no more than a sample drawn from a universe of artifacts manufactured by a society over some vaguely defined period of time. Other precautions to observe when using four-cell coefficients are discussed by Kroeber (1940).

Methods do exist which give answers expressing the combined result of the error involved in sampling and the extent to which the observed data fit the expected with respect to a hypothesis. The remainder of this paper will be devoted to illustrating the application of these methods to typological problems and some other archaeological data. All of the techniques presented are drawn from the literature of biological statistics dealing with the analysis of binomial distributions, especially the discussions of Mather (1947: Chapter XI) and Snedecor (1946: Chapters 9 and 16), and the reader is referred to these sources for an adequate explanation of the underlying concepts. The most practical method of recording and subsequently extracting the variety and quantity of data needed for a thorough analysis of any sizable collection would appear to be one of the mechanically or electrically sorted punch card systems.

Table 3. *Four-Cell Frequencies with Independence of Attributes*

	GRIT TEMPER	SHELL TEMPER	TOTAL
Stamped Surface	53	64	117
Smooth Surface	32	43	75
Total	85	107	192

Using Table 3 as an example, an analysis which fulfills the stipulated conditions can be made by means of a formula for computing a statistical entity known as chi square. The formula which is most convenient for a 2 x 2 table is

$$\chi^2 = \frac{n(ad - bc)^2}{(a + b)(c + d)(a + c)(b + d)},$$

or verbally, the number of specimens multiplied by the squared difference of the product of the diagonals divided by the product of the marginal totals. Substituting the values of Table 3 gives

$$\chi^2 = \frac{192[(53 \times 43) - (35 \times 64)]^2}{117 \times 75 \times 85 \times 107},$$

which reduces to

$$\frac{192 \times 231 \times 231}{117 \times 75 \times 85 \times 107} = 0.128.$$

With a χ^2 of 0.128 and one other argument, the number of degrees of freedom, it is possible to enter a table of χ^2 and read the probability of the occurrence of so large a χ^2 through the operation of sampling variation alone in a population having independent attributes in the ratios indicated by the marginal totals. The appropriate number of degrees of freedom is 1 because the computation imposes the restriction that the frequencies must add up to the marginal totals, so that as soon as a frequency is assigned to any cell those of the other three can be found by subtraction. The probability corresponding to a χ^2 of 0.128 with 1 degree of freedom is between .80 and .70, which means that a χ^2 this large would arise by chance alone between 70 and 80 times in 100 in a population having independent attributes. It seems reasonable to accept the hypothesis of independence of attributes and conclude that the marginal totals present a fair picture of the potters' habits, there being very little evidence that the individual cell frequencies fall outside the range expected in a random drawing from a homogeneous population having the proportions of attributes indicated by the marginal totals. In other words, there is no discernible tendency for the attributes to cluster into types. Here, in contrast to the coefficients of association mentioned above, it has been possible to make a statement in terms of numerical probability and a definite hypothesis, which reduces the data to their most comprehensible form.

Chi square for Table 2 would be computed as

$$\frac{100[(50 \times 50) - (0 \times 0)]^2}{50 \times 50 \times 50 \times 50} = 100,$$

a value exceeding by a large amount the tabled value of 10.877 for a probability of .001 for 1 degree of freedom, and the probability that the marginal totals fairly represent the potters' habits is astronomically remote. The attributes are not independent; inspection of the table shows that the sample is derived from two populations, one characterized by grit tempering and a cord wrapped paddle stamped surface, the other by shell tempering and a smooth surface. This is the same conclusion as that based on the coefficient of association, but again a numerical expression of the odds against the occurrence of such a distribution in a random drawing from a population having an independent distribution of the four attributes has been provided.

It is important to note that the proportions used in testing attribute independence or lack of it were derived from the sample, and consequently the calculations have not tested the proposition that the observed proportions exactly represent those of the population from which the sample was obtained. What has been tested is the hypothesis that the two samples, those in the two rows or the two columns, were randomly drawn from a common binomial population. In the first instance (Table 3) the hypothesis was accepted, in the second (Table 2) it was rejected. Acceptance in the case of the data of Table 3 indicates that both cord wrapped paddle stamped and smooth surfaced vessels were randomly drawn from a population of vessels having grit temper and shell temper in a ratio estimated to be in the neighborhood of 85:107, or alternatively, both grit tempered and shell tempered vessels were randomly drawn from a population of vessels having cord wrapped paddle stamped and smooth surfaces in a ratio estimated to be 117:75. The estimated ratios are simply the marginal totals, and the inferences about the nature of the parent population can be completed by finding confidence limits for these estimates. This can be accomplished easily by means of a calculation or by reference to a table of confidence intervals such as that presented by Snedecor (1946: 4). Rejection of the hypothesis of independence in the case of Table 8 leads to the conclusion that cord wrapped paddle stamped vessels were drawn from a population of vessels estimated to be exclusively grit tempered, and smooth surfaced vessels were drawn from a probably exclusively shell tempered population. Again confidence intervals can be assigned to the estimates.

The next question to be investigated is that of a suitable technique for situations involving combinations of more than two pairs of attributes. The method to be employed is closely related to that just illustrated, but the resemblance is obscured by the streamlined computing routine used for the 2 x 2 table. There are two basic steps required: (1) calculation of an expected frequency for the combination, customarily under the hypothesis that the combination in question does not constitute a distinctive type, i.e., that the attributes making up the combination have independent distributions; and (2) comparison of the expected frequency with the observed frequency to determine whether or not the difference between the two can be reasonably attributed to sampling error. If the observed frequency exceeds the expected frequency by an amount too great to be considered the result of mere sampling error, it will be concluded that a genuine tendency for the makers of the artifacts to combine the attributes in question has been discovered—that the existence of a type has been demonstrated.

The following data will be used to explain the working method: in a collection of 297 pottery vessels, it is suspected that a combination of grit tempering, stamped surface, and a collared rim occurs often enough to provide sufficient grounds for the definition of a pottery type. A count made of the frequency of the triple combination gives 83 vessels; of the frequency of grit tempering alone, 117 vessels; of stamped surface alone, 91 vessels; and of collared rims alone, 136 vessels.

Under the hypothesis of independent distribution of attributes (no type), the frequency of the combination would be expected to be a simple function of the relative frequencies of the component attributes. Calculation of the expected number is a straightforward problem in compound probability, here

$$\frac{117}{297} \times \frac{91}{297} \times \frac{136}{297} \times \frac{297}{1} = 16.42 \text{ vessels.}$$

In practice it is necessary to compute the proportion (p) characteristic of the combination for reasons to be explained below. The computation of p here is

$$\frac{117}{297} \times \frac{91}{297} \times \frac{136}{297} = .0553.$$

The next step is to obtain the deviation (d) of the observation from the expectation by subtracting 16.42 from 83.00, which results in a deviation of 66.58.

It is necessary here to introduce some new symbols required for the final comparison of the expected frequency (E) and the observed frequency (O). The proportion of vessels not expected to exhibit the combination will be designated q, which is simply $1 - p$ or $1.000 - .0553 = .9447$ in the example. The expectation for the various possible frequencies of two alternative types (in this example grit tempered, cord wrapped paddle stamped, collared rim vessels and vessels not having this combination) can be found by expanding the binomial $(p + q)^k$, where k is the symbol for the number of individuals in the group (297 vessels); in addition, and of immediate importance in the solution of the problem, is the fact that the variance of the expanded binomial distribution is pqk ($.0553 \times .9447 \times 297 = 15.52$). The standard deviation (σ) is $\sqrt{pqk}$, which makes it possible to compute easily either the deviate in units of standard deviation

as $\dfrac{d}{\sigma}$, or $\left[\dfrac{d}{\sigma}\right]^2$ as $\dfrac{d^2}{pqk}$. Both $\dfrac{d}{\sigma}$ and $\left[\dfrac{d}{\sigma}\right]^2$ can be converted into state-

ments of probability by means of widely available tables. In the case of d/σ, tables of areas of the normal curve or tables for t for infinite degrees of freedom may be used; $(d/\sigma)^2$ is the familiar χ^2 for 1 degree of freedom. Choice of formula is a matter of individual preference since the answers obtained are identical; tables for χ^2 are less closely computed than those for d/σ owing to their two dimensional character, but the precision of the latter does not appear to have any advantage for archaeological purposes. In both cases the tables were computed on the basis of a continuous curve rather than the binomial curve with discrete steps used here, and consequently they are not exactly applicable. A widely recommended procedure for avoiding excessive distortion is to group categories so that the expected numbers are not too small, say 5 or less. A partial correction (the Yates correction) can be made by adjusting d, and precise methods of adjustment for small numbers can be found in statistical literature. The simple adjustments do not seem to change the results markedly, but anyone planning to use these techniques should be familiar with informed discussions of the subject.

Calculations for $(d/\sigma)^2$ for the example are

$$\frac{(66.58)^2}{15.52} = \frac{4432.90}{15.52} = 285.62.$$

Entering a table of χ^2 with this figure and 1 degree of freedom, a probability of finding a fit with hypothesis through chance at least as bad [as, or] very much less than .001 is noted. A similar calculation for d/σ indicates that the odds are actually less than 1 in 400,000,000,000 that so large a difference between observed and expected frequencies would arise through random sampling in the expanded binomial. It can be concluded that the chance of a sampling vagary as the explanation is exceedingly remote, and the large number of vessels exhibiting the combination must be attributed to the habits of the potters. The calculation does show that a pottery type exists. Further research would be necessary to investigate whether (1) on the basis of other attributes it might not be possible to identify a group of pottery types sharing the specified combination, or (2) whether there are other combinations differing by only one attribute which should be included in the type description as variants. The original conclusion—that the existence of a pottery type was demonstrated—is not modified by either case.

The evaluation of probability can perhaps be clarified by two other examples. Had the observed frequency been 24 vessels, χ^2 would have been computed as

$$\frac{(7.58)^2}{15.52} = \frac{57.46}{15.52} = 3.70,$$

which for 1 degree of freedom represents a probability of between .10 and .05, but much closer to .05. The conclusion is not at all clear. There is an appreciable chance that no real preference for the combination was exhibited by the potters, and the evaluation must be made with the aid of all the experience which the archaeologist can muster. If related sites plainly show that the combination is elsewhere a valid type, the interpretation would probably be that in this case the type was just appearing or disappearing. In the absence of other data, one could say only that there is a very good possibility that a type has been discovered. In certain types of statistical investigation a χ^2 of more than 3.841 (the .05 level of probability for 1 degree of freedom) is considered significant, or in our terms the hypothesis of independence would be rejected. It would appear unwise to carry over blindly such concepts into archaeology. Had the observed frequency of the combination been 8 vessels, d would have been 8.42 and $\chi^2 = 4.57$ with a probability between .05 and .02. The same general reasoning applies again, but here the situation is reversed because the expected frequency exceeds the observed frequency; there is a strong probability that the potters tended to avoid the combination, and the examples observed might best be considered the work of unorthodox potters.

A thorough investigation of a collection requires the calculation of d/σ or χ^2 for every possible combination of presumably important attributes. The number of combinations possible can be found by grouping the mutually exclusive attributes and multiplying together the number of attributes in each of the groups. If the groups of attributes consist of (1) smooth surface, stamped surface; (2) incised rim, plain rim; (3) incised lip, plain lip; and (4) bowl shape, jar shape; the computation is 2 × 2 × 2

× 2 = 16 possible combinations. If the groups are (1) smooth surface, stamped surface; (2) rectilinear incising on shoulder, curvilinear incising on shoulder, plain shoulder; and (3) grit tempered, shell tempered; there are 2 × 3 × 2 = 12 possible combinations. These 12 combinations will be used in an example with the following data given: total number of vessels (k), 186; frequency of smooth surface, 121 vessels; of stamped surface, 65 vessels; of rectilinear pattern incised on shoulder, 47 vessels; of curvilinear pattern incised on shoulder, 28 vessels; of plain shoulder, 111 vessels; of grit tempering, 70 vessels; and of shell tempering, 116 vessels. Combination counts and computations are shown in Table 4. The computations are exactly like those described above. For example, p in the first combination is

$$\frac{121}{186} \times \frac{47}{186} \times \frac{70}{186} = .0619.$$

The expected number (E) is 186 × .0619 = 11.51, and so on.

Table 4.   Computation of d^2/pqk for Twelve Combinations of Attributes

ATTRIBUTE COMBINATION	O	E	d	d^2	pqk	d^2/pqk
Sm. surf., rect. sh., grit t.	0	11.51	−11.51	132.02	10.78	12.25
Sm. surf., curv. sh., grit t.	2	6.84	−4.85	23.52	6.59	3.56
Sm. surf., plain sh., grit t.	14	27.17	−13.17	173.45	23.21	7.47
Sm. surf., rect. sh., shell t.	38	19.07	+18.93	358.35	17.11	20.94
Sm. surf., curv. sh., shell t.	26	11.36	+14.64	214.33	10.66	20.11
Sm. surf., plain sh., shell t.	41	45.04	−4.04	16.24	34.13	0.48
St. surf., rect. sh., grit t.	3	6.18	−3.18	10.11	5.97	1.69
St. surf., curv. sh., grit t.	0	3.68	−3.68	13.54	3.61	3.75
St. surf., plain sh., grit t.	51	14.60	+36.40	1324.96	13.45	98.51
St. Surf., rect. sh., shell t.	6	10.25	−4.25	18.06	9.69	1.86
St. surf., curv. sh., shell t.	0	6.10	−6.10	37.21	5.90	6.31
St. surf., plain sh., shell t.	5	24.20	−19.20	368.26	21.04	17.50
Total	186	186.00	0.00			

Table 4 is to be interpreted simply as a list of χ^2 values, each of which has its corresponding probability for 1 degree of freedom. The individual χ^2 values, computed as d^2/pqk, do not have additive properties in contrast to the contingency table discussed below. Interpretation in terms of pottery types follows the principles already discussed. Three combinations have large positive deviations and large χ^2 values with probabilities well beyond the .001 level. These are stamped surface, plain shoulder, grit temper; smooth surface, curvilinear incised shoulder, shell temper; and smooth surface, rectilinear incised shoulder, shell temper. The last two combinations differ by only one attribute, and hence are to be lumped in one type. The same is true of the smooth surfaced, plain shouldered, shell tempered combination, which is important numerically but has a very small χ^2 value. Accordingly, there is definitely a smooth surfaced, shell tempered type having three kinds of shoulder treatment in a ratio estimated to be about 26:38:41. This can be confirmed by calculating a χ^2 for a 2×2 table testing the degree of association of smooth surface and shell temper. It will be found that they are very strongly associated, as are grit temper and a stamped surface. It can be inferred that the indifferent χ^2 value (0.48) of the shell tempered, plain shouldered, smooth surfaced combination is the result of the fact that plain shoulders are shared with and are rather more characteristic of the stamped surfaced, grit tempered combination. This conclusion is at sharp variance with conventional type analysis, where the shell tempered, plain shouldered, smooth surfaced combination would almost surely be distinguished as a separate type, as would the other two smooth surfaced, shell tempered combinations. The calculations above are intended to be an objective demonstration that the fundamental pattern of the type is the smooth surfaced, shell tempered vessel. Shoulder treatment can be described only in terms of estimated ratios of a group of mutually exclusive attributes.

The stamped surfaced, plain shouldered, grit tempered vessels constitute a second definite type; χ^2 for the combination is very high (98.51) and it can be shown that stamped surface and grit temper are strongly associated. The 14 vessels having smooth surfaces, plain shoulders, and grit temper would not be assigned to either type; they are genuinely intermediate and would be so described. The same reasoning applies to the 5 vessels having stamped surfaces, plain shoulders, and shell tempering. The remaining few vessels share two attributes with one or the other of the types and would be assigned accordingly as somewhat aberrant examples. Combinations of this sort, characterized by negative deviations and crossing over of attributes from two types, offer interesting evidence on the degree of conventionality of the potters. In this connection the combinations with a frequency of 0 are highly informative.

A second sort of table can be computed which offers summary evidence on the total pottery making habits of the group. For this table, the individual contribution of each combination would be computed as d^2/E, which for the first combination of Table 4 is 132.02/11.51. The total of these contributions is a χ^2 value for the 12 combinations taken together, for which a probability can be found in the χ^2 table using 7 degrees of freedom. A verbal explanation of the appropriateness of 7 degrees of freedom is too cumbersome for inclusion here, and a clear graphic presentation of a $2 \times 3 \times 2$ table is also difficult, but it can be stated that the particular restrictions imposed by the attribute totals used as basic data allow 7 of the 12 cells of the table to be filled in freely within the general limitations of the attribute totals. The remaining five can be determined by subtraction and hence do not contribute to the degrees of freedom. A χ^2 computed in this manner gives an over-all measure of the tendency of the potters to group attributes and offers cogent material for comparison with other sites having the same categories. Other sorts of comparisons between sites can be made by using the observed number for each combination from one site as the expected number for the other and calculating the resulting χ^2 or by calculating a χ^2 testing the proposition that both sets of observed values could reasonably be considered random samples from a common population. The latter process is illustrated below in the example dealing with the problem of site homogeneity (Table 6).

All of the examples have been concerned exclusively with attributes which are physical properties of the artifacts. It is well known, however, that artifacts have other kinds of attributes, notably provenience, which can be pertinent evidence for the existence of a type. Thus a site might yield two kinds of vessels which differed only in the presence or absence of a single physical attribute, say a lip flange on one. If nothing but physical properties were considered, both kinds would be included in one pottery type because a difference of one attribute is not sufficient evidence for separation. But if the flanged lip appeared only on vessels found in graves and the plain lip was confined to village debris, it would be obvious that the potters had in mind two types with different functional connotations. Provenience furnishes the second attribute required to differentiate two types. The attributes "found in graves" and "found in village refuse" can be included in a probability calculation in exactly the same way as can any physical property of an artifact.

An example, this time not fictitious, of the application of this technique to a non-typological problem will be presented. The data of Table 5 are from the Columbia University excavations at the Arzberger Site, Hughes County, South Dakota, and summarize provenience data of grooved paddle stamped body sherds and other types of surface finish. The problem

Table 5. Surface Finish of Body Sherds by Provenience, Arzberger Site, South Dakota

EXCAVATION UNIT	SURFACE FINISH		
	GROOVED PADDLE STAMPED	OTHER	TOTAL
House I	396	1,279	1,675
House II	135	546	681
House III	172	532	704
House IV	178	657	835
Ditch	0	4	4
Unknown	22	79	101
Total	903	3,097	4,000

to be investigated is one of site homogeneity. If the site is homogeneous, one excavation unit should be much like another within the limits of sampling error. With respect to the data given on surface finish of body sherds, a hypothesis of independence can be set up: the proportion of grooved paddle stamped sherds will be a function of the frequency of the totals and will be independent of the locus from which the sample is drawn if the site is truly homogeneous. Chi square is computed by the d^2/pqk method used above, although this is not the most common technique for a $2 \times n$ contingency table such as given. The value of p is $903/4,000 = .2258$, $q = .7742$, and k is successively the total number of sherds for each sample. The values are shown in Table 6 (a few rounding errors have not been adjusted). The result is good evidence that the hypothesis of independence is correct. Individual values are small, and the total for 4 degrees of freedom (this is a 2×5 contingency table) corresponds to a probability of between .20 and .10, which does not give any very convincing reason to suspect significant differences in the various excavation units. It can be concluded that so far as the evidence at hand is concerned, the site may reasonably be considered the product of a single occupation over a restricted period of time.

Table 6. Test of Homogeneity of Excavation Units, Arzberger Site, South Dakota

	O	E	d	d^2	pqk	d^2/pqk
House I	396	378.21	17.79	316.48	292.81	1.08
House II	135	153.77	18.77	352.31	119.05	2.96
House III	172	158.96	13.04	170.04	123.07	1.38
House IV	178	188.54	10.54	111.09	145.97	0.76
Other[1]	22	23.70	1.70	2.89	18.35	0.16
Total	903	903.00			$\chi^2 = 6.34$	

[1] The expected frequency for "Ditch" is less than 6, and accordingly it is incorporated in a new category by adding its value to "Unknown."

An attempt to appraise the usefulness of this approach to typological and related problems should consider the amount of labor necessary in making the computations. In view of the general availability of computing machines, this seems trivial. The writing of the exposition was far more tedious than the computing of the examples. There is a great deal of work required in making, recording, and assembling the observations needed for a thorough study, but this is not the fault of the statistical methods. It is rather an inevitable part of any detailed study. The methods of calculation used here were selected on a basis of clarity of exposition, not economy of labor; those interested in computing routine are referred to the statistical textbooks cited.

With regard to the more serious question of general usefulness, these are the methods generally recommended for handling data of this sort, although no claim is made that the particular procedures illustrated here completely exhaust the resources of statistics. The information derived from them is important in an earnest attempt to discover the cultural significance inherent in archaeological remains, and there is no other way in which such information can be obtained. There is no magic involved, however; the usefulness of the result is entirely dependent upon the wisdom with which attributes are observed and investigated and on the relevance of the context to meaningful archaeological problems. Moreover, the inference to be drawn from a statement of probability is sometimes not altogether clear, but at least the degree of uncertainty is put into objective form.

A source of uncertainty which has been mentioned is the fact that the proportions on which the hypothesis of independence is evaluated are derived from the sample and hence are themselves subject to sampling error. This difficulty is inescapable; we can work only with the samples we have, and the observed proportions are surely the best estimate of the proportions of the population, the properties of which must be inferred from the sample. Nevertheless, the cautious student will interpret his results with one eye on a table of confidence limits. To add to this uncertainty, the dimensions of which can at least be estimated on the basis of statistical theory, there is the purely archaeological problem of the nature of the relationship of the sample to the living culture which produced the artifacts. The whole problem is summarized by the often repeated warning that statistics are never a substitute for thinking. But statistical analysis does present data which are well worth thinking about.

Bibliography

Brainerd, George W.
   1951 "The Place of Chronological Ordering in Archaeological Analysis," *American Antiquity*, Vol. 16, No. 4, pp. 301–313. Salt Lake City.
Krieger, Alex D.
   1944 "The Typological Concept." *American Antiquity*, Vol. 9, No. 4, pp. 271–288. Menasha.
Kroeber, A. L.
   1940 "Statistical Classification." *American Antiquity*, Vol. 6, No. 1, pp. 29–44. Menasha.
Lehmer, Donald J.
   1951 "Robinson's Coefficient of Agreement—A Critique." *American Antiquity*, Vol. 17, No. 2, p. 151. Salt Lake City.
Mather, K.
   1947 *Statistical Analysis in Biology*. New York: Interscience Publishers.
Newell, H. Perry, and Alex D. Krieger
   1949 "The George C. Davis Site, Cherokee County, Texas." *Memoirs of the Society for American Archaeology*, No. 5. Menasha.

Robinson, W. S.
  1951 "A Method for Chronologically Ordering Archaeological Deposits." *American Antiquity*, Vol. 16, No. 4, pp. 293–301. Salt Lake City.
Rouse, Irving
  1939 "Prehistory in Haiti, A Study in Method." *Yale University Publications in Anthropology*, No. 21. New Haven.
Snedecor, George W.
  1946 *Statistical Methods Applied to Experiments in Agriculture and Biology.* Ames: Iowa State College Press.
Taylor, Walter W.
  1948 "A Study of Archaeology." *Memoirs, American Anthropological Association*, No. 69. Menasha.

CHAPTER SEVEN

𝔯𝔯𝔯𝔯𝔯𝔯𝔯𝔯𝔯𝔯𝔯𝔯𝔯𝔯

Settlement Archaeology

The field of settlement archaeology
is assuming increasing importance. Rather
than a group of specific case studies,
this section is comprised of one paper
which surveys the subject.

SETTLEMENT PATTERNS IN ARCHAEOLOGY

BRUCE G. TRIGGER's paper on the determinants of settlement patterns has been described by Gordon Willey as "a basic and definitive treatment" of the subject in his summary of a recent series of papers on settlement archaeology. It is quoted in full here, for it represents the clearest statement of a new and rapidly developing aspect of archaeology.

📖 This survey paper is concerned with exploring the range of ways in which the concept of settlement patterns can be useful for the interpretation of archaeological data. My primary interest is in the nature of settlement patterns and the relationships they bear to the rest of culture. I shall analyze (1) the relationships that exist between settlement patterns and other aspects of culture, and (2) the ways in which archaeologists can use the knowledge of such relationships to further an understanding of the cultures they are investigating. The first step requires a cross-cultural investigation of (a) the range of factors that correlate significantly with settlement patterns, and (b) the manner in which these factors articulate with one another to produce the settlement pattern of an individual society. Our main interest will be the determinants of settlement patterns, by which we mean those classes of factors that interact with each other to

"The Determinants of Settlement Patterns" by Bruce G. Trigger *in* K. C. Chang, *et al., Settlement Archaeology,* National Press (1968), pp. 53–78. Reprinted by permission of the author, the editor, and the publisher. This edition of the paper has been slightly revised (1969) from the original (1964) by the author. We are grateful for his cooperation in this regard.

produce the spatial configurations of a social group. This interaction is not simply complementary. Since individual determinants may tend toward results that oppose as well as reinforce one another, a settlement pattern may be a compromise among a number of conflicting determinants. There are, still, other factors that are functionally related to the settlement pattern but whose relationship is a dependent rather than a determining one. These, however, lie beyond the scope of this study.

Before we proceed with our investigation it is necessary to clarify what we mean by settlement patterns. To do this we must here review some of the work that has been done to date. The concept of the settlement pattern was first put to substantial use in the field of archaeology by Gordon R. Willey in his book *Prehistoric Settlement Patterns in the Virú Valley* (1953). There, Willey delineated changes in the form and distribution of sites in a small Peruvian valley during the course of several millennia, and related these changes to socioeconomic trends and to historical events. In his Introduction he described settlement patterns as a "strategic starting point for the functional interpretation of archaeological cultures" that reflect "the natural environment, the level of technology on which the builders operated, and various institutions of social interaction and control with the culture maintained" (p. 1). Since then, a considerable number of studies have been concerned with settlement patterns. Some are basically factual studies aimed at ascertaining the types of settlement patterns associated with a given culture. Others have attempted to use settlement patterns to reconstruct the social (Chang 1958; 1962) or religious (Sears 1961) institutions of ancient cultures. Some have concentrated on the layout and house types associated with individual sites (Willey 1956b); others, on the distribution patterns of large numbers of sites (Trigger 1963a). The cultures studied range from small hunting and gathering ones (Chang 1962) to complex civilizations (Coe 1961), and the interpretive approaches range from simple, straightforward analogy to systematic cross-cultural comparisons using ethnographic material.

One of the chief merits of Willey's definition of settlement patterns lies in its breadth and its clearly functional view of settlement pattern phenomena. The value of settlement patterns for reconstructing prehistoric cultures is seen as a result of the variety of institutions that are "reflected" in the settlement pattern. In another work, Willey suggests that there is no settlement pattern approach as such, but that settlement patterns should be treated as a class of data available for analysis through a variety of approaches (Willey 1956a: 1).

Despite such a healthy emphasis on variety and on a range of possible uses of data, it seems that in recent years two approaches have dominated settlement pattern studies.

The first is primarily ecological and often appears to be based on the assumption that the settlement pattern is a product of the simple inter-action of two variables—environment and technology. This sort of eco-logical determinism has been actively promoted as a determinant not only of settlement patterns but also of culture in general, by Leslie White and his students, and, in archaeology, particularly by Betty Meggers. The eco-logical approach is primarily an investigation of how the settlement pattern reflects the adaptation of a society and its technology to its environment.

In the second kind of approach, settlement pattern data are used as a basis for making inferences about the social, political, and religious organi-zation of prehistoric cultures. Chang (1958; 1962) and Sears (1961) have used the term "community pattern" to refer to "the strictly social aspects of settlement patterning." E. Z. Vogt (1956: 174–175) has even suggested that these two approaches, along with studies of process, might be con-sidered as separate branches of the study of settlement patterns. These two kinds of study are distinguished not only by approach but also to a large degree by their choice of data. The first tends to be concerned with the size and distribution of whole sites, whereas the second concentrates on the patterning within individual settlements. Mayer-Oakes (1959: 167) has distinguished between *community types* and *zonal patterns*; Sears (1961: 226) between *site* and *areal* patterns, referring to the former as *microcosmic* and the latter as *macrocosmic*. Chang has used the terms "microstructure" and "macrostructure" to describe the sociocultural systems of individual settlements and those made up of a number of settlements, respectively.

I believe, however, that archaeologists and other anthropologists also can more profitably conceive of settlement patterns in terms of three levels. The first of these is the individual building or structure; the sec-ond, the manner in which these structures are arranged within single com-munities; and the third, the manner in which communities are distributed over the landscape. Each of these levels appears to be shaped by factors that differ in kind or degree from the factors that shape other levels, and hence the combined study of all three is likely to shed more light on archaeological cultures than is the study of a single level.

Although work to date has done much to advance the study of settle-ment patterns, the heavy concentration on only two approaches has not been without its disadvantages. So far, archaeologists have been more interested in using settlement patterns as a basis for reconstructing indi-vidual cultures than in studying the nature of settlement patterns for its own sake. Hence there is little in the way of a systematic understanding of settlement patterns to guide the archaeologist. In the long run, however, settlement pattern data can be used with a full knowledge of their pros-pects and limitations only when some attention has been given to the nature of this phenomenon in living societies. My aim in the first part of this paper is to assemble a list of the various factors that scholars have suggested play a part in determining the structure of individual buildings, settlements, and overall distributions. This list is based on the work of geographers, sociologists, and historians. Material from both simple and complex societies will be considered, since circumstances peculiar to each may help to point up problems common to settlement pattern studies as a whole. Since this part of my paper is essentially a survey of other people's ideas, my illustrations are drawn from many different parts of the world. In another study I have tried to analyze to what degree similar factors have determined the settlement patterns of a single region over a long period (Trigger 1965).

DETERMINANTS

INDIVIDUAL BUILDINGS. There has been relatively little in the way of a systematic investigation of our most basic unit, the individual structure. Perhaps the most common use that has been made of house types has been in tracing historical connections among different groups. Therefore, much that we say here must be in the form of queries rather than answers. There is great variety in the structures of complex societies—various types of houses, as well as temples, forts, tombs, etc. In the simplest societies, there may be only one, quite uniform, house type and no special-purpose buildings. Yet even this single house type may represent an accommodation to a considerable variety of factors.

One of these factors is the subsistence regime of the society. Migratory peoples tend to have houses that are either transportable or easy to build, and even semisedentary swidden agriculturalists may be less inclined to invest in buildings than would a completely sedentary population. For migratory societies, there seems to be an even more specific correlation between house types and the availability of building materials. In areas where such materials can be come by easily, a new shelter can be erected at each camping place, but in deserts or steppe country where such materials are scarce, buildings tend to be of a sort that is usually moved from place to place. Examples are the portable tepee of the Plains Indians, the light goat-hair tent of the Arab Bedouin, and the *yurt* of the Mongolian herdsmen. In the *yurt*, insulation against the cold climate is provided by two layers of felt stretched, one on the inside, the other on the outside, of a collapsible wooden trellis (Fitch and Branch 1960: 141–142).

Thus a house represents an attempt to meet the challenge of an environment with the building materials that same environment offers. In a short but important study of primitive architecture, James Fitch and D. P. Branch (1960) have noted that the structural design of many primitive buildings "reflects a precise and detailed knowledge of local climatic conditions . . . and . . . a remarkable understanding of the performance characteristics of [local] building materials" (p. 134). They suggest that the principal climatic factors to which houses adapt are the diurnal and yearly variations in ambient and radiant temperatures, air movement, and humidity. They find that houses in different regions of the world often show adaptations that are of "surprising delicacy and precision" (p. 136).

The dome-shaped igloo of the Central Eskimo, for example, is built quickly and easily of local material that is readily available. The dome offers minimum resistance and maximum obstruction to winter gales. This shape also exposes as little of its surface to the cold as possible, and can be heated effectively by a point source of heat, such as an oil lamp.

In hot deserts, there are marked differences between day and night temperatures, as well as between seasons. In such regions, buildings with heavy walls of stone and clay absorb heat during the day and reradiate it at night in a manner that helps to flatten out the uncomfortable diurnal fluctuations of the coldest months. Such buildings are common among the Pueblo Indians of the American Southwest, in North Africa, and in the Middle East. Roofs are either of vaulted mud brick or of mud slabs laid on beams. In moister regions, such as Nigeria, a mud dome is frequently covered with thatch so that it sheds water.

In wet, tropical regions, temperatures vary rather little, but shade and ventilation are essential to comfort. Walls are therefore reduced to a minimum to allow for ventilation, while a large, steeply sloping roof projects beyond the living space as protection against sun and rain. A raised floor also serves to fend off dampness and wild animals. Houses of this sort can be constructed easily out of available saplings and fibers.

In some of the preceding examples, not only the general structural principles but also the shapes of the houses are adaptations to the environment. The igloo and the sloping roofs of rainy regions are cases in point. The Naskapi house is a conical wigwam braced by a ring of stones and covered with bark or skins. G. I. Quimby (1960: 383–384) has observed that no other shape would be as efficient in an environment where frozen ground and the lack of soil make it impossible to sink poles into the ground. Moreover, certain types of more complex structures, such as houses built around an open court, are less practical in cold climates than in warm ones. Not only is the usefulness of the courtyard, which is normally the center of a good deal of family activity, reduced in a cold climate, but also heating such a house is considerably more difficult than heating a compact one. Climatic factors may also influence the orientation of houses. Doors or windows may face toward the sun, away from an unpleasant prevailing wind, or toward a lake or river. Such practical considerations certainly enter into the Chinese art of *fung-shui*, or geomancy, although there they are embedded in an elaborate system of symbolism and magic (Durkheim and Mauss 1963: 68, 73).

But a building is more than an adaptation to climate. It also reflects the skills of its builder and his technology. This technical know-how affects the range of materials that are available, and through the materials the shape and design of buildings. Skill in stone and brickwork permits the erection of larger and more elaborate structures. In different societies, building techniques may develop along divergent paths that, in part, reflect the different materials used. The brick and stone architecture of Europe and Western Asia gave rise to buildings whose weight rested primarily on the walls. In Eastern Asia, however, a tradition of wood architecture was developed in which walls tended to be "hung" on a pole-and-beam construction that supported the roof (Willetts 1958: 689–723). Specific techniques also make new designs possible. The dome, for example, made it possible to roof over unencumbered spaces of considerable size.

The size and layout of buildings may also reflect the structure of the family. A house occupied by a nuclear family may contain one or more rooms, but the function of these rooms will relate to the needs of a single family. If the house belongs to a lineage, then nuclear family units are likely to be found repeated within the house, although such things as food stores may be common to the whole unit. Chang (1958) has suggested that even in large houses, such as those of the Witoto of South America, which house a whole village, the household can be distinguished by (1) interpreting the use of equipment, (2) distinguishing the partitions that separate households, and (3) identifying separate kitchens. In a polygynous household, on the other hand, each wife may have her own living area and kitchen, but the rooms belonging to the head of the household will be without a kitchen, since he will be fed by his various wives in turn. Alternatively, a polygynous family may have a common cookhouse (Murdock 1934: 559). From archaeological evidence it might be difficult to distinguish a household consisting of a master and his resident servants from that of a lineage, especially if social differences within a society are not strongly marked in material terms. Moreover, although various forms of multi-family houses may be indicative of lineages or polygynous families, similar institutions are also found associated with nuclear family houses and so can go undetected. Particular forms of houses may also be related to forms of family organization. The longhouse as a unit of residence seems closely associated with lineage organizations. Here, the main archaeological problem is to distinguish residential longhouses from buildings such as men's clubs. In Melanesia, some of the latter have not only the outline of a longhouse but also a row of fireplaces down the center, associated not with nuclear families but with particular status groups within the club (Codrington 1957: 101–105). Any site in which a few "longhouses" are associated with a large number of nuclear family houses should be suspect, and the buildings subjected to careful investigation before functions are assigned to them.

The structures in a community may reflect differences in wealth and rank, as well as various social institutions. The economic egalitarianism of many primitive societies is reflected in uniformity in the design and size of shelters, but with increasing social complexity the design and functions of buildings become increasingly differentiated. Among the Huron, the most important chiefs in a village occupied the largest longhouses, which served as gathering places for meetings and rituals (Trigger 1963b: 156). In societies where authority or class divisions are more pronounced, the houses of the elite become larger and more elaborate. In such places as the Marquesas, for example, the elaborateness of the platform on which a house was built reflected the importance of its owner in the social hierarchy (Suggs 1960: 124). In addition to such differentiations in house types, special-purpose structures are more common in a class-divided society. Some of these structures are also residential. Visitors or bachelors may sleep inside the clubhouses that are common in Oceania (Codrington 1957: 69–115); and in Sparta and more recently in some parts of Hungary (den Hollander 1960), adult males normally lived apart from their wives and families. The age grade system of the Masai found expression in the special camps where the warriors and unmarried girls of a village lived together until they reached the age when they were permitted to establish homes of their own (Forde 1934: 302–333).

Elsewhere, various special-purpose structures that are not lived in may serve the needs of the community as a whole or of some of its members. The Arab guest house, which is used to feed and accommodate travelers, functions primarily as a meeting place for the men of a tribe or village (Salim 1962: 72), as did the sweat house among the Pomo. The Plains Indians constructed large triple tepees where some of the ceremonies of their men's societies were performed (Forde 1934: 57). Huts or houses may also be built to isolate members of society. Among the Indians of the Northwest Coast, girls were frequently secluded for a time at puberty, either in a small hut or behind a curtain. In complex societies, there is often a considerable variety of public buildings devoted to secular group activities, such as schools, libraries, stadia, public baths, and museums. Once their function has been determined, these buildings permit us to say a good deal about the nature of community life and the values of ancient civilizations.

The specialization of production is also reflected in the individual structure, in the form either of workshops added on to houses or of separate buildings that serve as workshops and storerooms. Likewise, the transportation and sale of goods stimulates the growth of marketplaces, stores, and caravanserais. By determining the use that was made of individual buildings, the archaeologist can recover a good deal of solid information about patterns of production and trade in ancient societies.

The religious beliefs of a society may affect house types and may also result in the construction of shrines, temples, or tombs. The royal funerary temples of the Khmer civilization were built as a model of the universe. The central structure with its five towers on a large pyramid represented Mount Meru, the center of the universe; the surrounding walls were the rock wall that surrounded the universe; and the moat beyond was the great ocean (Coe 1961: 71). Mircea Eliade (1960) and others see houses as a representation of a people's conception of the universe. Eliade notes that such "habitation symbolism" is very clear among the subarctic peoples of North America and Siberia. Among them the center post is symbolically identified with the "pillar of the world"; among the pastoralists of Asia, and the "archaic Chinese," the mythico-ritual function of the pillar has been "passed on" to the overhead smoke hole. Special religious buildings include temples and plazas where rituals can be performed. The *kivas*, or ceremonial lodges, found among the Pueblo tribes of the American Southwest are interesting for two reasons: first, the *kiva* may be a retention of an earlier form of round house, long abandoned as a dwelling; and second, the *kivas* were owned by religious fraternities that were associated with the various clans of the community. Sears (1961) has already demonstrated the value of studying temple and tomb complexes as representations of ritual. In this way, much can be learned about the religious practices of prehistoric societies. Nevertheless, the whole field of the relationship between structures and ritual remains to be studied in a comparative fashion both on a worldwide basis and within particular culture areas. In any case, archaeologists must beware equating the study of religious buildings with the study of religion itself. The importance of cult buildings varies a good deal from society to society. Gods may have no temples at all, and ceremonies may be performed in the open or in public places that normally have other uses. To understand religious practices, the archaeologist must also look for household shrines and cult images and symbols, whatever the architectural complex may be.

Political institutions also affect house styles. In areas where crime is common and police controls ineffective, houses will often tend to be built with an eye to security. The inward-facing house is one example of this sort of building. A few fierce dogs will also provide protection for a house or tent, but this sort of defense would not likely be obvious in the archaeological record. The lack of proper defenses on a higher (community or national) level may result in houses themselves being adapted for such purposes. The towering, thick-walled dwellings found in Southern Arabia were often strong enough to hold off attacks by Bedouin. A more complex political organization will also generate buildings to serve its own needs, such as administrative offices, jails, and barracks.

Nor can the influence of secular tastes and fashions be ignored. These are reflected in the design and layout of houses, and may account for the spreading of particular types of buildings into areas for which they were not originally designed and may not even be well suited. The layout of a house may also reflect such tastes as a desire for individual or group privacy. The former will be reflected in the clear division of a house into rooms and the separation of the rooms by doors. Secular tastes may also produce special summer or country houses that may differ a good deal from normal ones. Huron women are described as going with their children to live in the fields during the summer, not merely to be nearer their work but also to be away from the crowded conditions of village life (Trigger 1960: 18).

COMMUNITY LAYOUTS. The next level I deal with is the layout of the structures constituting a single community. By a community I mean "the maximal group of persons who normally reside in face-to-face association" (Murdock 1949: 79). In general, a community corresponds to a single settlement and therefore can be identified with the archaeologist's *component* (Willey and Phillips 1958: 21, 22). However, in areas of dispersed settlement such an equation may not hold, nor will it hold for migratory hunting and gathering peoples who reestablish their community in several settlements in the course of a year, or among whom the community may be forced to scatter into small family groups at least during certain seasons. In these cases, the community, as socially defined, would be associated with more than one settlement or site. The archaeological definition of the aggregate of settlements associated with such a community would depend on ascertaining at what time of year different settlements were occupied and what kinds of settlements are associated with each season. In dispersed patterns, the solution may depend on the definition of whatever nuclei exist in the pattern and on estimations of the size of a community that could be associated with a particular mode of subsistence. Then, on the basis of complementary distributions, the pattern itself could be worked out, at least as a statistical possibility. Despite some violence to the sociological concept of community, I extend the term to cover the whole of large stable units of settlement, such as cities, which, if they cannot be defined as communities, at least represent stable interaction patterns.

The maximum size and stability of a community are quite obviously limited by the environment and the effectiveness of the subsistence technology. The latter includes the means of acquiring or producing food, as well as storing, processing, and transporting it. The three last factors are often crucially important: effective means of storing food allows the population to expand beyond the numbers that could formerly survive the period of least production; processing allows foods to be used that otherwise would be inedible (e.g., acorns and bitter manioc); and transportation determines the size of the area in which food can be collected and concentrated. These ecological factors play an important role in determining the major types of community pattern as they have been defined by Chang (1962: 30). They determine, for example, whether or not a community can complete its annual subsistence cycle at a single site, and whether a single site can be inhabited permanently, as would be the case with irrigation agriculture, or only semipermanently, as with most swidden agriculture. When such sedentary life is not possible, a community may have to occupy a network of scattered settlements in the course of a year. In some cases the annual subsistence region in such a network will remain unchanged from year to year, and even the main seasonal settlements within it will remain unaltered. In other cases the group will exploit and exhaust the ecological potential of one region and therefore be forced to move on to fresh territory.

Within any region, people will tend to establish their settlements in places that are close to drinking water, sources of food, and, as far as possible, in places that are safe and pleasant. Even the hunters and gatherers of the temperate forests sought to locate their camps on sand banks by the edge of lakes or rivers, where they would be dry, and where the breeze would keep away bothersome insects. Agricultural groups seek locations where the soil and weather are favorable to their crops and their methods of cultivation.

Whereas community size and location are influenced to a large extent by ecological factors, the layout of communities appears to be strongly influenced by family and kinship organization—especially in primitive societies. These relationships are not necessarily totally independent factors, since kinship relations are at least partly determined by ecological factors that operate through the relations of production.

In a study of circumpolar groups, Chang (1962) has distinguished between communities of a "Siberian" type and those of an "Eskimo" type. The Siberian type is composed of individuals "unilineally determined by descent and/or unilocally recruited by marriage. It is a basic unit of economic cooperation and is strongly integrated as a cohesive body" (p. 33). This type of society often occupies a multidwelling village with individual or multifamily houses laid out in a planned fashion. When there is more than one lineage present, each one occupies its own section of the village, and when the community splits up for its seasonal movements it splits along lines of kinship, with the same groups returning to their winter base year after year. The Eskimo type of community is characterized by the looseness of its organization, by fluctuations in group membership, and by bilateral kinship. Such communities tend to be an incoherent conglomeration of families, each family settling where it likes and moving when new districts offer greater advantages. Even the winter settlements are characterized by this irregularity. Chang's distinction between "Siberian" and "Eskimo" community types is similar in many ways to Steward's (1955) distinction between patrilineal and composite bands. The first type of community, by either distinction, is associated with a more stable and more sedentary subsistence pattern than is the second, and the subsistence is more often based on fishing than on hunting. Chang suggests that the kind of solidarity associated with the Siberian type "tends to call for a symbolic projection of the community structure in the lay-out of the settlement site" (p. 37).

This same theme forms the basis of Chang's (1958) now-classic study of neolithic village patterns, which suggests a high degree of correlation between community plans and village social organization, and postulates land ownership as an important determinant of neolithic community types. In particular, his survey of neolithic societies demonstrates a strong correlation between planned villages and communities composed of a single lineage, and between segmented planned villages and communities composed of more than one lineage. Although there are perhaps more neolithic societies with a scattered homestead pattern than Chang's sample suggests, his conclusions remain valid so long as they are presumed to read: the absence of x settlement pattern does not necessarily imply the absence of y community type, but the presence of x strongly suggests that y is present also. The idea that kinship organization is reflected in village plans or in the distribution of communities is not new in anthropology: the relationship between social and geographical space was one of the main themes explored by Evans-Pritchard in *The Nuer* (1940). Nor is this phenomenon confined entirely to primitive societies. In medieval Arab cities, different quarters were sometimes laid out for different tribes. Likewise, the city of Tenochtitlan was divided into sections, each with its own temples and schools and belonging to a *calpulli*, probably an endogamous deme (Soustelle 1962: 7–8).

In complex societies, not only classes but religious and ethnic groups may live in well demarcated areas of the community, which societies are even separated from one another by a wall. In these communities, special sections may be set aside for foreigners or for ethnic groups such as Jews. In these areas, such groups are able to live under the protection of city officials (Sjoberg 1960: 100). Ethnic areas may also be found within modern communities, where they develop as a result of associational patterns rather than formal rules. Although divisions of the community resulting from disparate levels of wealth may be defined fairly easily from the quality and size of dwellings, the more informal ethnic divisions may be hard to trace in the layout of a site. A district populated by prosperous foreign traders could perhaps be distinguished from the local elite quarter by a preponderance of store rooms, by alien house plans, or by evidence of foreign cults. The section of the Spanish settlement of Nueva Cadiz in Venezuela that was inhabited by Negro and Indian slaves was identified by Indian pottery representing various tribal groups and by the lack of such permanent habitations as were found in the European quarter (Rouse and Cruxent 1963: 134–138). The best hope of identifying ethnic groups at an archaeological site seems to lie in investigating artifacts to discover whether particular symbols or written materials are associated with houses in one part of the site but not in another. But even where these efforts prove fruitful, it is difficult to demonstrate that an ethnic difference—as opposed, for example, to a religious or tribal difference—is involved. The presence of Huron captives in historic Seneca villages is attested in the archaeological record by the presence of many Huron-style potsherds among those of native design. Without historical documentation, however, it is likely that these sherds would have been described as trade sherds and their real social significance overlooked (MacNeish 1952: 46).

In more complex societies, subsistence factors, in the narrow sense, are less important as determinants of the size and location of communities. Trade may provide a source of wealth and stimulate the growth of large cities in remote regions, and the wealth amassed from such trade may in turn serve either to finance the development of novel agricultural systems in areas where they would otherwise be impractical, or to effect the importation of food from distant regions. Settlements may also spring up in wastelands where rare and valuable minerals are discovered. In ancient times, copper smelters were built at Aqaba on the shores of the Red Sea, a region rich in copper but lacking in agricultural potential.

Specialization on a local or village level can develop in relatively simple societies. When a number of villages are linked together in a trading network, for example, they are better able to transcend local limitations in natural resources; and a trading network also fosters greater specialization and better products than does an autonomous village economy. Thus a careful investigation of trade and of the nature of production is prerequisite to explaining of the size and the social and cultural complexity of communities. The archaeologist must determine what goods were present and produced in his sites. Data concerning production relationships can be obtained through study of the layout of workshops and stores within a community. The study should note whether places of work and residence are together or separated; whether the workshops of one trade are in the same part of the community or at scattered points; the degree to which the production and sale of goods are handled as a single operation or as separate functions; the importance of public markets, as opposed to stores; and so forth. Data of this sort, considered together with what can be learned about the social organization of the community from other sources, will permit more detailed and faithful reconstructions of ancient social organizations.

Graveyards also provide interesting clues to social and political organizations. For example, status differences can often be traced in graves even better than in house types or village patterns. This is especially true at a neolithic or advanced collecting level where there may be considerable differences in status but little difference in standards of living. Social relations and kinship may also be reflected in the relationship between communities and their cemeteries. Chang (1963: 65) has noted that in the Yangshao phase in North China each village had its own cemetery, but as the population increased and villages split, villages that had shared a common ancestry often continued to share a common graveyard, so that the ratio of cemeteries to villages declined. In historic times, the tribes of the Huron confederacy held a ceremony every decade or so in which all the members of the various member tribes who had died in the interim were reinterred in a common ossuary as an expression of political solidarity. A careful cross-cultural study of the relationship between burial practices and social structure might reveal correlations of considerable interest and value.

Little formal work has been done by archaeologists on the relationship between special-purpose structures and the community as a whole. Gideon Sjoberg (1960) has noted that in most preindustrial cities the major temples and palaces and the homes of the elite are concentrated in the center of the community. In support of this observation, one can quickly call to mind the location of the agora and the acropolis in Athens, the Roman forum, the temple center of a Sumerian city, or the palaces and temples of a Chinese city like Peking. In the New World, similarly, the center of Tenochtitlan was occupied by the main temples, palaces, and markets of the city, and Cuzco, the Inca capital, appears to have consisted of palaces, temples, and a ritual square surrounded by villages of royal retainers (Rowe 1944). But in cities like Tenochtitlan that were organized on a segmental principle, each of the divisions of the city also had a secondary center. Moreover, in some cities the elite center appears to have been at one side or in one corner of the city. In some of the cities of Chou China the elite center was a walled-off corner of the city (Chang 1963: 180–195), and in the cities of the Indus Valley civilization the citadel was to one side (Wheeler 1960: 18), as was the elite center in the ancient Egyptian town of Kahun (Smith 1958: 96–98).

The *kind* of buildings associated with such civic centers also provides some indication of the values and orientation of a particular society. In simpler societies, houses are often grouped around a central plaza that may serve as a market, a work area, and a meeting place, and may contain or be bordered by such public buildings as temples or council houses. In the dispersed pattern of the American farming community, such special-purpose buildings as schools, churches, and general stores are foci of public activity. However, as we noted in the discussion of individual structures, the reconstruction of community activities on the basis of the layout of public buildings within the community must be undertaken with caution. For one thing, it may be difficult, from archaeological evidence alone, to determine the full range of uses that was made of a plaza; and for another, norms may require that various structures important in community life be located outside the settlement, as for example the clubhouses of the secret societies in Melanesia. Temples or cult centers may also be located in sacred spots outside the residential area. The Egyptian pyramid complexes, with their small colonies of attendant priests, were built as the foci of royal mortuary cults. The priests lived near the pyramid and maintained themselves through agriculture and craft occupations (Kees 1961: 157–160). Monastic communities, with carefully organized routines and often with rigidly laid-out buildings, are still another example of whole communities that are religiously based. Pilgrimage centers like Mecca would be humble desert villages were it not for the tourist industry that sustains the local population.

The development of complex political organization gives rise to similarly specialized communities. Isolated forts and garrison towns are built to guard frontiers or to police the countryside. Royal courts are commonly established within cities, but some constitute independent communities. The king of Buganda, for example, lived in an oval enclosure over a mile long that also housed his guards, retainers, and slaves. The roads leading to this compound were lined with the houses of important chiefs and officials (Murdock 1934: 525). Warfare and defense play important roles in determining the site and layout of communities in many parts of the world. Where warfare is endemic, as it was among the Iroquois, villages were commonly built on hilltops or in the bends of rivers. Where walls or stockades are used for defense, houses are often crowded together to conserve space. When the Roman empire was adequately defended by its armies, cities tended to grow into sprawling agglomerations, but when the defense system collapsed in the third century A.D. the inhabitants of cities such as Barcelona were forced to abandon their suburbs and crowd together behind hastily built walls (Weiss 1961). Large numbers of pastoralists often camp together for protection, and smaller groups of Bedouin will camp with their tents arranged in a circular fashion (Forde 1934: 317). Similarly, the Masai *kraal* consists of a thorn fence and a ring of houses surrounding a central area where the domestic animals are secured for the night. The central area of a city is often similarly walled off, both to separate it from the city as a whole and so that it can serve as a place of last retreat. In Mexico, temple platforms served the latter purpose, and the capture of the main sanctuary symbolized the capture of a city (Soustelle 1962: 211). The presence or absence of fortifications cannot be considered as direct evidence of the prevalence of warfare, since the effectiveness of such means of defense depends in part on whether offensive of defensive warfare is in the ascendant.

It is also argued that community patterns, like house plans, reflect cosmological conceptions. According to Eliade (1960), communities are often laid out as an *imago mundi*. In Hindu culture, the central feature of any town is regarded as a symbol of the pillar of the universe. When a village is constructed in Bali, a space is left vacant in the center to be used for a cult house whose roof symbolizes the sky. Likewise, Roman cities were laid out according to a divine plan, their division into four quarters being the earthly manifestation of a heavenly prototype (Müller 1962). In all such examples, either the community is laid out in some general fashion according to a prescribed pattern, or there is a tendency to read such a pattern into an existing plan. In a very interesting paper, Lévi-Strauss (1953: 534) has argued that the elaborate layout of a Bororo village— where houses are arranged around a circle according to moieties, clans, and ranked subdivisions of clans—is a reflection not of unconscious social organization but rather of a model of society consciously existing in the Bororo's minds. Unfortunately, many of these symbolic plans would be difficult, if not impossible, for the archaeologist to detect, let alone explain, without non-archaeological sources of information.

ZONAL PATTERNS. The overall density and distribution of population of a region is determined to a large degree by the nature and availability of the natural resources that are being exploited. As long as other land is available, settlers tend to avoid areas that are naturally poor or where diseases or other dangers are common. Factors such as availability of game have a strong bearing on the size of hunting territories and on the distribution of permanent and transient bases. The attractions of fishing and collecting shellfish and the difficulties of overland travel through bush or jungle may result in concentrations of population along bodies of water (Kroeber 1953: 143–146). In Ontario, for example, the late Iroquoian occupation, which was based on agriculture, was confined to the warm and fertile regions in the southern part of the province, and to areas that were close to rivers and had light soil. Such populations were notably absent in central southwestern Ontario, which is relatively high and cold and also an area of hard clay soils, few rivers, and flat, forested lands. At best, such areas were used as hunting territories by the neighboring tribes (Trigger 1963a). Similar correlations have been noted between the neolithic Danubian culture and loess soils in Europe (Narr 1956: 139–140); the Sangoan culture and the tropical forest zone in Africa (Cole 1954: 26); and the eastern Gravettian culture and the mammoth in ice-age Europe (Hawkes and Woolley 1963: 83–86). In complex societies, fertile regions become centers of population and hence of political and cultural importance. In Japan the main fertile areas have been the Kanto, Nobi, and

Kinai plains on the east side of Honshu Island. The chief cities and cultural centers have been located on these plains, and Japanese history has been largely a struggle for control of these areas, and through them, of the country (Sansom 1958: 5–6).

Because archaeologists and geographers have had fairly good success in reconstructing both prehistoric subsistence patterns and prehistoric environments, the study of the relationship between these two sets of factors has become popular. Since the relationships of production strongly influence many other aspects of culture, even more stress has been placed on the ecological approach to the reconstruction of prehistoric societies (see, e.g., Kehoe 1964). This is a perfectly legitimate approach so long as it is used in an objective manner, but it should not inhibit anthropologists from following other avenues of research that also may shed light on prehistoric cultures. For example, if we know that a prehistoric society depended on shifting agriculture, it is reasonable to suggest that it had a lineage-based social structure, and if longhouses are excavated the statement becomes even more reasonable. But determining whether the society was matrilocal, like the Iroquois, or patrilocal, like the Tupinamba, is much more difficult. Knowledge about the division of labor may shed some light on the problem (White 1959: 150–152), and useful correlations may also someday be found between art styles or religious practices and lineality.[1]

As contiguous regions become more interdependent, zonal patterns are modified to an increasing degree by economic factors, as opposed to merely subsistence factors. In particular, trade plays an important role in establishing new communities and in increasing population density. Many of the most densely populated industrial regions of the modern world produce neither enough food to support their own population nor the raw materials needed to support their industries; both are obtained through trade and production. Trade, however, can be important even between very simple societies. Among the Alaskan Eskimo, trading partnerships between sea-oriented and inland hunters helped to level off periods of poor hunting for both groups and induced greater community stability (Dunning 1960: 26). In northeastern North America, agriculturalists and hunters occupying contiguous but different ecological zones exchanged their respective products to such an extent that even before the European fur trade began, the Huron villages in southern Ontario were clustered in a small area favorable for this kind of trade. Long-distance trade has been seen as a major factor in the rise of medieval European cities, e.g., Venice (Pirenne 1925) and the coastal cities of the ancient Levant, e.g., Tyre (Revere 1957). In the Hellenistic period, a series of cities including Petra, Palmyra, and Hatra, all of which depended on trade, grew up around the

[1] When this paper was written, James Deetz's (1965) important study of stylistic change in Arikara ceramics had not yet appeared.

margins of the Arabian Desert. Many of the important cities in ancient southern Arabia were built in the desert east of the fertile mountain region but along a major trade route to the north (Bowen 1958). Even earlier, special colonies were established for trade in foreign regions; examples are the Assyrian *karums* in Anatolia (Ozguc 1963) and the self-sufficient colonies established by the Greeks around the Black Sea and in the western Mediterranean.

The overall distribution of settlements is also affected by political organization. Internal security may require garrisons or administrative towns in the various sections of the country. Hsiao-tung Fei (1953: 90–100) describes the *ch'engs* or administrative towns in imperial China as instruments of power in the hands of the ruling classes. The emperor's representatives and the state bureaucracy lived in these towns and administered the countryside from them. Landowners, living off the rents from their estates, also frequently lived there for protection. In a centrally organized state, such towns would form provincial nuclei within a milieu of villages and scattered homesteads, and the national capital would be characterized by its greater size and luxury. Although the relative wealth of city states may differ considerably, it is doubtful that a single city state would predominate to the same degree as the capital city in most national states (Lambert 1964: 17). In civilizations where cities are less important, the distribution of shrines or ceremonial centers may reflect political organization. Although little is known about Maya political organization, the distribution of a large number of minor ceremonial centers around the large centers reflects unmistakably the subordination of the former to the latter. On the other hand, even without written records, one may presume that such immense undertakings as the Egyptian pyramids of the Fourth Dynasty would be interpreted as reflecting a powerful central government controlling a vast dominion. This impression is strengthened by noting that the tombs of the nobles in this period are not to be found elsewhere in Egypt but cluster around the pyramid of the reigning king in a fashion as centralized as that of the government they served (Baer 1960: 301).

Warfare is another factor shaping the overall distribution of settlements. Hunting bands may have a strong sense of territory, and so avoid one another. Since most of these groups have little in the way of immovable property they may simply move out of the way or scatter when danger threatens. Pastoralists, on the other hand, often band together in larger groups so as to be able to defend their herds. Agricultural peoples can respond in a number of different ways. Scattered communities may join together to build a common fort to which they can all flee in times of danger. In Bronze Age Palestine, these forts were often the headquarters of a local chief (Albright 1960: 205). Where there are a number of small villages, the people may choose to fortify one of the larger ones, which, like the fort, can be used as a place of refuge in times of danger. In most city states the capital serves this purpose.

One feature of warfare may be the development of buffer zones between belligerent factions. Where the population density is low, warring neolithic groups are often separated from each other by lakes or broad stretches of forest. During the Middle Ages, the rich plains of Burgundy, which had been thickly populated, were abandoned because of the repeated incursions of the Vikings (Bloch 1961: 41–42). In large states the defensive system may become an important specialized feature of the overall settlement pattern. The Roman limes and the Great Wall of China were Maginot Lines of their day, designed to keep out the marauding tribes to the north. Both required elaborate constructions and the establishment of garrison communities. Similar frontier defense systems had been built by the Egyptians as early as the Middle Kingdom (Kees 1961: 317). Moreover, the need for quick movement of troops and messengers may result in extensive road systems.

Religious factors can also affect the overall settlement pattern. Among the Maya, ceremonial centers served as community and state foci for the population that lived around them. In the Middle East, Judaeo-Christian religious communities, driven by persecution or a desire to escape the world, established settlements in forbidding and lonely regions, which they developed, often with great difficulty, to produce their needs. European monastic orders pioneered settlement in many parts of northern Europe; the Benedictines were active in clearing the forests of the Dauphine and the Ile de France, and were followed in other regions by the Cistercians (Darby 1956: 194). In North America, utopian religious communities had curious and erratic careers, and Mormonism played an important role in the colonization of Utah.

Taste and symbolic factors appear to have a fairly limited role in determining zonal patterns. They are involved to some degree in determining the location of villas or pleasure resorts serving the main centers of population, in the establishment of summer and winter capitals in some tropical countries, and in the preference for suburban living among the more affluent in western cities. It has been suggested that the twelve great cities making up each of the three Etruscan leagues in Italy were not an accidental number but a ritually auspicious one, perhaps in emulation of the league of twelve cities in Ionia (Pallottino 1956: 131–135). The designation of the twelve cities appears to have taken place after the fact, and hence played no role in their foundation or location. In general, social, economic, and political factors seem to find more expression on the zonal level than do ideational ones.

So far, we have been considering settlement patterns as a reflection of a variety of more or less stable conditions. To the factors we have already noted as determinants, we must add the more dynamic factors of migration and population change. These may alter the settlement pattern of a region more or less completely. Homans (1962: 127–181) has argued that two contrasting types of settlement in medieval England, the compact village of the central region and the dispersed settlement of Kent and East Anglia, were the result not of geographical or technological variations but of different traditions of land use that were brought from the continent; neither was sufficiently unsuited to the new environment to be forced to change. The rise or fall of population in response to economic factors or disease may also affect the settlement pattern in various ways. Land crowding may be an important factor stimulating migration to urban centers. As a result of wars and bubonic plague, large areas of farmland in central Europe reverted to thick forest between 1350 and 1450 (Darby 1956: 198).

INTEGRATION

It is clear that settlement patterns represent responses to a number of different kinds of factors that influence them in different ways and degrees on different levels. For example, ecology, warfare, and religion have an influence on individual structures, community plans, and zonal patterns, whereas symbolic factors tend to affect only the first two of these levels. Certain factors leave a very clear imprint on one or more of these levels: war may result in fortified houses, walled settlements, or large defensive works, and trade may be reflected in special buildings and communities. At the same time, these factors may also be reflected indirectly, in terms of the prosperity or lack of prosperity associated with them.

If we conceive of the settlement pattern as an outcome of the adjustments a society makes to a series of determinants that vary both in importance and in the kinds of demands they make on the society, we must consider not merely the range of factors affecting settlement patterns but also the manner in which different factors interact with one another to produce a particular pattern. Factors vary in importance according to both the local situation and the temporal relationship that they have to one another.

We have already noted that primitive agricultural communities threatened by attack may respond in a number of different ways. A number of different solutions then, are possible to the same problem. In other situations the range of choice may be considerably more restricted. Let us consider a shift in the settlement pattern of the Shukriya Bedouin, one that is especially interesting because it was brought about primarily by political changes rather than by economic or environmental ones. The Shukriya, an Arabic-speaking people, live in the Butana Desert, east of Khartoum in the Sudan. In the last century their camps and their herds were constantly menaced by raiding parties. In self-defense, they began to move about in groups that were two to three hundred tents strong. Because the sparse, scattered desert pastures could support the correspondingly large herds for no more than 15 to 20 days, the groups were forced to move frequently from one place to another. With the establishment of British rule, the threat of raids was lifted, and the large tribal groups broke up into smaller family units, each able to occupy a single stretch of the pasture year-round without exhausting it. As a result, these smaller groups tended to become sedentary; some even took to agriculture in a small way (Crowfoot 1920: 86–87). In terms of subsistence patterns, two alternatives had always been open to the Shukriya: large groups could exhaust individual pastures one by one and move on, or smaller groups could occupy a larger number of pastures simultaneously, each group remaining on the same pasture throughout the year. But was this choice really open to the Shukriya? The answer would seem to be No, inasmuch as the fear of raids necessitated a defense best achieved by staying together. Moreover, even if neighboring tribes had agreed to remain at peace, it is unlikely that conflict could have been avoided prior to British rule. Slow increases in population would have begun to tax the grazing areas, and new outbreaks of fighting would have resulted. The same British rule that brought peace also provided the Shukriya with new opportunities in a national economy. Conflict and a subsequent need to band together for defense would appear characteristic of pastoral economies in areas where pasturage is limited. A culture wherein a potential variety of settlement patterns is limited by a restricted range of possibilities in one or another of the culture's aspects can be said to exhibit a principle of functional limitation.

A variation on this pattern is one in which a form of settlement may be highly desirable in some respects although unfavorable in most others. For example, an area well-placed for trade may be ill-equipped to support a large population. Nueva Cadiz has already provided one example of such a situation. The town was founded on an island off the coast of Venezuela that was close to pearling areas and protected from the Indians on the mainland. On the other hand, both food and water had to be imported. As a result, the colony survived only so long as the pearl fisheries were profitable. Similarly, the city of Samarra was founded in 836 A.D. by the Caliph Mu'tasim, on a site removed from the major trade routes of the Middle East but considered to be a safer residence for the Caliph than the turbulent city of Kufa. Despite the removal of many merchants and artisans to the new site, the city endured for less than fifty years before it was abandoned and its inhabitants drifted back to the "natural" centers of population in Mesopotamia. Likewise, the city of Akhetaton, which was founded in honor of the new god of the Egyptian Pharaoh Ikhnaton, was inhabited for only 17 years. The trading cities in Arabia and desert mining outposts like Aqaba flourished in regions poorly suited for agriculture. Each of these communities was abandoned when the function it was de- signed to serve ceased to be important. In other cases, the determination of a settlement pattern may involve a choice between opposing considera- tions: modern cities, for example, are utterly vulnerable to bombing attack, and therefore a liability to their military defenders, but they are essential for efficient industrial production. In such cases, the course of develop- ment reflects the relative importance attached to different functions: ad- vantages gained through trade may make a large investment in land development worthwhile, or the agricultural worth of an area may justify elaborate defenses. We may call this the principle of hierarchical resolu- tion of conflicting tendencies.

When a problem may be solved by one of several alternatives, the solution may be determined by the manner in which a previous problem was resolved. A city, for example, is functionally distinguished from a town or village in that it contains a high concentration of the facilities needed for the specialized functions characteristic of complex societies, such as temples, administrative buildings, the residences of the elite, work- shops for artisans, and defense facilities. It is evident, however, that some early civilizations, such as those of ancient Egypt and Peru, and of the Maya, existed without true cities. In such societies the main temples might be located in one place, forts in another, and the royal court in still an- other. Craftsmen, both full- and part-time, could live in the scattered vil- lages and exchange their produce at market places or through a state- operated redistribution network. Such a settlement pattern, though clearly workable at a certain level, is nevertheless cumbersome, and one would expect that with increased cultural complexity there would be a tendency for different functions to converge toward a common center. The pattern of convergence may differ considerably from one society to another. A fort may become the residence of a chief and his retainers; as immovable property accumulates, the well-to-do may move into the fort, so that a town begins to develop; and artisans may settle in the town so as to sell their wares to the townsfolk and to farmers who come to trade and to worship at local shrines. In other cultures, the cult center may come to serve as a fort or marketplace and in this way become the nucleus of a city. In Shang China the city apparently consisted of a walled elite center surrounded by villages that were probably self-sufficient in terms of sub- sistence and local handicrafts, but because many of these villages were also centers of particular occupational specialties, the whole tended to be bound together as a unit (Chang 1963). In the Chou Period, probably largely in response to warfare, these specialist villages tended to cluster close to the elite enclosures, producing finally a true city. Even without the stimulus of war, a court may attract public servants, attendants, and the merchants and menials who serve them, as well as temples and state buildings. If such nuclei attract trade, or serve as forts or administrative centers, they may eventually become viable cities, whether or not the court remains.

There is considerable variation in the rate and degree of this concentration in different areas. In Mesopotamia, large urban communities arose at an early period within a context of warring states. In Egypt, where a strong territorial state was established early, there was no need for fortified towns, and less of a tendency for these functions to coalesce around common centers (Frankfort 1956). In Mexico, cities seem to have developed quite early. This tendency was stimulated perhaps primarily by the growth of interregional trade. In the lowland Maya region, this tendency seems to have been much weaker. Thus, a flourishing center, whether established first for political, economic, religious, or defensive reasons, or for a combination of these, may gradually take on other functions until it becomes an important and diversified center of population serving the needs of a complex society. The basic patterns of growth within a given culture may be directed by local circumstances or by general configurations of development. This sort of development can be seen as illustrating a third principle, that of the convergence of functions.

CONCLUSIONS

In the foregoing, I have ranged rather widely in time and space. I should like now to emphasize several points concerning the nature of a settlement-pattern approach to the study of prehistoric societies.

HABITATION, COMMUNITY, SOCIETY. I have defined three "levels" that are the object of settlement-pattern studies: the individual structure, the layout of communities, and the manner in which communities belonging to a culture or society distribute themselves over the landscape. The patterns displayed at each of these levels can be viewed as being functionally related in some way to all aspects of a culture and therefore able to shed light on a variety of problems. But, in fact, each level displays tendencies especially appropriate to the study of particular aspects of society: individual structures furnish information about family organization, craft specialization, and perhaps the relative importance of different aspects of the social structure; the layout of shrines or temples may elucidate religious rituals; community plans have yielded useful information about lineage organization and a community's adaptation to its physical and cultural environments; and areal patterns reflect a good deal about the social and political organization of complex societies, as well as about trade and warfare. Problem-oriented approaches exploiting the potential of each of these levels simultaneously would seem to be highly desirable—

though the investigation of settlement patterns must of course be aided by the study of artifacts, which often yield supplementary data about subsistence patterns, warfare, trade, beliefs, and the division of labor.

DIACHRONIC AND SYNCHRONIC VANTAGE POINTS. Second, I have observed that the interpretation of various aspects of the settlement pattern can be meaningful from a diachronic, as well as a synchronic, vantage point. Many aspects of a settlement pattern can be interpreted using functional ethnographic correlations, but other aspects can be understood only as the result of a historical process of development. For example, the development of Mesopotamian civilization from a neolithic base, through a system of city states, to the level of empire or national state is quite different from the direct transition of Egypt from a neolithic base to a large territorial kingdom. Although ecological differences have been suggested as the primary cause for their dissimilar development (Coe 1961: 84), it seems to me that the explanation lies largely in the nature of their political and social development. In Mesopotamia, social, political, and economic institutions tended to grow in complexity concurrently, and in this way villages or groups of villages grew into city states with multicentric sources of power. In Egypt, where a large territorial state was established while the country was at a relatively primitive stage of cultural development (an analogy might be drawn with Shaka's Zulu empire), further economic and cultural progress took place under the aegis and control of the royal court and the government administration. Membership in the elite culture was long restricted to this bureaucratic class, and the development of cities as independent nuclei of an elite culture was inhibited.[2] In the course of time, with Egyptian society becoming less court-centered and Mesopotamia moving toward national state configuration, there was a marked degree of convergence between the two cultures. The diachronic study of settlement patterns in a region can shed light on the development of social and economic institutions, and may provide similar genetic explanations for cultures that are not as well documented.

UNIVERSAL AND LIMITED CORRELATIONS. In the interpretation of prehistoric settlement patterns, two kinds of correlations are of value. The first are functional correlations of universal applicability; examples of this sort are found in Chang's "Study of the Neolithic Social Grouping" (1958). Correlations of the second kind are limited in their applicability to a particular area. Within such an area the nature of artifacts or aspects of the settlement pattern may be worked out by analogy with related ethnographic cultures. This method is limited in time and space, and is further dependent on the degree of cultural continuity in a particular area: for example,

---

[2] Since this paper was written, I have published a more detailed account on my views on the origin of Egyptian civilization. See B. G. Trigger, *Beyond History: The Methods of Prehistory* (New York, 1968).

many features in Eskimo, Pueblo, or Polynesian archaeological sites can be identified by comparison with the modern cultures in the area. Even particular mythological figures can be identified in the pre-Columbian art of the southwestern United States. Through cultural persistences of this sort, the identification of structures and their use in various parts of the world may be accomplished at least as effectively—and perhaps more so—as they might be through universal correlations. If the more limited correlations are less universal (i.e., less scientific), they are no less valuable to cultural historical studies, and are therefore no less deserving of serious attention.

References

Albright, W. F.
    1960   *The Archaeology of Palestine.* Harmondsworth: Penguin Books Inc.
Baer, K.
    1960   *Rank and Title in the Old Kingdom.* Chicago: University of Chicago Press.
Bloch, Marc
    1961   *Feudal Society.* Chicago: University of Chicago Press.
Bowen, R. L.
    1958   "Ancient Trade Routes in South Arabia." In *Archaeological Discoveries in South Arabia,* R. L. Bowen and F. P. Albright, editors. Baltimore: Johns Hopkins Press.
Chang, K. C.
    1958   "Study of the Neolithic Social Grouping: Examples from the New World." *American Anthropologist,* Vol. LX:298–334.
    1962   "A Typology of Settlement and Community Patterns in Some Circumpolar Societies." *Arctic Anthropology,* Vol. I:28–41.
    1963   *The Archaeology of Ancient China.* New Haven: Yale University Press.
Codrington, R. H.
    1957   *The Melanesians.* New Haven: HRAF Press.
Coe, M. D.
    1961   "Social Typology and Tropical Forest Civilizations." *Comparative Studies in Society and History,* Vol. IV:65–85.
Cole, Sonia M.
    1954   *The Prehistory of East Africa.* Harmondsworth: Penguin Books Inc.
Crowfoot, J. W.
    1920   "Old Sites in the Butana." *Sudan Notes and Records,* Vol. III:85–93.
Darby, H. C.
    1956   "The Clearing of the Woodland in Europe." In *Man's Role in Changing the Face of the Earth,* W. L. Thomas, editor. Chicago: University of Chicago Press, pp. 183–216.
den Hollander, A. N. J.
    1960   "The Great Hungarian Plain: A Frontier Area." *Comparative Studies in Society and History,* Vol. III:74–88; 155–169.
Dunning, R. W.
    1960   "Differentiation of Status in Subsistence Level Societies." *Transactions of the Royal Society of Canada,* Vol. LIV, Section II:25–32.
Durkheim, E., and M. Mauss
    1963   *Primitive Classification.* Chicago: University of Chicago Press.
Eliade, Mircea
    1960   "Structures and Changes in the History of Religions." In *City Invincible,* R. M. Adams and C. H. Kraeling, editors. Chicago: University of Chicago Press, pp. 351–366.

Evans-Pritchard, E. E.
    1940 *The Nuer.* Oxford: Clarendon Press.
Fei, Hsiao-tung
    1953 *China's Gentry.* Chicago: University of Chicago Press.
Fitch, J. M., and D. P. Branch
    1960 "Primitive Architecture and Climate." *Scientific American,* Vol. XXIII, No.
        6:134–144.
Forde, C. D.
    1934 *Habitat, Economy and Society.* London: Methuen & Co., Ltd.
Frankfort, Henri
    1956 *The Birth of Civilization in the Near East.* New York: Doubleday and Com-
        pany, Inc.
Hawkes, Jacquetta, and Leonard Woolley
    1963 *Prehistory and the Beginnings of Civilization.* New York: Harper and Row.
Homans, George C.
    1962 *Sentiments and Activities.* Glencoe: The Free Press.
Kees, Hermann
    1961 *Ancient Egypt: A Cultural Topography.* Chicago: University of Chicago Press.
Kehoe, Alice B.
    1964 "A Worm's-Eye View of Marriage, Authority, and Final Causes." *American
        Anthropologist,* Vol. LXVI:405–407.
Kroeber, A. L.
    1953 *Cultural and Natural Areas of Native North America.* Berkeley: University of
        California Press.
Lambert, W. G.
    1964 "The Reign of Nebuchadnezzar I." In *The Seed of Wisdom,* W. S. McCullough,
        editor. Toronto: University of Toronto Press, pp. 3–13.
Lévi-Strauss, Claude
    1953 "Social Structure." In *Anthropology Today,* A. L. Kroeber, editor. Chicago: Uni-
        versity of Chicago Press, pp. 524–553.
MacNeish, R. S.
    1952 "Iroquois Pottery Types." *National Museum of Canada Bulletin,* No. 124.
Mayer-Oakes, W. J.
    1959 "A Developmental Concept of Pre-Spanish Urbanization in the Valley of
        Mexico." *Tulane University Middle American Research Records,* No. 18, p. 2.
Müller, Werner
    1962 *Die Heilige Stadt.* Stuttgart: Kohlhammer Verlag.
Murdock, G. P.
    1934 *Our Primitive Contemporaries.* New York: The Macmillan Company.
    1949 *Social Structure.* New York: The Macmillan Company.
Narr, K. J.
    1956 "Early Food-producing Populations." In *Man's Role in Changing the Face of the
        Earth,* W. L. Thomas, editor. Chicago: University of Chicago Press, pp.
        134–151.
Ozguc, Tahsin
    1963 "An Assyrian Trading Outpost." *Scientific American,* Vol. CCVIII, No. 2:
        96–106.
Pallottino, M.
    1956 *The Etruscans.* Harmondsworth: Penguin Books, Ltd.
Pirenne, Henri
    1925 *Medieval Cities.* Princeton: Princeton University Press.
Quimby, G. I.
    1960 "Habitat, Culture, and Archaeology." In *Essays in the Science of Culture,* G. E.
        Dole and R. L. Carneiro, editors. New York: Thomas Y. Crowell Company,
        pp. 380–389.
Revere, R. B.
    1957 "No Man's Coast: Ports of Trade in the Eastern Mediterranean." In *Trade and
        Market in the Early Empires,* K. Polanyi, editor. Glencoe: The Free Press.

Rouse, Irving, and J. M. Cruxent
    1963   *Venezuelan Archaeology.* New Haven: Yale University Press.
Rowe, John Howland
    1944   "An Introduction to the Archaeology of Cuzco." *Papers of the Peabody Museum of American Archaeology and Ethnology,* Harvard University, Vol. XXVII, No. 2.
Salim, S. M.
    1962   *Marsh Dwellers of the Euphrates Delta.* London School of Economics Monographs on Social Anthropology, No. 23.
Sansom, George
    1958   *A History of Japan to 1334.* Stanford: Stanford University Press.
Sears, W. H.
    1961   "The Study of Social and Religious Systems in North American Archaeology." *Current Anthropology,* Vol. II:223–246.
Sjoberg, Gideon
    1960   *The Preindustrial City.* Glencoe: The Free Press.
Smith, W. S.
    1958   *The Art and Architecture of Ancient Egypt.* Baltimore: Penguin Books, Ltd.
Soustelle, Jacques
    1962   *The Daily Life of the Aztecs.* New York: The Macmillan Company.
Steward, J. H.
    1955   *Theory of Culture Change.* Urbana: University of Illinois Press.
Suggs, R. C.
    1960   *The Island Civilizations of Polynesia.* New York: Mentor Books.
Trigger, B. G.
    1960   "The Destruction of Huronia." *Transactions of the Royal Canadian Institute,* Vol. XXXIII, Pt. 1, No. 68:14–45.
    1963a "Settlement as an Aspect of Iroquoian Adaptation at the Time of Contact." *American Anthropologist,* Vol. LXV:86–101.
    1963b "Order and Freedom in Huron Society." *Anthropologica* N. S. V:151–169.
    1965   *History and Settlement in Lower Nubia.* New Haven: Yale University Publications in Anthropology, No. 69.
Vogt, E. Z.
    1956   "An Appraisal of *Prehistoric Settlement Patterns in the New World.*" Viking Fund Publications in Anthropology, No. 23:173–182.
Weiss, A. H.
    1961   "The Roman Walls of Barcelona." *Archaeology,* Vol. XIV:188–197.
Wheeler, Mortimer
    1960   *The Indus Valley Civilization.* Cambridge: University Press.
White, L. A.
    1959   *The Evolution of Culture.* New York: McGraw-Hill Book Company.
Willetts, William
    1958   *Chinese Art.* Harmondsworth: Penguin Books, Ltd.
Willey, G. R.
    1953   *Prehistoric Settlement Patterns in the Virú Valley.* Washington: Bureau of American Ethnology, Bulletin 155.
    1956a Editor, *Prehistoric Settlement Patterns in the New World.* Viking Fund Publications in Anthropology, No. 23.
    1956b "Problems Concerning Prehistoric Settlement Patterns in the Maya Lowlands." In Willey, 1956a.
——, and Philip Phillips
    1958   *Method and Theory in American Archaeology.* Chicago: University of Chicago Press.

CHAPTER EIGHT

Culture Change, Social Change, and Analogy

This concluding section
is devoted to the interpretation
of archaeology. Included are papers
on three broad sectors of
interpretation—culture change,
social change, and analogy—which
represent a cross-section of
the enormous amount of literature
on these subjects.

WHAT HAPPENED IN PREHISTORY?

V. GORDON CHILDE was one of the great figures of European archaeology, and his syntheses of Old World prehistory and the origins of civilization are known far outside the narrow circle of professional archaeologists. The following exposition of the processes of culture change, the understanding of which is fundamental to the interpretation of the archaeological record, comes from one of his last books.

📖 Having rigged a culture up with the trappings of personality and set it on the stage of archaeological history, what acts shall the archaeologist present it performing? It should be exhibited developing, changing before the spectator's eyes. It may move about, and enter into relations with other cultures, but archaeologically these too are just changes, changes in the distribution of the diagnostic types and changes in the composition of the assemblages they characterize or in those types themselves. Only the latter changes can strictly speaking be termed changes in culture or cultural changes though distributional changes may promote these.

Distributional changes should reflect displacements of population, the expansions, migrations, colonizations or conquests with which literary history is familiar. The simplest case may be termed expansion. Any population may be expected to multiply, but the new mouths can be fed only

Reprinted from *Piecing Together the Past* by V. Gordon Childe (1956), pp. 135–158, by permission of the publishers, Routledge & Kegan Paul Ltd., London, and Frederick A. Praeger, New York. Footnotes and references are omitted.

by exploiting new territory or by intensifying the productivity of the original habitat. Even on the second alternative, since the productivity of any area is limited, the population, if it continue to grow, must eventually overflow. On the other hand the human population of our globe was once exceedingly sparse—*Homo sapiens* was originally a rare animal. In prehistoric and even in early historical times immense tracts of land were totally or virtually uninhabited. Even in the European Middle Ages the gradual clearance of forests and appropriation of wastes by European peasantries was a familiar phenomenon; it continued for many centuries and must have begun millennia before the Roman Conquest.

Such gradual encroachment of humanity on the wilderness would theoretically be represented archaeologically by a more or less continuous distribution of types, diagnostic of one culture round a primary nucleus. In so far as a typological development is detectable in these relics, the later stages should of course be more widely distributed than the earlier ones, but save in relatively recent times, technological progress has been far slower than the expansion of population.

In practice it would be hard to draw any logical distinction between this hypothetical expansion and colonization or migration. The distribution pattern is not really likely to be continuous, since regions where the favorite game was scarce or hard to catch, less fertile soils, patches of swamp or desert, bare rocks and rugged mountains will be avoided or passed over. So the distribution of find-spots will be interrupted by empty spaces.

If the search for a congenial habitat, whether hunting or fishing-grounds, cultivable soils, pastures or trading posts, involve traversing deserts, mountain ranges or stretches of sea, the migrants may quickly and even suddenly be brought into an environment diverging seriously from that of their starting-point. But even continuous expansion, if pushed far enough, would eventually bring the settlers into a novel environment. Now in so far as a culture is an adaptation to a specific environment, it must be modified by transfer to a different environment, and the degree of modification is likely to be inversely proportional to the culture's technological level. In no case can it be expected that one and the same culture should be represented by an identical assemblage of types in two contrasted environments. Conversely all cultures under identical environmental conditions are liable to exhibit quite a number of common traits—behavior patterns and archaeological types expressing them that are imposed on men by external natural conditions such as raw materials, or are at least adaptations peculiarly well fitted to securing survival in a particular environment. Step by step expansion, just as much as migration, is likely to bring a society into a habitat so different from its starting-point that adaptation to it will require an assemblage of types so different from those appropriate to the homeland that we seem to be confronted with distinct cultures.

Fortunately for archaeologists even quite progressive societies are often reluctant to relinquish cherished customs, however unsuitable they may have become. In Australia I remember in my youth eating turkey and plum pudding at Christmas when the temperature was over 95° F and seeing judges walking through the blazing sun in black coats and top hats. In the southern hemisphere the traditional diet for a European Christmas was cherished and the dress then approved for an English gentleman remained obligatory.

Thus distributional change, as much as the lapse of time, may result in cultural change, and in either case differentiation may proceed so far as to raise the question of the relation between two cultures. In principle there need be no difference between the cultural changes observed as one proceeds from the basal to the superficial layers of a stratified site and those distinguishing the starting and terminal points of an expansive or migratory movement. Both are presented in the archaeological record as changes in the assemblage of types, the replacement or modification of old types and the emergence of quite novel ones. But in stratified sites, not all observed changes are changes in culture; they may be changes of culture. In other words the phenomena observed in successive layers may represent the replacement of one culture by another as much as the progressive development of a single culture. And not all the observed phenomena document cultural change at all. In an inhabited site we may discover a layer of ashes and debris reflecting the violent destruction of the whole settlement. The destruction layer records a historical event— a hostile attack or a natural catastrophe. The same or a parallel event may be recorded in homotaxial layers at several sites. Even so, the destruction is not itself a cultural change; it may be the prelude to one, but only if the assemblages from the re-occupation layers diverge from those beneath the debris.

No doubt all cultural changes, from a slight modification of a traditional pattern or deviation from a customary rite to a major invention like the wheel or a bold strategic innovation, originated with an individual who was naturally a member of a community. They are recognizable archaeologically only if they have been adopted by, or imposed upon, a whole society. Recognizable changes in culture may be said to result from the internal genius of the society itself or to be provoked by some external event whether that be a change in the non-human environment or some sort of relation with another society.

The recognizable changes in culture whether between basal and superficial layers in a group of stratified sites or between the initial and terminal points of an expansive or migratory movement are presented in the archaeological record as variations in assemblages of types and so could serve equally well as the bases for chorological as for chronological distinctions. In practice archaeologists infer from observed divergences between assemblages from consecutive layers in one or more stratified sites either the development of one culture or the replacement of one culture by another. These opposing inferences are of course equivalent to the alternatives of peaceful internal development or military conquest. The former alternative is to be preferred on the following conditions: the distributions of the two assemblages should be concordant . . . ; a substantial number of the new types distinguishing the later assemblages should be logically derivable from the old—ideally all the stages in typological series linking them should be discoverable locally. In this case, subject to reservations mentioned above, prehistorians do not regard the innovations in the upper layer as distinctive of a new culture nor apply a new name to the assemblages they characterize; they receive the same name as those from the lower levels but qualified by a numeral or chronological adjective as "Magdalenian VI," "Upper Solutrean," "Middle Minoan." If on the other hand sufficient typological continuity cannot be established between consecutive layers a change of culture is assumed and a new name introduced. As soon as adequate study showed that the types distinctive of consecutive layers in French caves could not logically be presented each as members of typological series, the old terms "Lower," "Middle" and "Upper Aurignacian" were replaced by "Perigordian I–II," "Aurignacian" and "Perigordian IV–V," or even by "Chatelperronian," "Aurignacian" and "Gravettian." . . .

When the distributions are discordant or exclusive—and such must result from expansive movements—a decision between the alternative interpretations is less easy. English culture of the twentieth century differs both from contemporary American culture and from sixteenth-century English culture. The last differed so superficially from sixteenth-century American culture, that the latter could be termed a colonial variant of English culture. So the contrast recognized today could be regarded as the result of divergent developments of one and the same culture in different environments. "Environment" not being qualified by "natural" includes relations to other cultures—Spanish, Dutch, French, Pre-Columbian —that markedly affected the development in the New World. When communications were more difficult, divergence between spatially separated groups must have proceeded faster and farther. Some early Neolithic cultures in Europe provide examples.

The earliest and simplest Danubian pot-forms and decorative patterns are replicated with surprising uniformity all over the löss-lands from the Bakony in Hungary to the Harz in central Germany and from the Vistula to the Meuse and are associated everywhere with equally uniform house types, stone adzes and personal ornaments. The settlements being confined strictly to the löss, the distribution is interrupted by considerable blank spaces, but is as continuous as it could possibly be, given that restriction on habitat. In the sequel in various parts of this territory the old ceramic repertoire of forms and patterns develops into divergent local styles, each associated, albeit in varying degrees, with parallel innovations in architecture, armament, burial rites and so on. Some of the latter innovations, associated with most local ceramic styles, appear as complete novelties while others are at least as clearly typological developments from the older inventory. The local divergence of ceramic styles then seems to denote the break up of one original Danubian culture into a family of new cultures. Provided these new ceramic styles be exclusively associated with two or three other equally differentiated diagnostic traits and exhibit definite and mutually exclusive distributions, each must be accepted as characterizing a distinct culture. . . . Consequently each culture thus characterized deserves a name of its own, however obvious be its descent from the original Danubian and consequently its status as a phase in that culture's development.

All these cultures may be considered *genetically* related, *directly* to the original Danubian, *colaterally* to one another. The totality of genetically related cultures constitutes the simplest case of what I propose to designate a *cycle* (of cultures) or culture-cycle. A more objective definition would be: All cultures, characterized by the same families of types, belong to the same cycle. If then the habitat of a culture be termed a *province,* let us say that cycles occupy *spheres.* . . .

Our discussion of changes in the distribution of cultures, reflecting the movements of peoples, and of the consequent cultural changes, has thus brought us to relations between spatially distinct cultures, or rather to the specific kind of relation termed *genetic.* Most archaeologists are so far diffusionists as to admit some relation between any two cultures which share even one reasonably improbable type. But that relation need not be genetic.

The first English trader who presented a bottle of gin and a necklace of beads to the chief of a Pacific Island, even though he had no successor, established a relation between the island culture and British civilization that archaeologists could recognize if they could not define precisely. A regular repetition of such trading visits might not only multiply recognizable imports, but also lead to the replacement of stone adzes and shell knives by metal ones with an inevitable reaction on the art of wood carvers and perhaps some modification of native costume. The island culture would thus share several types with British and Australian cultures, but no archaeologist would be tempted to infer the same sort of relation between the former and the latter as subsisted between the last two. The relation would be still patently external.

Japan, Australia and Britain are shown to be related by sharing quite a large number of highly improbable types like railways, textile factories and policemen's uniforms, and nearly all the types or families of types common to Japan and Australia before 1914 could be shown to have originated in and been derived from Britain. The industrialization of Japan and the "westernization" of her police force did involve the temporary settlement there of expert operatives, engineers and instructors. But these temporary immigrants were not colonists, and formed a tiny minority in Japan's population. Though industrialization reacted on dress, architecture and several other facets of Japanese culture, it left its essential fabric intact. The relations of Japanese to Australian and British cultures were still different in kind from those subsisting between the Australian and the British, though all would be attested archaeologically by the same types or by types of the same family. Only Australian-British relations should be described as genetic. And they would be attested by more common types and types different in kind. Japanese culture did not share with Australian those behavior patterns expressed for instance in shower-baths, house-plans, golf-courses and churches that are common to Australia and Britain. It is these that disclose Australian culture as a local variant of British culture, or, if you will, a provincial variant of British civilization.

In comparing simpler societies (which are not likely to include craft groups of full-time specialists), archaeologists may infer genetic relations, despite separation in space, from communities of arbitrary types that are the home-made products of domestic industries or ideological behavior rather than from types that have been imported, produced by specialized crafts or are imposed by their superior efficiency or by environmental circumstances. Imported manufactures or raw materials, as such, are obviously irrelevant. Even among preliterate societies, specialists such as metal workers or tile-makers may leave one community to work for another; inventions that enhance efficiency like the rotary quern or the cut-and-thrust sword can be communicated from one society to another with even less interchange of personnel than textile factories and police helmets; any society that moved into the treeless Orkney islands would have to translate its traditional wooden houses and furniture into stone. So good indicators of genetic connection between two spatially separated cultures should be (1) home-made, (2) peculiar to the cultures to be related, and (3) not environmentally conditioned. But at least two traits thus qualified are requisite for any plausible inference and the inference would remain very provisional unless further common types can be identified.

Hand-made pots seem to conform ideally to the above requirements because they are not suitable for transport for any distance and therefore for trade articles and moreover are believed—on ethnographic analogies—

to be normally made by women who are reputedly more conservative than men. Nevertheless pots, though not themselves likely to be traded, often imitate vessels of more valuable and portable material such as metal. Indeed, in the Early Bronze Age of many parts of Asia and Europe painted and incised decoration went out of fashion in pottery, and vases were given a plain burnished surface as if to mimic metal ware. . . .

The expansion of early Danubian culture . . . led by divergent local developments to the emergence of a cycle of collateral cultures. Direct relation to a single ancestral culture seems the most obvious way of explaining the relations between cultures sharing several families of types of the kind indicative of genetic relations when direct descent of the several types from one another is impossible. Such cycles are common enough, but all too often the common ancestor remains a postulate. In northern Holland, Jutland, Denmark, Central Germany (Saxo-Thuringia), Silesia, Sweden, with the east Baltic coasts and Central Russia we find cultures all characterized by local types of battle-axes of the same family with downward drooping blades associated in each case with four or five types from six equally distinctive families. These cultures are usually grouped together as a single cycle and termed "the battle-axe cultures." Admittedly neither drooping-bladed battle-axes nor any other single type of the remaining five families are exclusively associated with cultures of this cycle, but in no culture outside the battle-axe cycle are types of so many of the six families associated together. The simplest way of accounting for the observed agreements between the six cultures is to regard all as derived by local divergence from a single "Battle-axe culture" spread by the migrations of a single "Battle-axe folk." So far, however, no such ancestral culture has been identified, and, until it be, the "Battle-axe people" remain a highly speculative postulate.

It should indeed be remembered that cultural change may result in convergence as well as divergence and that in historical times the formation of what we may term British or French culture was due not to the differentiation of a local culture out of a wider cultural continuum, but to the assimilation of a series of already differentiated local cultures. Russian archaeologists would explain in some such way the rise of the Andronovo culture in southwestern Siberia and Kazakhastan. Over this vast area uniform assemblages characterized by a very distinctive ceramic style and scarcely less distinctive metal types succeed a multitude of small but easily distinguishable local cultures, while the diagnostic Andronovo types do not seem derivable from any one of the earlier local cultures rather than another nor from any one known culture outside their area. So the observed cultural unification is interpreted by some Russian authors as the reflection of a federation of autonomous local groups, by others as the consequence of the adoption by such groups of stock-breeding, agriculture and metallurgy. Nevertheless cultural assimilation and unification has in historical times been effected by the absorption of one or more cultures by another. Normally some recognizable types of the absorbed cultures survive locally. In that case the process of absorption produces hybrid cultures which are genetically related as colaterals.

We have in fact assumed that the distributional changes in the cultures whose expansion was discussed [above] were taking place in a human and cultural vacuum. That very seldom was true. Usually the expanding or migrating societies in the end came up against other societies with distinct cultures. On reaching the territory occupied by the others the migrants may halt. In this case the distributions of the types distinctive of the two cultures should when mapped, reveal a recognizable frontier between two provinces. . . . Thus, for instance, in southwest Finland the distribution of boat-axes discloses a sharp frontier between the intrusive battle-axe farmers and the older hunter-fishers who made comb-ornamented pottery. Alternatively the immigrants may advance into the other people's territory, into a different cultural province. In this case they may either drive out or exterminate the former occupants and so extinguish the previous culture of the province. Or they may subdue or fuse with the former occupants.

In the first case the archaeological result will be the replacement of the former culture of the province by the intrusive culture—the most drastic form of cultural change that may be observed in a stratified site. In the second the consequence will appear in the formation of a *mixed culture*, characterized by types derived from both components and genetically related to each. In such a hybrid when the intrusive types predominate over those previously characteristic of the province, prehistorians are inclined to speak of dominance or conquest and to assign the composite culture to the cycle to which the predominant types belong. In the reverse, they may use the term absorption.

Estimates of dominance are liable to be highly subjective, its interpretation in "political" terms as conquest is always speculative. When the two cultures are on different technological levels, the more efficient types expressive of such superiority will almost inevitably predominate in the resultant mixed culture. So when barbarians conquer a civilized province, their political and military success may scarcely be registered in the archaeological record. Again in so far as one culture is a good adaptation to an environment, the adaptive types will be taken over and preserved by an intrusive culture that had been adapted to a different environment. In this case too invaders, though most probably also conquerors, are likely to appear to archaeologists to have been absorbed.

Quite often the culture of the invaded region is both technically superior to and better adapted to the environment than that of the invaders. So both factors combine to promote the predominance of the native types. This is what makes it so hard to detect archaeologically the invaders from the temperate forest zone who in the course of history have so often conquered parts of the more civilized Mediterranean world. Hence in Lombardy Lombard culture looks more Roman than Teutonic, even more than Frankish culture in France appears predominantly Gallo-Roman.

· In fact the ultimate and historically most significant consequence of conquest is the formation of a mixed culture, normally richer than either of the components and usually more progressive. If the immediate result be the imposition of an upper class ruling over a subject population, the best hope of recognizing the latter is from their graves; the burial ritual, the weapons and personal ornaments buried with the deceased in some graves may be contrasted not only with those previously current in the province but also with those of other contemporary graves. In the Usatova culture of the Pontic steppe the mass of the types from domestic sites could logically be interpreted as adaptive developments of the Tripolye culture with some borrowings from neighboring "steppe" or battle-axe cultures. The contrast of a few burials under large barrows accompanied by human sacrifices and predominantly "steppe" pottery and weapons with cemeteries of flat graves in which pottery painted in the Tripolye technique predominates, seems to prove that the "steppe" elements in the Usatova culture are really due to a fusion between Tripolye peasants and Steppe pastoralists and that the latter enjoyed social and political preeminence over the cultivators. Again in cemeteries of the Bylany culture of Bohemia the contrast between the majority of rather poorly furnished cremation graves in the established Urnfield tradition and a few burials by inhumation accompanied by wheeled hearses, weapons and rich grave-goods clearly reflects the imposition of a military aristocracy upon an established Urnfield population; indeed by this time in the Iron Age it may be possible to distinguish within the latter "kings" and their "knights."

Such unambiguous cases are very exceptional. Fusion need not necessarily lead to the formation of a society stratified into ruling and subject classes. Even if it does, there remains the horrid possibility that the subjects received no ceremonial burial at all, so that only the aristocracy would be represented in the archaeological record, but could not be recognized as such for lack of contrast with "commoners" or subjects! Archaeologists have been too prone to "explain" cultural change by migrations or conquests and to interpret all relations between cultures as genetic, in the hope it would seem of disguising prehistory in the semblance of nineteenth-century politico-military history. Recent instances cited [above] have already shown that not all relations between cultures are genetic in the foregoing sense and not all typological communities are to be explained in "political" terms.

When two peoples are spatially juxtaposed, when, that is, the archaeological types diagnostic of the two cultures, respectively plotted on a map, exhibit exclusive distributions, archaeologically recognizable relations will almost inevitably be established between them. These may take the form of a mere interchange of products, recognizable by stray types of the one culture on the territory of the other and, at least when associated with types proper to the latter, conventionally interpreted as "trade." Secondly types of one culture may be adopted by its neighbor. In southwest Finland beyond the frontier dividing the boat-axe farmers from the hunter-fishers and on the territory of the latter some boat-axes do occur. These, being made in the materials and by the techniques proper to the hunter-fishers, are easily distinguishable from the farmers' products and identifiable as copies of alien forms. But on a few hunter-fisher encampments, located near the frontier, some pots, decorated with cord-impressions in the style of the farmers, were manufactured as well as the native comb-impressed vessels. Äyräpää has plausibly explained this phenomenon as a result of intermarriage between the two distinct societies. In both cases we have positive instances of *acculturation* without any political fusion or domination—a phenomenon exemplified by British-Japanese relations as quoted [above], and illustrated just as clearly by the contacts between the Greek colonists on the Sicilian coasts and native tribes in the interior and again all along the frontiers of the Roman Empire. When the cultures concerned are relatively poor in distinctive archaeological types, the results of such external contact could easily be mistaken for mixed cultures and as indicative of genetic relations to the component cultures.

In their reaction against an exaggerated appeal to migrationist explanations and their abuse to further the ends of German imperialism, Russian prehistorians for a time tended to deny migrations and conquests altogether and so to rule out genetic relations between prehistoric cultures. This sort of approach in fact obliges the prehistorian to undertake a much profounder study of the cultures concerned than is demanded for facile migrationist interpretations and so leads to a deeper appreciation of neglected aspects of the data. Krichevskiĭ's brilliant essay on the so-called "Nordic cultures" in Central Europe illustrates this point well. The agreements among the several Late Neolithic cultures of the Danubian province both with one another and with those of Northern Europe had traditionally been explained by German prehistorians as resulting from conquests of the löss lands by successive bands of warlike invaders from the North European plain. Krichevskiĭ proposed to account for the general resemblances between the Central and North European cultures by the undoubted fact that in Late Neolithic times there was a general shift in emphasis from tillage to stock-breeding that had actually proved the more productive pursuit under the prevailing environmental and technological conditions; the rest of the observed changes would be more or less ideological reflections of the economic revolution. To document this thesis he was able to show that far more of the types, distinctive of the Late Neolithic cultures, could be reasonably derived from those current in the province, albeit in rather embryonic forms and previously neglected, during the Middle Neolithic stage. This documentation at least represented a substantial contribution to knowledge, even if the author's thesis cannot be accepted in its entirety on factual and methodological grounds.

This contrast between Russian Marrist (not Marxist!) and German imperialist interpretations is after all just a special case of the controversy between evolutionists and diffusionists that has divided ethnographers as well as archaeologists for the last fifty years and that raged with unusual fury in the English-speaking world in the twenties. Extreme adherents of both schools have become sectaries and converted their respective hypotheses into irreconcilable but undemonstrable dogmas. But in so far as evolutionism and diffusionism are heuristic principles, prehistorians should be at the same time both evolutionists and diffusionists.

On the one hand, observed changes in the archaeological record from any one province should be explained as far as possible by reference to the local data. That is, innovations in each period should, wherever possible, be treated as developments of tendencies discoverable in the previous period. So assemblages from the latter should be closely scrutinized with a view to finding therein embryonic precursors of the new types and the intermediate stages in typological series linking these to the old. Gratuitously to invoke migrations or "influences" from outside may be a mere cloak for laziness and has the effect of relegating to the wings all the action of the prehistoric drama.

On the other hand, a single type common to two cultures, however remote, establishes a presumption that some sort of relation subsisted between them and is thus a challenge to prehistorians to demonstrate this relation and clarify its nature. A type is the concrete embodiment of an idea, so the same type at two points in space or in time should document the diffusion of an idea on the useful heuristic hypothesis that each invention has been made but once. Of course no archaeological evidence could rigorously demonstrate the diffusion of an idea. It can prove opportunities for diffusion and it can enhance the probability that diffusion in a specific case has taken place.

Intercourse, carrying with it opportunities for the communication and diffusion of ideas between two provinces and their inhabitants, is irrefutably attested by the transportation of natural substances far from the places where they occur in nature. Documented already in the Upper Paleolithic stage by Mediterranean shells in Central France and the vertebrae of Atlantic fish in caves in the Riviera, such intercourse notoriously became ever more frequent and of wider scope in subsequent archaeological periods. From the Neolithic stage onwards manufactured articles of specialized types afford equally reliable evidence. Opportunities for diffusion and external relations between cultures can thus be rigorously proved, but only under rather exceptional circumstances or within a narrow geographical range.

To enhance the probability of diffusion distributional, quantitative and qualitative criteria may be invoked. The nearer together the find-spots of a single type be, the less likely is it that the type in question was invented or devised independently at each.

(1) When the challenge comes from two remote sites, a first response should be to look for specimens in intermediate regions. In the third millennium B.C. double-spiral headed-pins are found both in Greece and in the Indus valley. The probability that the type was diffused from one region to the other or to both from a third center has been enhanced by the discovery of examples in Turkey, Turkmenia and Persia.

(2) The more types that are common to two sites or cultures, the less likely it is that any or all of them arose independently in each region. Having found one common type or trait we should therefore look for others. By 1300 B.C. chariots on four-spoked wheels were driven by warriors both in China and in Central Europe. When it appeared that in both regions they were drawn by horses, often interred in "royal tombs" and regularly associated with socketed celts of tin-bronze, the inference to direct or indirect connection between these two widely separated cultural provinces became virtually inevitable.

(3) The more improbable a type be, the more improbable is its independent invention two or more times. But probability cannot be determined *a priori* or by inspection. A type that is absolutely rare or that is confined to regions between which relations have been suggested by the previous criteria, may rank as improbable. Greater significance may be attached to double-spiral headed-pins when it is remarked that such pins were not worn in Mesopotamia, Palestine or Syria in the third millennium nor in the Western Mediterranean and Temperate Europe till the second.

Archaeologists can thus go quite a long way towards proving diffusion— but only of concrete types and specific patterns of behavior. The diffusion of wheat-cultivation is in fact proven; for all cultivated wheats are derived from two species of wild grasses with a quite restricted distribution in Southwest Asia; cultivated in Europe or China wheats constitute a case of "the transportation of a natural substance far from the places where it occurs in nature." It would be vain to try and prove "the diffusion of agriculture." "The diffusion of the wheel" might provoke interminable controversies and appeals to contradictory abstract arguments. Substitute for "the wheel," "tripartite disk wheels" or "four-spoked wheels" and the foregoing criteria can be invoked. These terms denote concrete types, definable by ostensive definition and capable of plotting on a map; no figure will adequately represent all the varieties of "the wheel" actually known from the archaeological record.

Indeed a fourth and virtually conclusive criterion is potentially available to establish almost conclusively the diffusion of such concrete types. If only the chronological framework be sufficiently comprehensive and the individual finds fixed in it closely enough, the earliest find-spots should be arranged along consecutive *isochrons* round the focus where the type originated. (An isochron, like an isobar or an isohyet, is just a line joining up find-spots on the map to which the same date relative or absolute is assigned.) In other words, the farther a region be from the center where the type was invented, the later should be its first appearance (naturally the distance must not be measured in abstract units, but by reference to the effective communications established). Such distribution maps would not only provide the most conclusive evidence for diffusion imaginable, but would also define in what culture, i.e., among which people, the diffused idea originated. Yet it must always be remembered that the distributional pattern disclosed on such maps is liable to distortion by the differential capacities of local cultures to accept and incorporate what diffusion offers.

A culture-trait cannot be diffused to another culture unless it harmonizes with the latter's pattern. A culture is not like a formless pin-cushion into which a new invention, a novel rite or a fresh fashion can just be stuck. They just will not stay in place unless they fit organically into the highly complex but always flexible structure of the recipient. Double-spiral headed-pins will not be worn by people whose traditional costume or coiffure does not require any pins at all! So they were in fact not adopted in Crete or Egypt. Wheeled carts were not needed in the narrow valley of the Nile where the river, never far away, offered far more economical means of transport for heavy goods; in fact wheeled vehicles were not adopted in Egypt till more than a thousand years after their first use in Mesopotamia, and then as war-engines rather than transport devices. There is no use turning out *en masse* cheap pots on the wheel until population be dense enough to provide a local market to consume such fragile articles!

So the degree of proneness to adopt foreign ideas when exposed thereto by diffusion must itself rank as a significant item in a culture's description, just as the results will enrich the inventory of culture-contents. At the same time diffusion establishes a relation between cultures. But the precise nature of this relation, that is, the mechanism of diffusion, has to be inferred from the archaeological data in each concrete case; traders, raiders, missionaries, conquerors, wives, colonists, imported slaves, returned mercenaries and many others may have been the agents.

PEOPLE IN PREHISTORY

IRVING ROUSE's paper is based on the assumption that the study of "people" is basic to prehistory. He asks four questions about such people, and attempts to show how they can be answered. To some degree this paper is a critique of V. Gordon Childe's approach to prehistory, and the reader is advised to study this paper in conjunction with the preceding one.

🀒 Prehistorians are regional specialists. Our discipline is so broad that none of us can, in his own research, encompass the whole field. The specialists in each region have tended to develop somewhat different aims, for their data lead them in different directions. Specialists in Polynesia, for example, are preoccupied with problems of migration, since the people of that area were great canoeists and moved from island to island. By contrast, specialists in the prehistory of the Near East have devoted little attention to migrations. Their main concern is with the rise of civilization, since this was the most important event in their region.

Each group of regional specialists has worked out its own methods of achieving its aims. Many have developed their own peculiar terminologies, examples of which will be given below. These regional differences are intensified by the tendency of paleolithic and protohistoric specialists to work in relative isolation.

The differences are as true of the New World as of the Old. For example, Willey & Phillips's . . . book on *Method and Theory in American*

"The Place of 'Peoples' in Prehistoric Research" by Irving Rouse, *Journal of the Royal Anthropological Institute* 95, Part 1 (1965) 1–15. Reprinted by permission of the author and the Royal Anthropological Institute of Great Britain and Ireland.

Archaeology (1958) reflects the procedure and terminology which its authors use in their own specialities, the protohistory of Nuclear America and of the southeastern United States. Different terms and different methods are used by the specialists in Paleo-Indian archaeology and in the protohistory of other parts of the New World, such as the midwestern United States on the one hand, and California on the other (Heizer 1959).

Nevertheless, if one surveys the entire range of methods in the New World and compares it with the range of methods in the Old World, as my visit to England is giving me the opportunity to do, one finds that they are alike. This has surprised me. Before coming here, I had assumed that there were significant differences between the methodology of the two hemispheres, but I have encountered British counterparts for almost all we do in America and vice versa.

Personally, I find this most encouraging. Not only does it indicate that we should eventually be able to develop a single, unified discipline of prehistory, covering the whole world, but also it is a sign that prehistorians in both hemispheres are on the right track; if we were not, we could hardly have developed similar methods while working in relative isolation.

We cannot, however, hope to become a unified discipline until we have achieved a greater measure of agreement about our concepts and about the terms we use for them. The current variety of terms has been particularly troublesome to me because I am working on a synthesis of world prehistory. It has been necessary for me to devise a special terminology for this purpose, encompassing in so far as possible all the regional variations. I present this terminology here, and shall attempt to show how it fits into the trends of prehistoric research in both Old and New Worlds, in the hope of pointing the way towards greater uniformity within our discipline.

My terminology is based upon an assumption that the study of people is basic to prehistory, as it is to all other branches of anthropology. The first prehistorians, to be sure, were simply collectors of artifacts, but we have long since passed beyond this stage. We now dig sites not only to obtain artifacts but to learn all we can about the peoples who lived in the sites. Following Childe (1956), I would suggest that we ask four main questions about each people: (1) who were they, (2) when did they live, (3) what culture did they have, and (4) how did that culture change? I shall discuss these four questions in turn.

1. WHO WERE THE PEOPLE?

According to Childe (1956: 28), interest in the question "who?" first arose on the continent of Europe towards the close of the last century. Childe attributed its development to the rise of nationalism, and certainly this was true in Germany where Kossina (1920), for example, attempted to identify the prehistoric ancestors of the German people. Comparing the collections from different sites, he found that many of them were characterized by similar traits, which he took to be evidence of habitation by Germans.

The interest in peoples assumed a somewhat different form as it spread from Germany to Great Britain. It had been easy enough for the Germans to trace themselves back into the past, because their country has a relatively homogeneous population. But it would not have been possible for the British prehistorians to do the same thing because their origin is too diverse. Too many different prehistoric peoples have fused to produce the historic British people. Moreover, British prehistorians have always been as interested in paleolithic as in later time, and it would obviously have been impossible to trace any historic people as far back as the paleolithic. Hence, the British focused their attention not upon the historic peoples and their antecedents but upon the recurrent traits by means of which the Germans had traced themselves back into prehistory. The British used these traits to distinguish entirely new groupings of people, which were peculiar to prehistory.

Childe's *The Danube in Prehistory* (1929) provides a good example of this. Childe was able to treat some of his sites as single units but had to break others down into several components, each characterized by a different assemblage of artifacts. At the site of Vinča near Belgrade, for example, he marked off the bottom metre of the deposit as a single component, which he called Vinča I (Childe 1929, Figs. 9–12). This component was characterized by jars with anthropomorphic lids, curvilinear incised designs, female clay figurines, etc. Childe found that these same traits occurred in components of other sites, grouped all such components with Vinča I, and named the group Vinča I after the type component. He then proceeded to discuss the culture of the group, which he likewise called Vinča I (Childe 1929: 26–27).

In effect, Childe started out to answer my first question "who?" but did not work all the way through to the answer. After having classified the components, he assumed the answer to the first question and shifted to the third, "what culture did the people have?" In order properly to answer the first question, he would have had to apply the name "Vinča I" to the people of the components as well as to their culture, and would have had to specify which traits are diagnostic of the Vinča I people. The diagnostic traits would have comprised a complex considerably smaller in scope than the Vinča I culture.

Childe (1956: 15, 173) termed his procedure "chorological classification." He adopted the word "chorology" from Menghin (1931: 7), though he deplored its ugliness. It is not very appropriate either. Chorology means the study of geographical distributions and Menghin used it because he and Kossina had relied upon the geographical distribution of traits in defining their peoples. But this was not true of Childe. If he had carried through to definition of the Vinča I people, for example, he would have based that definition on the recurrence of diagnostic cultural traits in a number of components. In effect, he would have defined the people in terms of these traits. It is appropriate, therefore, to call his procedure "ethnic classification."

We have seen that ethnic classification began in Europe around the turn of the century. American prehistorians did not become interested in it until the 1930s. Then, it developed in two forms, one in the southwestern United States (e.g., the Gladwins 1934) and the other in the midwestern part of the country (e.g., McKern 1939). The southwestern approach resembled the original German development, in that it aimed to trace the historic Amerindian peoples back into the past. Hence, it has limited applicability, as in the case of Germany. It can only be applied to late protohistoric peoples and under exceptionally favorable circumstances, which happen to exist in the southwest. The midwestern approach, on the other hand, resembles that which developed in Britain. Like Childe, the midwesterners set out to define purely prehistoric units. As a result, their approach has more general applicability and is worth considering in more detail.

Midwestern prehistorians became interested in peoples because of the presence in their area of large mounds and the prevalence of a belief that these mounds had been built by a different and more advanced people than the American Indians, who were popularly called "the Mound Builders." Many early writers, including a former president of my university (Stiles 1933: 101), believed that the Mound Builders were descended from the Phoenicians, the Israelites, or some other people of antiquity. Midwestern prehistorians had to spend much time in refuting this belief, which they did by excavating mounds and showing that they contain artifacts comparable to those of the modern American Indians.

Eventually it became apparent that several groups of American Indians were involved in the construction of the mounds. The mounds are so variable in structure and content that they cannot all have been produced by the same people. So the problem arose of distinguishing various groups of mound-building Indians.

Midwestern prehistorians first attempted to solve this problem by the use of chorological classification, in the Kossina-Menghin sense of the term. They studied the distribution of traits from mound to mound, in the hope of being able to distinguish geographical groupings of people. This study, however, failed to reveal any consistent patterning of traits. The reason was soon recognized: the peoples who produced the mounds had lived at different times and had overlapped in geographical distribution. The overlaps were obscuring the boundaries between the peoples.

One way out of this difficulty would have been to set up periods and to study the geographical distribution of the peoples period by period. However, the midwesterners had spent so much time on the problem of defining the peoples, i.e., in answering the first question I have posed, that they had not yet been able to do anything with the second question, "when did the people live?" Therefore, they decided to disregard both temporal and spatial distributions and to define their peoples purely in terms of cultural traits, i.e., by means of ethnic classification.

The method they developed has become known as the midwestern taxonomic system (McKern 1939). It was in two parts, only the first of which is comparable to the British approach. In this first part, the midwesterners isolated components and classified them in terms of traits. Like Childe, they did not distinguish, as I am doing, between a people and its culture. They simply applied the name of a type site to the culture of each group of components, and called this culture a "focus." But they did recognize that they had not based their definition of a focus on all of its traits; they referred to the traits diagnostic of each focus as its "determinants."

With the components and foci as a base, the midwesterners went on to erect a superstructure consisting of aspects, phases, and patterns (e.g., Wilford 1941, Table 1). These were hierarchic units and, like the foci, were based solely upon similarities and differences between the foci, not upon geographical or chronological distinctions. Foci which shared most of their determinants were grouped into a single aspect; aspects which shared most of their diagnostic traits were grouped into the same phase; and phases which shared most of their diagnostics were placed in the same patterns.

This superstructure of aspects, phases, and patterns was considered a temporary expedient. It was designed to serve as a sort of filing system within which to organize the various foci until such time as it should become possible to arrange them in chronological order. After the Second World War, a chronology was set up, the superstructure was then abandoned, and the foci were arranged in their proper chronological and geographical order (e.g., Griffin 1952, Fig. 205). The only traces of the taxonomic superstructure which survive are the names of the three patterns, Archaic, Woodland, and Mississippi, which now serve to designate periods.

The basic part of the midwestern system has spread westward to the prehistorians specializing in the plains of the west-central United States, eastward as far as New England, and southward to the Caribbean region, in which I specialize. In my own New England research, I have retained the midwestern terminology, in accordance with local practice, but have modified it in the Caribbean region. There, Cruxent and I have substituted the terms "complex" and "style" for "focus," since our data are not sufficient to reveal the total culture of the components. We have set up chronologies of complexes and styles, which are equivalent both to the midwestern sequences of foci and to the chronology of cultures established by Childe for the Danubian region (cf. Rouse and Cruxent 1963, Fig. 3; Griffin 1952; and Childe 1929, Table opp. p. 418).

But I am getting ahead of the argument. We are concerned at this point not with the question of when each people lived but with the question of who they were. Our problem is how to define peoples. We have seen that most British prehistorians do so by setting up "cultures" and most Americans, by working out "foci" (alternatively called "phases" or "facies"; Heizer 1959). Cruxent and I substituted the terms "complex" and "style" for "focus" because we wished to make it clear that we have been unable, for lack of evidence, to define our peoples in terms of their total cultures and have had to work instead with complexes of stone, bone, and shell artifacts, in the case of non-ceramic peoples, and with pottery styles, in the case of ceramic peoples. In this, we have followed the lead of the Paleo-Indian and Peruvian specialists respectively (Rouse and Cruxent 1963: 16). Alternatively, we might have used the terms "industry" and "assemblage," which are preferred by the Old World prehistorians who lack sufficient evidence to work with full configurations of culture (Piggott 1959: 87).

Reviewing the terminology of Cruxent and myself since arriving in Britain, I have come to believe that we were wrong in assuming that any prehistorian uses total cultural configurations to define peoples. For one thing, it is not possible to know the total culture of any prehistoric people; one can only expect to obtain more or less information about those aspects of each culture which have been preserved in the form of remains or which can be inferred from the remains (e.g., Childe 1956: 118–128). For another thing, I doubt whether, when one classifies sites in order to distinguish peoples, one ever uses all the available cultural information. The midwestern taxonomists recognized this when they distinguished between a focus and its determinants. Kluckhohn (1962: 75–76) has independently expressed the same point as follows: "Observation of the actual operation of archaeologists suggests that in many cases the classification of sites is actually made on the basis of pottery complex or architectural style (including masonry type). If this fact is explicitly stated, the procedure may well be the most convenient and quite unobjectionable. If, however, there is assertion or implication that the classification has been made on the basis of the total cultural complex, this is misleading, for what occurs is that other cultural elements found associated with the critical pottery complex or architectural style are simply dragged in after the crucial step has been taken. If we are really operating with pottery or masonry-architectural complexes (or a combination of these two) only, it would be in the interests of clear thinking to bring this circumstance into the open, either through terminology or explicit statement. It seems possible that classificatory operations based solely upon these apparently somewhat more sensitive and more consistent criteria would be the most useful. The associated culture elements (not used in cultural classification) could then be studied apart from the prejudice of a question-begging nomenclature, and, after the trends toward uniformity had been unequivocally ascertained, the operations for definitions in terms of total culture . . . could be rigorously set up." Kluckhohn was referring in this passage to the protohistory of the southwestern United States, but his words would apply equally well to the protohistory of other areas, such as the Near East (e.g., Braidwood 1952, Figs. 26–27).

In the passage quoted, Kluckhohn has, in effect, recognized the need to distinguish between my questions "who?" and "what?" but has not expressed this need in terms of the concept of "peoples." Reformulating his statement in these terms, I would say we ought to recognize that we are primarily concerned with peoples, that we define each people by establishing a "complex" of its traits, and that each complex comprises only a small part of the people's "culture." In some cases, we are able to learn little more about a people's culture than its complex; in others, we recover information about many additional aspects of the culture; but in no case are we able to reconstruct the entire culture of a prehistoric people.

In summary, I would suggest that the procedure of distinguishing peoples be termed "ethnic classification." The traits diagnostic of each people may similarly be called an "ethnic complex" in order to avoid confusion with burial or religious complexes, for example. The procedure of ethnic classification is as follows:

First, each site must be broken down into components, as is currently the practice in both Europe and America. If the site has yielded a homogeneous assemblage of artifacts, it should be treated as a single component, but if not, it will have to be divided into several different components, each with its own homogeneous assemblage. All components that have yielded similar assemblages are grouped together. Each group is defined by listing its distinctive traits and is given the name of a typical site. The name applies not only to the group of components but also to the traits which characterize it and to the people who lived in the components. The traits constitute a complex which is indicative of the people. Whenever one discovers a new site, one can identify the people who lived there simply by determining which complex it contains.

The crucial part of this procedure is the selection of the traits to be used in setting up complexes. In actual practice, as I have observed it, each investigator selects the traits which best enable him to classify his components and thereby to distinguish peoples. He must choose traits which occur in all the components, or else he will not be able to include all components within the classification; traits which are relatively frequent, or else the classification will not be reliable; and traits which were significant to the people, or else he will be unable adequately to distinguish peoples. Chipped stone artifacts best meet these requirements in the case of paleolithic and Paleo-Indian remains, and pottery in the case of neolithic and Neo-Indian remains, but there are exceptions. Specialists in Eskimo prehistory have come to rely primarily upon harpoon heads, and Polynesian specialists, upon fish hooks or adzes. In some areas, the traits are obtained from refuse deposits and in others, from graves. In my opinion, it does not matter what sort of traits or what kinds of materials one uses to classify one's components, providing that these traits and materials do the job they are supposed to do: permit one to distinguish peoples and to identify additional settlements (components) of each people as they are found.

In my country, prehistorians are criticized, even by some colleagues (e.g., Taylor 1948), because we devote so much effort to chipped stonework and potsherds. I do not believe it is sufficiently realized that these bits of artifacts do not interest us for their own sake but because they provide us with a means of identifying peoples. We have not made it clear that we must study the stones and potsherds in order to define ethnic groups.

2. When Did Each People Live?

Interest in the question "when?" arose long before anyone had become concerned about the first question "who?" Not only classical Greek and Roman writers but also a contemporary Chinese scholar speculated that there had been a sequence of stone, bronze, and iron ages (Chang 1963: 2). This theory was revived during the Renaissance and was documented archaeologically by the Danes Thomsen and Worsaae in the first half of the nineteenth century (Daniel 1943).

When the three-age system, as the stone–bronze–iron sequence is called, was first established, it was assumed to be worldwide. Subsequent research has shown that it is applicable only to certain regions, such as Scandinavia. Prehistorians in other parts of the world have had to construct their own regional chronologies. Both in the Old and New Worlds, this process began immediately after the First World War. Childe's Danubian chronology, already mentioned, was one of the first in the Eastern Hemisphere. The first in the Western Hemisphere was the so-called Pecos classification, set up in the southwestern United States in 1927 (e.g., Rouse 1962: 36).

The original three-age system had a second feature which I find objectionable. It is defined in terms of individual artifact types and not of cultures or peoples. As the system subsequently gave way to a series of regional chronologies, there was a tendency to shift from artifacts to cultures. I have already illustrated this trend in my discussion of Childe's chronology and of the one set up by the midwestern taxonomists; it is also true of current usages of the Pecos classification in the southwest. But the trend has not been universal. In England, for example, Hawkes (1959, Fig. 2) has subdivided the Iron Age by studying the distribution of individual types of artifacts, rather than cultures. Specialists in the prehistory of the southeastern United States use a similar approach and object to the practice of midwesterners and southwesterners in basing their chronologies upon foci, i.e., upon cultures.

The research of James A. Ford (1962), a leading southeastern prehistorian, will serve to illustrate this point. Ford works solely with types of pottery. He divides his region of study into local areas and collects potsherds from the surfaces of as many sites as possible in each area. He seriates the collections from each area in terms of their pottery types, thus producing a number of local sequences, each of which he proceeds to divide into units he calls "periods" (e.g., Ford and Willey 1949, Fig. 4). Then he synchronizes the "periods" of each local area in order to form a regional chronology.

In the terminology I am using here, each of Ford's local "periods" corresponds to a culture, but not to the culture of a single people. Instead, it refers to the culture of a single area and period. Ford's approach does not allow for the possibility that two peoples may have lived side by side in the same area and period, or that a people may have lived in more than one area or period (Rouse 1955, Fig. 2). Hence, I do not believe that his approach can give an accurate picture of prehistory.

Indeed, I would suggest that the approach to chronology in terms of individual types of artifacts is an anachronism—a survival of the time when prehistorians were simply collectors of artifacts. If it is true, as I stated at the beginning, that we have moved on from the study of artifacts *per se* to focus upon the people who made the artifacts, we ought to base our chronologies upon peoples and not upon artifacts. In my opinion, Childe, his European colleagues, the midwestern taxonomists, and the specialists in southwestern prehistory, all took a step in the right direction when they based their regional chronologies upon cultures rather than upon artifacts. But I would go one step further and substitute peoples for cultures. It seems to me logical to date the peoples before working out their cultures. In fact, I do not believe that one can properly reconstruct a people's culture until one has determined when and where the people lived, for one will not be able to understand the culture until one has acquired some knowledge of its physical and cultural environment. I doubt that a historian would discuss a people's culture without first informing himself about the period in which the people lived. Why should a prehistorian do so?

The proposed shift in the construction of chronologies from cultures to people is largely a matter of terminology. It requires one to work in terms of complexes rather than cultures, but most of us already do this. The procedure is as follows. First, one delimits the region and time to be studied (Rouse 1957, Fig. 1). Next, one divides the region into areas. One arranges the complexes of each area, and hence its peoples, in chronological order by use of the standard techniques such as stratigraphy, seriation, and radiocarbon dating, thereby producing local sequences of peoples. One determines which peoples in each sequence were contemporaneous by a study of trade sherds and other evidences of relative age. Then, one enters the sequences in a chronological chart, one to a column, placing all the contemporaneous peoples on the same level within their respective columns. One divides the chart into periods by drawing horizontal lines between the levels, i.e., between each group of contemporaneous peoples. Comparing the peoples' complexes within each period, one will find that they share a number of traits, which may be regarded as time-markers for the period. When new peoples are discovered, they can be dated simply by determining which time-markers are present in their complexes.

3. What Culture Did the People Have?

It did not take the early prehistorians long to develop an interest in the life of prehistoric time. When, for example, Lord Avebury wrote his pioneer synthesis of prehistory in 1865, he included three chapters on "Modern Savages" in order, as he put it, to "throw light on the ancient remains found in Europe, and on the condition of the early races which inhabited our continent" (Avebury 1900: 408). Subsequently, Sollas (1911) juxtaposed chapters on Eoliths and Tasmanians, Middle Paleolithic and Australian aborigines, Aurignacian and Bushman, and Magdalenian and Eskimos, thus using the cultures of modern peoples to illustrate life during various periods in the three-age system.

As the three-age system gave way to regional chronologies, it became necessary for British prehistorians to use other frames of reference in reconstructing the lives of prehistoric peoples. Some began to study the culture of each region during a particular period of time, but this has not proved to be very satisfactory, because there is too much variation in culture from one part of a region to another (Jope 1963). Others have analyzed the development of different aspects of culture from one period to another (e.g., Clark 1940, 1952). This is a fruitful approach, but has the disadvantage that it fails to reveal the interrelationships between various aspects of culture within single societies. Probably for this reason, the current trend is to study individual societies, i.e., "cultures" (Childe 1951: 30–53; Piggott 1959: 80–100). In the terminology of the present paper, this means (1) defining a people in terms of its diagnostic traits of material culture, (2) dating the people's remains, and (3) reconstructing as much as possible of the rest of the people's culture. It is this third step in the procedure—answering my question "what?"—that concerns us here.

In answering the question "what?" British prehistorians no longer rely, as Lord Avebury and Sollas did, upon vague general analogies to modern primitive peoples. Instead, they focus on the remains of a particular prehistoric people ("culture") and draw inferences from those remains, with the help of specific analogies to European folk customs and to the cultures of comparable people living in other parts of the world (Clark 1951). Documentary evidence and place-names have also been used to interpret the remains of the latest protohistoric peoples (Wainwright 1962).

Interest in the reconstruction of culture arose in the United States about the same time as in Britain, but in a very different manner. There was no need for Americanists to draw general analogies to modern primitive peoples, as Lord Avebury and Sollas were doing. Many American Indian tribes still retained their aboriginal cultures, and it was only necessary to project these cultures into the past by identifying sites occupied by the ancestors of the modern Indians. In this way, American prehistorians were able to produce a number of "prehistoric ethnologies," as they were sometimes called (e.g., Smith 1910).

Recently, there has been a tendency to substitute the term "anthropology" for "ethnology" in this connection. The reason, I suspect, is that American prehistorians have always maintained a closer professional association with cultural, linguistic, and physical anthropologists than is the case in Britain. We have come to feel we must justify this association by reconstructing the entire anthropology of our sites—their cultures, physical traits, and languages—instead of limiting ourselves to the relatively few traits utilized in ethnic classification and in the construction of chronologies (Taylor 1948; Binford 1962).

Until the 1930s, it was the practice to reconstruct the cultures—and, where possible, the races and languages—of individual sites. With the establishment of the midwestern taxonomic system and other methods of ethnic classification, Americanists began to reconstruct the cultures of peoples ("foci") rather than sites. This was a great improvement, since it meant that each reconstruction no longer had to be based upon the evidence from only a single site. One could dig a number of sites belonging to the same people, put the evidence from all of them together, and be reasonably sure that, in so doing, one was dealing with the same culture.

The digging of additional sites offered four advantages: (1) It enabled one to obtain rare artifacts which had not turned up in the original excavation. (2) It provided the opportunity to search for conditions under which perishable objects have been preserved. (3) It also became possible to utilize alternative techniques of excavation. In digging to define a people or to construct a chronology, for example, one normally employs stratigraphic techniques. Subsequently, it may be necessary to move to other sites in order to apply different techniques which better reveal structures and burials. (4) New sites may also provide evidence about activities not carried on at the site originally excavated. In regions where the original excavations were in burial mounds, for example, it has been necessary to move on to dwelling sites, and vice versa.

Up to this point, I have been discussing simple peoples, who were relatively self-contained. The digging of additional sites has proved to be even more necessary in the case of complex societies, comprising several peoples who lived side by side in a dependent relationship (Mayer-Oakes 1963). The specialists in classic Maya civilization, for example, concentrated upon ceremonial centers during the time when they were primarily concerned with the question "when?" After turning to "what?" they began to realize that the Maya actually consisted of two ethnic groups, the civilized people who lived in the ceremonial centers and the peasants of the forests, who lacked monumental architecture, writing, astronomy, sculpture, and the other attributes of Maya civilization. They have had to supplement their research in the centers with excavation of the forest sites, in an effort to work out the peasant as well as the civilized culture (Willey 1956: 107–114).

To sum up, British and American prehistorians originally approached the problem of reconstructing culture in very different ways. The British drew vague, general analogies, whereas Americans were able to project the cultures of historic Indian peoples back to individual prehistoric sites. From these separate beginnings, both the British and the Americans seem to be trending in the same direction, towards reconstruction of the cultures of specific groups of people, distinguished by means of ethnic classification. The procedure may be summarized as follows:

The aim is to reconstruct all aspects of a people's culture, material, social, and mental. As I have already indicated, a fuller picture of the material culture, beyond the people's diagnostic complex, may be obtained by digging widely in search of rare types of artifacts, especially in sites where perishable materials have been preserved (e.g., Clark 1939: 50–85). Social culture may be reconstructed by investigating the loci in which a people carried on each of its activities, e.g., eating, sleeping, the manufacture of artifacts, and burial. Examination of the artifacts and other debris of each locus will reveal much about the activities that took place there. Study of the relationships among the loci, which may be called the "settlement pattern," provides information concerning the people's ecology and social structure (Sears 1961). Something can be learned about the people's mental culture by studying its art; design motifs, for example, provide clues as to deities (e.g., Ucko 1962).

These procedures require two kinds of reasoning: inference from the remains and the drawing of analogies to present-day conditions (Thompson 1956). In reasoning by analogy, one must resist the temptation to go farther than the available evidence permits, but one may go quite far, especially in the study of economic life, by the use of direct historic analogy, in which one projects a particular people's culture back into its own prehistoric sites (Tax *et al.* 1953: 250–254). One has to be more cautious in reasoning by analogy from one people to another (Ascher 1961).

To a lesser extent, it is also possible to reconstruct a people's racial, political, and linguistic affiliations. Races can be inferred from the skeletal material found in the sites (e.g., Neumann 1952), and political or linguistic groupings can be projected back from historic time (e.g., Caldwell 1958: 4).

The success of one's reconstruction will depend to a considerable extent upon how well one has defined the people and thereby delimited the culture to be reconstructed. It is essential to begin a tightly defined, local group of people, having so restricted a distribution in time and space as to eliminate the possibility of temporal and spatial variations. Only in this way can one be reasonably sure of dealing only with communities which had the same culture and the same tribal and linguistic affiliations. If, on the contrary, one defines a people broadly and loosely, one is liable to produce a grouping which is ethnically, politically, and linguistically so variable that one's reconstruction will be quite meaningless (e.g., Fairbanks 1952: 294–298).

4. How Did the Culture Change?

Though prehistorians can and do study changes in race and language as well as in culture, I shall here limit myself to culture. Piggott (1960) has pointed out that the remains of material culture provide our best evidence of change. The most reliable results may be expected from the study of ethnic complexes, since these consist by definition of the most common and the most reliable traits available for study. Hence, I shall divide the following discussion into two parts, dealing respectively with (1) changes in ethnic complexes and (2) changes in the other aspects of culture associated with each complex, i.e., in the rest of a people's culture.

(1) If the procedures outlined in the previous sections of this paper have been followed, each complex will be relatively uniform. Our problem, therefore, is not to study variations within complexes but to examine the changes that took place as one complex gave rise to another.

Comparing one complex with another, one will find both similarities and differences. The similarities are indicative of continuities between the complexes and the differences are an expression of change from complex to complex. Let us consider the continuities before examining the changes.

It is not uncommon in both Old and New Worlds to refer to the continuities between complexes as "traditions." For example, paleolithic specialists apply the phrase "Mousterian of Acheulean tradition" to one of the Mousterian "industries" in order to indicate that it was marked by a survival of the Acheulian-type hand-axe, which the "typical Mousterian" did not have (e.g., Bordes 1956: 5). Caldwell (1958: 3–4) has similarly distinguished a series of "regional traditions" in the eastern United States.

Europeans think of traditions in terms of any continuity between complexes ("industries") but Americans tend to restrict the term to continuities between the complexes of single areas, as in the example given. This area restriction is most marked in the Peruvian field, where it is now customary to distinguish between "tradition" and "horizon," the former referring to the continuities of traits from one period to another within an area, and the latter to the continuities from one area to another within a period (Willey and Phillips 1958: 29–40).

Working in Venezuela, Cruxent and I have combined the concepts of tradition and horizon in the European manner (Rouse and Cruxent 1963: 23–26). We started by defining peoples and working out their chronology, as already explained. Then we compared the peoples' complexes and found that we were able to arrange them in lines of development, which we called "series." Each series shows a marked continuity of culture, like the traditions and horizons of Peruvian prehistory, but none is limited to a single area or period, as in Peru (Rouse and Cruxent 1963, e.g., Fig. 28). Segments of certain series do constitute traditions or horizons in the Peruvianist sense, but the entire series do not. Assuming that the same situation exists in Peru, I would suggest that the Peruvianists have given us a somewhat distorted picture of the cultural continuities in that region by distinguishing between the concepts of tradition and horizon.

The procedure that Cruxent and I used was to compare the Venezuelan complexes in terms of their distributions within our chronological charts. Wherever we found a strong continuity of traits between two adjacent complexes, whether in the dimension of time or space, we concluded that the two belonged to the same series. Wherever we encountered a marked discontinuity, we assumed that the series had come to an end. We named each series by adding the suffix "-oid" to the name of a typical complex. For example, one series is called "Saladoid" after its earliest known complex ("style"), which is Saladero.

Having established series in this fashion, we proceeded to study the changes that had taken place from one complex to another within each series. We noted the principal changes and attempted to determine their causes: were they due to internal development (invention) or to acculturation under the influence of another people (diffusion)? We also attempted to show the extent to which each foreign trait had been modified to conform to the preexisting native traits. We were prevented by paucity of data from carrying this approach very far except in the case of the Saladoid series, where we were able to produce a rather detailed picture of the changes in ceramic traits from one complex to another (Rouse and Cruxent 1963: 116–125).

It is, of course, not necessary to use series as the frame of reference in studying changes from complex to complex, as Cruxent and I did, but I believe it is more consistent with the nature of culture to do so. Culture is traditional and tends to resist change. If, therefore, one concentrates upon the changes from one complex to another without also studying instances of lack of change, one will acquire an incomplete picture of what has happened. For example, Childe's preoccupation with the spread of traits of Mediterranean civilization to the barbarians of central and northern Europe led him to overlook the purely local developments among the barbarians, until he finally became aware of the continuities in barbarian complexes that had survived in the face of Mediterranean influences (Childe 1958: 74).

(2) Turning now from changes in complexes to changes in the rest of the culture, we come to the subject which is customarily called "cultural evolution." British prehistorians have long been active in this field (e.g., Childe 1950) but Americans have tended to shy away from it. Indeed, there was an implicit taboo against the subject in the United States during the period between the two World Wars. This, I believe was due to a misunderstanding on our part about the nature of evolution. It was generally supposed at the time to have followed the same course throughout the world—to have been an absolute process that had affected all mankind in the same way, though to a differing extent in different parts of the world. We in America believed strongly in the relativity of culture and therefore could not accept this absolute theory of evolution. We knew, for example, that American Indian civilization had developed differently than European civilization, and we suspected that our own American civilization was likewise trending in a somewhat different

direction. But instead of creating a new theory of evolution to account for the differences, we turned our backs on the subject and concluded that there has been no such thing as cultural evolution.

With the revival of American interest in cultural evolution after the Second World War, Willey and Phillips (1958: 61–78) set up a system of stages to express the development of the Amerindian civilizations. This system has the great merit of demonstrating that cultural evolution has proceeded rather differently in the New World than in the Old, but it has been criticized for failing to take into account differences in evolution in various parts of the New World. Willey and Phillips (1958, Fig. 2) had assumed that the cultures of the peripheral parts of the New World were simply stagnant versions of the earliest cultures in the centers of civilizations, but this is not true. Instead, the peripheral cultures have developed in different directions than the central cultures.

To correct the error, several authors (e.g., Braidwood 1960, Fig. 1) have suggested setting up a separate system of stages for each region. Other writers (e.g., Hester 1962, Fig. 3) have thought it better to set up a different system for each kind of environment in the New World. I think myself that we would do better to create a separate system of stages for each series of peoples (Rouse 1964). Systems of stages like this have already been set up in the southwestern United States, one for the Anasazi series of peoples, a second for the Hohokam peoples, and a third for the Mogollon peoples; and they provide a good picture of the evolution of culture in that region (e.g., the Gladwins 1934, final chart; Rouse 1962, Fig. 2).

The southwestern approach may be termed "ethnic," since it is based upon peoples. Some may find it too specific, but it seems to me the only way to avoid ethnocentrism and to look at cultural change from a relative point of view. It is also more compatible than the general approach with the regional orientation of modern prehistory. It enables one to study cultural evolution in terms of the special conditions within each region, as well as those within each group of people, and thus to take into consideration all the factors which have affected cultural development.

CONCLUSIONS

This paper has been based upon an assumption that people are the proper subject of prehistoric research. I have suggested that we need to answer four main questions about them: who were they, when did they live, what cultures did they have, and how did the cultures change?

The question "who?" may be answered by means of ethnic classification, i.e., by grouping together sites or components of sites which have yielded similar assemblages of artifacts. The inhabitants of the components grouped together in this fashion may be termed a "people" and may be defined by setting up a complex of diagnostic traits.

The answer to the question "when?" is obtained by construction of a regional chronology. The complexes of each local area, and through them, its peoples, are arranged in chronological order. The resultant sequences are synchronized in the form of a chronological chart, and this chart is divided into periods. The periods are defined by distinguishing "time-markers," i.e., a number of traits which occur in all of a period's complexes and which therefore can be used to date its peoples.

Part of the answer to the question "what?" is supplied by the complexes. It is necessary to reconstruct the rest of each people's culture from its complex, much as a paleontologist reconstructs the fleshy part of an extinct animal from its skeleton. This is done by inference from the remains and by the use of anthropological analogies. In some cases, it is also possible to project an historic people's culture, race, and language back to its prehistoric ancestors.

For the answer to the question "how?" one should study the continuities and changes in (1) the complexes and (2) the rest of peoples' cultures. I have cited the research of Cruxent and myself in Venezuela to show that the complexes may be arranged in series, based upon their continuities, and that the changes may then be studied from complex to complex within each series. I have further suggested that the best way to examine changes in the rest of cultures, beyond the complexes, is to set up stages of development within each series.

The four questions I have discussed are not the only ones that can be asked about prehistoric remains. For example, one may want to define religious instead of ethnic complexes, to map the geographic distribution of traits or complexes period by period, or to study changes in settlement patterns rather than in ethnic complexes. I would contend, though, that the four questions are basic to prehistoric research and that all other questions follow logically from them.

References

Ascher, Robert
    1961 "Analogy in Archaeological Interpretation." *Southwestern Journal of Anthropology* 17: 317–325.
Avebury, Lord
    1900 *Prehistoric Times, as Illustrated by Ancient Remains and the Manners and Customs of Modern Savages.* London, 6th ed.
Binford, Lewis R.
    "Archaeology as Anthropology." *American Antiquity,* 28: 217–225.

Bordes, F.
1956 "Some Observations on the Pleistocene Succession in the Somme Valley." *Proceedings of the Prehistoric Society*, n.s., 22: 1–5.

Braidwood, Robert J.
1952 *The Near East and the Foundations for Civilization: An Essay in Appraisal of the General Evidence.* Eugene, Oregon.
1960 "Levels in Prehistory: A Model for the Consideration of the Evidence." In *Evolution after Darwin: The University of Chicago Centennial,* Sol Tax, editor. Chicago, Vol. 2, pp. 143–151.

Caldwell, Joseph R.
1958 "Trend and Tradition in the Prehistory of the Eastern United States." *Memoirs, American Anthropological Association,* No. 88.

Chang, Kwang-chih
1963 *The Archaeology of Ancient China.* New Haven.

Childe, V. Gordon
1929 *The Danube in Prehistory.* Oxford.
1950 *Social Evolution.* London.
1956 *Piecing Together the Past: The Interpretation of Archaeological Data.* London.
1958 "Retrospect." *Antiquity* 32: 69–74.

Clark, Grahame
1939 *Archaeology and Society.* London.
1940 *Prehistoric England.* London.
1951 "Folk Culture and the Study of European Prehistory." In *Aspects of Archaeology in Great Britain and Beyond: Essays Presented to O. G. S. Crawford,* W. F. Grimes, editor. London, pp. 49–65.
1952 *Prehistoric Europe: The Economic Basis.* London.

Daniel, Glyn E.
1943 *The Three Ages, An Essay on Archaeological Method.* Cambridge.

Fairbanks, Charles H.
1952 "Creek and Pre-Creek." In *Archaeology of Eastern United States,* James B. Griffin, editor. Chicago, pp. 285–300.

Ford, James A.
1962 "A Quantitative Method for Deriving Cultural Chronology." *Pan American Union, Technical Manual,* No. 1.
——, and Gordon R. Willey
1949 "Surface Survey of the Virú Valley, Peru." *Anthropological Papers of the American Museum of Natural History,* 43, Pt. 1.

Gladwin, Winifred, and Harold S. Gladwin
1934 "A Method for the Designation of Cultures and Their Variations." *Medallion Papers,* No. 15.

Griffin, James B.
1952 "Culture Periods in Eastern United States." In *Archaeology of Eastern United States,* James B. Griffin, editor. Chicago, pp. 352–364.

Hawkes, C. F. C.
1959 "The ABC of the British Iron Age." *Antiquity* 33: 170–182.

Heizer, Robert F.
1958 "Classification Systems for Archaeological Cultures." In *A Guide to Archaeological Field Methods,* Robert F. Heizer, editor. Palo Alto (3rd ed., revised), pp. 97–101.

Hester, James J.
1962 "A Comparative Typology of New World Cultures." *American Anthropologist* 64: 1001–15.

Jope, E. M.
1963 "The Regional Cultures of Medieval Britain." In *Culture and Environment, Essays in Honour of Sir Cyril Fox,* I. Ll. Foster & L. Alcock, editors. London, pp. 327–350.

Kluckhohn, Clyde
  1962 *Culture and Behavior: Collected Essays of Clyde Kluckhohn,* Richard Kluckhohn, editor. New York.
Kossina, Gustav
  1920 *Die Herkunft der Germanen; zur Methode der Siedlungsarchaologie.* Leipzig.
Mayer-Oakes, William J.
  1963 "Complex Society Archaeology." *American Antiquity* 29: 57–60.
McKern, William C.
  1939 "The Midwestern Taxonomic Method as an Aid to Archaeological Study." *American Antiquity* 4: 201–213.
Menghin, Oswald
  1931 *Weltgeschichte der Steinzeit.* Vienna.
Neumann, George K.
  1952 "Archaeology and Race in the American Indian." In *Archaeology of Eastern United States,* James B. Griffin, editor. Chicago, pp. 13–34.
Piggott, Stuart
  1959 *Approach to Archaeology.* London.
  1960 "Prehistory and Evolutionary Theory." In *Evolution after Darwin: The University of Chicago Centennial,* Sol Tax, editor. Chicago, Vol. 2, pp. 85–97.
Rouse, Irving
  1955 "On the Correlation of Phases of Culture." *American Anthropologist* 57: 713–722.
  1957 "Culture Area and Co-tradition." *Southwestern Journal of Anthropology* 13: 123–133.
  1962 "Southwestern Archaeology Today." In *An Introduction to the Study of Southwestern Archaeology* by A. V. Kidder. New Haven, pp. 1–53.
  1964 "Archaeological Approaches to Cultural Evolution." In *Explorations in Cultural Anthropology,* Ward H. Goodenough, editor. New York, pp. 455–468.
———, and José M. Cruxent
  1963 *Venezuelan Archaeology.* New Haven.
Sears, William H.
  1961 "The Study of Social and Religious Systems in North American Archaeology." *Current Anthropology* 2: 223–231.
Smith, Harlen I.
  1910 "The Prehistoric Ethnology of a Kentucky Site." *Anthropological Papers of the American Museum of Natural History,* 6, Pt. 2.
Sollas, W. J.
  1911 *Ancient Hunters and Their Modern Representatives.* London.
Stiles, Ezra
  1933 *Letters and Papers of Ezra Stiles, President of Yale College, 1778–95.* New Haven.
Tax, Sol, Loren C. Eiseley, Irving Rouse, and Carl F. Voegelin, editors
  1953 *An Appraisal of Anthropology Today.* Chicago.
Taylor, Walter W.
  1943 "A Study of Archaeology." *Memoirs, American Anthropological Association,* No. 69.
Thompson, Raymond H.
  1956 "The Subjective Element in Archaeological Inference." *Southwestern Journal of Anthropology* 12: 327–332.
Ucko, Peter J.
  1962 "The Interpretation of Prehistoric Anthropomorphic Figurines." *Journal of the Royal Anthropological Institute* 92: 38–54.
Wainwright, F. T.
  1962 *Archaeology and Place-Names and History: An Essay in Problems of Coordination.* London.
Wilford, Lloyd A.
  1941 "A Tentative Classification of the Prehistoric Cultures of Minnesota." *American Antiquity* 6: 231–249.

Willey, Gordon R., editor
    1956 "Prehistoric Settlement Patterns in the New World." *Viking Fund Publications in Anthropology,* No. 23.
_____, and Philip Phillips
    1958 *Method and Theory in American Archaeology.* Chicago.

CULTURE CHANGE

BRUCE G. TRIGGER's essay on culture change is an admirable exposition of the basic principles of invention, diffusion, and migration as applied to archaeological data. What are the criteria for establishing any one of these three concepts in the archaeological record? How do archaeologists explain the changes observed in the archaeological record? These are questions Trigger discusses in this extract.

🔲 Among prehistorians, the study of culture change is primarily an examination of invention, diffusion, and migration (Kroeber 1948:344–571). It is generally believed that these three concepts, judiciously applied, can be used to explain all of the changes observed in the archaeological record. A large literature has grown up around each of them and an even larger one around the controversies concerning the relative importance of each as a factor in culture change.

INVENTION

By the term invention or innovation is meant the creation of any new idea, that is, the conceiving of something not previously known to the inventor. An invention is a "mutation" that comes about through the modification of an idea in the light of experience or the combining of several old ideas to produce a new one (Kroeber 1948:352–374; R. B. Dixon 1928:33–58). The concept definitely excludes the acquisition of new ideas from a source external to the individual. Most innovations, like the majority of biological mutations, are minor ones and are unimportant, either because they remain idiosyncratic or because they replicate something that is already known to others. The solving of a crossword puzzle is an innovation of the latter sort.

The term invention is, therefore, most often reserved for a socially significant innovation, whether it be a new machine or technical process, an institutional change—such as the development of representative government—or a scientific or philosophical discovery. Innovations may be the result of either planned research or accidental discovery. Many important changes, particularly in the social sphere, do not come about as the result of a single discovery but rather are the cumulative product of many small innovations, often made simultaneously by different people.

Diffusion and Migration

Diffusion is the name given to the process by which an invention gains social acceptance. It refers to the spread of new ideas or new units of culture from one person or group to another. If a parallel can be drawn between innovation and mutation, diffusion may be described as the process of selection by which a trait either is added to those that are already part of a culture or else manages to replace an existing trait. The successful diffusion of a trait is the result of a process of evaluation in which individuals and groups come to appreciate and accept it. This evaluation is made in terms of the needs and belief systems of the culture involved and the choices made by one culture may not be the choices made by another (Erasmus 1961:17–97). Particularly in the area of technology, the acceptance of new traits depends on whether or not they are perceived as promoting a culture's more effective exploitation of its environment.

Some anthropologists distinguish between primary diffusion, which takes place within the culture in which a trait was invented, and secondary diffusion, which is the diffusion of a trait beyond it (R. B. Dixon 1928:59, 106). It is argued that the chances of a trait diffusing within its culture of invention are greater than the chances of it being accepted by other cultures, where needs and values may be different. Traits may spread independently of one another or in clusters. When an entire foreign culture is accepted by a group, the process is called assimilation (Kroeber 1948:415–428). A cluster of traits which spread together may or may not be functionally interrelated. The former are usually called a "logical trait-complex." One example is the horse-complex, which seems to have evolved in Central Asia, and comprises, in addition to the horse itself, the bridle and bit, saddle, quirt (whip), harness, cart, and the use of mare's milk for food (R. B. Dixon 1928:158). This collection of traits spread throughout much of Northern Asia and, with the exception of the use of mare's milk, throughout Europe. Other clusters of traits may not be functionally related but merely travel together since various contacts exist between groups which permit them to do so. Accidental trait-complexes tend to be more ephemeral than logical ones and are subject to more drastic changes and substitutions.

Diffusion involves the spread of ideas and, as such, must be distinguished from the spread of goods as a result of trade or warfare. The Eskimos, for example, trade with the Europeans for iron goods and these goods have become an important part of their culture. In spite of this, they have never learned to make these tools for themselves. In other words, while the idea of using iron tools has spread to the Eskimos, the ideas of iron production have not. From a cultural point of view, the statement that iron tools have diffused to the Eskimos is incorrect. What we mean is that the Eskimos obtain iron tools from the Europeans. The fact that they do so, means that Eskimo culture is no longer self-sufficient, but has become dependent on European technology. This illustrates another characteristic of diffusion.

As a trait moves from one culture to another, it is rare if all of its attributes move with it. The idea of adding an outrigger to a canoe may diffuse from one culture to another, yet in the second culture the boat will probably be built according to local traditions of carpentry, which may be very different from what they were in the original culture. The basic idea of the chemical composition of gunpowder spread from China to Europe, but because the technology and political structure of Europe were different from those of China, gunpowder was developed differently and came to play a very different role in Europe from what it did in China. An extreme example of limited diffusion is the spread of writing from the Americans to the Cherokee in 1821 (Kroeber 1948:369–370). A half-breed Indian by the name of Sequoya did not learn how to read English, but by observing his American neighbors he grasped the basic idea that it was possible to represent sounds with written symbols. Working on his own, he invented a syllabary of 86 characters (many borrowed from the English alphabet, but in no case used to represent their original sound values), which he then used to write his own language. In this example, only the *idea* of writing, not that of the alphabet, let alone the original sound values of the letters, spread from one culture to another. Such extreme examples are sometimes called stimulus diffusion or stimulus invention (Kroeber 1940; 1948:368–370), meaning that only general principles, rather than all of the details associated with a complex invention are diffused, and that these general principles stimulate what is in most respects a new invention. In one sense, almost all examples of diffusion between cultures are examples of stimulus diffusion, since a trait rarely manages, or is required, to carry all of its technological, let alone, conceptual attributes with it from one group to another. In order for a nation, such as China, to build its own atomic bomb, it is not necessary for its scientists to learn how Americans produce a nut or bolt.

It is also important to note that, while diffusion frequently results in the spread of a trait over vast distances, it does so because an idea is transmitted from one person to another. The expansion of a people who carry their culture with them may likewise result in the geographical spread of a trait, but the spread is not diffusion, since no new individuals or groups share the trait after the movement has taken place. By contrast, the learning of the English language and American patterns of behavior by an immigrant to the United States *is* an example of cultural diffusion, although it is one that in no way involves the geographical spread of a trait or trait complex. Diffusion refers to the spread of traits socially from individual to individual, and ultimately from group to group, rather than to their geographical movement.

Because of this, we must thus distinguish between the spread of ideas and the movement of peoples. The latter is usually called *migration*. Often these two concepts are not clearly separated since, it is argued, the spread of ideas always comes about through people meeting and interacting. Frequently, migration is classified as a subset of diffusion and distinctions are drawn between the diffusion of culture that is accomplished through large-scale movements of people and that which is accomplished without it (MacWhite 1956:17). In fact, the situation is more complex and definitions of this kind merely blur the distinction between the spread of ideas and the movement of people. The spread of a people can, for example, lead to the geographical expansion of a culture, without the spread of elements of this culture to new groups (such as was the case with the Viking settlements in the New World); on the other hand, movements of population can be an important agent of cultural diffusion (as in the Spanish conquest and settlement in Mexico). In still other cases, cultures can diffuse without people moving (such as the spread of Latin culture throughout the western Roman Empire) or people can move without the diffusion of culture taking place (the total assimilation of immigrants). The various combinations that are observed of these suggest that the migration of people and the diffusion of ideas are independent concepts that are better kept conceptually separate when we interpret historical phenomena.

Distinguishing Independent Invention, Diffusion, and Migration

The prehistorian is interested in formulating rules that will allow him to distinguish changes in culture resulting from diffusion, migration, and independent development. The data he uses come either from archaeological excavations or from distributional studies. By and large, the prehistorian is not interested in investigating these processes on an interpersonal level, but rather in distinguishing how they are involved in the interaction between cultures or large societal units. On this level independent development normally means that the trait was invented inside the culture being investigated, and diffusion means diffusion between cultures.

Evidence of the act of invention is rare in the archaeological record. Where it occurs, it most often takes the form of idiosyncratic creations that are distinguishable because of their uniqueness, but which, because they did not gain acceptance in any culture, are historically inconsequential (Rouse 1960:313). It is more frequently claimed that an invention occurred in a particular culture because likely prototypes for some new trait can be found in an earlier related culture. Mud-covered baskets, for example, are often argued to be the forerunners of pottery (Arkell 1957). In the majority of cases, however, such proposals remain at the level of speculation.

Similarly, clear-cut evidence of diffusion or migration is frequently lacking in the archaeological record. Where substantial changes take place in a short period of time, the prehistorian seeks to discover if these result from the arrival of a new people with an exotic culture, or if the new traits appear as a result of local invention or trait diffusion from somewhere else.

Much of the theoretical literature that discusses how to distinguish between diffusion and independent development has grown out of attempts to provide historical explanations for trait distributions in the absence of archaeological evidence. There is general agreement that if a trait has a continuous distribution over a wide area, it probably had a single origin, followed by diffusion. If evidence of the trait is not found outside its present area of diffusion, there is also a tendency to assume that it originated somewhere within that area. Where archaeological evidence is lacking, culture historians have tended to assume (much as linguists do about the origin of language families) that, all other factors being equal, a trait probably originated somewhere near the center of its present distribution or else in the area where it presently has the greatest elaboration and complexity. Principles such as these were first enunciated by Edward Sapir (1916) in his paper on *Time Perspective in Aboriginal American Culture* and have since been used by Nelson (1919), Kroeber (1925), Wissler (1926) and many other anthropologists. The principle that older traits generally have wider distributions than more recent ones is now generally recognized as having too many exceptions to be useful (R. B. Dixon 1928:69–72). Likewise, the once popular theory that trait-complexes develop and spread from a common center has been criticized because it ignores the fact that new traits can be added to a complex anywhere throughout its distribution (R. B. Dixon 1928:167–181). In spite of this, there is general agreement that, when used with caution, distributional analyses can produce results of historical value, particularly when traits are analyzed one at a time.

Serious disagreements occur when ethnologists attempt to deal with discontinuous trait distributions, and it is in this area that various techniques have been developed which it is claimed can distinguish between diffusion and parallel development. These theories, none of which has ever proved quantifiable, are based for the most part on general and unproved assumptions about the nature of culture and human psychology. Those who believe that different human beings can easily arrive at similar conclusions tend to assume that parallel inventions are common in human history; while those who believe that man is uninventive and that any sort of complex invention is unlikely to be arrived at twice, stress diffusion as the main process underlying culture change. Attempts to evaluate these positions from a psychological point of view have been, and for the most part remain, highly impressionistic.

The first anthropologist to expound the theory of parallel development was Adolf Bastian (Daniel 1963:107; Lowie 1937:30–38). Bastian, who had travelled widely, believed all minds were much alike and concluded that under similar circumstances human beings would arrive at similar solutions for the same problem. As a result, cultural development in different parts of the world tends to follow similar lines, whether or not there is any communication between these regions. De Mortillet had this sort of idea in mind when he proposed his "law of similar development," on the basis of which he argued that the paleolithic sequence found in France would prove to be a universal sequence of cultural development. The same concept of human nature underlies all unilineal theories of cultural evolution with the exception of that of the Vienna school, which postulates a single line of development producing cultures which then diffused throughout the world (Graebner 1911; Schmidt 1939).

Bastian's view of human nature has been objected to, not because anthropologists disagree with his assumption that human beings are much alike, but because environmental conditions vary from one region to another and the range of alternative cultural solutions for most problems is usually quite broad. Hence, different cultures evolve alternative solutions to the same problem and thereby undergo divergent development.

The more extreme diffusionists have based their work on the assumption that human beings are totally lacking in inventiveness. Innovations are believed to be so rare that even very general traits such as pottery, domestic plants, or mummification can have had only one origin. This concept underlies the work of the Vienna school and that of the "extreme diffusionists" in England during the early part of this century. The latter constructed schemes of culture history which saw all civilization derived from ancient Egypt (G. E. Smith 1915; Perry 1923) or Mesopotamia (Raglan 1939), and believed that all supposedly "advanced traits" (such as mummification, no matter what form it took) could be traced back to a place of origin in one of the ancient civilizations of the Old World (R. B. Dixon 1928:244–264; Daniel 1963:104–127). Vestiges of this sort of thinking can still be found in A. J. Arkell's (1957) claim that pottery was invented only once, or in Munro Edmonson's (1961) attempt to compute a diffusion rate for culture during the neolithic period by plotting the distance between the points at which traits such as pottery and metal tools are known to appear first in different parts of the world.

One anthropologist who attempted to study human inventiveness was A. L. Kroeber (1948:341–343; 364–367). He observed that many things were not only invented more than once, but that in the scientific field the same discovery was often made within the same year by scientists who had no knowledge of each other's work. This obviously happens because scholars throughout the world are conscious of similar problems and have a common pool of ideas to draw from. Generalizing from this, Kroeber postulated that the more two cultures are alike, and the more their needs are the same, the more likely they are to come up with similar solutions to the same problems. The initial similarities, however, can arise from different sources. Two cultures can be alike because they spring from a common source, and, under these conditions, similar inventions merely help to offset the differences that inevitably must arise as a result of separate development. On the other hand, similarities can develop in historically unrelated cultures that have a similar general adaptation to their environment. Formal similarities can thus result from historical interconnections, functional similarities, and finally from similar cultures (for either of the two reasons given above) generating further similar inventions. In order to distinguish which of these factors is at work in a given situation it is necessary to have either detailed historical information or a highly sophisticated understanding of the nature of culture change. In most situations where historical reconstructions are attempted, the information in neither category is adequate to produce fully satisfactory results. All too often in the past, anthropologists have tried to supplement a lack of historical information with theories of culture that would allow them to reconstruct the past from present-day distributional evidence alone. In the next section I will discuss why most of these efforts have proved futile.

THE WEAKNESS OF THE "CULTURE HISTORICAL" APPROACH

Many debates about historical connections have centered on the nature of the evidence that is needed to prove that similar traits in two cultures are historically related. Graebner argued that the probability of traits found in different areas being historically related varies according to the resemblances in form and function that they exhibit (which are not simply in the nature of the phenomenon) and also according to the number of such traits that the regions involved can be found to have in common. He called these his criteria of "quality" and "quantity." While few ethnologists would deny the general validity of these principles, there is much disagreement as to the way they can be applied. It is sometimes argued, for example, that a large number of similar traits, although not proven to be of common origin, create as great a probability of historical connections between two cultures as do close resemblances in a small number of items.

Ethnologists usually begin by trying to discover whether or not similar traits in two or more cultures are genetically related (that is, derived from a common source), rather than by trying to prove independent invention. One basic assumption, contained in Graebner's criteria of quality, is that the more complex an item of culture is, the greater is the chance of being able to prove common origin. The literature is full of comments to the effect that a particular sort of object is too complicated to have been invented twice. These statements, however, almost invariably turn out to be personal judgments, with little in the way of scientific theory or a reliable estimate of probability to support them. The result is that objects that one anthropologist believes are related, are considered by another not to be. At present, clear-cut decisions are possible only in a limited number of cases, and these are determined largely by the nature of the evidence being considered.

Some objects found in two or more cultures may be shown not only to be "genetically" related but to be products of the same culture. In the recipient cultures these objects are usually called "trade goods," regardless of the means by which they passed from one culture to another. Such objects can usually be distinguished from indigenous material through differences in form and manufacture and also by the fact that they lack historical antecedents in the local culture. No one doubts, for example, that the Roman coins or Central Asian Buddhas that are found in archaeological sites in Scandinavia are trade goods (Stenberger n.d.; 124–130). Such objects are similar in every way to other examples known to be of foreign origin and there are no stylistic or technological antecedents in Swedish culture that could account for such a perfect parallelism in design and workmanship. The presence of the same kind of trade goods in two cultures demonstrates contact (however indirect) between them, and this strengthens the chances that ideas could have been exchanged as well as objects. Trade goods thus provide evidence of the existence of channels of communication that can be used to argue the possibility of cultural diffusion.

Zoologists, likewise, may show that domestic plants or animals are not indigenous to certain areas, since the wild species that gave rise to them do not, and probably never did, occur there (McCall 1964:91–101). The genetic constitution of plants and animals frequently constitutes an effective means of distinguishing varieties that share a common origin from those that are the result of parallel development. Moreover, the genetic relationship between tame plants and animals and their wild ancestors provides evidence of their place of origin. The absence of both native wild goats and ancestral forms of wheat or barley in North Africa in post-Pleistocene times indicates, for example, that these items must have been brought into this area, probably in domestic form, from Southwest Asia (Reed 1960:130–134). Plant and animal studies, like trade goods, produce irrefutable evidence of contacts between different regions and, thus, are useful for demonstrating the possibility that traits could have diffused along the same routes. Care is needed, however, not to generalize indiscriminately on the basis of such evidence.

In order to demonstrate historical connections, one must first eliminate the possibility that the similarities in the items being compared are in fact products of convergent development. For many years, diffusionists argued that all pyramidal structures had their origins in ancient Egypt. The fact that the Egyptian pyramids were tombs covering the graves of kings, while the Mesopotamian ziggurats were platforms supporting the temples of important deities did not deter such speculation. It was assumed that whatever differences, in form and function, were found among pyramidal structures in different parts of the world, were the result of divergent development and that all these structures could be traced back to a common prototype. Since that time, archaeologists have shown that the Egyptian pyramid developed from the mounds of sand that were originally used to cover individual graves. These developed into an elaborate sun symbol, which in functional—although perhaps no longer in conceptual—terms served the same purpose. The ziggurat, on the other hand, appears to have been an elaboration of the low platforms used (and still used) in southern Iraq to raise houses and public buildings above the level of the river. Far from being the result of divergence from a common prototype, any similarities between the Egyptian pyramid and the Mesopotamian ziggurat appear to be the result of historically unrelated convergent development from totally different origins.

Once upon a time it was believed that similarities in social organization were indications of widespread historical connections. Morgan (1871:387), for example, argued that since many North American Indian tribes have the same general system of kinship system as have the Tamils in southern India, both groups were historically related. It is clear, however, that since social organization is limited in its variations and is highly correlated with economic organization, it is often convergent in its evolution. No one would argue that since the Nyoro of Central Africa have an Omaha kinship system, they are historically related to the Winnebago of the United States, or would even suggest that the idea of the state had a single origin. Mere typological similarities in social or political organization are no proof of an historical relationship among different groups.

Languages provide an even more instructive example of the lack of historical significance that can be attributed to structural similarities. In the last century it was often argued that typological or structural similarities between languages were indications of historical relationship. Today, it is clear that tone languages have evolved independently in Africa and the Far East and that sex gender is no proof that the Khoisan (Bushman) and Indo-European languages are historically related. Demonstrably related languages, such as those of the Indo-European family, display a wide variety of structural variation, from Latin, which is essentially a synthetic language, to English, which is essentially analytic.

Such structural principles are poor evidence of historical relationships among languages, because types are limited in number and therefore the possibility of convergence is high. Much more reliable proofs of historical relationships can be found in those features of language in which chances of arbitrary association play a significantly greater role. Each word or morpheme (except perhaps for the words "mother" and "father") (Murdock 1959b) is a completely arbitrary association of sound and meaning. In any two vocabularies a linguist expects that no more than four percent of the words will share the same association of form and meaning because of coincidence. Any greater degree of similarity indicates either that words have been borrowed between these two languages or that they share a common origin. According to Greenberg (1957:39–40), an examination of the core vocabulary of the languages involved, and a comparison of the degree to which linguistic similarities between two languages are shared with others that are equally related, will allow the linguist to distinguish the latter kind of relationship from the former. Proof of either sort of historical relationship between languages thus depends not on structural similarities but on a significant number of arbitrary associations between form and meaning.

Unfortunately, in the nonlinguistic domains of culture it is frequently impossible to estimate how arbitrary a trait is and what is the likelihood that the same form could have evolved independently several times. We frequently do not have enough understanding about the behavior of culture to apply Graebner's criteria of quality and quantity intelligently. It is even far from clear, in many cases, to what degree these criteria are distinct. The margin of doubt concerning whether similarities are due to convergence or diffusion is therefore frequently very great.

Applying the criterion of quality, one expects that the more resemblances there are between traits from different cultures, the greater is the chance that they are derived from a common historical source. It has become apparent that general categories, such as pottery or mummification, are meaningless units of comparison, since they cover broad areas of culture and often share few similarities in content. They are, therefore, extremely susceptible to multiple invention. Comparisons must consider specific traits or a complex of closely related traits.

The first task is to determine whether traits that look alike, really are. Just as in linguistics, meaningful lexical comparisons are based on words similar in sound and meaning, so with culture: the categories being compared should be alike both in form and function (Steward and Setzler 1938). Form and function are possibly less arbitrary, yet vary with respect to each other more in the field of culture than they do in linguistics. Hence, the possibility of disparate origins and "false convergence" should be investigated, when any category is found whose members lack a one-to-one correlation in these two (Steward 1929). For example, through a careful analysis of the wear patterns on 300 so-called "celts," J. Sonnenfeld (1962) found that these objects had been put to very different uses in different cultures. Moreover, in this instance, he found no evidence of a significant correlation between form and function. The analysis of the function of a trait, in the sense of both its technological use and its role in the culture as a whole, should be carried out, wherever possible, independently of form so that these two categories of information can later be compared.

It is also obvious that, to constitute satisfactory evidence of a historical relationship, the traits being compared should be nonfunctional. Arrowheads are manufactured out of only a few materials and have a limited number of shapes; hence, it is not inconceivable that various combinations of these attributes have been reinvented many times. Some functions, particularly technological ones, can be determined fairly easily; others are more subtle and it would be folly to pretend that the present state of anthropology can take account of all of them. For example, little is understood about such relationships as those between art styles and social structure, which require a more sophisticated understanding of psychological mediations than is possible at present. For this reason, it is not always possible to distinguish functional and nonfunctional criteria.

Various studies indicate that the possibility of convergent development of elaborate trait-complexes, is greater than common sense would lead one to believe. Therefore, complex similarities in related traits do not necessarily indicate a historical relationship between two cultures.

In 1913, Alexander Goldenweiser enunciated his "principle of limited possibilities" which proposed that parallel and convergent developments are likely to occur for two reasons. The first reason was the usual psychological one, namely, that the range of human reactions to similar problems is frequently limited; hence the chances of the same trait being invented more than once are quite high. The second reason was modelled after the biological concept of selection. It proposed that since the range of traits that any one culture may be able to integrate successfully is limited, features that are different to begin with, often end up being channelled along similar lines. Just as natural selection causes animals having very different origins (such as bats and birds) but occupying similar ecological niches to develop along similar lines, so cultural traits that are different in origin may grow alike if they find themselves in a similar cultural environment. Since anthropologists, unlike biologists, usually are unable to distinguish similarities resulting from convergent development from ones that indicate common origin, they are often unable, from analysis of form and function alone, to determine which of these two factors has been at work.

The principle of limited possibilities is the basis of Rands and Riley's (Riley 1952; Rands 1961) concept of pattern elaboration. These men argue that most innovations are extensions of previously existing patterns, rather than creations along completely new lines. Hence the choices among various alternatives that have been made at any one period will tend to restrict the range of choices that are possible later. Once the nucleus of a complex has been established through a set of primary choices, later traits will tend to develop sequentially from it. Rands and Riley (1958) have illustrated this concept with a comparison of the methods of torture employed by the Iroquois, Aztecs, and Tupinamba (the latter a Brazilian tribe). This complex is analyzed by breaking it into component traits on varying levels of generality. The authors conclude that many of the detailed similarities in ritual and technique found in the methods of torture employed by these three groups may be convergent elaborations of a limited number of more general traits that may or may not be historically related. Hence, limitations of choice, as well as functional necessity, may be a factor promoting convergence and thus helping to increase the difficulty of determining whether or not similar traits are historically related.

In a paper discussing two similar games of chance, the first an Aztec, the second a Hindu one, Charles Erasmus (1950) has argued that it is impossible to use probability theory to estimate the likelihood of diffusion as opposed to independent development. In particular, this argument is directed against Tylor's (1879) suggestion that the probability of the recurrent invention of an item of culture varies inversely with the number of common elements that are involved in the complex. In order to apply Tylor's formula one would have to know (1) the exact number of possible alternative combinations that each element in these two games has, (2) all of the opportunities for their combination, and (3) that each of these elements is independent of the others, in the sense that the occurrence of one does not bias the probability of the occurrence of any of the others. The growing understanding of limited possibilities and of pattern elaboration emphasizes how difficult it would be to satisfy the last of these requirements.

Graebner's second criterion, that of quantity, proposes that the greater is the number of qualitative resemblances between two areas, the greater is the chance of there being an historical connection between them. The traits being compared ideally should be independent of each other, if each is to constitute a separate piece of evidence. It is frequently difficult, however, to determine if traits are, in fact, independent. Royal brother-sister marriages, retainer burials, the restriction of gold for the use of the upper classes, and the employment of dwarfs as household servants may be considered as individual traits or as part of a pattern related to a highly stratified society. Since it is difficult to determine whether the elements being compared are truly independent, the same problems that beset the statistical use of quantitative evidence burden the use of qualitative evidence. In fact, it becomes impossible to separate these two categories of data.

In addition to accepting interrelated traits as independent evidence of a historical relationship, there is also frequently a tendency to ignore the relative significance and validity of the individual relationships being proposed and to concentrate mainly on the number. The basic assumption seems to be that if enough similarities are discovered, a few mistaken ones will not greatly bias the evidence. This of course is fallacious. The significance of no item that is used in a quantitative argument is any greater than its individual qualitative value as established in terms of the criteria stated above.

Moreover, when culture areas are being compared, there is all too frequently a tendency to compare traits collected from different cultures within the area and even from different periods. It is argued that proof of historical connections need not depend on detailed comparisons between individual cultures, since traits probably diffused between the two areas gradually and over different routes. Statistically, however, by increasing the number of cultures that traits are selected from, one naturally increases the probability of finding cultural parallels and the value of the evidence is thereby diminished. Rowe (1966) has recently compiled a list of 60 traits common to the Andean and ancient Mediterranean civilizations in order to illustrate the danger of assuming that even a large number of casual similarities between two remote regions is proof of a historical connection between them. Taken individually, and subjected to careful scrutiny in terms of the criteria we have discussed, scarcely any of these traits would escape elimination. They are either too general, too obviously functional, or too interdependent. Considering the vast array of cultures involved and the nature of the traits, any that are not eliminated using these criteria could easily be attributed to chance. Evidence that one plant of Peruvian origin, such as the potato, was known in Europe prior to 1492 would constitute infinitely better evidence of a historical connection between these two areas than do 60 doubtful traits.

A final criterion, often employed in distinguishing between diffusion and independent development, is the ease of communication between the regions involved. Graebner called this the criterion of continuity. While distance and the nature of the terrain undoubtedly affect communication, it is not easy to estimate the effect that these factors have on diffusion, since many cultural variables intervene. Estimates of the ability or desire of ancient peoples to travel frequently vary. An illustration of this is the recent dispute between Sharp (1957) and Suggs (1960) concerning the ability of the Polynesians to use astronomical sightings to chart courses across long stretches of the Pacific Ocean. The notion of routes also causes difficulties. R. B. Dixon (1928:231) argued that it would be unlikely for various traits to have diffused from Southeast Asia to the tropical regions of the New World, since they would have been forgotten during their bearers' long sojourn in the intervening Arctic and temperate regions. However, if recent suggestions of trans-Pacific connections prior to 1492 (Ekholm 1964) are ever confirmed, the significance of this argument would be greatly diminished.

It is clear, then, that even close formal similarities in traits or trait-complexes do not necessarily indicate a common origin. The limitation of possibilities, through various functional constraints, and the similar needs and nature of man, all conspire to make repeated invention, parallel development, and convergence not only possible, but fairly common. When two cultures share many specific, seemingly nonfunctional traits, it seems logical to postulate some sort of historical relationship between them, just as when two languages contain many words with similar sounds and meanings, it is possible to infer some sort of historical relationship between them, either genetic or diffusionary. When dealing with material culture, we must be more cautious, however, since the make-up of few items of culture is not functionally determined, or at least influenced, in some way. Sometimes, historical relationships can be demonstrated by discovering artifacts in one culture which can be demonstrated to be local imitations of objects originally manufactured in another. An example is the crude, but detailed, imitations of Greek coins found in the La Tene culture of western Europe (Powell 1958:100–102). Even so, without the perspective that only archaeology can provide, it is often impossible to tell whether close similarities, even between nearby cultures, are the result of their divergence from a common ancestor, the convergence of two originally different cultures, or a combination of both. We have already seen in our discussion of pyramids that, in the absence of archaeological evidence, very wrong conclusions may be reached, but once such evidence becomes available, the answers to most problems concerning the types of artifacts that are preserved in the archaeological record are quickly forthcoming. These, in turn, provide the basis for a reasonable discussion of the history of those items of culture that have not been preserved.

It was suggested not long ago that proof of diffusion or independent development does not rest on archaeological evidence but rather on "a set of theoretical principles that must be objectively applied to each case" (Meggers 1964:522). Linguistics has almost reached the point where this is possible. When dealing with other areas of culture and with artifacts, however, present theories are clearly insufficient to allow us to reconstruct the past using ethnological evidence alone. Solid inferences must be based on archaeological evidence, which, if it is sufficient, may allow us to distinguish between the alternative hypotheses that the study of trait distributions raises. Moreover, the further we move into the past the more completely we must rely on purely archaeological evidence.

What are the criteria that can be used to determine whether similar objects in noncontiguous cultures are historically related?

(1) It must be demonstrated that the objects or traits in question are genuinely similar in form and function and have enough nonfunctional criteria in common to at least suggest that the similarities between them are likely to result from a common origin. Occasionally, a particular trait or trait-complex is sufficiently unique that its very nature demonstrates a historical relationship. No one doubts that maize or tobacco came from the New World or that the English spoken by the inhabitants of Bombay is of British origin. Most traits, however, are not clear-cut.

(2) Where proof of diffusion seems likely, it must be shown next that the objects that appear to share a common origin are not the products

of convergent evolution. To answer this question, detailed archaeological data are required concerning the historical antecedents of the objects in question in the various cultures in which they are found. We have already noted how archaeological evidence shows that the Egyptian and Mesopotamian "pyramids" developed from entirely different, and historically unrelated, antecedents. Historical analysis also shows that certain highly stylized Mayan motifs, which G. Elliot Smith (1924) claimed were the heads of elephants (and hence were evidence of Hindu influence in Mayan culture), were in fact curvilinear stylizations of the head and bill of a native parrot. Archaeological evidence, by allowing prehistorians to trace the local antecedents of various traits, makes a valuable contribution toward distinguishing traits that are genetically related from those that result from convergence.

(3) It is fair to presume that whenever a trait capable of surviving in the archaeological record diffused from one area to another over land, it left traces of its passing along the way. Hence, even if a trait now has a discontinuous distribution, it should be possible to prove archaeologically that at some period its distribution was not discontinuous. This evidence should take the form of a series of archaeological sites, which either marks the route along which the trait moved or else shows its former distribution to have embraced the gaps between the regions of its present occurrence (Rouse 1958). The sites within this area should be dated so that one can discover where the trait originated and how it spread. If, for example, a trait turns out to be older at two ends of its total distribution than it is in the middle, the archaeological evidence would favor multiple origins with an overlapping distribution rather than a single origin. The same test might profitably be applied to traits with presently continuous distribution, a few of which may turn out to have had more than one origin. It is obvious that it is impossible to find any archaeological evidence for many traits, and for others the evidence will be very scanty. In these cases, proof of historical connections cannot be ascertained. Nevertheless, if archaeological evidence of historical connections between two areas is forthcoming, then the possibility is enhanced that various other traits, of which no archaeological evidence remains, may have had the same history. It is also clear that, even when we are dealing with ethnographic traits that undoubtedly share a common origin, only archaeological evidence can demonstrate at what period and by what route they diffused.

(4) When intervening areas are not susceptible to archaeological investigation (as is the case in Polynesia where islands are separated by vast stretches of ocean) the argument that similar traits are genetically related must rest largely on the proof of the historical relatedness of traits, such as languages and crops, whose nature is such as to permit

no doubt of their common origin. The fact that a Malayo-Polynesian language is spoken on Easter Island, and that typical Polynesian crops are grown there, is infinitely better proof of the close historical relations between that island and the rest of Polynesia than Heyerdahl's reed boats and stonework are proof of a historical connection with South America. The genetic relationship of the former traits is assured but the genetic relationship of the ones listed by Heyerdahl is only a matter of conjecture.

Distinguishing Diffusion and Migration

Various criteria have been established to help to distinguish pure trait diffusions from cultural changes brought about by movements of people. Most of these criteria are designed to pinpoint major discontinuities resulting from the total replacement of one population by another. This kind of treatment, as we have noted before, ignores the fact that movements of people and traits at times take place quite independently of each other, and consequently disregards the variety of situations in which movements of population and of cultural traits can and do occur. In 1939, W. M. Flinders Petrie listed nine types of culture change (excluding independent invention) all but one of which involved migrations of people. Although this list reflects a rather melodramatic view of culture change, it has the merit of recognizing the wide variety of circumstances under which culture change can come about. Its categories include: (1) general substitution of population, (2) killing the men and scattering the women, (3) killing the men and capturing the women, (4) enslaving the men and taking the women, (5) victors ruling over slaves, (6) victors ruling over stable populations, (7) mixture of diverse peoples, (8) assimilation of immigrants, and (9) merely the adoption of foreign ideas. Another list, anthropologically more sophisticated, was drawn up by Eoin MacWhite in 1956. It distinguished between various types of organized invasions, casual immigration, and the different ways trait diffusion (acculturation) can come about through raiders, foreign visitors, or local groups being in contact with neighboring cultures. These lists differ from the one below in that they treat the entire problem from the point of view of culture change and fail to include instances where changes in population took place with little or no corresponding change in material culture. From the point of view of human history, population movements of the latter sort are as significant as the ones that bring about major cultural changes. The particular categories we discuss are obviously points on a continuum, and not a set of rigidly defined situations.

I. The first kind of change is the total replacement of one population and their culture by another. Normally, a change of this sort involves one group driving out another and occupying its former homeland.

This probably happens most frequently between adjacent and culturally similar groups and under these conditions "culture change" (as opposed to population change) is minimal. When the invaders are culturally different from their predecessors, the break is usually quite apparent in the archaeological record and where distinct populations are involved there may even be a noticeable discontinuity in physical type. While total changeovers of this sort are relatively rare, one would think they could be detected easily in the archaeological record. Such, however, is not always the case.

To begin with, one must be certain that the sharp break in the cultural continuity of the archaeological record is real and not merely apparent. Evidence from one site or from only a small area may not adequately reflect what has happened elsewhere. Thus, the first task of the archaeologist is to determine that the discontinuity he has noted holds true in terms of the whole culture. Secondly, he must determine that the total sequence has been recovered and that no period has been overlooked. It is possible that for ecological reasons, or perhaps because of unstable political conditions, a region was abandoned for a time before a new population moved in or the old one returned. The failure to note this temporal gap could result in a misunderstanding of the relationship between the cultures occupying the region before and afterwards and might even result in interpreting the same local tradition at two stages in its development as being two unrelated cultures. Such problems can be reduced to a minimum by extensive excavations and a careful study of the stratigraphic and chronological evidence. Finally, the archaeologist must examine the content of the cultures he is studying as thoroughly as possible. You may recall that archaeologists in Nubia failed to see the historical relationship between the Meroitic and Ballana cultures, because they concentrated on burials and tomb types, the particular area of culture where the greatest discontinuity existed.

Secondly, whenever it is possible to do so, it must be demonstrated that there was a genuine change in population. This requires evidence that the previous population was abruptly replaced by a new one. Where racial differences are noted between the skeletons associated with the two cultures, it must be shown that the change in physical type took place abruptly and at the same time the change in culture came about. Evidence of only a gradual change in physical type would, of course, weaken the argument that a total (or almost total) replacement of population took place.

Thirdly, something must be found out about the nature of the replacement. Often, the clues will consist of evidence of widespread destruction, followed by the settlement of people with a different culture. This evidence must be more convincing than the small collection of apparently unburied bodies that Mortimer Wheeler has suggested indicates that the

Indus Valley city of Mohenjodaro was sacked (Dales 1964). The documentation of how replacement took place requires extensive and carefully controlled excavations, and it appears that the archaeological record for few cultures is equal to this task.

As further proof of the intrusive nature of the new culture, the archaeologist not only must demonstrate that it suddenly replaced an older one, but, must also show where and from what antecedents the intrusive culture developed. In short, the new culture must be shown to be native to another region. This requirement rules out attempts to attribute the origins of "new" cultures to unknown regions. This is particularly important in Northeast Africa where little archaeological work has been done outside the Nile Valley, and where many a hypothetical antecedent of some Nile Valley culture is said to exist in some region that is archaeologically unknown. While no prehistorian must be denied the right to controlled speculation, the tendency of some scholars to pile one unsubstantiated hypothesis on another, often to the point where they ignore meaningful evidence close at hand, has incited a rather positivistic reaction among their less romantic colleagues.

Finally, Rouse (1958) is correct in suggesting that the route of any migration should be worked out and the distribution of all the sites checked to see if the resulting pattern makes sense historically. Furthermore, the archaeologist should attempt to find out if environmental and cultural conditions would have permitted a migration to take place. Such environmental factors are especially important in ecologically marginal regions, such as North Africa, where there have been considerable variations in climate.

The difficulties that replacement hypotheses can run into when there is a lack of detailed archaeological data are demonstrated by the recent questions raised concerning the validity of the "Neanderthal hypothesis" (Brace 1964; Coon 1965:52, 53). For a long time, many physical anthropologists believed that the Classic Neanderthal men of western Europe differed radically from *Homo sapiens*, perhaps even constituting a separate species of hominid. Although relatively few skeletons had been found, and few sites were excavated that belonged to the transitional period, it was widely accepted that Neanderthal man, along with his Mousterian culture had been swept aside between 30,000 and 40,000 years ago by modern *Homo sapiens*. It was assumed that these latter types, coming from the east, brought with them the earliest Upper Paleolithic [blade] cultures found in Europe. Even those who did not consider the Classic Neanderthals to be a separate species, saw them as being brushed aside, much as the North American Indians were by the Europeans, with only a few of their racial traits managing to survive in a very diluted form in remote regions.

Today this theory is being widely challenged. It has been suggested not only that the Classic Neanderthals of western Europe may have evolved into *Homo sapiens* in that area (aided perhaps by genetic drift from other regions), but also that the Mousterian culture evolved of its own accord into the Upper Paleolithic Perigordian I culture of western Europe. Once the theoretical issue is framed in this way, the current lack of archaeological data becomes evident, since it renders virtually impossible any final solution of this problem at this time.

II. The second type of culture change is that resulting from the movement of an organized group of people into a new area. Such groups settle down alongside the native population, as conquerors and rulers—as the Tussi were in Ruanda (Murdock 1959a:350; Willey 1953a); as subjects of the native population—as Bedouin groups from Palestine and Arabia often were in ancient Egypt; or else they interact with the local population on a basis of equality. Under these conditions, the incoming group may preserve its sense of ethnic identity and much of its own culture for a long time. Eventually, however, the old and the new cultures blend and may produce a single culture made up of various traits from each of the ancestral ones. In general, the relative importance of the contribution made by the two cultures will depend on the size and importance of the groups involved as well as the degree to which the incoming culture is adapted to its new environment. Various factors, such as the desire of the dominant minority group to preserve their sense of identity vis-à-vis their subjects, may impede the total blending of the two cultures. Special situations may also produce highly distorted forms of cultural blending. If, for example, large numbers of men from a particular tribe are killed in war and the women of the tribe marry outsiders, various traits from the old culture that are associated with women will be more likely to survive than those associated with men. An example of this is reported in the Lesser Antilles, where the Caribs are said to have killed off the Arawak men, but married the women (Rouse 1964:502). While the Caribs adopted the Arawak language, their arrival appears to have terminated the relatively elaborate, priestly religion of earlier times which centered on the worship of deities known as *zemis*. In this instance, cultural merging could be expected to take place quite rapidly.

In these situations the problem of proof is even more difficult than it is with total replacements. At one time there was a tendency to attribute almost every change in culture to the intrusion of some new groups or "master race" (Daniel 1963:104–127, 139–153). Unfortunately, using this model of culture change uncritically, almost any new trait can be attributed to the intrusion of a new group, while cultural continuities in the same culture can be ascribed to the survival of the native population. Thus, this sort of explanation can be read into almost every example of cultural change that is found in the archaeological record. To avoid un-bridled speculation, strict rules are needed to govern such interpretations. The purpose of these rules—which are simply a modification of the ones required to prove total replacement—is to help the prehistorian to dis-tinguish culture change that really does result from the arrival of new populations from changes that come about as a result of internal develop-ments or trait diffusion.

In order to demonstrate that the innovations observed in the archaeo-logical record were brought in by an organized migration, sites belonging to the intrusive culture associated with this group must be found and dated to the period when, or just before, the new traits became general in the local culture. These sites must be shown to belong not only to a culture that is different from contemporary cultures in the area, but also one for which a homeland and place of origin can be located elsewhere. In addition, the route of the migration must be found, its direction traced, and conditions shown to be such as to permit a migration over the route proposed (Rouse 1958). Finally, it must be shown that the culture is genuinely intrusive, in the sense of permanently occupying the region. In the seventeenth century, hunting bands from Northern Ontario fre-quently spent the winter living in encampments outside Huron villages, where they traded dried meat and skins for corn meal. This interaction between the Huron and Algonkians may have introduced various items of Algonkian culture to their hosts, but their settlement in Huronia was merely part of their annual cycle and did not result in any permanent Algonkian settlement in this region. Proof of population movement re-quires a demonstration that the incoming groups actually settled in the region (which may be done in part by showing that their settlements were permanent ones) and that they and their culture gradually mingled with the indigenous one. This in turn, requires archaeological evidence of the gradual mingling of cultural traits over time and (assuming that the intrusive groups were different to begin with) physical anthropo-logical evidence showing genetic mingling.

Clearly, it is sufficiently difficult to satisfy these criteria so that certain instances of major culture change resulting from the blending of two groups (especially when this went on quickly and, therefore, is hard to detect in the archaeological record) are likely to be ruled out for lack of evidence. The validity of this hypothesis can be considerably reduced, however, if, as more archaeological data accumulate, it can be demon-strated that the individual traits that were assumed to be brought in by the intrusive culture (and hence all at one time) actually appear in the archaeological record at different times. This is often the case. It is felt by many prehistorians that it is better to have criteria that are sufficiently strict so that certain (apparently) good cases are ruled out for lack of evidence, rather than to have rules so loose that any instance of culture change can be interpreted as being of this type. The logic behind this is that situations where proof of membership in this category is not forthcoming fall into a recognizable residual category. Later, when more evidence is available, they may be restudied and assigned to this one. Confusion reigns when none of the categories being used is clearly recognizable as a residual one.

III. A third type of change involves the organized migration of large numbers of people, but is characterized by little cultural change in the region they enter (at least of a sort that is detected in the archaeological record). In these instances the intrusive population accepts the material culture of the area it moves into. This can occur either because the group moves rapidly and carries little of its own culture along with it, or because the area into which it moves is ecologically different from the one it left and its old culture is unsuited to the new conditions. It can also happen where the culture of the new area is considered by the migrants to have greater prestige than their own. When nomads, such as the Hebrews, settled in Palestine, they quickly adopted the material culture of the farming and urban groups who already lived in the area. Likewise, the Philistines, who settled in the Canaanite cities along the coast, after what appears to have been a rapid flight from their original homeland, adopted the native culture of the region so completely that only a new style of tomb and a few artistic motifs can presently be used to distinguish them from the original population (Kenyon 1960:221-239). To the archaeologist who has no knowledge of historical records, the archaeological evidence, consisting mostly of towns pillaged by the invaders and later rebuilt in much the same style as before, would probably be insufficient to suggest that important ethnic and linguistic changes had taken place. Similarly, the Germanic invasions of much of the western Roman Empire led to such a swift adoption of Latin culture by them that the period of invasion might easily appear in the archaeological record as merely one of political instability and cultural decline, rather than as a period that also saw considerable movements of population.

Clues that suggest the intrusion of organized groups are signs of war, cultural decline, and fairly rapid cultural change, the latter being induced, in part by the decline in culture and in part by social and cultural innovations introduced by the intruders. This sort of evidence is rarely sufficient, by itself, to prove that new groups settled in the region. Evidence of rapid changes in physical type may increase the probability of migration, but here again caution must be exercised against unwarranted speculation based on inadequate data. Archaeological evidence of intrusion may be found in the form of the temporary camps and settlements of the invaders prior to acculturation. These sites are probably scarce and difficult to identify. It seems more difficult to find evidence of this sort of change than to find evidence of types I and II. The evidence is also often more ambiguous and difficult to interpret, since it is hard to tell the difference between the sites of an intrusive mobile population and those of groups of raiders who merely passed through a region.

In some cases, the intrusive population may adopt the local material culture, yet impose its own language on the region. In such instances, lexicostatistical data may reveal when a particular speech community underwent expansion and thus may provide clues concerning population movements. Such evidence, along with historical accounts, suggests that the Nubian-speaking peoples arrived in the Nile Valley from the southwest sometime during the Ballana period, although there are few indications of cultural discontinuity at this time. Apparently, they adopted the culture of the region and yet arrived in sufficient numbers to replace the earlier local language, Meroitic (Trigger 1966a). A similar situation seems to hold with the arrival of the Greeks in Crete, an event that appears to have preceded rather than brought about the collapse of Minoan culture. Commenting on this situation, Fritz Schachermeyr has observed:

> It is a great mistake to assume that historical events are always reflected in the archaeological record of stylistic phases. Many historical upheavals occurred without leaving any such traces behind them (Palmer 1965:180–181).

The absence of linguistic evidence does not, or course, prove that population movements never occurred, since the intrusive people may have adopted the language as well as the material culture of the region into which they moved.

IV. A fourth type of culture change is that resulting from an influx of outsiders who do not enter a culture as an organized group, but rather as individuals or families who find a place for themselves within the existing social order. These people may come as settlers, refugees, missionaries, slaves, or as the foreign husbands or wives of members of the indigenous group. Some may acculturate very quickly, others, for religious or other social or cultural reasons, may seek to preserve certain aspects of their old culture within a new social setting. Such people, especially those who possess special skills, can be important agents of diffusion. In Tudor times, the English government offered substantial incentives to foreign craftsmen to induce them to settle in England and teach their skills to English workers (Hodgen 1952:174–176). This is an example of the deliberate encouragement of migration in an effort to effect culture change. When such migrations continue from a single source over a long period of time, they can result in a considerable amount of cultural convergence. The conversion of the northern part of Lower Nubia from Christianity to Islam appears to have come about as more and more Egyptian Moslems bought land in that region and began to settle down and convert their neighbors (Trigger 1965:149). The main characteristic of this sort of change is that all the various traits being introduced do not appear at the same time, as they do when introduced by population replacements and organized migrations. Moreover, it does not interrupt the essential continuity of the indigenous culture. For this reason, it is extremely difficult for the archaeologist to distinguish between this sort of culture change and the results of simple trait diffusion.

Since the newcomers of unorganized migrations are usually absorbed directly into the fabric of the existing society, intrusive sites are not associated with them. Only rarely is it possible to find ghettos made up of numbers of such immigrants, who lived together in order to retain certain aspects of their old way of life. Such situations are hard to distinguish from the results of organized migration and in many ways they represent, socially as well as archaeologically, an intermediate type. Even if foreign households can be discovered within communities, it may be difficult to tell whether they belonged to itinerant groups visiting the community or to immigrants who came to live there. Where the native people and the migrants are physically different, the discovery of significant numbers of new skeletal types, and of the gradual mingling of new physical characteristics with those of the local population, may shed light on this problem. While the effect of this sort of migration on the genetic constitution of the population may be significant, the cultural effects are probably little different from those of trait diffusion. Hence, the difficulties of distinguishing the two do not create a serious problem. Moreover, the more massive the migration is, the greater is the chance the prehistorian will be able to detect it. Thus, the chance of noting this kind of change tends to vary more or less directly in proportion to its historical importance.

V. Unorganized migrations take place that have no marked effect on the recipient culture. Under these circumstances, the immigrant accepts the general culture of the society into which he is moving. This normally happens if he believes the latter culture to be more desirable than the one he has left. Unskilled prisoners, slaves, or migrant laborers are unlikely to possess any special skills that they can transmit to such a culture. At most, they may retain some of their old beliefs and personal habits and perhaps pass some of these on to their children. This is especially likely to happen if they are alienated from the new society by a sense of inferiority or are refugees forced to flee their native land but still sentimentally attached to it.

While movement from society to society, both forced and voluntary, is characteristic of complex societies, it is not unknown in primitive ones. Occasionally, it can take place on a large scale and yet leave little imprint on the recipient culture. Among the Iroquois, for example, large numbers of prisoners frequently were incorporated into the society of their captors, often so completely that they would refuse repatriation even when the opportunity for it was freely offered to them. From a cultural viewpoint such movements are often of minor importance, but in terms of understanding population dynamics and social organization they are of considerable interest. Unfortunately, it is very difficult to find evidence of such movements, although some work may be done in this direction, either through physical anthropology or through studies of shifts in the overall distribution of population.

VI. Our sixth category is trait diffusion. All culture diffuses as a result of contact between people, but trait diffusion involves no permanent shifts in population. Trait diffusion comes about either as a result of prolonged casual contacts between neighboring groups, or as a result of contacts between specialists such as traders or artisans. The itinerant craftsman, the wandering pilgrim, and the ambassador to a foreign country, all potential instruments of diffusion, do not represent any permanent exchange of population between two groups. Occasionally, the archaeologist may discover clear-cut evidence of mechanisms of diffusion, such as the Assyrian trading posts in Anatolia that we have mentioned already. Evidence of contact more often takes the form of trade goods or similar innovations appearing in nearby cultures at approximately the same time. Where traits have continuous distributions, and the possibility of diffusion from a single point of origin is high, it is necessary only to correlate each trait in time and in space in order to show where it originated and in which direction it moved. If the earliest point of occurrence coincides with a region where the trait has obvious cultural prototypes, the chances of it having evolved there are high. Where proof of continuous distribution is not forthcoming, individual traits must be judged according to the criteria set forth above, and some personal decision arrived at regarding the probability of independent development as opposed to common origin. Whenever possible, evidence should be sought concerning the nature of the contacts involved in trait diffusion. Unless they consciously avoid or reject foreign traits, adjacent cultures probably exert a wide range of influences over each other as a result of fairly continuous general contacts. The diffusion of some ideas over long distances may require considerably more specialized mechanisms.

Since all cases of diffusion, for which actual population movements have not been proven, form part of this category, it is in effect a final residual one. Within it, it is frequently impossible to distinguish between trait diffusion that definitely was unaccompanied by population movements of any type and those cases where migration may be involved, but is not proved to be.

VII. The final cause of culture change that must always be considered is independent invention. The problems of distinguishing traits that appear as a result of independent invention from those that appear as a result of diffusion have been discussed above. No further treatment is required here.

CONCLUSION

We have been examining the various cultural processes associated with movements of people and with the invention and dispersal of cultural traits. Although we have not examined in any great detail the idea of a culture as a functionally integrated system, we have stressed the importance for any sort of historical reconstruction of knowing the role that the various artifacts being studied have played within any particular culture. While the existing cultural system may affect the innovation and acceptance of new traits, this does not prevent us from studying the history of individual traits in their own right. The examination of these traits, both individually and in their cultural setting, provides a basis for making inferences about the processes of cultural change, such as we described in the last section.

We have also seen that even when the prehistorian makes full use of all the archaeological, physical anthropological, and linguistic data at his disposal, he is still often unable to discern all of the historical factors that have shaped cultural change. The reliability of deductive explanations, based on general theories of the nature of culture, is very low. Reliable explanations are only possible if we have detailed archaeological (both cultural and physical) and linguistic data. The solution to most problems requires increasingly refined local chronologies and the detailed investigation of the culture history of adjacent regions. The archaeological recovery and analysis of cultural and skeletal data is slow, painstaking work, but it is the basis on which most of the progress in prehistoric studies is built. The interpretation of this evidence is enhanced by a growing understanding of the nature of culture change, by the prehistorian's awareness of theoretical developments in the fields of ethnology and social anthropology, and by the creative application of these findings to the interpretation of the archaeological record. These problems of interpretation constitute the true theoretical domain of prehistory and represent a range of skills different from, but at least as extensive, as those that must be possessed by the field archaeologist.

References

Arkell, Anthony J.
    1957   "Khartoum's Part in the Development of the Neolithic." *Kush* 5:8–12.

Brace, C. Loring
    1964   "The Fate of the Classic Neanderthals: A Consideration of Hominid Catastrophism." *Current Anthropology* 5:3–43.

Coon, Carleton S.
    1965   *The Living Races of Man.* New York: Alfred A. Knopf.

Dales, George F.
    1964   "The Mythical Massacre at Mohenjodaro." *Expedition 6.*

Daniel, G. E.
    1963   *The Idea of Prehistory.* Cleveland: The World Publishing Company.

Dixon, Roland B.
    1928   *The Building of Cultures.* New York: Charles Scribner's & Sons.

Edmonson, Munro S.
    1961   "Neolithic Diffusion Rates." *Current Anthropology* 2:71–102.

Ekholm, Gordon F.
    1964   "Transpacific Contacts." In *Prehistoric Man in the New World,* Jesse D. Jennings and Edward Norbeck, editors. Chicago: University of Chicago Press, pp. 489–510.

Erasmus, Charles J.
    1950   "Patolli and Pachisi, and the Limitation of Possibilities." *Southwestern Journal of Anthropology* 6:369–387.
    1961   *Man Takes Control.* Minneapolis: University of Minnesota Press.

Goldenweiser, Alexander A.
    1913   "The Principle of Limited Possibilities." *Journal of American Folklore* 26:259–292.

Graebner, Fritz
    1911   *Methode der Ethnologie.* Heidelberg: C. Winter.

Greenberg, Joseph H.
    1957   *Essays in Linguistics.* Chicago: University of Chicago Press.

Hodgen, Margaret T.
    1952   "Change and History." *Viking Fund Publications in Anthropology* 18.

Kenyon, Kathleen
    1960   *Archaeology in the Holy Land.* London: Ernest Bern Ltd.

Kroeber, A. L.
    1925   *Handbook of the Indians of California.* Bureau of American Ethnology, Bulletin 78.
    1940   "Stimulus Diffusion." *American Anthropologist* 42:1–20.
    1948   *Anthropology.* New ed. New York: Harcourt, Brace and World, Inc.

Lowie, Robert H.
    1937   *The History of Ethnological Theory.* New York: Holt, Rinehart & Winston, Inc.

MacWhite, Eoin
    1956   "On the Interpretation of Archaeological Evidence in Historical or Sociological Terms." *American Anthropologist* 58:3–25.

McCall, Daniel
    1964   *Africa in Time-Perspective: A Discussion of Historical Reconstruction from Unwritten Sources.* Boston: Boston University Press.

Meggers, Betty
    1964   "North and South American Cultural Connections and Convergences." In *Prehistoric Man in the New World,* Jesse D. Jennings and Edward Norbeck, editors. Chicago: University of Chicago Press, pp. 511–526.

Morgan, Lewis Henry
    1871   "Systems of Consanguinity and Affinity of the Human Family." *Smithsonian Institution Contributions to Knowledge,* 17, No. 218.

Murdock, George Peter
    1959a   *Africa, Its Peoples and Their Culture History.* New York: McGraw Hill Book Company, Inc.

1959b   "Cross-language Parallels in Parental Kin Terms." *Anthropological Linguistics* 1(9):1–5.

Nelson, Nels C.
1919   "The Archaeology of the South-West: A Preliminary Report." *Proceedings of the National Academy of Sciences,* 5:114–210.

Palmer, Leonard R.
1965   *Mycenaeans and Minoans: Aegean Prehistory in the Light of Linear B Tablets.* London: Faber and Faber Ltd. (2nd edition).

Perry, William
1923   *The Children of the Sun.* London: Methuen and Co. Ltd.

Petrie, William M. F.
1939   *The Making of Egypt.* London: Sheldon Press.

Powell, T. G. E.
1958   *The Celts.* London: Thames and Hudson.

Raglan, Fitz Roy, R. S.
1939   *How Came Civilization?* London: Methuen and Co. Ltd.

Rands, Robert L.
1961   "Elaboration and Invention in Ceramic Tradition." *American Antiquity* 26:247–257.

——, and C. L. Riley
1958   "Diffusion and Discontinuous Distribution." *American Anthropologist* 60:274–297.

Reed, Charles A.
1960   "A Review of the Archaeological Evidence on Animal Domestication in the Prehistoric Near East." In *Prehistoric Investigations in Iraqi Kurdistan,* Robert J. Braidwood and Bruce Howe, editors. Chicago: University of Chicago Press.

Riley, Carroll L.
1952   "The Blowgun in the New World." *Southwestern Journal of Anthropology* 8:297–319.

Rouse, Irving
1958   "The Inference of Migrations from Anthropological Evidence." In *Migrations in New World Culture History,* Raymond H. Thompson, editor. Tucson: University of Arizona, Social Science Bulletin, No. 27, pp. 63–68.
1960   "The Classification of Artifacts in Archaeology." *American Antiquity* 25:313–323.
1964   "Prehistory of the West Indies." *Science* 144:499–513.

Rowe, John H.
1966   "Diffusionism and Archaeology." *American Antiquity* 25:313–323.

Sapir, Edward
   "Time Perspective in Aboriginal American Culture." Canada Department of Mines, Memoir no. 90.

Schmidt, Wilhelm
1939   *The Culture Historical Method of Ethnology.* S. A. Sieber, trans. New York: Fortury's.

Sharp, Andrew
1957   *Ancient Voyagers in the South Pacific.* Baltimore: Penguin Books, Inc.

Smith, Grafton Elliot
1915   *The Migrations of Early Culture.* Manchester: Manchester University Press.
1924   *Elephants and Ethnologists.* New York: E. P. Dutton and Company, Inc.

Sonnenfeld, J.
1962   "Interpreting the Function of Primitive Implements." *American Antiquity* 28:56–65.

Stenberger, Marten
n.d.   *Sweden.* London: Thames and Hudson.

Steward, Julian H.
  1929   "Diffusion and Independent Development: A Critique of Logic." *American Anthropologist* 31:491–495.
——, and F. M. Setzler
  1938   "Function and Configuration in Archaeology." *American Antiquity* 7:337–343.
Suggs, Robert C.
  1960   *The Island Civilizations of Polynesia.* New York: Mentor Books, New American Library.
Trigger, Bruce G.
  1965   "History and Settlement in Lower Nubia." *Yale University Publications in Anthropology,* No. 69. New Haven: Yale University Press.
  1966   "The Languages of the Northern Sudan: An Historical Perspective." *Journal of African History* 7:19–25.
Tylor, Edward B.
  1879   "On the Game of Patolli in Ancient Mexico and Its Probably Asiatic Origin." *Journal of the Royal Anthropological Institute* 8:116–129.
Willey, Gordon R.
  1953   "A Pattern of Diffusion–Acculturation." *Southwestern Journal of Anthropology* 9:369–384.
Wissler, Clark
  1926   *The Relation of Nature to Man in Aboriginal America.* London: Oxford University Press.

ARCHAEOLOGY AS ANTHROPOLOGY

American archaeology has always been closer to anthropology than to history, and so American archaeologists seek to explain their data in anthropological rather than historical terms. The following paper by LEWIS R. BINFORD argues that archaeology should increase its efforts to contribute to anthropology as a whole since the structure of an entire cultural system is reflected in its material culture. Binford demonstrates the applicability of this premise with an example from eastern North America.

回 It has been aptly stated that "American archaeology is anthropology or it is nothing" (Willey and Phillips 1958:2). The purpose of this dis-

"Archaeology as Anthropology" by Lewis R. Binford, *American Antiquity* 28, No. 2 (1962) 217–225. Reprinted by permission of the author and the Editor of *American Antiquity.*

cussion is to evaluate the role which the archaeological discipline is playing in furthering the aims of anthropology and to offer certain suggestions as to how we, as archaeologists, may profitably shoulder more responsibility for furthering the aims of our field.

Initially, it must be asked, "What are the aims of anthropology?" Most will agree that the integrated field is striving to *explicate* and *explain* the total range of physical and cultural similarities and differences characteristic of the entire spatial-temporal span of man's existence (for discussion, see Kroeber 1953). Archaeology has certainly made major contributions as far as *explication* is concerned. Our current knowledge of the diversity which characterizes the range of extinct cultural systems is far superior to the limited knowledge available fifty years ago. Although this contribution is "admirable" and necessary, it has been noted that archaeology has made essentially no contribution in the realm of explanation: "So little work has been done in American archaeology on the explanatory level that it is difficult to find a name for it" (Willey and Phillips 1958:5).

Before carrying this criticism further, some statement about what is meant by explanation must be offered. The meaning which explanation has within a scientific frame of reference is simply the *demonstration* of a constant articulation of variables within a system and the measurement of the concomitant variability among the variables within the system. Processual change in one variable can then be shown to relate in a predictable and quantifiable way to changes in other variables, the latter changing in turn relative to changes in the structure of the system as a whole. This approach to explanation presupposes concern with process, or the operation and structural modification of systems. It is suggested that archaeologists have not made major explanatory contributions to the field of anthropology because they do not conceive of archaeological data in a systemic frame of reference. Archaeological data are viewed particularistically and "explanation" is offered in terms of specific events rather than in terms of process (see Buettner-Janusch 1957 for discussion of particularism).

Archaeologists tacitly assume that artifacts, regardless of their functional context, can be treated as equal and comparable "traits." Once differences and similarities are "defined" in terms of these equal and comparable "traits," interpretation proceeds within something of a theoretical vacuum that conceives of differences and similarities as the result of "blending," "directional influences," and "stimulation" between and among "historical traditions" defined largely on the basis of postulated local or regional continuity in the human populations.

I suggest that this undifferentiated and unstructured view is inadequate, that artifacts having their primary functional context in different operational sub-systems of the total cultural system will exhibit differences and similarities differentially, in terms of the structure of the cultural system of which they were a part. Further, that the temporal and spatial spans within and between broad functional categories will vary with the structure of the systematic relationships between socio-cultural systems. Study of these differential distributions can potentially yield valuable information concerning the nature of social organization within, and changing relationships between, socio-cultural systems. In short, the explanation of differences and similarities between archaeological complexes must be offered in terms of our current knowledge of the structural and functional characteristics of cultural systems.

Specific "historical" explanations, if they can be demonstrated, simply explicate mechanisms of cultural process. They add nothing to the explanation of the processes of cultural change and evolution. If migrations can be shown to have taken place, then this explication presents an explanatory problem; what adaptive circumstances, evolutionary processes, induced the migration (Thompson 1958:1)? We must seek explanation in systemic terms for classes of historical events such as migrations, establishment of "contact" between areas previously isolated, etc. Only then will we make major contributions in the area of explanation and provide a basis for the further advancement of anthropological theory.

As an exercise in explication of the methodological questions raised here, I will present a general discussion of a particular systemic approach in the evaluation of archaeological assemblages and utilize these distinctions in an attempted *explanation* of a particular set of archaeological observations.

Culture is viewed as the extra-somatic means of adaptation for the human organism (White 1959:8). I am concerned with all those sub-systems within the broader cultural system which are: (a) extra-somatic or not, dependent upon biological process for modification or structural definition (this is not to say that the form and process cannot be viewed as rooted in biological process, only that diversity and processes of diversification are not explicable in terms of biological process), and which (b) function to adapt the human organism, conceived generically, to its total environment both physical and social.

Within this framework it is consistent to view technology, those tools and social relationships which articulate the organism with the physical environment, as closely related to the nature of the environment. For example, we would not expect to find large quantities of fishhooks among the recent archaeological remains from the Kalahari desert! However, this view must not be thought of as "environmental determinism" for we assume a systematic relationship between the human organism and his environment in which culture is the intervening variable. In short, we are speaking of the ecological system (Steward 1955:36). We can observe certain constant adaptive requirements on the part of the organism and similarly certain adaptive limitations, given specific kinds of environment. However, limitations as well as the potential of the environment must be viewed always in terms of the intervening variable in the human ecological system, that is, culture.

With such an approach we should not be surprised to note similarities in technology among groups of similar levels of social complexity inhabiting the boreal forest (Spaulding 1946) or any other broad environmental zone. The comparative study of cultural systems with variable technologies in a similar environmental range or similar technologies in differing environments is a major methodology of what Steward (1955:36–42) has called "cultural ecology," and certainly is a valuable means of increasing our understanding of cultural processes. Such a methodology is also useful in elucidating the structural relationships between major cultural subsystems such as the social and ideological sub-systems. Prior to the initiation of such studies by archaeologists we must be able to distinguish those relevant artifactual elements within the total artifact assemblage which have the primary functional context in the social, technological, and ideological sub-systems of the total cultural system. We should not equate "material culture" with technology. Similarly we should not seek explanations for observed differences and similarities in "material culture" within a single interpretative frame of reference. It has often been suggested that we cannot dig up a social system or ideology. Granted we cannot excavate a kinship terminology or a philosophy, but we can and do excavate the material items which functioned together with these more behavioral elements within the appropriate cultural sub-systems. The formal structure of artifact assemblages together with the between element contextual relationships should and do present a systematic and understandable picture of *the total extinct* cultural system. It is no more justifiable for archaeologists to attempt explanation of certain formal, temporal, and spatial similarities and differences within a single frame of reference than it would be for an ethnographer to attempt explanation of differences in cousin terminology, levels of socio-cultural integration, styles of dress, and modes of transportation all with the same variables or within the same frame of reference. These classes or items are articulated differently within an integrated cultural system, hence the pertinent variables with which each is articulated, and exhibit concomitant variation, are different. This fact obviates the single explanatory frame of reference. The processes of change pertinent to each are different because of the different ways in which they function in contributing to the total adaptive system.

Consistent with this line of reasoning is the assertion that we as archaeologists must face the problem of identifying *technomic* artifacts from other artifactual forms. Technomic signifies those artifacts having their primary functional context in coping directly with the physical environment. Variability in the technomic components of archaeological assemblages is seen as primarily explicable in the ecological frame of reference. Here, we must concern ourselves with such phenomena as extractive efficiency, efficiency in performing bio-compensatory tasks such as heat retention, the nature of available resources, their distribution, density, and loci of availability, etc. In this area of research and explanation, the archaeologist is in a position to make a direct contribution to the field of anthropology. We can directly correlate technomic items with environmental variables since we can know the distribution of fossil flora and fauna from independent data—giving us the nature of extinct environments.

Another major class of artifacts which the archaeologists recover can be termed *socio-technic*. These artifacts were the material elements having their primary functional context in the social sub-systems of the total cultural system. This sub-system functions as the extra-somatic means of articulating individuals one with another into cohesive groups capable of efficiently maintaining themselves and of manipulating the technology. Artifacts such as a king's crown, a warrior's coup stick, a copper from the Northwest coast, etc., fall into this category. Changes in the relative complexity of the socio-technic component of an archaeological assemblage can be related to changes in the structure of the social system which they represent. Certainly the evolutionary processes, while correlated and related, are not the same for explaining structural changes in technological and social phenomena. Factors such as demography, presence or absence of between-group competition, etc., as well as the basic factors which affect technological change, must be considered when attempting to explain social change. Not only are the relevant variables different, there is a further difference when speaking of socio-technic artifacts. The explanation of the basic form and structure of the socio-technic component of an artifactual assemblage lies in the nature and structure of the social system which it represents. Observable differences and changes in the socio-technic components of archaeological assemblages must be explained with reference to structural changes in the social system and in terms of processes of social change and evolution.

Thus, archaeologists can initially only indirectly contribute to the investigation of social evolution. I would consider the study and establishment of correlations between types of social structure classified on the basis of behavioral attributes and structural types of material elements as one of the major areas of anthropological research yet to be developed. Once such correlations are established, archaeologists can attack the problems of evolutionary change in social systems. It is my opinion that only when we have the entire temporal span of cultural evolution as our "laboratory" can we make substantial gains in the critical area of social anthropological research.

The third major class of items which archaeologists frequently recover can be termed *ideo-technic artifacts*. Items of this class have their primary functional context in the ideological component of the social system. These are the items which signify and symbolize the ideological rationalizations for the social system and further provide the symbolic milieu in which individuals are enculturated, a necessity if they are to take their place as functional participants in the social system. Such items as figures of deities, clan symbols, symbols of natural agencies, etc., fall into this general category. Formal diversity in the structural complexity and in functional classes of this category of items must generally be related to changes in the structure of the society, hence explanations must be sought in the local adaptive situation rather than in the area of "historical explanations." As was the case with socio-technic items, we must seek to establish correlations between generic classes of the ideological system and the structure of the material symbolism. Only after such correlations have been established can archaeologists study in a systematic way this component of the social sub-system.

Cross-cutting all of these general classes of artifacts are formal characteristics which can be termed stylistic, formal qualities that are not directly explicable in terms of the nature of the raw materials, technology of production, or variability in the structure of the technological and social sub-systems of the total cultural system. These formal qualities are believed to have their primary functional context in providing a symbolically diverse yet pervasive artifactual environment promoting group solidarity and serving as a basis for group awareness and identity. This pan-systemic set of symbols is the milieu of enculturation and a basis for the recognition of social distinctiveness. "One of the main functions of the arts as communication is to reinforce belief, custom, and values" (Beals and Hoijer 1955:548). The distribution of style types and traditions is believed to be largely correlated with areas of commonality in level of cultural complexity and in mode of adaptation. Changes in the temporal-spatial distribution of style types are believed to be related to changes in the structure of socio-cultural systems either brought about through processes of in situ evolution, or by changes in the cultural environment to which local socio-cultural systems are adapted, thereby initiating evolutionary change. It is believed that stylistic attributes are most fruitfully studied when questions of ethnic origin, migration, and interaction between groups is the subject of explication. However, when explanations are sought, the total adaptive context of the socio-cultural system in question must be investigated. In this field of research archaeologists are in an excellent position to make major contributions to the general field of anthropology, for we can work directly in terms of correlations of the structure of artifact assemblages with rates of style change, directions of style-spread, and stability of style-continuity.

Having recognized three general functional classes of artifacts: technomic, socio-technic, and ideo-technic, as well as a category of formal stylistic attributes, each characterized by differing functions within the total cultural system and correspondingly different processes of change, it is suggested that our current theoretical orientation is insufficient and inadequate for attempting explanation. It is argued that explanations of differences and similarities between archaeological assemblages as a whole must first consider the nature of differences in each of these major categories and only after such evaluation can adequate explanatory hypotheses be offered.

Given this brief and oversimplified introduction, I will turn to a specific case, the Old Copper complex (Wittry and Ritzenthaler 1956). It has long been observed and frequently cited as a case of technological "devolution" that during the Archaic period fine and superior copper utilitarian tools were manufactured, whereas during Early and Middle Woodland times copper was used primarily for the production of non-utilitarian items (Griffin 1952:356). I will explore this interesting situation in terms of: (1) the frame of reference presented here, (2) generalizations which have previously been made concerning the nature of culture change, and (3) a set of hypotheses concerning the relationships between certain forms of socio-technic artifacts and the structure of the social systems that they represent.

The normal assumption when thinking about the copper artifacts typical of the Old Copper complex is that they are primarily technomic (manufactured for use in directly coping with the physical environment). It is generally assumed that these tools were superior to their functional equivalents in both stone and bone because of their durability and presumed superiority in accomplishing cutting and piercing tasks. It is a common generalization that within the realm of technology more efficient forms tend to replace less efficient forms. The Old Copper case seems to be an exception.

Absolute efficiency in performance is only one side of the coin when viewed in an adaptive context. Adaptive efficiency must also be viewed in terms of *economy*, that is, energy expenditure versus energy conservation (White 1959:54). For one tool to be adaptively more efficient than another there must be either a lowering of energy expenditure per unit of energy of conservation in task performance, or an increase in energy conservation per unit of performance over a constant energy expenditure in tool production. Viewed this way, we may question the position that copper tools were technologically more efficient. The production of copper tools utilizing the techniques employed in the manufacture of Old Copper specimens certainly required tremendous expenditures of both time and labor. The sources of copper are not in the areas of most dense Old Copper implements (Wittry 1951), hence travel to the sources, or at least the establishment of logistics networks based on kin ties extending over large areas, was a prerequisite for the procurement of the raw material. Extraction of the copper, using the primitive mining techniques exemplified by the aboriginal mining pits on Isle Royale and the Keewenaw Peninsula (Holmes 1901), required further expenditure of time and labor. Raw materials for the production of the functional equivalents of the copper tools was normally available locally or at least available at some point within the bounds of the normal exploitative cycle. Extraction was essentially a gathering process requiring no specialized techniques, and could be accomplished incidental to the performance of other tasks. Certainly in terms of expenditures of time and energy, as regards the distribution of sources of raw materials and techniques of extraction, copper required a tremendous expenditure as opposed to raw materials of stone and bone.

The processing phase of tool production appears to present an equally puzzling ratio with regard to expenditure of energy. The processing of copper into a finished artifact normally requires the separation of crystalline impurities from the copper. Following this processing phase, normal procedure seems to have been to pound and partially flatten small bits of copper which were then pounded together to "build" an artifact (Cushing 1894). Once the essential shape had been achieved, further hammering, grinding, and polishing were required. I suggest that this process is more time consuming than shaping and finishing an artifact by chipping flint, or even the pecking and grinding technique employed in the production of ground stone tools. It follows that there was a much greater expenditure of time and energy in the production of copper tools than in the production of their functional equivalents in either bone or stone.

Turning now to the problem of energy conservation in task performance, we may ask what differentials existed. It seems fairly certain that copper was probably more durable and could have been utilized for a longer period of time. As far as what differentials existed between copper and stone, as regards cutting and piercing functions, only experiments can determine. Considering all of the evidence, the quality of durability appears to have been the only possible realm which could compensate for the differentials in expenditure of energy between stone and bone as opposed to copper in the area of procurement and processing of the raw material. What evidence exists that would suggest that durability was in fact the compensatory quality which made copper tools technologically more efficient?

All the available evidence suggests the contrary interpretation. First, we do not have evidence that the raw material was reused to any great extent once an artifact was broken or "worn out." If this had been the case, we would expect to have a general lack of battered and "worn out" pieces and some examples of reworked pieces, whereas evidence of use is a common characteristic of recovered specimens, and to my knowledge reworked pieces are uncommon if not unknown.

Second, when found in a primary archaeological context, copper tools are almost invariably part of burial goods. If durability was the compensatory factor in the efficiency equation, certainly some social mechanism for retaining the copper tools as functioning parts of the technology would have been established. This does not appear to have been the case. Since durability can be ruled out as the compensatory factor, we must conclude that copper tools were not technologically more efficient than their functional equivalents in both stone and bone. Having reached this "conclusion," it remains to explore the problem of the initial appearance of copper tools and to examine the observation that there was a shift from the use of copper for the production of utilitarian tools to non-utilitarian items.

It is proposed that the observed shift and the initial appearance of copper tools can best be explained under the hypothesis that they did not function primarily as *technomic items*. I suggest that in both the Old Copper and later cultural systems to the south, copper was utilized primarily for the production of *socio-technic items*.

Fried (1960) discusses certain pertinent distinctions between societies with regard to systems of status grading. Societies on a low general level of cultural complexity, measured in terms of functional specialization and structural differentiation, normally have an "egalitarian" system of status grading. The term "egalitarian" signifies that status positions are open to all persons within the limits of certain sex and age classes, who through their individual physical and mental characteristics are capable of greater achievement in coping with the environment. Among societies of greater complexity, status grading may be less egalitarian. Where ranking is the primary mechanism of status grading, status positions are closed. There are qualifications for attainment that are not simply a function of ones's personal physical and mental capabilities.

A classic example of ranking is found among societies with a ramage form of social organization (Sahlins 1958:139-180). In such societies status is determined by one's proximity in descent from a common ancestor. High status is accorded those in the direct line of descent, calculated in terms of primogeniture, while cadet lines of descent occupy positions of lower status depending on their proximity to the direct line.

Another form of internally ranked system is one in which attainment of a particular status position is closed to all except those members of a particular kin group who may occupy a differentiated status position, but open to all members of that kin group on an egalitarian basis.

Other forms of status grading are recognized, but for the purposes of this discussion the major distinction between egalitarian and ranked systems is sufficient. I propose that there is a direct relationship between the nature of the system of status grading within a society and the quantity, form, and structure of socio-technic components of its archaeological assemblage.

It is proposed that among egalitarian societies status symbols are symbolic of the technological activities for which outstanding performance is rewarded by increased status. In many cases they will be formally technomic items manufactured of "exotic" material or elaborately decorated and/or painstakingly manufactured. I do not imply that the items could not or were not used technomically, simply that their presence in the assemblage is explicable only in reference to the social system.

Within such a system the structure of the socio-technic component as regards "contextual" relationships should be simple. Various status symbols will be possessed by nearly all individuals within the limits of age and sex classes, differentiation within such a class being largely quantitative and qualitative rather than by formal exclusion of particular forms to particular status grades. The degree to which socio-technic symbols of status will be utilized within an egalitarian group should largely be a function of group size and the intensity and constancy of personal acquaintance among all individuals composing the society. Where small group size and general lack of interaction with nearby groups is the normal pattern, then the abundance of status symbols should be low. Where group size is large and/or where between-group interactions are widespread, lowering the intimacy and familiarity between interacting individuals, then there should be a greater and more general use of material means of status communication.

Another characteristic of the manipulation of status symbols among societies with essentially egalitarian systems of status grading would be the destruction at death of an individual's symbols of status. Status attainment being egalitarian, status symbols would be personalities and could not be inherited as such. Inclusion as grave accompaniments or outright destruction would be the suggested mode of disposal for status items among such groups.

Among societies where status grading tends to be of a nonegalitarian type, the status symbols should be more esoteric in form. Their form would normally be dictated by the ideological symbolism which rationalizes and emphasizes the particular internal ranking system or the means of partitioning the society. The structure of the socio-technic component of the assemblage should be more complex, with the complexity increasing directly as the complexity of the internal ranking system. Possession of certain forms may become exclusively restricted to certain status positions. As the degree of complexity in ranking increases there should be a similar increase in the differentiation of contextual associations in the form of differential treatment at death, differential access to goods and services evidenced in the formal and spatial differentiation in habitations and storage areas, etc. We would also expect to observe differentiation among the class of status symbols themselves as regards those which were utilized on a custodial basis as opposed to those that were personalities. Similarly, we would expect to see status symbols more frequently inherited at death as inheritance increases as the mechanism of status ascription.

Certainly these are suggestions which must be phrased as hypotheses and tested against ethnographic data. Nevertheless it is hoped that this discussion is sufficient to serve as a background against which an explanatory hypothesis concerning the Old Copper materials can be offered as an example of the potential utility of this type of *systemic* approach to archaeological data.

I suggest that the Old Copper copper tools had their primary functional context as symbols of achieved status in cultural systems with an egalitarian system of status grading. The settlement patterns and general level of cultural development suggested by the archaeological remains is commensurate with a band level of socio-cultural integration (Martin, Quimby, and Collier 1947: 299), that level within which egalitarian systems of status grading are dominant (Fried 1960). The technomic form, apparent lack of technomic efficiency, relative scarcity, and frequent occurrence in burials of copper artifacts all suggest that their primary function was as socio-technic items. Having reached this "conclusion," we are then in a position to ask, in systemic terms, questions concerning their period of appearance, disappearance, and the shift to nonutilitarian forms of copper items among later prehistoric socio-cultural systems of eastern North America.

I propose that the initial appearance of formally "utilitarian" copper tools in the Great Lakes region is explicable in terms of a major population expansion in the region following the Nipissing stage of the ancestral Great Lakes. The increase in population density was the result of increases in gross productivity following an exploitative shift to aquatic resources during the Nipissing stage. The increased populations are generally demonstrable in terms of the increased number of archaeological sites ascribable to the post-Nipissing period. The shift to aquatic resources is demonstrable in the initial appearance of quantities of fish remains in the sites of this period and in the sites of election for occupation, adjacent to prominent loci of availability for exploiting aquatic resources. It is proposed that with the increasing population density, the selective pressures fostering the symbolic communication of status, as opposed to the dependence on personal recognition as the bases for differential role behavior, were sufficient to result in the initial appearance of a new class of socio-technic items, formally technomic status symbols.

The failure to perpetuate the practice of the manufacture of copper tools on any extensive basis in the Great Lakes region should be explicable in terms of the changing structure of the social systems in that area during Woodland times. The exact type of social structure characteristic of Early Woodland period is at present poorly understood. I would suggest that there was a major structural change between the Late Archaic and Early Woodland periods, probably in the direction of a simple clan and moiety basis for social integration with a corresponding shift in the systems of status grading and the obsolescence of the older material means of status communication.

The presence of copper tools of essentially nonutilitarian form within such complexes as Adena, Hopewell, and Mississippian are most certainly explicable in terms of their socio-technic functions within much more complex social systems. Within the latter societies status grading was not purely on an egalitarian basis, and the nonutilitarian copper forms of status symbols would be formally commensurate with the ideological rationalizations for the various ascriptive status systems.

This explanatory "theory" has the advantage of "explaining": (1) the period of appearance of copper and probably other "exotic" materials in the Late Archaic period; (2) the form of the copper items; (3) their frequently noted contextual relations, for example, placement in burials; (4) their disappearance, which would be an "enigma" if they functioned primarily as technomic items; and (5) the use of copper for the almost exclusive production of "nonutilitarian" items in later and certainly more complex cultures of the eastern United States. This explanatory theory is advanced on the basis of currently available information, and regardless of whether or not it can stand as the correct explanation of the "Old Copper Problem" when more data are available, I suggest that only within a systemic frame of reference could such an inclusive explanation be offered. Here lies the advantage of the systemic approach.

Archaeology must accept a greater responsibility in the furtherance of the aims of anthropology. Until the tremendous quantities of data which the archaeologist controls are used in the solution of problems dealing with cultural evolution or systemic change, we are not only failing to contribute to the furtherance of the aims of anthropology but retarding the accomplishment of these aims. We as archaeologists have available a wide range of variability and a large sample of cultural systems. Ethnographers are restricted to the small and formally limited extant cultural systems.

Archaeologists should be among the best qualified to study and directly test hypotheses concerning the process of evolutionary change, particularly processes of change that are relatively slow, or hypotheses that postulate temporal-processual priorities as regards total cultural systems. The lack of theoretical concern and rather naive attempts at explanation which archaeologists currently advance must be modified.

I have suggested certain ways that could be a beginning in this necessary transition to a systemic view of culture, and have set forth a specific argument which hopefully demonstrates the utility of such an approach. The explanatory potential which even this limited and highly specific interpretative approach holds should be clear when problems such as "the spread of an Early Woodland burial cult in the Northeast" (Ritchie 1955), the appearance of the "Buzzard cult" (Warning and Holder 1945) in the Southeast, or the "Hopewell decline" (Griffin 1960) are recalled. It is my opinion that until we as archaeologists begin thinking of our data in terms of total cultural systems, many such prehistoric "enigmas" will remain unexplained. As archaeologists, with the entire span of culture history as our "laboratory," we cannot afford to keep our theoretical heads buried in the sand. We must shoulder our full share of responsibility within anthropology. Such a change could go far in advancing the field of archaeology specifically, and would certainly advance the general field of anthropology.

Bibliography

Beals, Ralph L., and Harry Hoijer
    1953 *An Introduction to Anthropology.* New York: The Macmillan Company.
Buettner-Janusch, John
    1957 "Boas and Mason: Particularism versus Generalization." *American Anthropologist,* Vol. 59, No. 2, pp. 318–324. Menasha.
Cushing, F. H.
    1894 "Primitive Copper Working: An Experimental Study." *American Anthropologist,* Vol. 7, No. 1, pp. 93–117. Washington.
Fried, Morton H.
    1960 "On the Evolution of Social Stratification and the State." In *Culture in History: Essays in Honor of Paul Radin,* Stanley Diamond, editor. New York: Columbia University Press, pp. 713–731.
Griffin, James B.
    1952 "Culture Periods in Eastern United States Archaeology." In *Archaeology of Eastern United States,* James B. Griffin, editor. Chicago: University of Chicago Press, pp. 352–364.
    1960 "Climatic Change: A Contributory Cause of the Growth and Decline of Northern Hopewellian Culture." *Wisconsin Archeologist,* Vol. 41, No. 2, pp. 21–33. Milwaukee.

Holmes, William H.
1901 "Aboriginal Copper Mines of Isle Royale, Lake Superior." *American Anthropologist*, Vol. 3, No. 4, pp. 684–696. New York.

Kroeber, A. L.
1953 "Introduction." In *Anthropology Today*, A. L. Kroeber, editor. Chicago: University of Chicago Press, pp. xiii–xv.

Martin, Paul S., George I. Quimby, and Donald Collier
1947 *Indians Before Columbus.* Chicago: University of Chicago Press.

Ritchie, William A.
1955 "Recent Suggestions Suggesting an Early Woodland Burial Cult in the Northeast." *New York State Museum and Science Service, Circular* No. 40. Rochester.

Sahlins, Marshall D.
1958 *Social Stratification in Polynesia.* Seattle: University of Washington Press.

Spaulding, Albert C.
1946 Northeastern Archaeology and General Trends in the Northern Forest Zone. In "Man in Northeastern North America," Frederick Johnson, editor. *Papers of the Robert S. Peabody Foundation for Archaeology*, Vol. 3, pp. 143–167. Phillips Academy, Andover.

Steward, Julian H.
1955 *Theory of Culture Change.* Urbana: University of Illinois Press.

Thompson, Raymond H.
1958 "Preface." In "Migrations in New World Culture History," Raymond H. Thompson, editor, *University of Arizona, Social Science Bulletin*, No. 27, pp. v–vii. Tuscon.

Waring, Antonio J., and Preston Holder
1945 "A Prehistoric Ceremonial Complex in the Southeastern United States." *American Anthropologist*, Vol. 47, No. 1, pp. 1–34. Menasha.

White, Leslie A.
1959 *The Evolution of Culture.* New York: McGraw-Hill Book Company.

Willey, Gordon R., and Philip Phillips
1958 *Method and Theory in Archaeology.* Chicago: University of Chicago Press.

Wittry, Warren L.
1951 "A Preliminary Study of the Old Copper Complex." *Wisconsin Archeologist*, Vol. 32, No. 1, pp. 1–18. Milwaukee.

——, and Robert E. Ritzenthaler
1956 "The Old Copper Complex: An Archaic Manifestation in Wisconsin." *American Antiquity* Vol. 21, No. 3, pp. 244–254. Salt Lake City.

PREHISTORIC SOCIAL SYSTEMS

*A recent trend in American archaeology has been the inference of
social structure through studies of artifact patterning in archaeological sites. These studies are based on the assumption that patterned
behavior will be reflected in artifacts as a whole or some of their
attributes. This selection by JAMES DEETZ is a clear and concise
example of this form of interpretation.*

The recent interest in the reconstruction of prehistoric social systems
has served to call attention to the nature and possible causes of patterning
as it is seen in archaeological materials. Whether inferences are drawn concerning social institutions based on settlement pattern, tool groupings
which indicate patterning that suggests particular activities, or the clustering of attributes indicative of the nature of social units, they all stem from
an awareness, perhaps implicit, of consistent and meaningful patterning
of certain modular units—houses, tools, or attributes. The purpose of this
paper is to make explicit the types of patterning encountered in archaeological data, to suggest possible applications of these types to the refinement of method, and to explore, in a preliminary way, the nature and significance of patterning at the level of individual behavior as it relates to
the inference of rules of residence and descent.

It is generally agreed that meaningful inference from the archaeological
record concerning the cultural systems responsible for its existence depends on an understanding of the manner in which culture is reflected in
its products. Behavior is a product of culture which is perishable and
therefore beyond recovery to the archaeologist in a direct sense, but the
products of this behavior—sites, structures, artifacts—reflect behavior in
a systematic manner. By acknowledging how different levels and types of
behavior might affect their products, one is provided with valuable insights regarding the behavioral significance of archaeological assemblages.
Four levels of behavior, and their archaeological equivalents, can be de-

fined and shown to have particular relevance to four types of inferential problems.

The first of these levels is that of the *individual*. Individual behavior is reflected at the attribute level, since the patterning of attributes exhibited by a group of similar artifacts results from similar patterned behavior on the parts of a number of individuals. While this behavior is shared by these individuals, as it would have to be if a pattern were to exist, it is the individual alone who is responsible for combining, for example, side notching with basal concavity on a projectile point. It is unlikely that more than one individual was responsible, in a direct sense, for the attribute configuration of any given artifact of the type commonly encountered in archaeological analysis. For this reason, patterning of attributes at the level of individual activity, is archaeology's only case of perfect association. Neither rodent activity, incorrect excavation procedure, nor improper laboratory sorting can destroy the association of cord-impressed decoration and lip thickening on a rim sherd. This perfection of association does not obtain with such an absolute guarantee at any of the three higher levels of patterning to be considered.

The second level of patterning is that which results from the actions of members of various minimal groups of interacting individuals—lineages, families, hunting groups, males, or females. Individuals grouped into such aggregates share in sets of behavioral patterns which can be seen in the patterned combination of artifacts as coordinate groups, as well as in the attributes of these artifacts. Such artifact complexes result either from individual or group action. Therefore, while only individuals are responsible for attribute groupings, both individuals or groups of individuals can produce artifact clusters. Unlike attribute groupings, artifact groupings are vulnerable to mixing and imperfect recovery due to field and laboratory procedural error.

The third level of patterning, that of the community, reflecting behavior of a face-to-face group of individuals, and including in most cases a number of minimal groupings as described above, is most frequently observed in the patterning of individual sites at the level of a single component. For example, the spatial arrangement of houses and the form of their architecture are a function of behavior at the community level, although one must also consider patterning at the individual and minimal-group levels in forming coherent inferences.

The fourth level is that of the entire society as a coordinate unit, and behavioral patterning at this level is a function of those patterns which are universal to the society as a whole. This level is seen archaeologically in settlement pattern, as the term is used by Chang (1958) distinct from community pattern, as well as in certain aspects of patterning at the three lower levels.

Examples of each of these four levels will make their definition more clear. At the level of the individual, recent studies of attribute patterning in ceramics (Deetz 1965; Longacre 1964) have demonstrated that tight clustering of attributes might result from the orderly transmission of behavioral pattern relating to pottery manufacture along female lines, permitting the postulation of matrilocal residence, a social convention which expectably would lead to such a phenomenon. Patterning of individual behavior manifested in attribute patterning can also provide information concerning culture-contact situations. During the excavation of a tanning vat complex at La Purisima Mission, Lompoc, California (Deetz 1963), a series of beamers was recovered from the vat floors. These had been used in the removal of hair from hides tanned for use in the mission ships, a technology introduced to the Chumash neophytes living at the mission. The particular attribute combination exhibited by these tools is quite illustrative of the nature of aboriginal conversion to European practices. The beamers are made from ribs; bone was a commonly used raw material by pre-Mission Chumash for tool manufacture. While the material was one familiar to the Indians, it was used to make a tool which formed a part of an introduced technological process, although the general form of the implement is similar to native ones used in similar activities, including bone-sweat sticks. The ribs used, however, were from cattle, an introduced animal. The pattern here is that of an aboriginally used raw material (bone) from an introduced animal (cow) to fashion an aboriginally known tool (bone beamer or scraper) to accomplish an introduced technological process (hair removal for vat tanning).

Patterning in artifact groupings is demonstrated by several recent studies. At La Purisima Mission during the nineteenth century, male Chumash neophytes were employed in a complex of roles introduced by Europeans —farming, cattle herding, and various crafts in the mission shops—while female neophytes continued in an occupational tradition not dissimilar from the aboriginal one, involving food preparation and the production of artifacts involved in this and related activities. Excavations in the neophytes' quarters (Deetz 1963) produced data which provide a striking demonstration of this differential shift in roles according to sex. While it is known that nuclear families resided in the barracks, a classification of the aboriginal artifacts according to activity by sex reveals that all artifacts associated with male activities had vanished from the inventory of the missionized Chumash, while female-associated artifacts were as numerous as they had been in pre-contact and contemporary aboriginal sites. Baskets, mortars, pestles, manos, metates, and comales formed the vast majority of the aboriginal assemblage, while scrapers, projectile points, arrowshaft straighteners, and chert flakes resulting from the manufacture of stone implements were exceedingly rare. It was possible to determine that one portion of the barracks had been used earlier in time, and this earlier occupation produced almost all of the few male-associated artifacts recovered. One other aspect of these data is of significance to those inferences regarding acculturation on a sexually differential basis. When one considers the nature of the complete assemblage from the barracks structure, including European and aboriginal artifacts, it is obvious that in the case of female material culture change, this was an additive process. European objects such as pottery, scissors, and knives were added to the aboriginal female tool kit, resulting in a complex actually somewhat richer than before, while change in male material culture was largely substitutive, with the European objects replacing rather than supplementing aboriginal items.

Other examples of this level of patterning are to be seen in the recent analysis of Mousterian sub-assemblages by Sally Binford (1965 and in [New Perspectives in Archeology]) and in Longacre's analysis of materials from the Carter Ranch Site in eastern Arizona (Longacre 1964). That the level of minimal group behavior depends in part on individual behavior is shown by Longacre's demonstration that different ceramic attribute groups which are a function of individual behavioral patterning have spatial significance, in that attribute clusters resulting from different modal individual behavior tend to group in artifact clusters which are a function of the shared behavior of segments of the community.

Examples of the third level of patterning are provided by those artifacts which represent an entire community, and are usually encountered in settlement-pattern studies. The artifacts in this case are usually structures, and their number and arrangement provide an indication of community behavior. The clustering of houses and storage pits within tightly formed defensive moats and palisades seen in the Middle Missouri Region late in the eighteenth century reflects defensive behavior in the part of the community as a whole.

Chang's study (1958) of the correlation between certain social systems, classified according to residence and descent rules, and community layout is another case which demonstrates the manner in which community behavior might be expected to reflect in the physical arrangements of material objects.

At the fourth level of behavioral patterning, that common to an entire society, emphasis shifts to the nature of patterning of whole communities into larger groups. The patterning seen in contemporary archaeological sites in a region is a reflection of the manner in which the society represented by those sites grouped its community units on the landscape, a form of patterning which in its formal analysis might reasonably be expected to reflect certain aspects of the behavior of the members of the society in certain universal categories. Examples would include the nature of ceremonial center distribution in Middle America or the relationship between seasonal camps and semipermanent villages in the Santa Barbara Channel region of southern California. In the latter case, small camps in the area inland from the foreshore suggest a seasonal division of the larger communities into smaller more economically efficient units during part of the year, probably during the dry summer months and early fall.

The brief examples cited above are intended only to serve as an indication of the nature of the four levels of patterning inherent in archaeological data. What is of primary importance is the realization that different levels require somewhat different analytical approaches, and that certain questions are better answered at certain levels of analysis. Basic to inferential method based on the analysis of patterning is that the very term *pattern* denotes repetition. Unless a number of examples of similarly patterned phenomena can be produced, sound inferences cannot be drawn, since the patterning must be demonstrated by numerous cases.

The remainder of this paper will be concerned with patterning at the lower two levels as it might permit the inference of rules of residence and descent in prehistoric societies. While it can be argued with considerable effect that to concentrate on the aspects of descent and residence in a social system is at least potentially dangerous, in that it can lead to an undesirable narrowing of perspective, certain recent archaeological analyses have been directed at the inference of either or both of these institutions. For this reason, it is perhaps advisable at this time to inquire into the possibility as well as the feasibility and practicality of such efforts. As has been suggested above, residence might be expected to be inferred from the individual level of patterning, that of attribute-clustering phenomena. While unilocal residence is in a sense a group activity, the effect which this practice might have on material objects would be the production of a series of similar artifacts resulting from family-based microtraditions of style, reflected in the attribute patterns produced by the individual. This assumption underlies both Deetz's (1965) and Longacre's (1964) recent ceramic studies. It is also demonstrated by the patterning observed in assemblages from historic Chumash sites in southern California. In this case, objects manufactured by males, particularly projectile points, exhibit a high degree of stylistic similarity within single sites, although intersite formal variation is high. While one might explain such variation as the result of different functions served by projectile points at different sites, our knowledge of Chumash subsistence patterns would suggest a highly homogeneous tradition within the area represented by the sites in question. This is almost certainly true of two of the sites, which are but ten miles apart, and located in identical environmental situations. At most, functional differences would only be a matter of virtually identical problems being met with alternate solutions and, as a result, explaining the variation as primarily due to social factors is more economical and efficient. In contrast to chipped-stone implements, made and used by males, milling equipment and basketry are strikingly similar throughout the entire range of the Chumash as they were known during the early nineteenth century. This pattern of high intersite variability but low variation within an assemblage shown by projectile points, and of the converse pattern seen in basketry and milling equipment is at least in agreement with the known facts of Chumash social organization, which was characterized by patrilocal residence and community exogamy. In this case, highly distinctive microtraditions of projectile-point manufacture might have been preserved by patrilocality, and similar isolated microtraditions in female manufacture prevented by a continuous circulation of females between communities.

. This example serves to place emphasis on one important aspect of inferring residence rules from modes of attribute patterning. It would seem to be most urgent that one investigate patterning in objects known or thought to have been manufactured by both sexes or, lacking this, to investigate the nature of patterning of single-sex traditions over time. By doing this, one avoids the difficult question: How much is enough? That is, to what degree must one demonstrate clustering to be certain that matrilocality or patrilocality has been reasonably established? A simple statement that the patterning can be shown not to be random is not sufficient, since theoretically one might expect a significant degree of attribute association to result from bilocality, particularly if combined with a unilineal descent rule, which might tend to bias residence in either an uxorilocal or virilocal direction. Most bilocal situations could reasonably be expected to produce significant attribute clustering in both male and female manufactures, particularly if accompanied by bilateral descent and a nearly even distribution of uxorilocal and virilocal modes of residence. To infer relatively rigid unilocality of either type in the absence of a controlled chronological series, one must not only demonstrate clustering of attributes in the products of one sex, but also a corresponding lack of clustering in the products of the opposite sex. In this sense, unilocal residence is an asymmetrical institution, and the existence and degree of asymmetry must be shown.

An alternative approach to the problem is provided by an analysis of change in patterning in ceramic attributes among protohistoric Arikara (Deetz 1965). In this instance, although patterning in only female cultural objects was considered, it was shown that over time this patterning became more random, and was accompanied by a reduction in house size. Furthermore, a reasonably sound historical reconstruction of later Arikara kinship change was made to provide the necessary control. Even in this case, however, one cannot say with certainty that residence was the sole causal factor in attribute clustering, nor to what degree clustering must occur to demonstrate matrilocality conclusively. The study does demonstrate that as matrilocality became less frequent, association of attributes became more random. No inference was formed from the data alone regarding residence; two simultaneous aspects of change were demonstrated, and their probable systematic relationship suggested. Relative degrees of clustering and association are indicated, but absolute frequencies cannot be postulated as reliable indicators of unilocality.

Inference of descent from archaeological data, at least in terms of patterning, is a much more difficult and complex problem. Unlike residence, descent is a group function, and therefore fits the level of group behavioral patterning described above. As such, it requires more meticulous care in handling the data, since this level is subject to the problems of mechanical mixing discussed earlier. Furthermore, descent is a subunit of residence, in a sense, since some but not all unilocal societies have a consistent residence rule. Therefore the demonstration of residence rule should be firmly established prior to the postulation of a rule of descent. The study of unilineal descent systems is, of course, the focus of much of ethnological theory, and many of the classics of ethnological writing treat the subject. As yet, there is not unanimous agreement on just what is meant by unilineal descent, or what purpose it serves in those societies which utilize it. It is very likely that there has been a confusion of cause and effect underlying much of the controversy in this area, and it can be suggested that unilineal descent is but a manifestation of another process, that of the formulation of clear-cut corporate groups which are structured in such a way as to function efficiently in a certain rather special social context. It is highly unlikely that a member of the most highly unilineal society would in fact deny *biological* descent from both parents, but at the same time, he would indicate that certain corporate rights and responsibilities reach him through either his mother's or his father's side. In this sense, descent is but a means to an end of corporate group formation, and perhaps if the term *descent* had not become one of general usage, clearer understandings would have been forthcoming more rapidly. Part of the cause is historical; the first workers concerned with unilineal descent worked in those areas, particularly Africa, where it was most clearly developed, and only later did it become apparent that there is more than one type of corporate kin group, and that unilineal descent is an organizing principle of only some.

If unilineal descent is seen as a mechanism by which sharply bounded corporate units are formed, then what must be demonstrated archaeologically is a group concept of corporate participation. Even if a means of accomplishing such an end were devised, it would not necessarily indicate unilineal descent, but only corporate membership in one or another social group, organized on the basis of residence, descent, or voluntary participation, to name but three possibilities. Conversely, the presence of an extended family unit in the same dwelling over a long period of time, using similar artifacts and perhaps sharing in a subsistence pattern from the same parcel of land, does not necessarily indicate the existence of a corporate concept. Unlike residence, which can be described in terms of purely *physical* and *spatial* relationships between people and objects, descent, at least in its corporate sense, involves in its description certain essential *conceptual* relationships between people and objects *held by the people* and, as a result, there is a dimension of patterning which may well not be reflected in the tangibles of archaeological data.

In conclusion, it is perhaps legitimate to ask why we are so concerned with the reconstruction of prehistoric social systems at all. There is always the danger of a certain method or area of inquiry becoming an end unto itself. The true value of such inferences would seem to lie in the direction of the ultimate benefit to general anthropological theory; the elucidation of system and orderly process in culture, past and present. Until and unless this type of inquiry is joined in a systematic fashion to the main body of ethnological theory, the danger is always present of such reconstructions entering the realm of ultimately sterile methodological virtuosity. This *should* not happen, but it must be kept in mind at all times that such a pursuit must relate in some way or another to the attainment of a broader understanding of culture. There is every reason to be confident that such will in fact take place but, at the same time, the possible pitfalls should be kept in mind. At the present point in our progress in this direction, perhaps the most significant value of recently gained understanding is that they indicate the nature of articulation between objects and people, and man's behavior in the larger sense. If this behavior is social, all well and good, but it must be studied regardless of the realm of culture it relates to. Studies such as those cited above, particularly in relationship to residence patterns, are of less value in their present imperfect state to social reconstruction than they are to indicating the nature of patterning and process in prehistoric cultures as shown by their material remains. Only with refinement will they become truly incisive and truly useful in the detailing of extinct social systems. However, though the route will be a long and difficult one, the longest journey must begin with a single step, and these first steps seem to lie in the right direction.

References

Binford, Sally R.
1965 "Social Groupings and Settlement Systems in the Mousterian." Presented at the American Anthropological Association Annual Meeting. (Unpublished.)

Chang, K. C.
  1958 "Study of the Neolithic Social Groups: Examples from the New World."
    American Anthropologist 60: 298–399.
Deetz, James
  1963 "Archaeological Investigations at La Purisima Mission." *Annual Report 1962–
    63*, UCLA Archaeological Survey.
  1965 *The Dynamics of Stylistic Change in Arikara Ceramics.* Urbana: University of
    Illinois, Series in Anthropology, No. 4.
Longacre, William
  1964 "Archaeology as Anthropology." *Science* 144 (3625): 1454–55.

ANALOGY IN ARCHAEOLOGY

The basis of all archaeological interpretation is analogy, that is, the assumption that nonobserved behavior can be discovered through the study of relevant observed behavior. In the past, archaeologists sometimes applied this principle recklessly, with extraordinary results. However, modern researchers, realizing the limitations of analogy, restrict its use to comparisons between peoples with similar material cultures and environments. In this paper ROBERT ASCHER examines both the history and future potential of analogy in archaeology.

回 The work of the archaeologist can be divided into four tasks. First there is the formulation and refinement of concepts; second, data gathering and processing; third, the interpretation of the data; and finally, synthesis. The four tasks are obviously related in a hierarchical scheme: concepts enable meaningful synthesis, synthesis depends on interpretation, and interpretation is ultimately founded on archaeological data.

Substantial progress has been made in approaches to the first, second, and fourth tasks in recent years. Productive work on concepts is illustrated by the successful *Seminars in Archaeology* of the Society for American Archaeology. The appearance of the new journal *Archaeometry* under the auspices of The Research Laboratory at Oxford, with its concentration on

"Analogy in Archaeological Interpretation" by Robert Ascher, *Southwestern Journal of Anthropology* 17 No. 4 (1961) 317–325. Reprinted by permission of the author and the Editors of the *Southwestern Journal of Anthropology.*

the application to archaeology of instruments developed in other disciplines, indicates how vigorous the attack on the second task has been. The ambitious work *World Prehistory* by Grahame Clark, if not wholly successful, demonstrates that a synthesis of human prehistory on a global scale is now feasible. What can be demonstrated for concept formulation, data gathering, and synthesis, cannot be easily shown for archaeological interpretation. If it is granted that acceptance of synthesis must vary with confidence in interpretation, it becomes apparent that interpretation warrants attention.

The most widely used of the tools of archaeological interpretation is analogy. In its most general sense interpreting by analogy is assaying any belief about non-observed behavior by referral to observed behavior which is thought to be relevant. The purpose of this paper is to examine this single interpretative tool. Concentration is on analogies where no historical records are available as aids. Evidence which suggests that there is cause for concern with the present status of analogy as an interpretive tool is presented and some suggestions are sketched.

The introduction of analogy into archaeology can be traced to the era of the classical evolutionary ideology. Analogy in this period was elementary: if it were true that certain living peoples represented early phases of human history, then the interpretation of the remains of extinct peoples could be accomplished by direct reference to their living counterparts. A monument to this logic is Sollas' *Ancient Hunters.* In this work the Tasmanians, Australian Aborigines, Bushmen, and Eskimos were enlisted as modern representatives of four successive paleolithic complexes. The question of the use of any class of paleolithic tools could be satisfied by direct referral to one of the four groups. For example:

> Anthropologists are generally agreed that the Palaeolithic "coup de poing" was not provided with a haft, but was held directly in the hand; and that it was not used simply as a "chopper": it is extremely gratifying therefore to find that the Tasmanians had no notion of hafting their homologue, or rather analogue, of the "coup de poing," and that it served a variety of purposes, among others as an aid in climbing trees.[1]

Interpretation in this mode, however, was not without its anachronisms. It was noted that living representatives of early periods occasionally enjoyed the use of classes of objects which were thought to be distinctive of later periods. In discussing the Australian Aborigines, for example, Sollas noted that polished stone axes ". . . are supposed to be the exclusive characteristic of the Neolithic period; but as the Australians are still in a Palaeolithic stage of culture, they present us in this case with an exception, for which various explanations may be found." In resolving this

[1] Sollas 1911: 74.

problem Sollas calculated that they might have invented it themselves or borrowed it from neighbors, but he eventually concluded with the suggestion that the Australian Aborigines learned to polish stone via an extensive network which at one time stretched from Australia to Europe.[2]

The critical reaction to the evolutionary assumptions, coupled with both the unexplained residues resulting from this early approach and the recovery of new data, forced reconsideration. As a result analogy was partitioned, and now at least two broad categories of analogy are recognized.[3]

The first category encompasses the classical evolutionary usage with appropriate shrinkages in the length and breadth of the time and space dimensions. In those areas of the world where history grades into archaeology, or where, in the absence of written documents, analysis of current or recent practices and archaeological data indicate continuity, archaeological data is interpreted by analogy to historical or living groups. In parts of the Near East, for example, archaeological evidence for the process of beer brewing can be interpreted by referral to both ancient texts and contemporary practices. The folk-cultures of Europe exhibit farming tools and practices, structures such as houses and granaries, and devices for transportation, which can be linked directly with the prehistoric past.

What is called the "folk-culture approach" by students of Old World archaeology is paralleled in the New World by the "direct historical approach." Both approaches admit the initiation of study from either end of the time scale. It is legitimate, presumably, to study the historically known prior to close examination of the archaeological unknown, or, reversing the order, to proceed from the archaeologically known to the historically unknown. If there is any subtle difference between the Old and New World approaches it is only that the longer time span in the Old World encourages the conception of smooth continuous passage from archaeology into history whereas in the New World the line between the two is more severely drawn.[4]

The withdrawal of the application of analogy from archaeological data where living representatives were assumed, to data where living or documented representatives could be demonstrated, left uncovered a vast temporal and spatial tract for which archaeological data existed. In order to cover this tract, consisting of over ninety-five percent of human history

---

[2] *Idem,* pp. 179, 207–209.

[3] A third category has sometimes been distinguished. This third category includes analogies to properties common to all men such as the need for capturing energy and the possession of a language. For purposes of interpretation this third category is meaningless. One does not need to undertake archaeological investigation to know that the individuals in a particular culture engaged in these activities. The question which the archaeologist seeks to answer is what were the particular patterns of a prehistoric people in carrying out these and similar activities.

[4] Compare Steward 1942 with Hawkes 1954.

and a large proportion of the globe, a second category of analogy came into use. This second category is here called the new analogy to distinguish it from analogy where historical continuity was assumed, as in the past, or is demonstrated, as in the present.

Anxious to avoid the mistakes of the early evolutionary school, and in the absence of any universal and unique model to guide in the recasting of interpretative tools, the new analogy has been set in a restrained format. In effect, the new analogy consists of boundary conditions for the choice of suitable analogs. A consideration of the canon for the selection of analogs, the qualifications placed on the power of the tool, and an example may characterize the theoretical posture of the new analogy.

According to Clark the archaeologist should ". . . restrict the field of analogy to societies at a common level of subsistence," and should ". . . attach greater significance to analogies drawn from societies existing under ecological conditions which approximate those reconstructed for the prehistoric culture under investigation than those adapted to markedly different environments."[5] Willey would select cultures on ". . . the same general level of technological development, perhaps existing under similar environmental situations."[6] V. Gordon Childe advised that an analog ". . . drawn from the same region or ecological province is likely to give the most reliable hints. . . ."[7] In summary, then, the canon is: seek analogies in cultures which manipulate similar environments in similar ways.

The qualifications on the new analogy are weighty. The mass of archaeological data yields subsistence or subsistence-connected information; hence, relevant analogies are to be initially restricted to this domain. The archaeologist is cautioned that the new analogy can provide only ". . . useful clues to general conditions, it can be a dangerous guide to the particular manifestations of culture . . .,"[8] or may ". . . in fact afford only clues in what direction to look for an explanation in the archaeological record itself."[9] The connection between the living culture or cultures and the archaeological culture in question is purely formal; there is no implication of direct generic relationship nor are any dimensions of space and time implied.

The following citation, from the interpretation of the mesolithic site of Star Carr, is an excellent example of the new analogy:

> The character of the finds suggests that we have to deal at Star Carr with a community rather than with the activities of a specialized group. The masculine element is sufficiently emphasized by the importance of hunting and by the evidence of great activity in the manufacture of tools and weapons.

[5] Clark 1953: 355.
[6] Tax, et al., 1953: 229.
[7] Childe 1956: 51.
[8] Clark 1953: 355.
[9] Childe 1956: 49. See also Clark 1951.

On the other hand, to judge from analogy with the hunting peoples of North America and Greenland, the importance of skin-working at Star Carr argues for the presence of women. Among the Eskimos generally women are mainly responsible for flaying the kill and preparing the skins for use. Men certainly play their part, especially in the hard task of thin-scraping caribou skins or when for some magical reason, as in preparing drum-skins among the Caribou Eskimos, it is considered wrong for women to undertake some particular task. Generally, though, it is agreed that the task is predominantly feminine and in fact constitutes the main part of women's labor.[10]

It would be misleading to imply that the restraint advocated in some quarters is practiced wherever archaeological data is interpreted by analogy. In fact, it would not be difficult to cite numerous cases in which less caution in the choice and use of analogs is clear. Consider, for example, the following attempt to interpret the *absence* of the caudal vertebrae of the otherwise well represented bovids in the important Australopithicine sites in the Makapansgat valley.

> To "tail" anything still signifies to "track it down." The leaders of Bushmen hunting parties, when tracking down their prey, signal to one another silently with the bushes or tails of the Cape fox. Tails spontaneously form flexible whips or flagella for beating thickets and grass-lands after game. The flagellum was one of the badges of the Pharaoh! The brush of a fox is the trophy of the chase. The warriors of Predynastic Egypt all wore bushy tails, that look suspiciously like fox-tails, and Pharaohs are delineated on Egyptian monuments retreating from the presence of gods looking back and trailing the bushy tails of an animal behind them. Horse-tails used to be emblems of rank formerly in Turkey, the rank depending on the number of tails (e.g., a pasha of three tails). Every South African witch-doctor carries an animal's brush preferably that of a wildebeste as every European witch carried a broom. It seems likely from the significance attached to tails universally by mankind in myth and history that their disappearance from the Makapansgat breccia is significant; they were all probably in great demand as signals and whips in organized group-hunting outside the cavern.[11]

In the engaging, less extreme example below an attempt is made to interpret the persistence of certain ceramic motifs in northern Georgia, U.S.A. Unlike the previous example, an awareness of boundaries is shown, if not rigorously adhered to.

> I am not quite sure to what extent we can measure general ethnic continuity in terms of ceramic continuity. Modern women of our civilization seem much bolder than men in quickly adopting new fashions which seem to display no continuing evolutionary or gradual developmental stages, although these fashions definitely run in cycles. Modern women's status and functions, however, are of course quite different from those of the average southern squaw. Per-

---

[10] Clark 1954: 10.
[11] Dart 1957: 167–168.

haps in the aboriginal Southeast, important new cultural traits that appeared suddenly and are the criteria for many of our major archaeological period designations were exclusively male interests: new weapons, pyramidal mounds, cult paraphernalia, things adopted by conquered or converted men; while the ladies stayed at home and made pottery that changed only gradually as the generations passed. Or perhaps we might better look at our own china dishware to see an expression of conservatism in spite of almost annual changes in foreign policy, Kinsey attitudes, hemlines, and hairdos. Even the atomic age will probably not change our chinaware, except maybe to break more of it.[12]

If the caution of the new analogy did not curb many, it did inhibit others to the point of not undertaking interpretation at all. In 1948 Taylor's *A Study of Archaeology* confronted New World archaeologists with their hesitancy to venture contextual interpretations. What Taylor did not realize was that to some conscientious archaeologists the strictures on interpretation, at least interpretation by analogy, may have in practice appeared formidable. More importantly, one student has argued that the new analogy is ineffectual in important areas, a second that interpretation by analogy is untenable; a third has abandoned hope of making any impartial judgment of the reasonableness of an archaeological interpretation. It will be instructive to consider these three points of view.

Hawkes perceives several kinds of cognition in archaeology. The distinction between them is marked by the degree to which history can be used in the interpretation of archaeological data. The kind of cognition for which the new analogy must be employed is ". . . a world wholly anterior to textual-historical evidence." In this world, Hawkes contends, interpretation cannot penetrate much beyond technology and subsistence. It is in these very aspects that man, according to Hawkes, is most similar to other animals. Where man is most unlike other animals, for example, in the possession of social, political, and in particular, religious institutions and systems, interpretative tools are near powerless.[13] An extreme position is taken by Smith: "It used to be thought," Smith writes, "that studies of surviving primitive peoples would provide the necessary analogies for interpreting prehistoric societies; but in the event the extension of ethnological studies has only served to show what an incredible variety of codes of behavior in fact actuate human conduct." Given this diversity, to ask for interpretation which utilizes living groups, is to demand "logical alchemy." Statements resulting from interpretations by analogy are assertions, not arguments, according to Smith. Imagine a situation in which at a given site one house structure is larger than all other house structures. If the larger structure is called an X, and not a Y or a Z, where X, Y,

---

[12] Wauchope 1949: 23.
[13] Hawkes 1954: 161–162.

and Z refer to uses of a single large structure in living groups, then "You can't really say that you *know* that it is [an X], and if someone criticizes your assertion, it is impossible to produce sufficient evidence to convince him you are necessarily right." Smith finds interpretation by analogy indefensible and argues for its abandonment.[14] A third position is taken by Thompson. He grants primacy to the role of analogy in interpretation but contends that an evaluation of its use in any particular instance can be made only by assessing the competence of the user. Thompson dismally maintains that there is no way to improve this situation other than hoping for ". . . improvements in the methods of measuring the amount of faith we place in an individual's work."[15]

From the foregoing discussion it is apparent that there is no general agreement on the new analogy, either in theory or practice. Certainly a call to abandonment is sufficient cause for discomfort. If it were not for the fact that analogy in archaeological interpretation has suffered chronic ambiguity since the nadir of classical evolutionary simplicity, an impasse could be said to exist. The following suggestions are sketched to aid in placing analogy on a firmer foundation.

1. For any given archaeological situation there usually exists more than a single analogy which can be used in the interpretation of the data. The real problem is to select from this finite range of possible analogs the one which offers the *best solution*. Selection of the best solution is most efficient when the least satisfying solutions are eliminated in a systematic way. Thus, a first elimination may be made on the basis of the economies, a second on the basis of the distances from the archaeological situation to the possible analogs as measured in terms of space, time, and form, and a third elimination may be based on the closeness of fit of the relationships between forms in the archaeological situation with relationships between forms in the hypothesized analogous situations. It may be that archaeologists in seeking analogs work in a systematic manner; but if they do it is seldom evident in the final solutions offered. Consider the following example:

> In this new soil, which was sticky and grey compared to the loose brown material in which the painted pottery had been deposited, we found polished-stone axes, polished-stone chisels, and flint sickle blades shiny from grain gloss. There was a brief alert when we thought we had come upon a burial, but it was a false alarm. Lying side by side in the soil were two large human thighbones, brown and shiny, polished from much handling. As they were completely alone, they were not part of a burial at all. All I could think of to explain their presence was that the ancient inhabitants of the Canary Islands, who were Neolithic people, had consecrated their kings by holding

[14] Smith 1955: 4–6.
[15] R. H. Thompson 1956: 331–332.

just such a pair of bones over their heads, and that pairs of thighbones were also used in the rituals of some of the Nilotic tribes of the Sudan. Perhaps the kings of Hotu had been similarly initiated into office. Who knows?[16]

If a systematic approach were used (it is not clear whether or not it was used in the above example), and the alternative solutions for a particular situation stated instead of the usual statement of a single solution (as above), there would be no need to examine credentials (which, in the above case, are extraordinary), but only the argument and the result. There is no touch of alchemy in the procedure outlined. Solutions to any problem are at best approximations arrived at by the elimination of those least likely. Simply, what is being suggested is the introduction of a clear systematic approach and considered statements of results in terms of degrees of likelihood.

2. It has been argued that the existing ethnological literature is inadequate for the purposes of archaeological interpretation because it contains either ideal descriptions of technologies, detailed descriptions without behavioral correlates, or no descriptions of technologies. On this basis it has been proposed that the archaeologist turn to the living community to compile his own inventories.[17] There is no question as to the merit of this suggestion.[18] If the argument which leads to the suggestion is valid, however, then the procedure outlined in section 1 above might be acceptable in theory but not possible in practice. Is the argument valid?

There does exist, as has been emphasized by Kidder and Forde, a rich and suitable literature which is neglected by the archaeologist.[19] The store of information on pottery manufacture and its associated behavior, for example, is copious. A codification of this literature and other similar information banks would be useful. There are, further, at least some quantitative models based on ethnographic data which are available and qualitative models can be designed to fit the needs of the archaeologist.[20] Behavioral interpretation, in terms of degrees of likelihood, beyond subsistence-connected activity, is only apparently remote.

3. The past and the present, it is often claimed, serve each other: archaeology depends on ethnographic data for interpretation; ethnology can make use of temporal depth that studies of the past may provide. This dogma, useful as it may be for certain purposes, has contributed to drawing a fast distinction between the ongoing and the extinct, the living and the dead. It is my contention that no clear distinction exists with regard to

[16] Coon 1957: 186.

[17] Kliendienst and Watson 1956: 76–77.

[18] This idea is of course not novel. For an excellent example see D. F. Thompson 1939. Unfortunately most of the studies of this type have been directed at demonstrating that many aspects of a culture are not preserved in archaeological data.

[19] Tax, et al. 1953: 231–232.

[20] For examples of the use of both types of models see Ascher 1959 and 1961.

the material evidence of culture. The point is not trivial, for the generally assumed polarity between the ongoing and the extinct has resulted in the total neglect of striking relevant data.

Every living community is in the process of continuous change with respect to the materials which it utilizes. At any point in its existence some proportion of materials are falling into disuse and decomposing, while new materials are being added as replacement. In a certain sense a part of every community is becoming, but is not yet, archaeological data. The community becomes archaeological data when replacement ceases. What the archaeologist disturbs is not the remains of a once living community, stopped as it were, at a point in time;[21] what he does interrupt is the process of decomposition. The observational fields of ethnology and archaeology overlap on that proportion of a living community which is in the process of transformation. It is the study of this very special corpus of data within the living community which holds the most fruitful promise for analogy in archaeological interpretation.

Bibliography

Ascher, Robert
    1959 "A Prehistoric Population Estimate Using Midden Analysis and Two Population Models." *Southwestern Journal of Anthropology* 15: 168–178.
    1961 "Function and Prehistoric Art." *Man* 61: 73–75.
Childe, V. Gordon
    1956 *Piecing Together the Past.* New York.
Clark, J. G. D.
    1951 "Folk-Culture and the Study of European Prehistory." In *Aspects of Archaeology in Great Britain and Beyond: Essays Presented to O. G. S. Crawford*, W. F. Grimes, editor. London, pp. 49–65.
    1953 "Archaeological Theories and Interpretations: Old World." In *Anthropology Today*, A. L. Kroeber, editor. Chicago, pp. 343–360.
    1954 *Excavations at Star Carr.* Cambridge.
Coon, Carleton S.
    1957 *The Seven Caves.* New York.
Dart, Raymond A.
    1957 "The Makapansgat Australopithecine Osteodontokeratic Culture." In *Third Pan-African Congress on Prehistory*, J. Desmond Clark and Sonia Cole, editors. London, pp. 161–171.
Hawkes, Christopher
    1954 "Archaeological Theory and Method: Some Suggestions from the Old World." *American Anthropologist* 56: 155–168.
Kleindienst, Maxine R., and Patty Jo Watson
    1956 " 'Action Archaeology': The Archaeological Inventory of a Living Community." *Anthropology Tomorrow* 5: 75–78.
Smith, M. A.
    1955 "The Limitations of Inference in Archaeology." *The Archaeological Newsletter* 6: 1–7.
Sollas, W. J.
    1911 *Ancient Hunters.* London.

[21] This erroneous notion, often implicit in archaeological literature, might be called the Pompeii Premise.

Steward, Julian H.
  1942 "The Direct Historical Approach to Archaeology." *American Antiquity* 7: 337–343.
Tax, Sol, L. C. Eiseley, I. Rouse, and C. F. Voegelin (editors)
  1953 *An Appraisal of Anthropology Today.* Chicago.
Thompson, Donald F.
  1939 "The Seasonal Factor in Human Culture." *Proceedings of the Prehistoric Society* 5: 209–221.
Thompson, Raymond H.
  1956 "The Subjective Element in Archaeological Inference." *Southwestern Journal of Anthropology* 12: 327–332.
Wauchope, Robert
  1949 "The Evolution and Persistence of Ceramic Motifs in Northern Georgia." *American Antiquity* 15: 16–22.

THE SUBJECTIVE ELEMENT IN ARCHAEOLOGICAL INFERENCE

RAYMOND H. THOMPSON's paper, which concludes this volume, is an attempt to analyze the processes whereby an archaeologist makes inferences from archaeological data. Thompson shows that the archaeologist proceeds from descriptive data to contextual inference by using the process of analogy. This article is an admirably concise statement of the limitations of inference in archaeology. Its significance is obvious, for the subjective elements in archaeological interpretation depend on many factors. One of them is the breadth of anthropological training possessed by the archaeologist, a point which has been made again and again throughout these readings.

▣ Willey[1] has described the two large problem fields of archaeology as the spatial-temporal arrangement of cultural materials and the reconstruction of cultural and ecological contexts. He points out that archaeology already

"The Subjective Element in Archaeological Inference" by Raymond H. Thompson, *Southwestern Journal of Anthropology* 12, No. 3 (1956) 327–332. Reprinted by permission of the author and the Editors of the *Southwestern Journal of Anthropology*.
  [1] Gordon R. Willey, in Sol Tax, Loren C. Eiseley, Irving Rouse, and Carl F. Voeglin, editors, *An Appraisal of Anthropology Today* (Chicago: University of Chicago Press, 1953), p. 229.

has the methods and techniques for the first of these. It is in the second that methodological explorations are necessary for it is here that the archaeologist operates by inference from the ethnographic present. There seems to be a healthy although sometimes overzealous appreciation of this need, but at the same time a surprising lack of interest in the equally important need for an examination of the conceptual tools for remedying the situation. This paper is a first step toward such an examination; it is an attempt to find out what an archaeologist does when he operates by inference.[2]

There are two related procedures involved in the establishment of an archaeological inference. First, the material evidence must be examined for suggestions or indications that an inference is possible. But an indicated conclusion cannot be established as an inference until its probability has been tested. Thus, the second process consists of the introduction of the probative material which contributes to this evaluation. The first step is a recognition of the indicative quality of the evidence; the second a full utilization of the probative analogy.

THE INDICATIVE QUALITY

An indication is that quality of the basic data which describes their inferential possibilities. The recognition of this quality is the starting point for any inference, for it is the indication which suggests that the inference is possible. The ability to recognize the indicative quality of the data is therefore a first requisite for the archaeologist who hopes to reconstruct the context of the specimen which he recovers. This ability is of course subjective. It is often described as the "feel" which an investigator has for the material.

The failure of archaeologists to define this individual sensitivity has caused other social scientists, and even some archaeologists, to seriously question its methodological validity. Attempts have been made to replace this subjective ability with more objective approaches. However, a devotion to objectivity cannot be substituted for the ability of the investigator to recognize that a certain cluster of the objectively described data is susceptible of yielding additional information.

Contrary to the folklore of the discipline, this sensitivity for the indicative quality is not an uncanny and inexplicable ability which only certain gifted individuals possess. Rather, it is the combination of the investigator's anthropological background or training in fact and theory, his archaeo-

---

[2] This paper was read at the 53rd Annual Meeting of the American Anthropological Association in Detroit, December 1954. It is a much abbreviated version of the introductory section of my doctoral dissertation (Harvard University, 1955), *Modern Yucatecan Maya Pottery: A Study of the Nature of Archaeological Inference*, [published] as a Memoir of the Society for American Archaeology.

logical experience which is often called familiarity with the material, and his intellectual capacity. It is the subtle combination of these three variables which makes the recognition of the indicative quality a subjective matter. This combination becomes such an intimate part of the individual archaeologist's analytical thinking that he is not conscious of the exact sources of the impression or indication that he expresses other than the cluster of data which initiated the indicative process.

The ability is therefore subjective or individual in that each investigator brings a different combination of skills to bear on any given problem. This does not mean that the ability to recognize the indicative quality is inexplicable, but it does mean that his ability is hard to define. It would be quite unnecessary to ask each archaeologist to set forth the details of his background, experience, and intelligence for the benefit of those who may wish to judge his work. It is not, however, too much to ask that he define the segment of the combination which contributes to a particular indication.

But as soon as an investigator begins to ask himself how and why he arrived at a particular indicated conclusion, he shifts from the indicative to the probative phase of the inferential process. This phase consists of specific statements of the evidence which enters into the substantiation of the inference. Some of them are explicit formulations of the indicative data; others are statements of entirely new material. In many cases the archaeologist would find it difficult to distinguish between the indicative material and the new evidence. In practice, the probative data represent a transition from the explicit declaration of the indicative background to the introduction of the new information, such that the documentation of the indicative reasoning leads to additional probative evidence. These observations parallel John Dewey's remark[3] on the conjugate relationship of the indicative and probative qualities of data, which I paraphrase: It is important that the material from which an inference is drawn should also be suitable as far as is possible to test the inference that is made, to indicate what new kinds of data are required, and to give some suggestion as to how they are to be obtained.

The Probative Analogy

The archaeologist who formulates an indicated conclusion is suggesting that there is a correlation between a certain set of archaeological material objects and a particular range of socio-cultural behavior. He must test this conclusion by demonstrating that an artifact-behavior correlation similar to the suggested one is a common occurrence in ethnographic reality. What actually happens is that he compares an artifact type which

[3] John Dewey, *Logic, the Theory of Inquiry* (New York: Henry Holt, 1938), p. 428.

is derived from archaeological data with a similar type in a known life situation. If the resemblance in the form of the two artifact types is reasonably close, he infers that the archaeological type shares the technique, behavior, or other cultural activity which is usually associated with the ethnographic type.

Thus the archaeologist proceeds from descriptive data to contextual inference by demonstrating the existence and validity of various degrees of relation of likeness. This similarity or parallelism of relations is called analogy. Archaeological inference is impossible without recourse to analogy.

It is of considerable theoretical importance to recognize that archaeological analogy is based on a comparison of abstractions rather than a resemblance between individual artifacts. In the translation of archaeological data into general anthropological terms artifacts are classified according to concepts which are designed to produce groupings of potential cultural significance. An artifact is not treated as an individual object but as a member of a group of objects called a type. A type, then, is an abstraction derived from a group of artifacts of similar form. The type, not the single object, serves as the basis for analogy.

Since the starting point of an archaeological analogy is an abstraction, it is a logical necessity that the other elements in the analogy be formulated as abstractions also. Thus, a type of archaeological objects must be compared with a type of ethnographic objects.

Just as the objects themselves, whether archaeological or ethnographic, are treated as types, so the associated cultural activity must be considered in terms of ranges and abstractions. The analogy cannot be established by invoking a single item of behavior any more than it can be based on an individual object. It can only be accomplished by the correlation of generalized ranges of behavior with types of artifacts.

Although a correlation between the artifact types and various cultural generalizations is the ultimate goal of an archaeological reconstruction the first inferences must be based on technological generalizations. The material bias of the basic archaeological evidence dictates this technological beginning of the inferential construct. The technical and ecological factors which condition the properties, source, and availability of raw materials define a specific range of possibilities for the manufacture of a class of artifacts. These technological possibilities have to be evaluated in terms of the archaeological evidence in order to narrow the range to fit the individual situation.

However, the information which is abstracted in a generalization is useless for analogy until it is organized to emphasize its relationship to the archaeological evidence. The probative value of any generalization is a function of the closeness of this relationship. It is therefore important that these abstract summaries be stated in precise and carefully chosen language. Technical data especially must be well organized not only because they begin the inferential construct but also because the significance of much technological information is often not readily apparent. Whenever an archaeologist receives technical or non-cultural information from another discipline he accepts the responsibility for identifying and exposing its interpretive significance.

The results of an analysis of the raw materials from which a group of artifacts is made are usually presented in terms of the properties of the materials. These data, like any other kind of non-cultural information, must be related to the archaeological problem. The archaeologist must shift the emphasis from a description of the technical property to a statement of some use which man makes of this property. In effecting this shift he introduces a cultural factor.

This transition from a technological to a cultural orientation is a fundamental step in archaeological inference because it establishes a cultural context for all of the probative material. But, the mere demonstration that this context exists does not define the nature or closeness of the relationship between the probative generalizations and the indicative archaeological evidence. This lack of definition results in a serious restriction of the probative value of these generalizations. Failure to recognize that culture is but one of three elements present in all archaeological concepts is responsible for this situation. These three basic properties are space, time, and culture. Phillips and Willey discuss the importance of this combination to archaeological theory:

> It is impossible to imagine an artifact type or a cultural "unit" that is not defined with reference to specific forms and does not also have distribution in space and duration in time. However, though invariably present, these three diverse properties may and do vary enormously in proportion one to the other. . . . It becomes essential, therefore, in the definition and use of archeological concepts of whatever nature to understand precisely what quantities of space, time, and formal content are involved in the mixture.[4]

These remarks have a particular significance for the related problems of the comparability of the ethnographic data used for analogy and the probability of the resulting archaeological inference. Both the indicative and the probative data are stated as abstractions in order to reduce all of the ingredients of the comparison to the same level of organization. But the system used to organize these data is also important. The abstractions must be formulated according to a single set of organizational criteria. Since the point of departure for the analogy consists of archaeo-

[4] Philip Phillips and Gordon R. Willey, "Method and Theory in American Archeology: An Operational Basis for Culture-Historical Integration," *American Anthropologist* 55: 615–633 (1953) 617–618.

logical evidence, the same theory and system used in the arrangement of this evidence must be used in formulating the comparative generalizations. It is, therefore, not enough to demonstrate the cultural nature of the probative information. The spatial and temporal boundaries must also be clearly defined before the generalizations can be used to maximum advantage for analogy with archaeological material.

Thus the archaeologist injects a subjective element into his inferential reconstruction at least twice. The importance of the archaeologist's particular skills and views in the recognition of the indicative quality has been particularly emphasized. These same faculties are employed in the probative phase of the inferential process, first in the search for analogous data, and then in the demonstration of the nature of the relationship between this material and the archaeological evidence. In both the indicative and probative phases the archaeologist makes increasingly greater use of the subjective element as he attempts inferences into the social and mental associations of his excavated material.

The subjective element serves as a kind of common denominator for archaeological inference. The individual investigator with his unique combination of interpretive skills provides the only possible means for the reconstruction of the cultural context of an archaeological collection. The final judgment of any archaeologist's cultural reconstructions must therefore be based on an appraisal of his professional competence, and particularly the quality of the subjective contribution to that competence. Our present method of assessing the role of this subjective element by an appraisal of the intellectual honesty of the archaeologist who makes the inferences is certainly inadequate. But, there does not seem to be any practical means of greatly improving the situation despite the insistence of many of the critics of archaeological method. We can only hope for improvements in the methods of measuring the amount of faith we place in an individual's work.

Fortunately, intellectual ability and integrity are not the only variables in an investigator's approach to a problem of archaeological reconstruction. These native qualities cannot be properly exploited without a rich background in anthropological theory and fact and a reasonable amount of familiarity with archaeological materials. Consequently, the best course to follow seems to be a continuation of the educational philosophy that an archaeologist is a general anthropologist who happens to prefer to pursue the study of man through an analysis of the unique documents of past human activity which can be found in prehistoric rubbish heaps.

INDEX

actuarial analysis, 51–52
Ahrensburgian, 96
air photographs, 33–43
  plotting of, 38–43
  stereoscopic examination of, 37–38
Allen, Major G. W. G., 33
American archaeology, 14–17
  relationship to anthropology, 14–15
analogy, 347–61
  definition of, 348
  ethnological, 287–88, 290, 348–55
  firm foundations for, 353–55
  folklore approach to, 349
  in archaeology, 347–55
  probative, 358
analysis
  methods of archaeological, 202
anthropology
  aims of, 326
  definition of, 10
archaeologist
  qualities of, 3–6, 49
  work of, 347
archaeology
  as anthropology, 326–38
  and cultural anthropology, 16–17
  and history, 6
  definition of, 3, 10–11
  dimensions of, 201–18
  explanation in, 327–37
  explication in, 326
  formal dimensions of, 203–9

  form-space-time interrelationships in, 217
  form-time relationship in, 215–17
  interrelationships of dimensions in, 212–17
  scope of, 6–7
  space-form relationships in, 213–15
  space-time relationships in, 217
  subject matter of, 202–12
archaeological theory, 14
archaic culture type, 25–26
Arretine pottery in India, 48
artifacts
  and archaeology, 326
  classification of, 185–98, 206–7
  comparison of, 208–9
  identification of, 194
  ideo-technic, 330
  qualitative, 204
  quantitative, 204
  socio-technic, 329, 333
  techniques for recognizing, 205–6
  type, 191–219
attributes, 186, 222–25
  ceramic, 344–45

bison-hunting, Paleo-Indian, 135–49
Blytt-Sernander series, 90
buildings
  adaptation of design to environment, 240–41
  fashion and, 244–45

buildings (*continued*)
  political institutions affect, 244
  reflection of structure of community,
    243
  reflection of structure of family, 242
  reflection of technology, 240–42
butchery techniques, 143–49

Childe, V. Gordon, 19, 28, 151, 265–78,
  279–81, 292
chi-square test, 223–31
Chumash sites, 341–44
classification of artifacts
  analytic, 186–88
  taxonomic, 188–93
  techniques of, 220
  utility of methods, 193–97
community
  definition of, 245
  factors affecting layout, 246–48
  factors affecting size, 245–46
  graveyards and special purpose-
    structures and layout, 249–51
  layouts, 245–51
  subsistence and layout, 248
component
  classification of, to form cultures, 195
  dating of (and cultures), 196
  determining the culture of, 194
Cortaillod, 150–51
Crawford, O. G. S., 33, 36
crop-marks, 34–35
cross-cultural types, 24–25
cultural distribution, 196
cultural ecology, 328
cultural periods
  dating of, 196
culture
  definition of, 12–13, 327
  genetic relationships between, 269–70
  indiscriminate use of prehistoric, 23
  patterns of, 23–24
  reconstructions of, 287–90
  relationships between, 274–76
culture change
  comparison in study of, 291–93
  conquest and, 272–73
  convergence and divergence in, 271–72
  distribution changes, a reflection of,
    266–69, 272
  independent invention in, 300–303
  invention in, 297–98, 301

migration and diffusion, 266–67, 272–
    78, 298–304, 313–22
  reflected in type variations, 267–68
  study of, 265–78, 290–93
  types of, 313–22
culture-historical approach, 304–13
culture traits, 277–78, 304–13

diffusion
  primary, 298
  secondary, 298
diffusionists, 305–6
direct historical approach, 14
Durotriges, 124

efficiencies in prehistory, 26
ethnic classification
  definition of, 281, 284

Federsee, 96
food, kinds and quantities of, 157
forest clearance
  identification of, 97–98
four-cell coefficient, 221–33

Galatea Bay, 154–61
Glastonbury, 121–23
Graig Lwyd, 179
Grand-Pressigny, 182
grave associations, 78–81
Gwisho, 168–74
  analogy to economy of modern
    hunter/gatherers, 172–74
  comparisons to other sites, 173
  description of plants found at, 168–
    72
  game animals at, 172–74

Hamburgian, 96
heirlooms, 78–79
Horgen, 150–51
horizontal excavation, 119–21
Huari, 59–60

imports
  at Maiden Castle, 128–30
  of stone axes, 175–82
independent development, 301–3
inference, archaeological, 356–61
inference of descent, 345–46
isochrons, 277
Iversen, Johannes, 97–98, 161

Jefferson, Thomas, 59

Kit Carson (town), 138
!Kung bushmen, 168-74

Lagerheim, H. C., 86
La Purisima Mission, 11, 341-42
law of strata identified by fossils, 59
literacy
  diffusion of, 7-8

Machu Picchu, 74-75
Maiden Castle, 120, 122, 124-32
Michelsberg, 150-51
Midwestern taxonomic system, 20, 282-84, 288
migration and diffusion, 266-67, 272-78, 298-304, 313-22
Moche pottery style, 80-81
mode
  definition of, 186
  types of, 188, 192-93
  use of, 188-91, 196-97
  versus types, 192-93
Mohenjo-daro, 54-55, 121-23
monte growth, 41
multilinear evolution, 24
Mycenae, 48

new archaeology in America, 22-24
New Zealand,
  prehistoric diet in, 154-61

old copper complex, 331-37
Olsen-Chubbuck site, 138-49
ordering, 63-67
Ordrup Mose, 164-66

Paleo-Indian cultures
  butchering techniques, 135-49
palynology, 83-99
parallel development, 302-3
patterning, 339-46
  types of, 340-42
people in prehistory
  how their culture changed, 290-93
  what their culture was, 287-90
  when they lived, 285-87
  who they were, 279-85
Pitt-Rivers, General, 33, 62
Plantago (cultivation weed), 167

Plymouth Colony, 11
pollen analysis, 83-99, 161-68
  slash and burn technique and, 98-99, 165-68
pollen samples
  collection of, 89-90
Préhistoire, 8
prehistory
  aims of, 8-9
  definition of, 10-11
processual interpretation, 17
protohistoire, 8

radiocarbon dating, 99-116
  experimental dating by, 108-13
  formation of radiocarbon, 99-100
  measurement techniques, 101-8
  samples of known age, 109-11
  some results from, 113-16
Redfield, Robert, 19
regional chronologies 285-87, 294

Sabratha, 47
Samian ware
  at Maiden Castle, 128-29, 131
seasonality, 158-61
seriation
  definition of, 61-62
  discussion of, 61-68
  evolutionary, 62
  of variations, 66-67
  similiary, 62-63
settlement patterns
  and archaeology, 237-61
  basis for inferences, 239-55
  concept of, 238
  determinants of, 237-38, 240-58
  ecological approach to, 238-39
  habitation, community and society, 258-59
  individual buildings, 240-45
  integration of determinants, 255-58
  natural resources and, 251-52
  political organization and, 253
  religion and, 254
  universal correlations of, 259-60
  warfare and, 254
  zonal patterns, 251-55
shadow sites, 34
Silchester
  horizontal excavations at, 121
social science archaeology, 19

social systems
  reconstructions of prehistoric, 339–46
soil-marks, 35–36
Soniche, 76
Southern California
  comparison with Galatea Bay environment, 156, 158
spores, 84–89
statistical analysis, 218–33
  applications to archaeology, 219–33
stereoscopic examination, 36–38
Steward, Julian, 19, 24, 328
stratigraphy
  principles of, 47–57
  theory of, 47–49
structural relationships, 306–7
subsistence regimes, 240
Superposition, law of, 38–39
  exceptions to, 59–61
Swiss prehistoric farming, 149–53

Thomsen, C. J.
  three-age system and, 70–71
three-age system
  theory of, 285–86

Tiryns, 48
trade, prehistoric, 175–82
  stone axes, 175–82
  trade goods, 304–5
Troy, 48
types
  concept of, 183
  definition of, 21
  general, 220
  kinds of, 191, 193

varves, 49
vertical excavation, 119–21
Vespasian, Emperor, 124–25, 131–32
Virú valley, 39–43
von Post, Lennart, 86

White, Leslie A., 201
Worsaae, J. J. A.
  statement of the use of archaeological associations, 72
Worsaae's law
  definition of, 69
  history of, 70–73
  limitations of, 77–79